African literature in French

Bakary Diallo in the garden of the poet Marcel Martinet, at Sceaux. The inscription on the back of the photograph reads: 'Bakary Diallo/auteur de la Maison Rieder/Pour Marcel Martinet/son ami/Bakary Diallo/6 Février 1928'.

African literature in French

A history of creative writing in French from West and Equatorial Africa

DOROTHY S. BLAIR

CAMBRIDGE UNIVERSITY PRESS

CAMBRIDGE

LONDON · NEW YORK · MELBOURNE

Published by the Syndics of the Cambridge University Press
The Pitt Building, Trumpington Street, Cambridge CB2 1RP
Bentley House, 200 Euston Road, London NW1 2DB
32 East 57th Street, New York, NY 10022, USA
296 Beaconsfield Parade, Middle Park, Melbourne 3206, Australia

First published 1976

Printed in Great Britain at the
University Printing House, Cambridge
(Harry Myers, University Printer)

Library of Congress Cataloguing in Publication Data
Blair, Dorothy S
African literature in French.
Includes bibliographical references and index.
1. African literature (French) – History and
criticism. I. Title.
PQ3980.B5   840'.9   75-39374
ISBN 0 521 21195 6

Contents

Preface

In spite of a proliferation of 'Studies in', 'Panoramas of', 'Introductions to' various aspects of African literature, which have appeared in English and French over the past decade and a half, as well as innumerable monographs on individual writers, there still remains a gap which this work is intended to fill: namely, to make a historical survey and objective critical analysis of the rise and growth of a literature in all its manifestations.

Existing critical works tend to concentrate on one genre – mostly the novel or poetry, or on a theme or influence appearing in the writings of a period or a group of authors – particularly the Negritude doctrine. In fact the tendency has been to consider 'Negritude' as synonymous with 'Negro-African'. Critics, as well as compilers of anthologies, have also treated French-speaking writers from the Caribbean and Madagascar as if they belonged to a common literary stock with those from the African continent, mainly because of the common cause they made at the birth of the Negritude movement. To continue to do so is to ignore the very different ethnic, geographic and cultural factors which have influenced the development of three distinct literary streams, long after the period when to be born with a dark skin, in a colonial or racially orientated society did influence the subjects, style and literary attitudes of emergent writers from the West Indies and Madagascar, as well as those from the French African territories.

In spite of Janheinz Jahn's contention that 'Geography does not provide literary categories' and that 'authors' complexions and birthplaces are also categories outside literature' (*Neo-African Literature*, p. 21),[1] it is defensible to propound the existence of an African literature (i.e. from the African continent) just as there undeniably exists a European literature, stemming from a common if distant ethnic ancestry, sharing a common stock of Judeo-Christian, Hellenic and Nordic mythology and flourishing under conditions of maximum interchange. This premise, if no other, will exclude from this survey certain White authors, who may claim from facts of birth, experience, inspiration and common cause that they are as 'African'

---

[1] See Bibliographical notes, p. 324, for full details of all general works quoted. Full bibliographical details of works of fiction studied are given at the head of the section in the text where they are discussed.

as the Black man. I consider that the creative writing of Black Africans alone comprise a homogeneous school of contemporary literature large enough now (in 1974) to justify in itself a comprehensive study.

Moreover, I shall speak only of works written in French. The comparative approach is often useful, sometimes desirable, not always practicable. In the present case it would expand this volume to unmanageable proportions. It is also a fact that African creative writing emerged earlier in French than in any other language of the European colonizers and, developing distinctly, grew independently in scope and maturity, variety of theme and genre. Far from there being any influences between them, when, at the height of the Negritude debate, African intellectuals from the two main European language groups began to be aware of each other's literary activities, bitter dissension raged between the French-speaking, pro-Negritude and the English-speaking, anti-Negritude partisans. Up to the beginning of the era of Independence there can be distinguished two main Negro-African literatures, developing in French and in English, with possibly less in common than, say, the Romantic literatures of Germany, France and Britain in the late eighteenth and early nineteenth centuries. This can be supported by a study of the different genres.

The folk-tale, the first manifestation of literary activity in French by African writers, primarily one of the most important means of assuring the survival of certain cultural and social traditions, is, of all the literary arts, the most intimately linked to the life of a people. It could be considered the most typically African of all the forms of literary expression if one could succeed in defining the term 'African'. However, we would have difficulty in finding a common denominator for regions as diverse as Mauritania, Nigeria, Mali, Sudan, Guinea, Somalia, Senegal, Ethiopia, Zaïre and Liberia, Sierra Leone, Cameroon, etc. In the first chapter of his study of Birago Diop's *Contes*,[2] Mohamadou Kane underlines the diversity of forms, themes and techniques adopted by story-tellers according to local traditions, beliefs and conditions. I shall examine these in the relevant chapter, finding certain common factors in those from the A.O.F. Suffice to note here that the main geographic, cultural and religious differences between the French and English-speaking regions of West Africa, where folk-tales are deeply entrenched in popular tradition, follow the distinctions outlined by Kane: those retold in English derive largely from forest and jungle areas, more fundamentally attached to fetishist cults and animist beliefs, with the Spider as the principal character of the folk-cycles. The English versions are limited to transcriptions and transla-

[2] *Les Contes d'Amadou Coumba* (sic), *du conte traditionnel au conte moderne d'expression française.*

tions from the oral sources, without personal stamp in style or form betraying the contemporary writer. The tales in French stem mainly from the Savannah regions, long subjected to Islamic penetration, and with the Hare or Antelope as the 'hero'. The narrators have usually done more than just preserve their people's cultural patrimony: they have made a recognizable, original contribution to contemporary African literature in French, in which it is possible to recognize individual style and expression in the versions by different writers.

While the folk-tale was a traditional part of African oral literature, the novel was, of course, an import from Europe. Having no indigenous models of either theme or narrative techniques to follow, African novelists using any of the West European languages, might well be expected to have much in common, particularly since the novels of both France and England have been the outcome of a certain amount of cultural cross-pollination since the eighteenth century. However, such common elements as can be found between the French and English African novel are limited to theme and situation ('Things-fall-apart'. 'Confrontations-of-civilizations', 'Fight-against-colonialism') and to the popularity of the autobiographical mode. But a novel with literary pretensions must be more than a set of characters and a situation. It is apparent that there are fundamental differences of personal treatment, emotional climate, individual structure and style in African novels inspired by the French and English colonial situation (including pre-1918 German Cameroon) and in a number of the more important post-Independence works of fiction.

Lastly, in the case of dramatic literature, there is further argument for considering plays in French as distinct from those in English. Drama published in French falls into two categories: on the one hand, works of epic, legendary and historical inspiration; on the other, contemporary, moral, satirical and political plays. The epico-legendary works with the exception of the Shaka dramas, are usually closely associated with the author's own country of birth or adoption. The comic, satiric and moral plays are even more definitely inspired by subjects, characters, situations, known to and closely observed by the writer in his own environment. A final reason for considering these as belonging to a school of French-African, rather than purely African drama (though I would not labour this point) is that there are sometimes slight, most probably unconscious traces of recognizable French influences owing to the author's having been steeped in French literary traditions as well as those of Africa – a hint of a 'Cornélien' sub-stratum, a Molièresque vein of comedy.

In short, while not denying the value of the comparative approach to African literature, I feel that there is justification and certainly enough material for this separate study of creative writing in French and an assessment of this contribution to contemporary literature as a whole.

As to what constitutes a French-African writer, my definition will be a person born in one of the French or Belgian colonized territories of West or Equatorial Africa, or whose parents come from these territories and who writes in French. (In the case of completely bilingual authors, such as Ola Balogun and Guillaume Oyônô-Mbia, only their works written originally in French will be discussed.)[3] I shall not differentiate between regions and shall make cursory mention of a writer's country of origin or birthplace, only enlarging on this when such details throw light on his subject, theme or treatment, or when appreciation of his cultural, geographic or ethnic origins are indispensable to a fuller understanding of his work. In any case, the French educational system, enforced in African colonies for the whole of the pre-Independence period,[4] helped to blur regional differences of culture and thought-worlds in the young Black intellectuals exposed to it.[5] At the time when creative writing in French first emerged from Africa in the 1920s and 30s, authors were all the product of a common primary and secondary school system, directed by the central Ministry of Education in Paris. Many of these promising youngsters from Cameroon, Ivory Coast, Senegambia, (then) Dahomey, Mali or Guinea, attended the same secondary or normal schools, coming with scholarships to the Lycée Van Vollenhoven in Dakar, the Lycée Faidherbe in Saint-Louis, the Ecole Primaire Supérieure at Bingerville in Ivory Coast or the William Ponty Normal School at Gorée (Senegal), which were the educational Meccas of the time. The brightest proceeded with bursaries to centres of higher education in France. It is now part of history how the Negritude movement was born on the Left Bank of Paris from the contact between Black students, intellectuals, budding authors, animated by a common desire to express their Black personality and solidarity in their writings. Geographic, regional, tribal, vernacular differences were ignored by them. After 1960 marginal regional features did begin to appear and, in the seventies, there is a noticeable tendency to encourage national pride in a local literature; but, in my opinion, this in no way invalidates my global approach to the history of French-African creative writing from its origins up to the early seventies, and a presentation by genres rather than by regions.

---

[3] The Cameroonian novelist, Mbella Sonne Dipoko, known to be equally at home in French and English, has, as far as I have been able to discover, only published in English.

[4] See note on French educational system on pp. 26–31 of Introduction.

[5] Also, where would David Diop – half Senegalese, half Cameroonian, who spent most of his life in France – really belong? The bibliographies of Zell & Silver and Jahn & Dressler both list him as Senegalese. Readers interested in the country of origin or adoption of the writers mentioned in my study should consult the table on page xxi.

It is perhaps more difficult to defend my exclusion of some of the West Indian writers, particularly in view of their important role in launching the Negritude movement. It is true their position in West African literature is complex and ambiguous. While their remote ethnic origins were in Africa, they themselves and their immediate forebears had been subjected to very different cultural and even geographic influences from their African counterparts. Yet, can we discount the fraternity that poets and intellectuals from Guadeloup, Martinique, Haïti and Guyana proclaimed with their contemporaries from West Africa whom they met in the Latin Quarter in the years between the First and Second World Wars? Or the common political and cultural cause they made with them as they founded their short-lived periodicals, launched manifestos, compiled anthologies and animated their own creative writings with the newly-found gospel of Negritude? Again, the first practical reason for not including the early writings from the French Caribbean is one of space, but there are certain cases where compromise cannot be avoided.

The definition I have adopted, if applied rigorously, would exclude René Maran, Étienne Lero, Aimé Césaire, Léon Damas and, more recently, Eugène Dervain and Gérard Chenet. Such hairsplitting would make nonsense of any serious attempt to trace the rise and development to the present day of Negro–African literature in French. Adequate mention will be made of West Indian writers, such as Lero and Césaire, who influenced the birth of Negritude. The question of how far the works of such writers should be considered, will require a rather arbitrary decision, as some cases are particularly ambiguous. Why, for example, include René Maran and exclude Bertène Juminer, who has settled in Dakar, where he exercises his profession as a specialist in parasitology as well as continuing to write novels? Is his case different from the Haïtian Gérard Chenet or the Martiniquan Eugène Dervain, settled respectively in Guinea and Ivory Coast? The criterion I have adopted, *grosso modo*, has been the degree of identity with a specific African region and its emergence as a source of inspiration in the work of the writer in question. In the case of Juminer, for example, loyal partisan of the Negritude cause as he was from his early student days and during his long friendship with Birago Diop, the situation, the characterization, the inspiration for his novels have always been drawn from his West Indian place of birth and not the Senegal of his adoption. Chenet and Dervain, on the other hand, have not only acquired Guinean and Eburnean nationality respectively, but take the inspiration for their plays solely from the folk-lore and epic tales of West Africa, with the result that their works are as truly African as those of Cheik Ndao, Bernard Dadié or Camara Laye.

Maran's case is more complex, Born in Martinique in 1887, educated almost entirely in France, while his father served as a colonial administrator in Togo, he was unofficially adopted by a French family and became the model of the assimilated West Indian, the exemplary pattern of the Black Frenchman. After leaving the University of Bordeaux, he entered the French Civil Service in the Colonial Office, like his father. From 1915–1921 he was employed as a high administrative official in the Oubangui-Chesi region of the Congo (the present Centrafrican Republic). Had it only been a question of Maran's colonial service in Africa, he could have been treated on the same terms as the colonial administrator F. V. Equilbecq, or authors such as Pierre Loti or André Gide, who drew inspiration for some of their works from their experiences in Africa. But Maran identified himself in a very special way with the people of Africa, and to him fell the honour of producing in 1921 what was acclaimed as the first '*véritable roman nègre*', *Batouala*, for which he was awarded the Prix Goncourt in 1922. The French-based critics of *Batouala* cautiously praised the emergence of a new African realism,[6] while the colonists and their sympathizers denounced his exaggerated description of the oppression of the natives of Oubangui.[7] All of Maran's subsequent works of fiction, including a sequel to *Batouala*, are situated wholly or partly in Central Africa, but only the two works mentioned above will be analysed for their place in the story of the French Negro-African novel.

One last word on Madagascar. Because of its geographical proximity, the island is usually considered as part of East African territory. Also, perhaps because there are so few Malagasy writers, these mostly poets, writing in French,[8] it has been expedient to include them in studies, anthologies and bibliographies devoted to Negro-African writings. Nevertheless, in spite of these precedents, I cannot justify making the Indian Ocean Islanders the literary bedfellows of the inhabitants of the African continent. Ethnically they are distinct from the African or Bantu peoples, having close kinship with the Pacific Islanders. Geographically isolated from Africa as well as from Europe, they have undergone cultural influences

---

[6] The publishers of the English version which appeared in 1922, without the name of the translator, think fit to warn the unsuspecting reader that, 'if some passages here and there appear a little outspoken to English taste, they form an integral part of the authentic portrayal of Negro manners'.

[7] M. Camille Guy, the then Governor of the Colony, in an article in 1922, demanding reform of the French Colonial educational system, remarks bitterly: 'It is this system that creates writers like this René Maran, who will one day produce more novels like *Batouala* – very mediocre from the literary point of view, childish in conception and whose general tendency is unjust and vicious' (see p. 9 of chapter 1).

[8] Some subsequent research may reveal why there are only a few works of prose fiction by Malagasy writers, none of which are of any significance, whereas the island has produced several outstanding poets writing in French as well as in Hova.

from both British and French colonization, but have drawn relatively little from personal experience in the mother country, compared with the large numbers of Africans who stayed and studied for long periods in France. It is worth noting that, of the three principal Malagasy poets of the first generation to write in French in this century, Rabéarivelo never left his native shores, Ranaivo emigrated to France only after the *coup d'état* of 1971, when he had long given up writing, and Rabémananjaro alone took part in the Negritude activities of his African contemporaries during his student days in Paris in the thirties. Malagasy writers have thus been far more exposed to local influences, climatic, scenic, sociological, cultural, which are very different from those of Africa. Their works are deeply impregnated with local linguistic and stylistic influences. Some of their poetry is simply a transcription and translation from Hova; some maintain in French the traditional *Hain-Teny* form; some epic poems and most of the dramatic works are inspired by a common ancestral past, resuscitating a local history and store of legend quite distinct from that of West or Equatorial Africa from which the works studied in the following pages emanate. So that, small as the corpus of writing in French from Madagascar is to date, it would be more scientific to consider the island poets as belonging to a separate regional literature.

All translations of quotations which illustrate my assertions or substantiate my judgements are my own. Where there are published translations in English of works discussed, I have included details of these in the citations at the head of each section, as well as listing them together on pp. 338–9 at the end of my Bibliographical notes.

The page references following my quotations are first to the original French edition, then, in [ ], to the published translation, if any.

February, 1975 D.S.B.

Former A.O.F.

Former A.E.F.

Former German colony under French trusteeship

Former German colony under Belgian administration

Former Belgian colony

[BAMBARA] = Main ethnic or linguistic groups.

0   200   400   600   800   1000   1200   1400   1600 km

French-speaking territories of West and Equatorial Africa, 1914–1975

Territory 1975 and date of Independence	Capital	Former name of territory	Authors associated with country (by origin or adoption)
Colonies comprising French West Africa ('A.O.F.')			
Islamic Rep. of Mauritania, Nov. 1960	Nouakchott	Mauritania	—
Rep. of Mali, Sept. 1960	Bamako	French Sudan	S. Badian, M. Gologo, A. Kourouma, Y. Ouologuem, F. D. Sissoko
Rep. of Niger, Aug. 1960	Niamey	French Niger	I. Issa
Rep. of Senegal, Aug. 1960	Dakar	Senegal	A. C. Dia, Bakary Diallo, B. Diop, D. Diop (half Cameroonian), M. Fall, A. A. Ka, Ch. H. Kane, M. S. M'Bengue, Ch. Ndao, O. Ousmane, A. Sadji, L. S. Senghor, O. Socé
Rep. of Guinea, Oct. 1958	Conakry	French Guinea	G. Chenet (Haitian by origin), C. Cissé, A. Fantouré (pseud.), K. Fodeba, C. Laye, C. Nénékhaly-Camara, D. T. Niane
Rep. of the Upper Volta, Aug. 1960	Ouagadougou	Upper Volta (1958–9 known as Voltaic Republic)	N. Boni
Rep. of the Ivory Coast, Aug. 1960	Abidjan	Ivory Coast	J. Bognini, B. Dadié, E. Dervain (Martiniquan by origin), C. Gadeau, A. Loba, Ch. Nokan
People's Republic of Benin (previously Rep. of Dahomey), Aug. 1960	Porto Novo	Dahomey	O. Bhêly-Quénum, P. Hazoumé, P. Joachim, M. Quenum
Colonies comprising French Equatorial Africa ('A.E.F.')			
Rep. of Chad, Aug. 1960	N'Djamena (formerly Fort Lamy)	Chad	J. Seid
Central African Republic, Aug. 1960	Bangui	Ubangi-Shari	P. Bamboté, R. Maran (by association)
Popular Rep. of Congo, Aug. 1960	Brazzaville	French Congo (Middle Congo)	J. Malonga, G. Menga, M. N'Débéka, M. Sinda, G. Tchicaya, U. Tam'si
Rep. of Gabon, Aug. 1960	Libreville	Gabon	—
United Nations Trust Territories under French administration, formerly German Colonies (except British Cameroon)			
Rep. of Togo, April 1960	Lomé	Togoland	D. Ananou
Federal Rep. of Cameroon, Jan. 1960	Yaoundé	British and French Cameroons	L. M. Ayissi, F. Bebey, M. Beti, D. Diop (half Senegalese), F.-B. M. Evembe, J. Ikelle-Matiba, B. Matip, R.-M. Mvomo, J. M. Nzouankeu, O. Oyono, G. Oyônô-Mbia, R. Philombé
Belgian Colony			
Popular Rep. of Zaïre (formerly Democratic Rep. of Congo), June 1960	Kinshasa (formerly Leopoldville)	Belgian Congo	H.-R. Bolamba, P. Lomani-Tchibamba
United Nations Trust Territory under Belgian administration, formerly part of German East Africa			
Rep. of Rwanda, July 1962	Kigali	Ruanda-Urundi	S. Naigiziki
Kingdom of Burundi, July 1962	Bujumbwa		

Abbreviations

A.E.F.   *Afrique Equatoriale Française*, the region originally comprising the French colonies of Equatorial Africa.

A.F.   *L'Afrique française* (Bulletin du Comité de l'Afrique française), official organ of commission dealing with French African colonial affairs.

A.O.F.   *Afrique Occidentale Française*, the region originally comprising the French West African colonies.

B.C.E.H.S.   *Bulletin du Comité d'Etudes historiques et scientifiques de l'A.O.F.* (Bulletin of the commission for historical and scientific studies in A.O.F.)

D.A.E.C. (in O.R.T.F.–D.A.E.C.)   Direction des Affaires Extérieures et de la Co-opération.

I.F.A.N.   *Institut Fondamental d'Afrique Noire*, a centre for ethnological study and research, with its headquarters and library at the University of Dakar, Senegal. This was originally, the 'Institut *Français* d'Afrique Noire' of the A.O.F. founded in 1938. The name was changed in 1965, after Independence, to the present rather clumsy compromise with the necessity to maintain the initials of the well-known 'IFAN' and to eliminate the colonial associations.

O.C.O.R.A.   *Office de la Co-opération Radiophonique*, an organization set up by France to foster cultural and creative activity, through the medium of radio, throughout the ex-colonies of Africa, with close links with the Metropolis.

O.R.S.T.O.M.   *Office de la Recherche scientifique et technique outremer* (Organization for scientific and technical research overseas).

O.R.T.F.   *Office de la Radiodiffusion et de la Télévision Françaises.*

Acknowledgements

I wish to express my sincere gratitude to the many people and institutions who have assisted me with advice, information, finances or access to material. I would like to mention in particular, in chronological order:

Mrs Peggy Rutherfoord who, back in 1956, suggested that I assist in the selection and translation of passages by French-African writers for what was to be the first anthology of African literature to be presented in English – *Darkness and Light* – so setting in motion the train of interest which has led to this study;

His Excellency Monsieur Léopold Sédar Senghor, whose generosity enabled me to attend the Seminar on African Literature and the Universities, in Dakar, in March 1963, and whose invitation to revisit Senegal in 1973 allowed me to bring my research up to date;

Monsieur Claude Wauthier, of Agence France-Presse, who put his considerable library of Negro-African writing at my disposal in Johannesburg in 1967;

Miss Moira Farmer, of the Gubbins Library of Africana at the University of the Witwatersrand, for her unfailing helpfulness in obtaining publications at all times;

The University of the Witwatersrand, whose research grant in 1968 assisted me with the purchase of books and whose grant out of the Ezrael Lazarus Foundation in 1973 helped me with the expenses of my visit to West Africa in 1973;

Monsieur Amar Samb and *Monsieur Zidouemba* of I.F.A.N., Dakar, for their courtesy and assistance in finding material out of their archives;

MM. Herbert Pepper and *Abdoul Diebel Diane* for similar assistance at the Archives Culturelles, Dakar;

the *Direction des Affaires Culturelles du Ministère des Affaires Etrangères*, who granted me a subsidy towards the expenses of my researches in Paris, 1973;

Monsieur Robert Cornevin, of the Centre de Documentation, Paris, who loaned me books from his private collection, which were otherwise unobtainable;

the *Library of the O.R.T.F.*, where I was able to obtain all entries to the Inter-African drama competition, and borrow all works in roneoed form as well as those published in volumes;

Dr Clive Wake, of the University of Kent, for assistance in obtaining copies of publications which are out of print;

Monsieur Robert Delavignette, the late *Mme Renée Martinet* and *Mme Marie-Rose Paupy* who shared their memories of Bakary Diallo with me; I must particularly thank Mme Paupy for permission to reproduce the photograph of Bakary Diallo taken in her parents' garden;

Professor Maurice Lubin, for giving me permission to translate the Louis Borno poem, 'Clair de lune' (see p. 144);

Finally my gratitude to *D. M.* and *N. M. B.* for their invaluable assistance with the typing of this book.

This book is dedicated to
my grand-children
THEMBE, ALEXEI and JOSHUA

whose names, by a happy coincidence, symbolize much of the inspiration behind the work that went into the following pages.

Aged 7, 6 and 4, you are too young to know the meaning of your names or the value of the written word, but one day you may read this, so I am allowing myself here a personal note which I have tried to exclude from the following work.

THEMBE (short for Thembekila) is Zulu for tactful, trustworthy and bringing hope.

ALEXEI (short for Alexander) in Greek means 'The Defender of Man'.

JOSHUA comes from the Hebrew, meaning 'Jehovah is Deliverance'.

So, collectively you represent Africa combined with the Greco-Latin and Hebraic traditions – three of the great civilizations of the world. It is my hope that one day you will see a world in which Man defends Man, a world delivered from hatred and prejudice, in which we can hope and trust.

Introduction: Background to a literature

In 1808 the Abbé Grégoire, former Bishop of Blois, published a book called *De la littérature des nègres*, the result of his researches into the 'intellectual faculties and moral qualities of the Negro'. He appended notices on the life and works of Negroes who had distinguished themselves in literature, arts and science and dedicated his book to 'all friends of Negroes and all those who have sought to prove that the black man belongs to the human race' and is not necessarily inferior morally or intellectually to the white man.

He devotes two chapters to an account of the Negro's skill in arts and crafts and his 'exceptional moral qualities', which consist, according to the Bishop, in a great aptitude for filial and paternal affection, generosity, love of work and courage – qualities which one does not expect to find the prerogative of any particular ethnic group. Finally, he turns to Negro literature. But he is hard put to illustrate his survey with examples of creative writing by Negroes. He draws attention to the now well-known cases of freed slaves who had written verse in English or Latin: Jacques-Elisa-Jean (Jacobus Elisa Joannes) Capitein and Phillis Peters. Capitein came originally from the Gold Coast and was bought as a child of seven or eight by a slaver and given to a friend who had him baptized and took him to Holland where he studied Latin, Greek, Hebrew and Theology at the University of Leyden. Eventually he went as a Calvinist missionary to Guinea. In the first half of the eighteenth century he composed neo-classic poems in Latin, of which one of the best is an elegy on the death of his friend and master who had meanwhile become a Minister at the Hague. Phillis Peters is even more interesting, in showing the grass-roots of a future poetic talent from Negro-African origins. A Senegalese, she was sold at the age of seven or eight to John Wheatley, a rich Boston merchant, whose name she eventually took. Her amiable disposition, sensitive nature and precocious intelligence caused her master to exempt her from the normal duties of a slave and to provide her with a good education, including the study of Latin and, of course, the Bible. From 1770 onwards she published various poems in English, in the languishing, sentimental style in vogue at the time.

Abbé Grégoire also mentions Mulattos from the West Indies who had written poetry, particularly one Castaing – whose verses 'adorned diverse anthologies' – Ernest Milcent, who took the *nom de plume* of Michel Mina, and Boisrend, author of *Précis des gémissements des sang-mêlés*, which is probably the very first 'protest poetry' from a Negro-African writer.

Some twenty years later, a retired colonial officer, Baron Jacques-François Roger, published African fables in French verse, collected during his period of office in Senegambia, 'with notes to introduce the reader to Senegambia, its climate, its principal products, its civilization and the customs of the inhabitants' (*Fables sénégalaises*, Paris, Nepven, Libraire, 1828). In his preface, Roger modestly excused his audacity in attempting to follow in the footsteps of his distinguished seventeenth-century master, hoping that the exotic interest of his material would be his justification. He thought that the raw material was interesting enough in itself to invite indulgence towards the execution of the verses, as everything that went into their composition belonged to the Negroes and was of such a different and original character that the French reader would find this sufficient to stimulate his curiosity. The Baron was perhaps too modest. In his forty-four fables, only the barest, most superficial allusions to local fauna and a few local terms indicate that they emanate from Africa. The temptation to emulate La Fontaine has drowned any affiliation with a true indigenous literature. The notes are, however, illuminating: the Baron points out certain traditions in the actual manner of relating the tales, which we shall find perpetuated in later written versions, when Black writers, such as Birago Diop, re-tell their own folk-lore. For example, he mentions the traditional prolonging of the story by repetitions, introductions of songs, riddles and ritual gestures and movements. He also comments on the fact that the Negroes attach more importance to the satirical than to the moral aspect of their fables, and that the local fabulists were *farceurs* whose intention was to amuse rather than to instruct or to edify their audiences.

From the middle of the nineteenth century, during the period of colonial expansion, are found the first tentative efforts at literary composition in the form of travel and tourist literature by 'indigenous' authors, who were, in fact, Mulattos. One Léopold Panet published an account of a journey from Senegal to Mogador which appeared in 1850 in the *Revue Coloniale*, and a half-caste priest, l'abbé Boilat, attempted to portray the life and people of his native region in his *Esquisses sénégalaises*, (published in Paris in 1853) where a more ambitious literary style can be detected. To these can be added a couple of other accounts of missionary or military expeditions to form the sum total of indigenous writing of the century.

Abbé Grégoire's postulate that 'Negroes belong to the human race' is now almost universally admitted, although prejudice lingered on in several continents for more than a hundred years after the appearance of his book – which probably did not reach a very large public in any case. It is now also recognized that the Negroes of what, for convenience, can be called 'Black Africa' had an original culture that went far beyond the limits of Baron Roger's *Fables*, although they did not develop literacy in the accepted sense of the term before the coming of the White man. We know a good deal more about the activities of the *griots* (troubadours), as professional chroniclers, praise-singers and story-tellers: of their responsibility for preserving the reservoir of fable, legend, folk-wisdom and history which formed the basis for an authentic popular literature, transmitted orally from generation to generation. The individual *griot*, through his talent, would add eloquence, lyricism, descriptive or dramatic detail to create a varied and rich poetic heritage.

The attitude of the early colonial – an attitude that persisted widely until the mid-twentieth century – was that the African only became 'civilized' with his coming. In fact the White man did not bring an 'Age of Enlightenment' to Africa, in the late nineteenth century, only the means for converting an oral tradition into a written literature. Furthermore, ignoring or despising the culture that existed prior to his coming, or at best simply not understanding that the origins and foundations of this culture were quite different from those of Europe, the White man superimposed his own in the colonial period, thus adding to the traditional literary heritage new themes, new attitudes and new inspirations, together with the adoption of a new language and new means of expression.

HISTORICAL REVIEW

An elementary knowledge of the pre-colonial history of West Africa, of the European conquests in the nineteenth century and of the restructuring of African society under the colonial rule of the twentieth century is essential for an understanding of the sources of much of the early creative writing, which were already preserved in the oral tradition, and of the climate in which literary inspiration grew and flourished in this century.

The generally accepted version of the history before the period of the French conquests in the late nineteenth century was that most of West Africa consisted of small, relatively feeble kingdoms or chieftainships, rarely larger than a confederation of villages, inhabited by isolated tribes bitterly hostile to each other, waging incessant destructive wars, engaging in inter-tribal slave-trading, and forming an easy prey to the more powerful invaders from the North: that for the three previous centuries internecine strife had reigned between the tribes inhabiting the valleys of the great rivers – the Senegal, the Niger, the Gambia, the Volta – and Islamic warriors keen to proselytize among the fetishists, merchants greedy for new markets and hordes of pastoral nomads seeking new pastures as they were driven south by the desert conditions of their origins: that when the French arrived, about the middle of the nineteenth century, they were widely seen as protectors and saviours and so their eventual conquests were facilitated. Although all this is not untrue, it is only part of the true picture.

If we go back before the sixteenth century, which in fact saw the fragmentation of West Africa into small hostile kingdoms, we return to the period of the Great Empires. First that of Ghana, which dominated most of West Africa south of the Sahara in the eleventh century and which saw the first great onslaught of Islam against the worship of the Serpent God Ouagoudou-Bida. This campaign inspired the Guinean historian Djibril Tamsir Niane in his dramatized version of the Sokamé myth, which is discussed in a later chapter. The religious tyranny of this period caused the eventual disruption of the vast Empire of Ghana which inaugurated a century and a half of anarchy, with perpetual wars between rival kings. In the thirteenth century the kingdom of Manding or Mali grew rich with the discovery of gold mines. The young king Soundjata Keita of Manding overthrew the cruel tyrant Soumaoro – reputed to owe his power to sorcery – and was proclaimed Emperor. The legendary exploits of Soundjata, together with the mystery associated with his birth, childhood and death, have made him one of the great mythical heroes of African epics. He was a warrior emperor, imposing his authority on warring kings, who submitted to his vassalage, thus putting an end to the ceaseless strife and establishing a peaceful, prosperous, well-organized society, whose greatness continued under his successors throughout the fourteenth century.

The fifteenth century is the period of the great Sudanese Empires. When the greatness of Mali declined, it was replaced by the rise of the kingdom of Gao, which had been successively a vassal of the Emperors of Ghana and Mali. Now, throwing off this vassalage, conquering a large area of Mali, Gao became the most powerful Empire of West Africa. It was during this period that the Portuguese, directed by Henry the Navigator, landed at Cape Verde on what is now the coast of Senegal (1444), and established trading centres. Henry's successor Don João set up a Portuguese Embassy at Niani, the capital of Mali. In the sixteenth century came the first French merchants, settling near the mouth of the Senegal River.

The final decline of the West can be dated from the sixteenth century onwards, synchronizing with the incursions of the slave-traders. The great Empires were finally broken up, and again a period of anarchy set in,

marked by the continuous tribal warfare between rival and usually usurping warrior kings. Great cities, such as Gao and Timbuktu, which had
been the centres of Islamic teaching and an important civilization, were
pillaged, and famine, misery and degradation spread far and wide. This
period of decadence continued through the seventeenth century, facilitat-
ing the invasions by the Moroccans who swept south to conquer Gao. Only
Bambara, with its capital, Ségou, remained as a powerful kingdom, which
returned to animist and fetishist practices. In the eighteenth century the
Touareg warrior hordes followed in the wake of the Moroccans. During
these two centuries the French had been increasing their trading posts near
the mouths of rivers and round the Gulf of Guinea and founding some
administrative centres, all of which flourished with the growth of slave-
trading. The Treaty of Paris in 1814 gave France the monopoly of all
trading (slaves and otherwise) of the Senegal region.

The first half of the nineteenth century was characterized by a new series
of Wars of Religion. The Fulani, nomadic herdsmen in search of fertile
pastures for their cattle and fanatical Muslims, had spread from the Upper
Nile over the Savannah regions, through the old Ghana kingdoms, into
what is now Mauritania. They were systematic Islamic proselytizers and
set up a series of theocratic states. This campaign against the remaining
vestiges of fetishism and animism was carried on by El Hadj Omar Tall,
who, on his return from Mecca in 1820, founded religious and military
communities called *zaouia*. Gaining a great reputation as a prophet and
democrat, he attracted huge numbers of disciples, mostly among Toucouleur tribesmen, including escaped slaves and victims of the oppressive
forces of a patriarchal society. From 1850 his Muslim Empire spread
through the Sudan, but inspired great hostility from neighbouring kings,
who feared his popularity. His final overthrow came from the French
general Faidherbe, with whom El Hadj signed a treaty in 1860, putting
an end to his ambition to spread his power throughout Senegal. He died
in 1864, fighting a Fula insurrection.

The second half of the nineteenth century was the period of the consoli-
dation of French power in West Africa, beginning with the conquest of
Senegal by Faidherbe between 1864 and 1870. After the interruption of
the campaign owing to the Franco-Prussian War, the putsch into the Sudan
was resumed from 1876 to 1885. In 1848 slavery had been officially
abolished in French territory by a decree of the Second Republic. In
practice the decree was never applied in Senegal and the colonization of
the area during the second half of the century had as its pretext the
humanitarian enforcement of the decree. Yet during the period of conquest,
up to the end of the century, slavery and slave-trading were widely and

openly practised through the purchase and sale of prisoners of war. The administration tolerated the practice, ostensibly to avoid awkward protests and uprisings, such as Paul Hazoumé describes in his historical novel, *Doguicimi*. A report issued in 1904 estimated that out of eight and a quarter million inhabitants of West Africa, two millions were *non-libre* to use the current euphemism. In some areas the proportion was probably something less than fifty per cent.

The French version of the history of this period is the glorification of the exploits of its military leaders, notably General Faidherbe and the explorers who followed in the wake of his victories, making possible the expansion of French settlement to the East and the North. By 1880 France could envisage an Empire stretching from Dakar to Dahomey, from Algeria to Timbuktu, from Lake Chad to the Nile. By the end of the century this Empire covered three million square kilometres of Africa.

The African side of the story is the courageous and obstinate resistance offered by the last of the warrior kings and sultans against superior forces and arms, in the series of wars that led to the final destruction of the last of the great organized African states. Particularly celebrated are two fiery, intransigent, intelligent rulers, who won the respect of their French adversaries and around whom an aura of legend was to grow: Lat Dior, the Damel (King) of Cayor, and the Almamy (Imam) Samory Touré, who, with El Hadj Omar, inspired some of the best dramatic literature from West Africa in the next century. Lat Dior is famed for his military strategy based on the policy of 'commandos' which harassed Faidherbe's armies. He was defeated in 1864 and Cayor annexed by the French, who allowed the Damel to return to his country under the Protectorate. However, when the construction of the railway from Saint-Louis to Dakar was decided upon, Lat Dior resisted bitterly the line running through his territory. War broke out again and he was killed in 1883, when Cayor was re-annexed.

Samory's story as soldier and statesman is even more remarkable. According to the Guinean historian, Suret-Canale, who compares him to Napoleon Bonaparte, he was the son of a modest pedlar and followed his father's trade. When his mother was captured in the course of a raid on his village by a neighbouring king, he went to plead for her release, which was granted conditional to Samory's being conscripted in the king's army, where he immediately distinguished himself by his innate military qualities. He left the king's services after seven years and recruited a small private army, by means of which, between 1870 and 1875, he unified the whole region from Upper Niger in the West to Sikasso in the East, to the kingdom of Ahmadou, ruler of Ségou (the son of El Hadj Omar) in the North, and South as far as the forest regions. Putting an end to the wars and dissensions that had ravaged the heart of the old Empire of Mali, he introduced a new era of peace and prosperity, encouraging agriculture and distributing justice. Wishing to impose Islam throughout his kingdom, he took the religious title of Almamy, and undertook the destruction of all fetishes and the construction of mosques. Although he established a permanent army, reinforced by reserves in case of war, Suret-Canale denied that he was basically bellicose, claiming that his military operations were limited to frontier raids to obtain prisoners of war, which were necessary currency as slaves to exchange with the British and French for arms, and with the Mauritanians for horses! His biggest campaign was the siege of Sikasso against the king, Tiébe, which failed. When the French conquered the neighbouring kingdom of Ségou and he saw his Empire threatened, Samory made terms with the French in 1887, abandoning all the regions west of Tinkasso and the Niger to their protectorates. But when the French showed signs of violating his territory more and more, after Ahmadou of Ségou had been finally overthrown, he again decided to make war. He adopted a 'scorched earth' policy, retreating into different regions already under his control, and leavng his enemies little advantage in their advances. By his qualities as a military strategist he won the great respect of his adversaries, whom he resisted for sixteen years, continually changing his headquarters in his retreat to the east. His final downfall was due to his one mistake in judgement: he did not believe in the possibility of a common front by an alliance with the neighbouring kings, who had long been divided by traditional enmity. In 1898 peace offers were made to him; he was captured and after an unsuccessful suicide attempt he was sent into exile in Gabon where he died two years later.

Meanwhile, under the Second Empire, Faidherbe had been establishing the administrative system of what was first known as 'Afrique Noire Française'. On 3 May 1854, the constitution was legalized of a system that was to operate for the next hundred years. All conquered and colonized regions were divided into *cercles* with White administrative officers, roughly equivalent to a district commissioner in the British colonial system. This administrative officer held superior rank to all other officers, of whatever professional qualifications, including doctors, engineers and teachers. Many of these governors and administrative officers were ignorant of local custom and tradition. Some were despotic, brutal and vicious. A few – like Baron Roger (pp. 2–3) and F. V. Equilbecq (see p. 13) – made serious and sympathetic attempts to understand the social background, tribal customs, local lore of their *circonscription*. The forced labour system was the common method of providing the necessary gangs for construction of roads, railways, exploiting plantations of all kinds, porterage, and also strengthening the armed forces, particularly at the time of the First World War.

Most of the education during the first period of the colonial era was in the hands of missionaries, who were instrumental in destroying much of the inherited, traditional, cultural values and institutions, which they considered to be manifestations of the devil. Faidherbe introduced lay-teaching into Senegal in 1854 to try to attract the Muslim chiefs who refused to send their sons to Catholic mission schools. Up to the end of the nineteenth century, during the whole period of conquest, very little progress was made with education, only a few primary schools being established in Senegal, Guinea, Ivory Coast, Dahomey and the Congo.

By the beginning of the twentieth century, the French were secure in their African territories. The period of conquest was over. Slavery was abolished *de facto* as well as *de jure*. An era of colonial development began, with the French sincere in their wish for co-operation with the African people in most areas. Big towns like Dakar and Abidjan developed. Roads and railways were built – alas, mostly with forced labour – linking the more important centres. Cars and radios and all the appurtenances of European life were introduced into the towns, where the tempo of life was irrevocably changed. Only in the *brousse*, (bush), existence remained unaltered. Apart from the superficial commodities of western living, the most important changes effected during the period of colonization were due to the introduction of the French educational system.

In 1903 a complete lay educational system was instituted in West Africa ranging from primary and secondary schools to normal colleges. In 1927 Senegal obtained permission from the French Ministry of Education for all urban schools to follow the same syllabus as in France, using the same text books. This was eventually applied to all the major schools in any of the French colonies, with the result that, in the second quarter of this century, Black boys sat on their school benches from Dahomey to Dakar, from Conakry to the Congo, reciting their lessons in French: multiplication tables, irregular verbs and the now proverbial history lesson beginning 'Our ancestors, the Gauls, had fair hair and blue eyes'. Teachers and inspectors for these schools were recruited in France; but in some of the village primary schools the teaching was in the hands of 'monitors' or student teachers, supplementing by the rod what they lacked in pedagogic competence. If the inspectors had often too little knowledge of local conditions to be very constructive in their criticisms and recommendations, the French

teachers were on the whole a dedicated, devoted and competent professional body. They felt it their duty to make their pupils so proficient in
the French language and so well versed in the official syllabus that the best
of them could proceed with bursaries to centres of higher education in
France. It is true that they felt they had a 'civilizing mission', to form
'French Africans', and it is easy to decry this attitude now with our
hindsight. At the time it seemed a valid policy, and not even the most
intelligent recipients of the system criticized it, except in retrospect. It was
only in the 1940s that they began to cast back Caliban's curse upon their
mentors. Be it said that in the Cameroon the Germans followed the same
policy up to the time of their defeat in 1918, when their colony came under
French control.[1]

In the primary schools the syllabus was based on a solid training in
French and arithmetic. Teaching was in French and the acquisition of a
good knowledge of the language was the first objective and an essential part
of the teaching programme. The main idea was that such educated Africans
should serve as intermediaries, interpreters and clerical assistants to the
colonial administrators. In French Equatorial Africa the granting of subsi-
dies to private primary schools was conditional to French being the only
language of instruction. Even as late as 1944 a Brazzaville conference on
education adopted the following resolution:

Instruction must be in the French language; the use of the local spoken dialects
being absolutely forbidden for teaching purposes, in private schools as well as in
public schools.[2]

In the same year, at Dakar, at the 'Conférence africaine de l'enseignement',
a certain Inspector Delage stated:

We must remember that the aim [of colonial education] is not so much to safeguard
the originality of the colonized races as to raise them up to ourselves.

I must point out that this principle was not supported by all colonial
administrators. I have already quoted, on p. xviii of the preface, Governor
Camille Guy's condemnation of Maran's *Batouala*. It is relevant here to
put the reference in its full context: M. Guy wrote:

More air! A good syllabus can only be obtained by pruning, not by additions.
Instruction in French, in elementary science, some professional and technical
training suitable to the environment. That is all that is required. Otherwise we
shall create not French citizens, but arrogant, disorientated, displaced persons [the

[1] For an account of life in the German Cameroon, see *Cette Afrique-là* [That Africa]
by Jean Ikelle-Matiba (Paris, Présence Africaine, 1963), in which the Prussian colonial
education system is described.
[2] Quoted by Jean Suret-Canale: *Afrique noire, occidentale et centrale*, vol. II: *L'Ere coloniale*
(*1900–1945*), 1968, p. 477. Paris, Editions Sociales. 3rd edition, 1968, p. 477.

words he uses are *désaxés, déclassés*] who have lost their indigenous virtues only to acquire the vices of their teachers and instructors...*A.F.*, 192.2, no. 1, p. 45.

This fear of the results of equality in the education offered to the indigenous people was probably fairly widespread too among the settlers and traders who saw a threat to their position as *Herrenvolk*. In his novel *Afrique, nous t'ignorons* [Our unknown Africa] situated in the Cameroon just before the outbreak of the Second World War in Europe, Benjamin Matip puts into the mouth of his European trader what was probably the common reaction. In a very contrived scene, M. Robert is criticizing the quality of the bananas brought for sale that day from the surrounding plantations. The 'Evolué' Sam, son of the local Chief, explains that it has been a bad season for all fruit and goes on:

'In any case, people like fruit for their vitamin content, I believe.' 'What?' retorted Robert, scandalised. 'Who's been telling you about vitamins?...People have been saying for a long time that there should be a special teaching programme adapted to the needs of you folk. I don't know what the hell your monitors are getting up to, or what the Director of Education in Yaoundé is getting at either, for that matter...When they've stuffed your heads full of fine words about vitamins, equality and liberty, there'll be no-one left in Africa except doctors, lawyers, magistrates...No one to dig the soil or serve tea...It's not surprising that you come to me with your cheeky talk, you ignorant monkey!' (pp. 30–1)

As a result of this purely French-orientated training, the idea was inculcated that Africans receiving such training were superior to their 'savage', uneducated brethren. The myth of French cultural superiority grew fast and firmly, and with it the belief that the acquisition of the French tongue and a French education was the only key to progress – which at the time was true. Works of fiction and of autobiography, appearing in large numbers from the end of the Second World War, hardly ever fail to include references, some bitter, some grateful, some few even objective, to the influence of the French schooling that the authors had received in their earlier years in Africa. To quote one example from many, Seydou Badian, the Malian writer, in his rather prosy, moralizing novel *Sous l'orage* (*Kany*) [Beneath the storm] (1963) makes one of the representatives of the young generation say: 'The white people only respect those who speak their language; they are the only ones who are civilized'. At a better literary level is the episode of the 'symbol' in Bernard Dadié's novel *Climbié* (1954), where he described the mental anguish the young pupils underwent, as their fellows were encouraged by the Principal to mock and victimize those who uttered a word of dialect. This school teacher had been inspired to think of the symbolic cube of wood, which the miscreant was forced to carry as punishment, until he could catch another child guilty of a linguistic lapse:

It was the end of the morning lessons. Outside the school premises each one could speak his own dialect. But Climbié had to carry the symbol, because he had spoken *N'zima* inside the school building. He could not show his resentment; the pupils who were ragging him were too numerous. His friends did not take part, but the most aggressive ones were those he had himself caught out several times. So he watched them dancing around him, until each one took his own way home.

Climbié went home alone, abandoned by his own friends, who were scared off by the presence of the symbol in his pocket, among the marbles and tops. Climbié could not eat his lunch, he was in a hurry to get rid of the little cube... If he didn't manage to before the end of the school day, he would have to stay behind to clean the yard and sweep all the class-rooms all by himself, with the symbol still weighing down his pocket. (pp. 106–7) [12]

Mongo Beti, who usually maintains a tone of comic irony in his novel *Mission terminée* [Mission accomplished], 1957 (see p. 206 for bibliographical details), allows a note of personal bitterness to penetrate the words of his hero Jean-Marie Medza, when he recalls, in the name of his generation, the school system of Cameroon in the years between the Wars:

Do you remember that period? Fathers took their children to school, like sheep driven to a slaughter-house. From villages deep in the bush, more than thirty miles away, little kids were brought by their parents to enter a school, any school. What a miserable crowd, those youngsters! Lodged by distant relatives near the school, or by distant acquaintances of their father, underfed, starving, thrashed all day by ignorant 'monitors', stupefied by books which presented them with a world which had no resemblance to their own, fighting all day among themselves, those kids were us, you remember?...

Catechized, confirmed, forcibly fed with communions like the Almighty's little geese, confessed at Easter and Trinity, enrolled beneath the banners of the Fourteenth of July processions, militarized, presented at all the national and international commissions as objects of pride, those kids were us, do you remember? (pp. 231–2 [1958, p. 188; 1966, p. 165])

This purely French-orientated education programme was based on two premises: that the Negro was a 'blank page', with no inherited personality, cultural values or institutions; or that what he had were barbarous, primitive or puerile; that, nevertheless, given the same opportunities, the African 'child' could become as 'civilized' as the French themselves, at which stage he should enjoy the same civic rights and advantages, including direct representation in the French Assembly.

Some of this prejudice was understandable, owing to ignorance among educationalists of the foundations of African culture or of the history of the indigenous people, which existed only in oral form. Some exception to this general prejudice was, however, made in the case of the Muslims, who were considered to be of superior civilization to the Negroes of other religions. This may be because, having assimilated some of the Arab culture with the study of the Koran, they could communicate by means of Arabic written characters, which were applied to some Bantu languages, such as Fula (in parts of Senegal) and Hausa (in Northern Nigeria).

In 1906 the Service des Affaires Musulmanes was created for regions with a predominantly Muslim population. One of its functions was the establishment of Franco–Arab schools (called *médersa*) for the sons of chiefs. Their main function was to train a few of the leaders of the community to act as interpreters and secretaries for the administrative officers, working with the Islamic tribes, and to translate into French the words and writings of the notables among them. The *médersa* in Saint-Louis was officially named in 1922 'École des Fils de Chef et des Interprètes' (School for Interpreters and Sons of Chiefs).

Koranic schools continued to exist side by side with lay schools – a situation illustrated by Cheikh Hamidou Kane's *Aventure ambiguë* [Ambiguous adventure, 1961], which describes the author's early education in Senegal in the thirties. Yet even these declined progressively under the pressure to westernize. Other African cults and cultures, unrecognized or misunderstood, took refuge in a clandestine existence, favoured by their esoteric character, and continued as 'secret societies'. The sacred forest, the fetishist cults, the initiation schools, were looked on as 'Schools for sorcerers' by the colonists and considered archaic by the younger generation of Africans. 'All that is out of date', says a young man in Seydou Badian's *Sous l'Orage*, referring to the tests of endurance that his elder brother Sibiri speaks of with pride, 'civilization demands something different. We are not made for the life Sibiri talks about. That's all right for ignorant folk.'

On the practical level, the new demands of existence made the young men's long period of training no longer feasible.

Since the economic conditions of life have changed, since recruitment has affected the young men, the period of training has been much reduced, to allow the villages to supply workers,

wrote Captain Duffner in 1934 in his *Croyances et coutumes religieuses chez les Guerzés et les Manons de la Guinée française* (*B.C.E.H.S.*, 1934, no. 4, p. 545).

FIRST AWAKENINGS OF BLACK CONSCIOUSNESS AND
INTEREST IN AFRICA

The first important factor in the re-awakening of the consciousness of Black
Africa to its own identity was the First World War, in which Black troops
took a conspicuous part. In 1857, General Faidherbe had formed the
tirailleurs sénégalais [Senegalese sharpshooters] finding them useful in the
conquest of the other African territories. In the early years of the twentieth
century they were used in military interventions in Morocco. At the
outbreak of war in 1914 there were 14,000 sharpshooters in service in
French West Africa and some 15,000 elsewhere in North Africa. All these
were sent to the front. Their service outside Africa somewhat shattered
the image of the invincible White man. For one thing, Whites were
fighting against Whites. White men were seen to exploit other White men.
Some Senegalese service-men took part in the mutinies in Champagne and
in the Black Sea. Echoes of the Russian Revolution reached them in 1917.

Meanwhile a revival of interest in African folk-lore was taking place in
Europe. This was encouraged by the researches of some of the more
enlightened colonial administrators, such as F. V. Equilbecq, by ethnologists – or social anthropologists as we would now call them – and then
spread to French writers and other scholars. In the course of his duties
as deputy colonial administrator of the French Sudan, Equilbecq travelled
widely before the war in Senegal, Upper Volta, Niger and Guinea. Wherever he went he made an effort to collect from the *griots* local folk-lore,
tales, proverbs and songs. In 1913 he published a collection of these,
translated into French, together with a long and most illuminating essay
in which he analyses the different categories of tales, their themes and
various major characters: *Aux Lueurs des feux de veillée, Essai sur la
littérature merveilleuse des noirs, suivi de contes indigènes de l'ouest african*
(Paris, Ernest Leroux, 1913). [By the light of the watch-fires, an essay on
the wonderful literature of the Negroes, followed by indigenous tales from
West Africa]. The success of this work was so great that Equilbecq was
encouraged to publish two further volumes of stories in 1915 and 1916.
It should be noted that the term 'Black literature' is used by Equilbecq for
the first time to refer to the authentic oral heritage, which he transcribed
and translated into French, without tampering with the original expression
and style. This work is invaluable to the student of folk-lore, particularly
to those interested in the comparison between different civilizations. A new
edition of the whole three volumes has been prepared recently by M.
Robert Cornevin and published by Maisonneuve et Larose in 1972.

The French poet Blaise Cendrars, in turn, undertook to compile a volume of legends, tales, fables, proverbs and other forms of folk-lore from all regions of Africa, all tribes, and all ethnic and linguistic groups, which he published in 1919 under the title of *Anthologie nègre* [Negro Anthology]. He, too, could not as yet find any original writings by Africans, and the contents are limited to transcriptions and translations from oral literature. A second edition of his anthology was called for in 1921, as the first went rapidly out of print. In 1947, with the even greater resurgence of interest in African folk-lore that followed the Second World War, Corrêa put out a completely revised edition. Many of the legends tell of the creation and origins of the world. There are fetishist and totemic legends, told as simple bald narratives with no attempt by the translator to intervene to add literary effects. There are tales based on popular 'science', such as 'Why the crocodile does not eat fowl' or 'Why monkeys live in trees'.[3] There are moral and humorous tales such as 'The crocodile, the man and the jackal', which appear in many forms in West African folk-lore and which later African writers tell in different versions and in their own styles. (Compare, for example, Birago Diop's story 'Le Salaire' [The Reward] and Benjamin Matip's more complicated 'Adieu Guerre, Adieu Paradis, in *A la belle Etoile* [Farewell to war, farewell to Eden, in Under the Stars]). There are some tales of fantasy, adventure and romance, which came close to the field of pure fiction. And there are, of course, examples from the traditional cycles of animal fables: those of the tree-frog, the hyena, the tortoise, the hare. On the whole this anthology is still of more interest to the student of social anthropology and folk-lore than of literature, except in as much as it proved a stimulus to Africans themselves to return to the inspiration of their own rich heritage of fables and legends and to retell these in French. For this was to be the basis of the first important creative writings in French by Africans.

In 1925 Roland Lebel presented a doctoral thesis at the Sorbonne on 'L'Afrique occidentale depuis 1870' [West Africa from 1870] (published Larose, 1925). His researches led him to explore the place of West Africa in French literature and then to examine colonial literature, as such, in a study published in 1928 (*Etudes de littérature coloniale*, Paris, Peyronnet & Cie). In the same year he produced the next significant anthology of African writing, under the title of *Livre du Pays noir* [Land of the Negro folk] (Paris, Edit. du Monde Moderne, 1928). But 'African literature' still meant predominantly writings by Frenchmen, about Africa, for Frenchmen. The authors of the passages included are mostly explorers, soldiers,

---

[3] Rudyard Kipling's *Jungle Books*, with similar themes based on Indian lore, were published in 1894–5, that is, about a quarter of a century before the African legends were discovered by Cendrars.

travellers, with a few professional writers and authors of stories for children. Lebel's comprehensive bibliography shows that much had already been written in French about the 'Pays des Noirs'. From these he chooses 'les plus belles pages' to quote his own words, which he thinks will be best suited to show the nature of the country and its inhabitants' lives in all their picturesque exoticism. His main aim seems to be to supplement brochures and books of propaganda as a source of information, in the hope of overcoming the ignorance of the average Frenchman about the 'Dark Continent'. This mild propaganda for future colonists is made more explicit in the preface by Maurice Delafosse, then colonial governor, who writes:

I should not be surprised if some of the readers of this book were inspired with a new vocation or if some of the inhabitants of the Metropolis felt the urge to visit these distant regions, which modern means of communication have brought so close to us, and perhaps then decide to stay as colonists in these attractive lands. (Lebel, *Livre du pays noir*, p. 8)

In Lebel's bibliography we find, for the first time, mention of completely original publications by Black writers, together with the editor's assessment of the interest and quality of the work: Ahmadou Mapaté Diagne's *Les trois volontés de Malic* (Collection des Livres Roses, 1920), Bakary Diallo's *Force bonté* (Rieder, 1926), R. Maran's *Batouala* (A. Michel, 1921) and its sequel *Djouma, chien de brousse* (1927).

The first of these works quoted by Lebel, Diagne's African version of the traditional 'Three Wishes' theme, was intended by the author to be an uplifting reader in French for primary school classes of Senegal, such as those he taught.[4] It would not occupy a place in a History of Literature, were it not for the fact that it is generally accepted as the first piece of original fiction written by an African, of modern times. The second, Diallo's *Force bonté*, is often described as the first novel written by a Negro, ignoring the fact that *Batouala* was published five years before it appeared. Is it that Maran was accepted as an 'assimilated Negro', a 'Black Frenchman', whose name did not even betray his colour, while Diallo corresponded to the archetype of the untaught, or self-taught, ingenuous Senegalese herdsman? Is it a more subtle refusal to accept Maran's corrosive, disconcerting work, which forced his readers out of their complacent paternalism *vis-à-vis* the Black colonies while Diallo reassured with his comforting message of gratitude to his White benefactors, and of peace, goodwill and understanding among men? These two attitudes are clearly

[4] In his autobiographical notes, published in the review *Awa*, no. 7, Dakar, Birago Diop records the impression that this little book made upon him as a schoolboy in Dakar (he was 14 when Diagne's book was published), recalling how it made him feel 'concerned for the first time in matters of "literature"'.

displayed in Jean-Richard Bloch's prefatory note. After explaining to the reader that Bakary Diallo is not one of the Negroes whom one might expect to try his hand at writing – a school-teacher or a civil servant – but a herdsman who only began to stammer a few words of French when he was conscripted as a *tirailleur*, Bloch goes on:

But it was in Africa that his heart opened. And these secrets he confides to us, in a language that is foreign to him, are dictated by *that admirable simplicity, that spontaneity, goodness, candour, guilelessness, which are the fragrant essence of the Negro soul*, when this has not been deformed by oppression . . . [my italics]

Force bonté is an autobiographical novel in a lyrical exalted mode. It opens with a Rousseauist description of the simple, contented life of a dreamy Fula shepherd boy, contemplating sky, trees and stars instead of watching his flock, which he continually loses, fascinated by the wonders of Nature and meditating on the Almighty who created it all. Even when his idyll is brutally shattered by conscription, and training for strange military manoeuvres, given in an incomprehensible language; even with the tribulations of active service at the Front, and when badly wounded with a fractured jaw that leaves him scarcely able to eat or speak, Bakary never loses his faith in the goodness of man in general and the White man in particular. He reacts with puzzled incomprehension to the acts of brutality or injustice which he witnesses or from which he suffers himself, and only retains finally the memory of kindness, generosity, loyalty, *force bonté*[5] and an ineradicable belief in the possibility of permanent co-operation and understanding between Black and White.

Apart from the noble sentiments expressed and the saintly character of the author, this book would be a remarkable *tour de force* on the linguistic and stylistic score alone, if it were the unaided and spontaneous composition of an ignorant herdsman, whose total knowledge of French was derived from his service in the armed forces and his sojourns in military hospitals and convalescent camps. However, it is impossible not to nourish some suspicion that the book was largely 'ghosted' or at least radically edited by a member of the staff of Rieders who published it, or by someone from the literary and intellectual circles of Paris which 'adopted' Bakary during his convalescence and the long period before demobilization. I have discussed these possibilities with M. Robert Delavignette, a former Directeur de l'Ecole Coloniale de la France d'Outre-Mer, now living in retirement in Paris, who knew Diallo well, and Mme Marie-Rose Paupy,

[5] This work is sometimes incorrectly quoted as 'Force *et* Bonté', as if meaning 'strength and goodness'. The 'Force' of the title is, in fact, used as an invariable adjective, with the sense of 'a considerable quantity'. I would thus translate Diallo's title as 'Abundant goodness'.

whose father, Marcel Martinet, was on the editorial staff of Rieders when *Force bonté* was being published. Mme Paupy, who was a young child at the time, and her mother, Mme Renée Martinet, have vivid memories of the frequent visits that Bakary Diallo made to their home in Sceaux, for many years after the First World War, between periods in hospital for surgical treatment of his shattered jaw. It was difficult to judge his command of French as his speech was impeded by his facial injuries. But they confirm his gentle, rather melancholic, poetic nature, which seems consistent with the lyrical outpourings of his prose, even if he could have been indebted for his final fluency to the good offices of some friend.

M. Delavignette met Bakary Diallo some years after the appearance of the novel. His memories are of a sensitive, poetic idealist, completely consistent with the personality that emerges from his writing, believing with deep sincerity in the possibility of understanding between France and Senegal, which at the time, did not increase his favour among his compatriots. He cannot confirm whether Diallo was, at the time of writing his book, in such complete command of the stylistic and grammatical resources of the French language, that he could have proceeded without substantial assistance. Monsieur Delavignette does, however, offer some interesting indirect evidence, from which some deductions can be made. In the early period of his conscription, Diallo attracted the attention of a colonial officer who made himself responsible for teaching him French; so his command of the language was not solely limited to barrack-room and drill-ground experience. He next became one of the African *protégés* of Mme Lucie Cousturier, the daughter of a high colonial official in French Guinea, who served as a nurse volunteer from 1914 to 1918 in hospitals in the South of France, where Diallo was being treated for his facial wounds. After the War she continued to serve as a god-mother to the expatriated *tirailleurs*, about whom she wrote a little book, *Des Inconnus chez moi* [Strangers in my home], showing an intuitive understanding of the African psychology of which the average Frenchman was quite unconscious. (Sympathetic as Jean-Richard Bloch was, the extract quoted from his Preface indicates this patronizing ignorance of reality). When Mme Cousturier later returned to Africa, she wrote another account of her impressions, *Mes Inconnus chez eux* [My strangers in their homeland], which was published by Rieder and caused a few ripples in *avant-garde* circles in Paris. The fact that the publishers were the same, and that Lucie Cousturier had literary pretensions, could lead to the conclusion that she had not only encouraged but had also assisted her *protégé* to write of his experiences. Finally, M. Delavignette rejects the idea that *Force bonté* could have been 'ghosted' by a member of Rieder's staff, as he knew well both Jacques Robertfranche, the director of the editorial division, and Jean-Richard Bloch, who was asked to write the Preface, and is convinced that they would both have respected the author's originality and spontaneity of expression. Even if this question cannot finally be resolved, it is important to note that the love of deliberately 'fine writing' continued to be fostered in Black Africa by the mediocre quality of the primary and secondary readers on which young pupils' literary appetites were nourished right up to the mid-sixties, and that these were probably responsible for the cliché-ridden, pseudo-romantic style of some African novelists. If French school-children were also fed on this same fodder, they were exposed to other correctives in the later stages of adolescence and in their higher studies.

After these promising and ambitious beginnings, Bakary Diallo gave no further signs of his literary talents, except for a longish poem, *Mon M'Bala*, an ode to his native village, written in Wolof with a literal translation in French on the facing page, composed at Podor in September 1948 and appearing in the periodical *Présence Africaine*, no. 6, in 1949.

Maran's work requires much closer and more serious consideration, not only for the important original contribution he made to French literature as a whole, but also for the influence he was to have on the development of a future generation of Negro-African writers in French. His *Batouala*[6] was the first *véritable roman nègre*, thus a brief analysis of this work, and its sequel, *Djouma, chien de brousse* [Djouma, a dog of the bush] will be useful, although I shall not deal with any of Maran's other writings, which include numerous novels, collections of short stories, poems and biographies of African explorers.

During his service as an administrative officer in the Oubangui-Shari region of French Equatorial Africa, Maran conceived the idea for his first novel, which took him six years to write. He called it a series of etchings, which is a most apt description, if one considers that etchings are the result of engraving an image *burned out in acid on a copper plate*. It tells the story of the life of the village of which Batouala is the headman. The author takes care to give precise details as to the geographical area in question, in order to ensure the authenticity of his narrative. It is an area formerly rich, but now reduced to poverty by seven years of French colonial exploitation. The inhabitants are debilitated by forced labour, which prevents them from attending to their own crops. There is a detailed description of the village life and customs. However, Maran's intention is not to perpetuate folk-lore, nor to evoke the picturesque, but to express Batouala's awakening to the abuses of the colonial system. Symbolically,

---

[6]   The original edition being long out of print, *Batouala* was re-issued in 1969 by Albin Michel. Now available in anon. trans. Heinemann, 1975. *Djouma* is still o.p.

the novel opens with a description of Batouala's physical awakening from sleep; a description which includes a wealth of Rabelaisian detail of his stretching, yawning, blowing his nose (without benefit of handkerchief), scratching and what in French is politely called *renvois retentissants*.

In spite of the Goncourt award, the average French reader reacted to this material with incredulity or contempt and the colonial administration was frankly indignant (see pp. xviii, 9). Lebel cautiously noted that the descriptions of the 'primitive life of the Negroes of Oubangui' were 'doubtless exaggerated'. The judgement of later decades as to the merits of Maran's novel has been somewhat different.

It is interesting that soon after this André Gide visited Central Africa and wrote his *Journey to the Congo* and his *Return to the Chad*, published in 1927 and 1928 respectively. There is no mention in Gide's *Journal* of his having read Maran's novel, but it is extremely likely that it was discussed in the literary circles which he frequented, if for no other reason than that a Negro had won the most coveted literary award in France. So it could well be that Gide's plan to go to the Congo and see for himself what conditions were like there may have been hatched, or at least encouraged, as a result of the controversy raging around *Batouala*. What we do know is that Gide visited the Eboués and that Maran, a close friend of Felix Eboué, who had provided him with much of the factual material for *Batouala*, must have been discussed.[7] So, what Maran expressed in the form of fiction, André Gide presented as a hard factual chronicle, written by a man who enjoyed tremendous prestige among his contemporaries and whose credentials could never be doubted: namely a severe, bitter indictment of the French colonial régime.

In the same year as Gide's *Journey to the Congo* appeared, Maran published the sequel to *Batouala*, *Djouma, chien de brousse*. The title is disarming, as it might lead the reader to expect a harmless animal tale – a French equivalent of Fitzpatrick's *Jock of the Bushveld*. But Djouma is Batouala's dog, and the story is the continuation of Batouala's life. Wrapped up in a series of *Decameron*-like episodes concerning the infidelities of Batouala's favourite wife, told with vigour and apparent guilelessness, one has a dog's-eye view, a *mondo cane*, of the ravages made in the colony by forced labour on the rubber plantations, on the roads, or in porterage for explorers, missionaries, travellers of all kinds.

What really concerns us here is to determine the contribution made by Maran in these two novels to Negro-African creative literature and, more

---

[7] For an account of Gide's visit to the Eboués, see B. Weinstein: *Eboué* (O.U.P. 1972) pp. 99–100. More light on the comparison between Gide and Maran can be obtained from the latter's article 'Gide et l'Afrique noire' in *Présence Africaine*, first series, no. v, pp 739–48.

indirectly, to the birth and development of the Negritude movement in the next decade. As to the former, we must recognize in these books, the first completely original, naturalistic works of fiction, set in tropical Africa, recounting the vicissitudes of Negroes without sentimentality or romanticism, written by a man who identifies himself with the suffering of his Black brothers. This is obviously an important achievement, especially in comparison with the best of earlier novels about Africa by French writers; for example, Pierre Loti's *Roman d'un Spahi* (1881), the first novel set in Senegal (*Madame Chrysanthème*, translated to Africa), the sentimental story of the liaison of a French soldier and a native of Saint-Louis, or *L'Atlantide* (1919), an adventure story in which Pierre Benoît symbolizes the mystery and attraction of 'deepest Africa' for the White man. Maran, on the other hand, writes sincerely and convincingly from the heart of his scene, from under the skin of his protagonists, and yet. . . the impression still remains that he is 'the Other', to use Sartre's expression.[8] In spite of his Negro forebears, in spite of his black skin, in spite of his sincere identification with the cause of the colonized people of Africa, he does not offer a positive manifesto, a rallying cry to which other aspiring Black writers and intellectuals will respond. The parallel between Maran and Gide has already been mentioned. For all his success in writing from the inside of Africa, Maran might just as well have been Gide – discounting differences of personality and literary style – or, for that matter, any traveller in Africa, or administrator equipped with the eyes to distinguish injustice and the pen to denounce it.

Maran's polemical fiction is in direct line with Voltaire, inspired by the same burning need to expose victimization, injustice and human suffering. A similar passion animates the poems of Aimé Césaire, David Diop and Léopold Senghor; however they do not stop at the denunciation of the evils of a system, at being 'the mouth of misfortunes that have no mouth', but propose the deliberate cultivation of pride of colour and race, expressed in poetry and prose that is profoundly African in subject, inspiration and style. To conclude then, I would range Maran among the important but marginal phenomena in the field of African writing.

The success of Maran's first two novels is indicative of the great interest in Africa that spread through Europe in the years between the wars. The subject of these works, moreover, cannot have failed to stimulate the Black intellectuals and students in Paris during this period, in their return to the

[8] In this respect it is important to note that some of his compatriots and fellow Blacks, reproached him for having illustrated only the most 'primitive' aspect of the Negro personality in *Batouala*. L. Damas, on the other hand, while judging his denunciations of colonial abuses as scarcely severe enough, adds that ' *it is as a Frenchman* that René Maran denounced them' (my italics).

inspiration of their common heritage. In this they were helped by the work of two ethnologists, the German scholar and explorer Leo Frobenius and the Frenchman Maurice Delafosse, both of whom had acquired a great reputation for objectivity in this new field of studies.

Frobenius[9] spent from 1890 to 1910 exploring in West and Equatorial Africa and was one of the first Europeans to admit that the peoples of these regions, so-called 'primitive savages', had a medieval culture equal to that of the West, that they were 'civilized to the marrow of their bones', to quote his own words. His works on the history and origins of African civilization appeared in the original German from 1894 to 1928. The first translation in French, *Histoire de la civilisation africaine* appeared in 1936 (Paris, Gallimard), so that his direct influence on the French-speaking world, particularly on the Black students in Paris, was anticipated by that of Maurice Delafosse. Delafosse was first a Colonial Governor in A.O.F., then Professor at the Ecole Coloniale des Langues Orientales in Paris. A linguist as well as an anthropologist, he published grammars and dictionaries of some African languages. He was largely responsible for encouraging native school-teachers, clerical assistants and interpreters to send in contributions to periodicals of a semi-technical nature: articles on African Languages, histories of the reigns of the sultans, and of the local wars of which oral tradition had preserved only fragmentary accounts. Although Delafosse's interests were primarily linguistic and sociological, he was indirectly responsible for the collection and preservation of material that had a literary importance. An interesting example is the *Petit Manuel français–bambara*, compiled by Moussa Travelé (1919) for which M. Delafosse wrote an introduction. It was intended as a reader for colonial administrators who wished to learn Bambara, and contained proverbs, riddles and tales translated into French. Delafosse tells the student that these are a correct but unfortunately not literal translation, as they should be in a volume destined for 'amateurs de linguistique', but perhaps on this account 'students of folk-lore will find plenty to satisfy their curiosity'.

Delafosse's own scholarly works date from 1912 to 1927, when he summarized the results of his personal experiences and researches in Africa. The most important, *Les Noirs de l'Afrique* (Paris, Payot, 1922),[10] was translated into English as *The Negroes of Africa, their History, their Culture*, by F. Fligelman (Washington, Associated Publishers, 1931). Delafosse also encouraged and guided the research of J. L. Monod, then Chief School Inspector for A.O.F., which resulted in his *Histoire de l'Afrique occidentale française*, adapted for schools in his region.

[9] Yambo Ouologuem satirizes him savagely under the name Fritz Schrobenius in his novel, *Le Devoir de violence* (Paris, Seuil, 1968).

[10] Also: *Haut-Sénégal-Niger*, 3 vols, Paris, Maisonneuve & Larose, repr. 1972.

The combination of these influences – namely the French educational system, particularly with its emphasis on the assimilation of Black intellectuals and the growth of a racial and cultural consciousness among the latter, simultaneously with the integration of Africans and Negroes from the Caribbean in common political and cultural organizations – resulted in the conception of an authentic Negro–African literature, whose birth is generally accepted to have taken place on the Left Bank of Paris in the early thirties. Its birth certificate can be said to be the review *Légitime Défense*, founded by the Martiniquan Etienne Lero; its godparents the Marxist branch of the Surrealist movement and committed literature of the time. It was baptized 'Negritude', but only some years later.

The Negritude movement has been analysed, dissected, studied, illustrated by countless critics and scholars over the past fifteen years. I shall therefore give here only an outline of its earliest aims and manifestations, reserving for a later chapter on poetry some comparison between its most important exponents.

The first number of *Légitime Défense* in 1932 was also the last. But before its premature demise (followed eight years later by that of its founder, at the age of thirty), it had launched the principle of 'thinking Black'. It offered the example of the fiery revolutionary verses of the two American Negro poets, Langston Hughes and Claude Mackay, who had brought to literature 'Marinated in red wine, the African love of life, the African joy in love, and African dream of death'. Lero was mainly concerned with denouncing the bourgeois society of his homeland, 'the mulatto society, intellectually and physically bastardized, whose literature was fed on white decadence', and for this reason he called on his compatriots to make common cause with the Senegalese and the Congolese. Their new writings were to be a literature of combat enrolled under the banner of Marxism.

The first true prophet of militant Negritude was Lero's compatriot, Aimé Césaire, who, with Léopold Sédar Senghor and Léon Damas, founded *L'Etudiant Noir* in 1932 to succeed *Légitime Défense*, as an organ for the publication of writings by fellow Black students. These were encouraged to write on the basis of colour rather than race. Césaire called on the Black writer to offer himself deliberately as the mirror of his birthplace, his environment and his people, Black *qua* Black; to use his special revelation to transmit the experience and emotions of his people. In his own *Cahier d'un retour au pays natal*, first published in 1939 [The English translation, *Return to my Native Land*, by Emile Snyder, appears in the bilingual edition published by Présence Africaine in 1971], and in which the word

'Negritude' first appears in print, he set the example, not rejecting the indignities, the shame and degradation of past history, but distilling out of the memory of the slave-ship, the slave-market, the overseer's whip, the marshes and the chain-gang, a new pride of race and colour.

One of the early manifestations of this attempt at 'decolonization' of the African mentality and literary inspiration, was a search for authentic African subjects, a return to the cultural heritage of legend, myth and folk-lore which certain White scholars had been instrumental in preserving. In the next chapter I look at creative writing in French inspired by these traditional sources (excluding dramatic works, which I treat separately in Chapter 2).

1. The transition from yesterday to today

When Europeans introduced writing into West Africa in the colonial period, this offered, in the first instance, a means of preserving traditional literary material which, up till then, had had no satisfactory method of transcription. Even in regions under a strong Arab influence, where the Arabic script was in use, this was reserved for religious teachings. The simultaneous introduction of a European tongue meant that the oral literature was most likely to be preserved in translation, which was often accompanied by a transcription of the original text in the vernacular, to assist the colonists to acquire a working knowledge of the latter. The emphasis was thus, as we have noticed with Moussa Travelé's translations from the Bambara, on the linguistic rather than the literary content.

We have seen, in the preceding chapter, how Europeans were at an early stage responsible for collecting and translating oral material and introducing it into France, beginning with Baron Roger, and his 'Fables in the manner of La Fontaine' to illustrate his researches into the Wolof language; then how, in the first two decades of the twentieth century, Equilbecq, Cendrars and Lebel compiled their anthologies which had more of an ethnological than linguistic emphasis. They were, incidentally, satisfying the taste for the picturesque and exotic in literature, which was inherited from the Romantic period, and given a new lease of life by Leconte de Lisle and the Parnassians; but primarily the success of these anthologies was due to the growing interest in folk-lore, which was the basis of the African oral literature. This consisted of proverbs, riddles, fables, myths, chronicles, legends, songs. The border-line between the different genres was tenuous. The story-tellers were poets and the poets were singers. Poetry was allied to song and history to legend. Incantatory songs of praise were a form of history as their substance was the genealogy of great families and the exploits of past heroes. As with the *chanson de geste*, elements of magic and the supernatural were indissolubly mingled with elements of fact. Mythological tales expressed the relationships that governed the creation and construction of the universe and the existence of its inhabitants. Stripped of its sacred element and some of its supernatural, and with an added dose of realism, the myth becomes the folk-tale, which is nevertheless still closely associated with obscure and mystical forces. Maxims and proverbs, rich in imagery, verbal sonorities, litanic repetitions and anaphora were close to poetry; or, in their epigrammatic concision could be miniature fables. The participation of the audience in the tale or recital of the professional singer and chronicler, by means of gestures, exclamations, repetitions, choruses and dances, could transform the occasion into a dramatic spectacle. It is not my intention, nor indeed is it within my competence, to attempt a study of the oral literature of Africa. This has been done by linguists, social anthropologists and ethnomusicologists. But it is interesting to note that, according to one of the most eminent of the latter, Monsieur Herbert Pepper, Africa was fortunate in that her poets and story-tellers long ignored or disdained the written form, in so far as writing tends to crystallize composition into too rigid categories, limit the form and impoverish the concept of reality:

...the mark of reality is its living, fluid, formless quality. The major art is that of speech. Speech expresses a vital force... It possesses a magic virtue, but only becomes poetry in so far as it is rhythmic.
(*Anthologie de la vie africaine, Congo-Gabon.* Documents recueillis et commentés par Herbert Pepper. Disques Ducretet-Thomson, nos. 320 C126–8. Sleeve notes)

If we accept Pepper's premise, then we immediately have an explanation of some of the limitations of African literature in French: once it has adopted a written form the richest and most original work will be found in poetry and folk-tales, that is, those genres nearest to the oral source, while that imported genre, the novel, with rare exceptions, will be enclosed in a pillory of social realism; dramatic literature will lose its spontaneous expressivity when it is transferred to the confines of a conventional theatre and will be most successful when it retains the attributes of total spectacle, such as it enjoyed in the days of the purely oral tradition.

In West Africa the *griots* were the story-tellers, chroniclers, praise-singers, poets, professional entertainers. A basic knowledge of the techniques and conventions of the recital was as much a part of their stock-in-trade as the content of their narratives. Both 'libraries' and skills would be transmitted from father to son in the caste. To these, the narrators would add new elements inspired by their own individual gifts – unexpected imaginative details to surprise and delight were introduced among the well-known traditional features. Some specialized in realistic descriptions; some in complex refined, courtly poetry; some inspired awe and admiration by their eloquence in recounting noble, heroic exploits; some diverted by their comic burlesque, colloquial language or bawdy episodes.

When aspiring African writers, encouraged by the Negritude movement in the thirties, looked to their national heritage for the content of their works, it was to the *griots* that they turned, and their reservoir of local lore. And for the next thirty years Negro-African writers continued to express their debt to these predecessors without whom the oral literature would have been lost. Some go so far as to attribute to the *griots* all the credit, not only for the literary material, but also for the form and style of their own work, claiming for themselves only the modest role of translator. Birago Diop called his first collection of tales from Senegal and Upper Volta *Les Contes d'Amadou Koumba*, Amadou Koumba being the *griot* of his family on his mother's side, whom he met by chance between 1935 and 1938, during his travels as a veterinary surgeon in the French Sudan.[1] Djibril Tamsir Niane, the Guinean historian, tells us that he owes his historical novel, *Soundjata ou l'épopée mandingue*, to an obscure *griot* of the village of Djeliba Koro, in the Seguiri district of Guinea, whose narrative he simply transcribed and translated. Niane adds this appreciation of the function of the traditional *griot*, whose great historical lore and narrative talents he had learned to value (his note evoking an irresistible reminder of Fénelon):

If today [in the nineteen-sixties] the *griot* is reduced to making a living from his music or even by working with his hands, this was not always the case in the Africa of former times. Then the *griots* were the Kings' Counsellors... It is from among the *griots* that the kings chose tutors for the young princes. (p. 5) [vii]

We shall see this role of the *griot* reappearing in a number of historical dramas written in the past decades. Jurist, professor of history and constitutional law, the *griot* was orator and stylist as well, showing as much concern for the literary form and expression as for the content of his teaching.

Niane's *griot*, the chronicler of *Soundjata*, will be the best to give us an example of his particular literary style, in which the imagery, the rhythmical phrasing and incantatory repetitions are very close to poetry:

I am a *griot*. It is I, Djeli, Mamadou Kouyaté, son of Bintou Kouyaté and of Djeli Kedian Kouyaté, master in the art of speech. Since time immemorial the Kouyaté have been in the service of the Princes Keita of Manding. We are sacks of words,

---

[1] It seems as if Birago Diop only borrowed the name from this chance encounter. In his autobiographical notes published in *Awa*, no. 7, he gives a different account of the origin of his Tales from that in the introduction to the first volume of *Contes;* 'Nevertheless I had to return home to Dakar for the holidays [from the Lycée Van Vollenhoven in Saint-Louis]. My mother made up for as much of the lost time as she could in making me aware of the world by "bringing me back to my origins", assisted in this task by the old *griot* genealogist-historian Guewel M'Baye and the "first neighbour", the story-teller Matabara Massamba Ali M'Baille.' This discrepancy is a detail of purely academic importance, as it is still to *griots* that Diop owes the inspiration for his revivals of traditional lore.

we are sacks that hold secrets many centuries old. The art of speech has no secrets for us; without us the names of kings would fall into oblivion; we are the memory of men; by words we give life to the exploits of kings for the young generations. . . . My words are pure and free from all lies; they are the words of my father; they are the words of the father of my father. I will tell you the words of my father, such as I received them; the *griots* of the king know no lies.

Listen to the History of the son of the Buffalo, the son of the Lion. I will tell you of Maghan Sonjata, of Mari-Djata, of Sogolon Djata, of Naré Maghan Djata; the man of many names against whom spells had no power. (pp. 9–11) [1]

One last example will illustrate the importance of the *griot* in forming the bridge between the oral literature of the past and the writings in French by Negro-Africans of today; that of Eugène Dervain, and his two plays on Da Monzon, one of the rulers of Ségou in the Empire of Mali. According to Lilyan Kesteloot's preface to *Saran, la reine scélérate* and *La Langue et le scorpion*, both plays are faithful reproductions of Bambara epics, told by two different *griots* (whence the differences in style and genre), transcribed and translated into French by Amadou Hampate Ba. Dervain claims simply to have dramatised Ba's translated narration, while maintaining the imprints of the *griots'* original literary style.

THE EVOLUTION OF THE FOLK-TALE, SHORT STORY AND FABLE

Interest in African folk-lore, already growing in France in the twenties, was given an additional stimulus by the Exposition Coloniale held in Paris in 1929. Those on the spot were best placed to feed this interest, and colonial officials continued to encourage interpreters and native clerks to collect material from their home regions. By the thirties school principals, teachers and even inspectors were encouraging pupils to do research during their school holidays into the legends, fables and local lore of their region of origin, which they contributed to a common stock on the resumption of classes.[2] These were used as linguistic exercises, for practice in French composition and, moreover, formed useful material for lessons in 'morals'. In the I.F.A.N. Archives in Dakar, there is a typescript (undated) of some thirty pages of folk-tales and moral fables, recorded in French by Boubou-Hama, Director of the local centre of I.F.A.N. at Niamey (Niger), to be used by teachers 'pour enseigner la morale universelle, une, partout dans le monde' [to teach morals that are universal, the same everywhere in the

---

[2] This tradition has been retained on a higher level. In Olympe Bhêly-Quénum's *Le Chant du lac*, which is supposed to take place in Dahomey after the Second World War, there is a reference to students from France spending their long vacations in 'sociological research' in their home regions.

world]. Among versions of the same tale told by different pupils we can already distinguish some who are conscious of picturesque detail and the possibility of improving the literary style on translating from the vernacular. In the forties certain stories began to appear in print in local newspapers, giving the name of the writer. Few of these early authors ever came to the attention of a wider public, but two publications in the paper *Dakar-Jeunes* for 1942 are worth noting: a short moral fable explaining why the hyena laughs when hungry and cries when replete, by A. Sadji, then a teacher or possibly already a school inspector in Senegal, whose first novel *Maïmouna* only appeared ten years later; and a Spider-story, *Araignée, mauvais père, ou l'histoire d'Ekébéba l'égoïste*, [Spider, the bad father, or the tale of selfish Ekébéba] signed by Bernardadie (*sic*).

These folk-tales, legends and local customs, borrowed from the repertoire of the *griots*, also formed part of the material for the first dramatic episodes and tableaux performed at the Ecole Normale Supérieure at Bingerville and at the William Ponty Normal School in Senegal. In *Climbié*, Bernard Dadié calls on his memories of his own schooldays at the former establishment, particularly when he tells how Saturday evenings at Climbié's school were given up to *théâtre*. We shall deal with these in more detail in Chapter 2.

It should not be thought that the majority of those responsible for preserving the indigenous folk-lore had any inkling that they were indirectly nourishing a future generation of creative writers. When the I.F.A.N. was founded in 1938, its aim was to serve as a base for research into Negro culture, art, music and folk-lore generally among Europeans. At first this interest was indeed limited to White scholars, the young generation of literate Africans and intellectuals tending to resist any suggestion of a return to traditional, tribal sources. Was it for this that they were acquiring, often with so much pain, effort, sacrifice and suffering, knowledge of western culture? The young man in Seydou Badian's *Sous l'orage*, who despises the initiation rites, also speaks disparagingly of all the artistic expression of his people. But Tiéman, a male nurse (obviously the mouthpiece of Badian, who was writing in the fifties),[3] reprimands the young men for abandoning their traditional culture. Meanwhile this was being brought back into honour among African intellectuals by the Negritude movement in Paris. The Black writer was encouraged to become the interpreter of his land, his people, his origins, and deliberately to foster a pride in race, colour and his own indigenous culture. In the *novella* of Olympe Bhêly-Quénum, *Le Chant du lac* [Song of the lake], this dialogue takes place

---

[3] *Sous l'orage* was published in 1963, but Badian completed his manuscript in 1954, while studying in Montpellier.

between students returning from Paris to spend their vacation in Dahomey early in the fifties, betraying a very different attitude from that of the contempt of the young *évolué* for his own culture, quoted above:

'We should be educated, cultured, civilized, if you like, but not snobs.'
'One should be irrevocably linked to the earth. I want to draw my strength from the archaic teachings of the traditions of my own country.'
'You'd have to be careful not simply to descend into folk-lore.'
'All folk-lore has its secrets which it is important to understand, and make simple and intelligible to people.' (p. 13)

In this allegorical and moralizing tale, Bhêly-Quénum opposes the emancipated generation of the nineteen-fifties, influenced by western science and logic, to their elders clinging to the reality of the folk-legends and deeply imbued with the superstitions of their forebears. His aim is to free people from the shackles of fear imposed by the cult of legendary monsters and maleficent gods. But he respects the poetic, imaginative element of folk-lore. As motto to the book is this quotation from James Joyce's *Portrait of the Artist as a Young Man*: 'Welcome, O life! I go to encounter for the millionth time the reality of experience and to forge in the smithy of my soul the uncreated conscience of my race.' But *Le Chant du lac* ends with the people's song of mourning for the death of the gods.

The *conte*, the short tale based on folk-legend, whose heroes are men or spirits, and the fable with a definite moral aim, form the first literary genre to be fully developed by French African writers. They are among the oldest to find publishers, after the novels of Diagne, Bakary Diallo and René Maran, mentioned in the preceding chapter, and were the source of inspiration for novels as well as short stories, during the whole of the pre-Independence era. After the first collection of tales to be published in French by an African, the *Contes et Proverbes Bambara* [Bambara Tales and Proverbs] of Moussa Travelé of 1923, we have to wait till after the end of the Second World War for more versions in French of African fable and legend. These then began to have real literary pretensions and were no longer mere transcriptions of more interest to social anthropologists than to students of literature.

It is difficult to credit any one author with pioneering in this field of African literature. Many publications were held up by the War, and even after the end of hostilities, publishing firms with a huge back-log of manuscripts, unsure of the interest of such new works to the French reading public, were for many years cautious of the financial risk involved in such publications. Many manuscripts were certainly prepared long before they appeared in print, or appeared in journals and periodicals long before being collected in book form. Birago Diop, during his student days at the National School of Veterinary Surgery at Toulouse, was already recalling the legends recounted to him by the *griots* of his mother's house. Senghor published in 1934 in *L'Etudiant noir* Diop's version of the *dits faits*[4] of the celebrated Senegalese sages: 'Kotje Barma ou les toupets apophtègmes' [The impudent adages]. In between his professional visits at his first post in the western Sudan, between 1935 and 1938 Diop was committing to paper more and more of these remembered tales, given renewed stimulus by his meeting with Amadou Koumba N'Gom. Returning to France, on his first leave, he found some of his old friends were also writing. Ousmane Socé (Diop) had already published his first novel, *Karim* (1935), and was busy writing *Mirages de Paris*, which included 'Rythmes du Khalam'. Judged by the actual date of publication, Socé was the first author of a complete collection of African tales in French, whose writing bears claim to be considered as literature.

THE HEYDAY OF FOLK-LORE IN FRENCH WEST AFRICAN LITERATURE

Ousmane Socé Diop

OUSMANE SOCE DIOP:*Contes et légendes d'Afrique noire*. Paris, Nouvelles Editions Latines, 1938, o.p. New edition in *Karim*, N.E.L. 1948. Separate edition, N.E.L. 1962.

Ousmane Socé Diop belongs to the generation of Senegalese intellectuals and writers who came to maturity in the years between the Wars and was a product of the student climate of Paris of the period. A close friend of Birago Diop and of Léopold Senghor, like the latter he turned to active politics, became a representative of Senegal in the French Parliament in 1937 and later a senator. In 1938 he published his first collection of traditional tales, *Contes et légendes d'Afrique noire*, after a first successful novel and some poetry. The majority of the stories which make up this collection belong to two categories that are characteristic of the oral heritage: heroic legends, of which there are five, and folk-fables of which there are three. There is also one original story that Socé calls 'Sara-Ba' (A *novella*), which is a forerunner of romantic fiction with some realistic details.

For the legends from the past, which form the biggest part of the collection, Socé claims to act as a faithful scribe to the 'guitarist' or traditional story-teller. Sometimes he even describes how the *griot* inter-

---

[4] *dits faits* could be interpreted as 'maxims translated into action', approximately 'sayings and doings'.

rupts his narrative with musical interludes, so that the reader can appreciate the atmosphere accompanying the story-telling and the nature of the popular entertainment. These heroic legends are the *chansons de geste* of Africa, which the minstrel sang to inspire similar feats of valour in his audience, challenging them to imitate the princes and warrior-knights of whom he sang. Some of Socé's stories are fairly close to historical fact or probability. Such a one is the legend of Maïssa Tenda Oueddj, sovereign of Cayor and Baol, who set out to punish the king of the neighbouring territory of Diobasse, who had refused to send the customary presents on his accession. The epic and poetic note is struck by the description of the extravagant preparations made for the battle and the picturesque hyperbole of the language – 'Yamba N'Dalla brandished a sword which his slaves had sharpened till it would cut your tongue simply to speak of it' – and the extravagant boasts of the warriors who promised each to bring back twenty slaves from Diobasse and to kill four of the enemy with a single shot. The Fula legend of Hans Bodédio, whether based on truth or myth, contains no supernatural elements. It has something of the *Roman courtois*, the romance of chivalry. It tells of the most famous of the pagan lords called *ardos*, who ruled over the region of the Niger in the nineteenth century, before the Mahometan conquests. These *ardos* were warrior-princes who combined a bellicose and sanguinary ferocity with an acute sense of honour, so that an affronted woman, even a stranger from a distant region, could infallibly call on them for redress of her wrongs, as is the case in this tale.

What basically distinguishes legend from historical chronicle is the introduction of supernatural forces. All of Socé's five historical legends extol courage, even bravado. In all, the adversaries are of equal valour and strength, so that the dramatic tension of the narrative and the heroic merit of the victories is maintained. But in some cases such victories are made possible only by the intervention of superhuman powers which act on behalf of the hero, as in the legendary epic of Greek antiquity. Silamakan, the son of the King of Macina, gave proof while still an infant that he was endowed with unusual and prodigious forces. As a man he routs an army of 400,000 without striking a blow, simply by the terror inspired by his *gris-gris* or charms. If we are looking for rationalization of the legend, this could perhaps be explained by mass hysteria which overcomes the enemy ranks. The most effective tale of legendary exploits is that of 'Tàra' (meaning 'he goes to War' in the Bambara language), the story of El Hadj Omar, who conquered three-quarters of West Africa for Islam. This is the *geste* of Omar in which, as with Charlemagne, the undisputed facts of his victories are ascribed to supernatural forces, rather than to superior military strategy. So history is put in the crucible in order to distil from it literature in the form of epic legend. Socé even takes the trouble to add factual details of dates, places and persons to correct the inaccuracies of the 'guitarist's' account. We are patently concerned with literature and not purely historical chronicle. For the reader, whether Western or African, these legends of heroism or bravado or chivalry have the stamp of literature: they are hymns of praise to an age of African valour with their elements of poetry and mysticism.

One of these so-called historical legends is in fact pure myth. It is the explanation for the end of the fabulous prosperity of the Kingdom of Ghana. Socé begins his 'Légende de Gana' with a note of historical authenticity as he situates his story in Timbuktu, where 'for centuries an authentic civilization was fashioned' to which it owed its 'mysterious aura of fame.' He passes imperceptibly into a mixture of realism and mythology, ascribing the miraculous prosperity of Ouagadou equally to the steady showers of rain which brought nourishment from the soil to enrich the sap of many trees, and to showers of gold that dispense the precious metal throughout the land. His descriptions of the dense mosaic of the cosmopolitan populations that inhabited the Kingdom of Ghana at that time are vivid and colourful. Then the mythological element dominates, according to which this prosperity of Ghana was due to the protection of a seven-headed snake which lived in a well and exacted the annual sacrifice of the most beautiful girl of the realm. When it is Sia's turn to be sacrificed, she is rescued from her martyrdom by her betrothed Amadou, whose love for Sia is greater than his fear of the taboo. After the slaying of the serpent a period of famine began. Thus, Socé tells us, ended the splendour of the empire of Ghana, the cradle of African civilization, a splendour which exists now only in the sad notes of the guitarists' songs which sometimes conjure it up from where it lies buried beneath a shroud of sand.

Socé's tale has many original aspects which can be ascribed to his literary gifts enriching the traditional source: vivid, realistic descriptions mixed with poetic imagery and a psychologically convincing portrayal of Amadou-the-taciturn, who becomes an unwilling hero to save the life of his betrothed.

The folk-tale or fable is both part of the traditional cultural heritage of African society and the basis of neo-African literature, the roots of a creative imaginative writing. The three fables in Socé's collection are of the traditional moral type. The story of the man who has a passion for cherries contains a lesson in good manners and a moral pointing to the need to avoid excess in all things. 'Penda' is the story of the girl who refuses all suitors because she will marry only a man who has no scar on his body – in a society and at a time when scars are the sign of valour in hunting or in battle. The third fable, entitled 'In the Time when Men and Beasts could Converse', is also a tale of loyal friendship and ingratitude. In two of the tales, magic and the supernatural are basic elements to enhance both the myth and the moral. In none are the characters more than fairy-tale types or extravagant near-caricatures. Mamadou, whose weakness for cherries is his undoing, is as flat as paste-board, although there is a comic realism in the description of his fight against temptation. However, this realism is rare. The setting of the stories is African only in nomenclature of persons, flora and fauna. Socé makes no more attempt to evoke atmosphere than to bring his characters to life. Nor have we any right to reproach him with this deficiency. Although writing for a European as well as African public, his function is still basically that of the *griot*. And the *griot* had his 'atmosphere' all around him as he told his tales in the African night. He had no necessity to evoke 'local colour'. His characters were well-known types, traditional *dramatis personae* acting out the moral lesson of the fable; they needed no individual personality, no closely observed psychology.

In 'Sara-Ba' the *novella* stripped of all supernatural, mythic or moral elements, the novellist in Ousmane Socé breaks through the translator and transcriber of the traditional *griot's* lore. This is a story of romantic love told with some realism. It is both timeless and universal, yet the background and setting is intrinsically West African and essential to the atmosphere. The story opens with a vivid and colourful description of the approach of a tornado over the town of Kayes in the Sudan. A group of youngsters play in the storm. Moussa takes advantages of the frolics to flirt with Safiétou, just in the flower of puberty. Their courtship progresses until she is married off to a man of her own caste and race. Eventually Safiétou has only one idea, to flee from the house of her husband, for whom her indifference borders now on hostility, to regain her freedom and if possible to rejoin her lover. The physical descriptions of the characters in Socé's story are still conventional and superficial. It is the relationship between the setting and the psychological mood of the tale that makes for the originality and the moving nature of the narrative and takes it out of the field of fable into that of creative fiction.

Short as it is, this story of 'Sara-Ba' has a progression of mood, character, psychology and situation which makes it a miniature novel. Although included in *Contes et légendes d'Afrique noire*, and in spite of the traditional situation of the girl married against her will to a husband of her father's choice, this is not a folk-tale, but a further proof, with his novel *Karim*, of Socé's gifts as an original fiction writer.

Les Contes et légendes d'Afrique noire is thus a landmark in the evolution of creative writing in French from Africa. It preserves in literary form, with the stamp of an author who is a conscious artist and not a mere scribe, two traditional aspects of the oral heritage: the historical legend and the folk-fable. By the success of these Socé encourages other African writers to follow his example, while in 'Sara-Ba' he paves the way for an original African fiction in depth, where certain universal, psychological truths and situations are allied to local realities of background and custom.

Maximilien Quenum

MAXIMILIEN QUENUM: *Légendes africaines: Côte d'Ivoire, Soudan, Dahomey* (Illustrated by P. Hardy). Rochefort, Imp. A. Thoyon Thëze, 1946, o.p.

The next volume of traditional African tales to appear in French was Maximilien Quenum's 'Three African Legends' published immediately after the War. There is nothing to indicate that the composition of these was in fact anterior to Birago Diop's *Tales of Amadou Koumba*, which we know he started collecting and writing in the early thirties. But for convenience I shall follow the chronological order of publication of these works.

Maximilien Quenum Possy Berry was born in Cotonou, Dahomey, in 1911, that is the same year as Ousmane Socé (five years after Senghor and Birago Diop) and so he is one of the older African writers who found their first incentive and inspiration in the Negritude doctrine. Most of his publications are academic ethnological studies; only his first, for which he was awarded a prize by the French Academy, can be considered a contribution to creative writing: these legends, which he recalls, as he explains, from his own childhood, were recounted by the elders of the village, who combined erudition with loquaciousness – he hopes that by transmitting them in turn, he will give his French readers a love and knowledge of Africa.

Quenum's three legends are all historical, each being characteristic of a different region of West Africa: Ivory Coast, Sudan and Dahomey. Each recounts the founding of a kingdom or a dynasty and the exploits of an early sovereign renowned for wisdom or military exploits. 'La Légende des Baoulé', of which many versions exist, recounts the origin of the name of the tribe which inhabited the centre of the Ivory Coast, the territory which was later colonized as the Gold Coast, now the Republic of Ghana.[5] The ruler, Queen Abra-Pokou, was celebrated for her wisdom and devotion to her country and subjects. Their prosperity attracted covetous pillagers from among neighbouring nomadic tribes. One year, when the invaders

---

[5] In fact Quenum does not himself explain how the incidents related gave rise to the name 'Baoulé'. See Dadié's version of the legend, p. 53.

were stronger and more numerous than usual, the queen ordered an exodus to save her people from complete annihilation and their flocks from plunder. With their pursuers hard behind them they came to the wild torrent of the River Comoé, whose god they had to placate in order to cross in safety. The soothsayer reported that the river required the sacrifice of a young male. As there were no volunteers, the queen offered her only son to save the tribe. The river god produced no alternative victim to this African Iphigenia, and so the young prince was hurled from the cliff to his death. Immediately a terrible and supernatural storm was unleashed, during which the huge baobab trees that lined the banks bent down to form a bridge over which the fugitives crossed in safety, the trunks separating again before the arrival of the pursuers. On the advice of the elders of the tribe, the Baoulé settled a little way beyond the river, in a fertile valley between the Comoé and the Banadama, after celebrating the apotheosis of the martyred prince.

Quenum tells the story with economy and simplicity of style, in keeping with the traditional legendary material. Without attempting to produce a piece of epic literature, he adds sufficient realistic and psychological detail to give life and personality to the narrative. As examples of the Queen's wisdom and foresight, he mentions the provisions of cereal she causes her subjects to stock up for lean years, whenever they have ample crops, so that they are well prepared for the eventual exodus. His descriptions of the terrors of the dense tropical forest and the rivers haunted by hippopotomi and crocodile are richly picturesque. The account of the sacrifice of the prince is fraught with dramatic tension as the soothsayer stays his hand in horror at his own task and admiration for the heroism of his victim, until, finally encouraged by the latter's steadfastness in his sacrifice, he hurls him to his doom.

The two other legends tell of great warrior-kings of Africa: Fama-Soundiata (the Alexander the Great of Mali) and Aho, the founder of the kingdom of Dahomey.[6] The first describes one episode from the legendary existence and reign of the King of the Manding: how by his upright life and avoidance of excess he was able to overcome his enemy, Soumangourou, given to over-indulgence and uxoriousness. The legend of the founding of Dahomey recounts how Aho-Dako-Dogbaglin, the strong, unscrupulous and cunning descendant of the panther (the royal fetish) was expelled from his own territory after a fratricidal struggle for power. He made his way north conquering all tribes and killing all their kings until he arrived in the land of Ghevi, ruled over by King Dan, who offered him traditional

[6] Aho is said traditionally to have founded the Kingdom of Dahomey, but Dan gave it its name.

hospitality. Under the pretext of extravagant funeral rites for his father, Aho suborned the subjects of his host by offering them presents and, by the ruse of dropping carcasses from a two-storey hut, maddened them with flesh. Eventually he hurled down his host, King Dan, himself. Then he fulfilled his boast to build a city on the belly of Dan, by dropping the King's body into the foundations of his new capital, which he called Dan-ho-mê – 'On-the belly-of-Dan'. Incidentally, this legend exemplifies the unenviable reputation enjoyed by the Dahoman sovereigns of being the most bloodthirsty of the local rulers, their addiction to human sacrifice being a constant pretext for French military advances and wars of suppression. However, Maximilien Quenum has no moral intent; he shows indeed little concern that the traditional founder of the kingdom may be thought less than admirable in the light of contemporary Western ethics.

His main aim is to introduce to the European reader legends which are as much woven into the fabric of African culture as the myths of the Old Testament and of Classical Greece and Rome are into Western Europe's. They make up a reservoir of 'Classical' allusion. Moreover, it is easy to make comparisons between the theme, incidents, characters and interpretation of these African legends and the bases of Hellenic or Hebraic mythology. The parallel between the parting of the Red Sea before the pursuing Egyptians and the bending of the baobabs to form a bridge for the fleeing Baoulé is one obvious example, as is that between the sacrifice of Iphigenia or of Abraham's son and that of Queen Abra-Pokou's child. People like Maximilien Quenum, who have transcribed and translated legends, but have done no further writing, have fulfilled, nevertheless, an important and two-fold literary function: they have preserved for future generations of African readers some of the best-loved elements of the traditional heritage, which might have fallen into oblivion with the decline of the *griots*; and they have established for Western readers a source of reference for the study of African literature, with its heroes and their epic or mythical exploits. To few of such readers would the name of Soundjata be as familiar as that of Alexander or Charlemagne, without this priming, nor would the name of the Prince of the Baoulé conjure up the same image or chain of associations as Iphigenia or Isaac. Nevertheless, we should not deprecate too much Maximilien Quenum's own contribution to the growth of this literature. While retelling the three tales with the economy necessary to the concise form he has adopted, he adds sufficient detail for them to read with lively dramatic tension and to stand on their own merits as a contribution to original creative writing in French, in the early years of the Negro-African renaissance.

Birago Diop

BIRAGO DIOP: *Les Contes d'Amadou Koumba*. Paris, Fasquelle, 1947. Re-issued Paris, Présence Africaine, 1960. *Nouveaux Contes d'Amadou Koumba*. Paris, Présence Africaine, 1958. *Contes et lavanes*. Paris, Présence Africaine, 1963. English translation: *Tales of Amadou Koumba*, trans.+intr. by Dorothy S. Blair. London, Oxford University Press, 1966, 20 tales selected from above.

To Ousmane Socé Diop's compatriot, partial namesake and friend of his Paris years, we owe the most important collection of tales in French, drawn from the rich reservoir of West African folk-lore. Birago Diop's name has become indissolubly linked with the *Contes* attributed to his household *griot*, Amadou Koumba.

Except for one volume of verse, *Leurres et lueurs*, pleasantly lyrical but rather derivative, Birago Diop's whole literary career (which for nearly thirty years he ran in harness with his professional activities as a veterinary surgeon) was devoted to recalling and recomposing the folk-tales and fables of his birthplace. It is not insignificant that these rivals for his interest both involved a preoccupation with animals. As a schoolboy at the Lycée Van Vollenhoven in Saint-Louis he showed equal potential for science and the arts. He read widely, encouraged by his older brothers as well as his teachers, and showing an early flair for writing. He chose to follow the model of brother Youssouffa, the doctor, in registering at the Faculty of Medicine at Toulouse, but admits that the younger Massyla's unpublished poems and works of fiction were his 'bush of fire'. When the deeply loved and admired Massyla died prematurely, Birago assumed his mantle, together with that of Youssouffa.

After qualifying in Veterinary Surgery at Toulouse, he was admitted to the Institut de Médecine Vétérinaire Exotique in Paris, where he was initiated by his compatriot and contemporary L. S. Senghor into the movement for African emancipation and the literary as well as political aspects of the Negritude movement. He contributed to *L'Etudiant Noir* an account of the *dits faits* of the Senegalese sage: 'Kotje Barma ou les toupets apophtègmes'. On his appointment to Western Sudan, his contacts in the course of his professional duties with people from many regions, his ready ear for the local story-teller, the meeting with Amadou, the son of Koumba, all contributed to re-prime the well of inspiration for the stories that he had started to recall in France as panacea for his homesickness and moments of loneliness as a student. Back in France at the beginning of 1942 and unable to return to Africa until after the Liberation, he linked up again with his old friends of the pre-war years, Damas, Senghor, recently released from the Stalag, and Alioune Diop, who was planning to produce *Présence Africaine*. Birago gave a talk in May 1944 on 'Le folk-lore noir' and the tales and legends of A.O.F., and this was illustrated by one of his own re-creations, 'N'Gor Niébé'. 'Un Jugement' and 'Sarzan' (which the author called 'Polyeucte Puni') appeared in *La Revue du Monde*, edited by Paul Morand and Ramon Fernandez. Senghor included 'La Lance de l'hyène' in the section of *l'Afrique noir* of the anthology *Les plus beaux écrits de l'Union française et du Maghreb*[7] for which he wrote an introductory essay where, incidentally, he criticized his friend's poetry for not being 'assez nègre'. The first number of the review *Présence Africaine*, which finally saw the light of day in November 1947, included the story 'L'Os'. After having been refused by Editions du Seuil, *Les Contes d'Amadou Koumba* was eventually published by Fasquelle in the series 'Ecrivains d'Outre Mer'. The year 1947 was a vintage one for Negro-African literature.

In 1950 Birago returned to West Africa, resuming his work as Chief of Veterinary Services in Ivory Coast, Upper Volta and Mauritania, until the constitution of the Independent Republic of Senegal, when he accepted the appointment as Ambassador to Tunis. In the preceding years he had put the finishing touches to the *Nouveaux contes d'Amadou Koumba* and four years later (1964) the last volume of the trilogy, *Contes et lavanes*[8], appeared. These three volumes, some fifty stories in all, made Birago Diop the most prolific of the African writers of folk-tales in French, and the most acclaimed. He was awarded the Grand Prix Littéraire de l'Afrique Occidentale Française for the *Contes d'Amadou Koumba* in 1947 (shared with Ousmane Socé's *Karim*) and the Grand Prix d'Afrique Noire in 1964 for *Contes et lavanes*. Since retiring from the Diplomatic Service in 1966 to open a veterinary clinic in Dakar, he has sketched the outline for an autobiography, which is to have the happy title, *Tous contes faits*,[9] but so far only brief notes under the heading 'Birago Diop raconte... Birago' have appeared in the Dakar periodical, *Awa*, nos. 7 and 8. In February 1973 he confided to me that with a lancet in one hand and a syringe in the other, he was unable to take up a pen again.

As we have seen, Birago Diop, if not one of the founders of the Negritude movement, was one of its earliest adherents, and his work showed an inflexible loyalty to the principles proclaimed by Césaire, Damas and Senghor. But his writing is never militant. For one thing he is too much of an artist, with too nice a literary sense to sacrifice composition

[7] Edited by Mohamed El Kholti, Léopold Cedar (*sic*) Senghor, Pierre Do Dinh, A. Rakoto Ratsimamanga & E. Ralahmihiatra, published by La Combe. See p. 243.
[8] 'Lavanes' are riddles in the form of short songs.
[9] Literally, 'all tales told'; but this is also a pun on the expression *tous comptes faits*, 'when everything has been taken into account'.

to commitment. An illustration of this is his own admission made in the course of the lecture on African folk-lore mentioned above:

Whenever, while transposing my stories, a word or expression in Senegalese did not come spontaneously in French to my satisfaction, I did not look for the equivalent in some contemporary author. But, falling back on the little I had learnt, I hurried to Rabelais and Montaigne, sometimes to Corneille, rarely to Voltaire, occasionally to Anatole France. And, as I presented my money, I always found an honest exchange, sometimes with no interest charged.

Equally honest in his turn, Diop could never betray the debt he owed to his literary as well as his linguistic masters, those poets respectfully listed: Shakespeare, Tennyson, Longfellow, Hugo, Musset, Racine, Boileau, Villon, Laforge, Baudelaire. Then too, his writings are marked by his own personal qualities, reinforced by the experiences of his travels and his professional activities: firstly his sense of humour, a sure guarantee against bitterness and anger; and then his deep sense of humanity, engendered or matured by his closeness to suffering in man and beast. So, when he returned to his origins, to his African sources of inspiration, deliberately setting out to preserve or revive the traditional wisdom of Africa, he produced what the critic Lamine Diakhaté hailed as 'the finest prose work of our literature' (in *Afrique en Marche*, juin/juillet, 1957). Diakhaté can be accused of dropping one of the casual superlatives of the over-enthusiastic critic, who had certainly not weighed the relative merits of Camara Laye's *Enfant noir* and *Le Regard du roi*, both of which had appeared by 1954; but it is undoubtedly true that the *Tales of Amadou Koumba* are solidly rooted in the African *terroir*, and express both in form and in content what Senghor recognized and acclaimed as '*la vraie pensée nègre*'. Unselfconsciously Birago Diop drew on all the sources that nourished his mental and spiritual growth. They became the warp and weft of the fabric that he wove – to use his own metaphor with which he introduces the *Tales*. The *pagnes* which he wove do not have to be labelled 'Made in Africa'. Moreover, it is here, in the three volumes of *Tales*, that Birago Diop the poet is clearly in evidence, rather than in his book of verses which, with the exception of those poems which formed part of the *Tales of Amadou Koumba*, are palely imitative of French nineteenth-century models.

Ismael Birago Diop's earliest influences were Islamic and he admits to having remained a traditionalist throughout his life. He attended the Koranic school before the French Primary School in Dakar. His step-father was El Hadj Pedre, Imam of Dakar, who defended him in the family tribunal before which he had to appear on his return from Europe with a White French wife. In spite of this one fall from grace, Diop's devotion to Islam is deep-seated, colouring the settings, choice of characters, situations, episodes and moral teachings of the majority of the stories, whether the characters are humans or animals. Allusions to religious practices and Koranic lore are intrinsic and casually spontaneous in the course of the narrative. The Islamic setting is essential to such stories as 'Le Prétexte' (*Nouveaux contes*), 'Serigne Khali et le voleur' and 'Le Fou du marabout' (*Contes et lavanes*). It adds the picturesque realism to the setting of 'L'Os' and 'Le Jugement', although the moral and the satire in these two tales are universal and they could be transposed into any society. The former is a story of excessive greed and unnatural lack of generosity. Rather than share a succulent shin-bone – a rare luxury in a community where meat had long been unknown – with his *plus-que-frère*, More-Lame shams illness and eventually, to save his face, has to allow himself to be buried alive rather than admit his ruse or be forced to share his feast. The comic tension is enhanced by the 'widow's' desperate attempts to prevent the final disaster, insisting on delaying the funeral rites in order piously to recite more and more *sourates* before the 'corpse' is washed, before it is enclosed in the shroud, before the coffin is lowered into the grave, and before the clods of earth are thrown in to fill up the pit. In 'The Judgement' the Solomon-like wisdom that resolves the dispute between the atrabilious husband and his repudiated wife is attributed to the most reputed marabout for miles around. These characters and incidents help to situate the stories, as do all the references to religious practices, ritual ablutions, sprinkling of the marabout's saliva in blessing. They form a natural part of the local colour and contribute to the realism of the stories whose characters are humans. But Diop's realism cohabits easily with fantasy to add to the sly humour of the animal tales. So we find M'Bam Hal-the-Warthog telling his rosary, M'Bott-the-Toad performing his ritual ablutions and saying his prayers at the water's edge before an important undertaking (this is a ruse to alert his fellow toads to come to his rescue); M'Bam-the-Ass, Bouki-the-Hyena, and Thile-the-Jackal are pupils at the Koranic school and Woundou-the-Cat undertakes a pilgrimage to Mecca, returning as el Hadji, complete with turban and holy water and hung about with rosaries.

In this way Birago Diop uses the Islamic setting for some of his most comic and satirical effects, while the universal validity of the comedy and the satire is in no way diminished. The comparison between Molière's hypocritical parasite and Diop's *faux dévot* in 'The Pretext' is most diverting. Serigne Fall, like Tartuffe, imposes on a credulous and generous host, who is the last person in the household to be undeceived as to the true character of his guest. But Serigne Fall is no pastiche. He is an authentic inhabitant of Diop's African world and, at the same time, he is universal.

'The species is always the same,' says Amadou Koumba, as he introduces the story, 'full of false and insinuating unction, the typical parasite, inconstant and vagabond.' But the detail that makes for the comic realism is purely Islamic. The comic and satirical effects are all the more cogent when we are in the world of the moral fables whose characters are animals, and when the false marabout is Woundou-the-Cat. The moral – that superficial religious observance, however apparently dutiful, never changed anyone's basic character – is also of universal application. The Islamic setting is just as realistic, but the animal characters add to the piquancy of the irony and the acerbity of the satire. Woundou is pure feline in his instincts but human in his actions, reasoning and sentiments. Thinking himself the victim of prejudice when mice and rats and young chickens have no confidence in his friendly overtures: developing an inferiority complex about the deplorable reputation of his cousin the Wild Cat, which Woundou thinks is harmful to himself, he decides to make the pilgrimage to Mecca, hoping that on his return the prejudice and ill-feeling will be forgotten. Having performed all the sacred duties according to rule and custom he returns full of wisdom, unction and compunction:

With a mellifluous voice, with slow, measured gestures, his rosary in his fingers, seated on a sheepskin, el Hadji Woundou-the-Cat, in his heavy turban recounted his long pilgrimage to an audience that grew more and more dense as his story was studded with more and more pious maxims and words of peace and humility. As the audience grew, el Hadji Woundou picked out some old acquaintances: Djinakhe-the-Mouse, Kantoli-the-Rat, Ounke-the-Tarantula, and others, all fat and prosperous, surrounded by their numerous offspring, whose embonpoint left nothing to be desired.

The new Hadji's words remained as edifying as ever; but his voice seemed to grow less and less unctious, hoarser and hoarser... (Woundou-El-Hadji, in *Contes et lavanes*, p. 146. Not included in my published translations of B. Diop)

And his eyelids, which until then had been devoutly lowered, opened more and more to the potential comestibility of his audience, until he frankly silenced his religious precepts, dropped his rosary and his turban and leapt from his prayer-mat onto Grandma Mouse. As she reached the nearest hole in safety: 'she declared in a voice that trembled as much from fright as from old age: "Mecca never changed anyone!"' (p. 147).

In 'Bouki et ses tablettes' from *Contes et lavanes*, Diop again places his animal characters in an Islamic setting for a two-fold comic effect. On the simplest level, the action of the tale is another variant of Bouki-the-Hyena getting the worst of an encounter, this time with the hind hoof of a camel, owing to the quicker wit of Thile-the-Jackal. Bouki and his fellow creatures are here pupils at the Koranic school at which Diop takes the opportunity

of launching some of the darts of his satire. M'Bam-the-Ass's slowness in
learning is condoned by his masters because of his usefulness in supplying
them with firewood. This is why he is encouraged to continue at school
well into his 'third childhood'. Diop implies that in some of these estab-
lishments the master's material welfare takes precedence over the pupil's
educational advancement. On the other hand, the parents of Bouki are more
ambitious for their offspring's education and progress. It is not in order
to make him a useful mendicant for his master, the Marabout, that they
send him to school, but for him to become a first-rate Arabic scholar. What
is more, they judge that the language spoken by the local Toucouleur master
is too far removed from the authentic sources:

too guttural, with too many dental and lingual sounds rather than nasals. Not only
could it not be the genuine Arabic of Mecca and Medina...but, what more, it
did not suit the hereditary nasal diction of the Hyena clan... (ibid. pp. 73–4)

The comic effects and the satire ricochet backwards and forwards from
animal characteristics (the Ass's proverbial stupidity, for example) to social
institutions (criticism of the Koranic school system), to human weaknesses
(over-ambitious parents), to academic hair-splitting, to finish – un-
expectedly – with animal characteristics (the nasal whine of the hyena,
just to remind us, when we were about to be misled into thinking this a
normal fable, that the characters in the story are in fact genuine inhabitants
of the bushveld and the savannah).

Paradoxically, Birago Diop the Muslim is at his most serious, and in
one case at his most militant, when he is defending the beliefs and practices associated with fetishism, animism and ancestor worship. But there
is no real ambiguity in this attitude. Serious Senegalese students of their
country's history and culture, themselves devout Muslims, have admitted to me that Islamization never completely eradicated the traces of the
previous 'pagan' religions. In 'Le Boli' (*Nouveaux contes*), Diop uses a tale
of fantasy and supernatural powers to illustrate the importance of continuing respect for the cultual objects that shelter the spirits of departed
ancestors. Even more so, 'Sarzan', the last story in the first volume of
Contes, one of those which Diop wrote for Ramon Fernandez during the
occupation, seems in many respects to be out of key with the others.[10] It
is true that he does not ascribe it to his *griot*, but tells it as his own first-hand
experience, gleaned in the course of his circuits on professional duties in
the West Sudan in the 1939–42 period. In spite of the difference in tone

[10] If I may be permitted a personal reminiscence here, when I submitted to Oxford University
Press the manuscript of my translations of *Les Contes d'Amadou Koumba*, they decided to
omit 'Sarzan' from the published selection, on the grounds that it was out of keeping in
a volume of folk-tales.

and in setting, 'Sarzan' is another, or one should say the original treatment of the 'Boli' theme, expressed in terms of contemporary realism. 'Le Boli' is a fantasy, with all the supernatural elements essential to a mythic anecdote: the man rejuvenated by magic processes; the spirits taking on the forms of human beings to punish or reward the latter. In 'Sarzan' the ancestors take their revenge in more credible manner in terms of modern psychology – by taking away the wits of the man who contemptuously refuses them the respect that is their due. So it is also an apologia for traditional, tribal, cultual practices, including the tests of endurance, the initiation rites for adolescent boys, which form an important episode in the story.

The irony is here more bitter, rigorously stripped of all effects of comedy. It is used as an instrument to prove to the Western reader how little right he has to condemn practices and beliefs different from his own. It is a lesson in tolerance generally, but more specifically a defence of traditional local practices. This is the only tale where Birago Diop seems to be addressing the Western reader directly. Perhaps this is the reason why the supernatural element (the power of the ancestors to take away a man's wits) takes on a different expression and has a different impact. In the story of the *boli*, the supernatural or magic element is part of an age-old mythology which has its counterpart in the folk-lore of many lands and cultures. This is typified by the god who can assume the form of a handsome young man, can metamorphose age into youth and all of whose miraculous interventions into the lives of men belong to the world of legend and at best can be interpreted as symbolic. But the spirits of the ancestors who haunt Sarzan are part of the reality of African life and Diop intends us to take them seriously and literally. So 'Sarzan' stands apart from the rest of the *Tales of Amadou Koumba*, whose satirical and moral effects are more indirect and are clothed in bonhomie and comic irony.

'Petit-mari' is another story which stands out from the rest in containing neither humour, fantasy nor the omnipresence of the spirits of the ancestors which haunt many of Diop's more serious tales, nor is there any direct moral. Its subject is only marginally traditional in situation and characters, in as much as the two protagonists are orphans, the emphasis being here not on Khary's orphaned state but on her incestuous love for her brother. Like 'Sarzan' it includes a detailed description of the circumcision rites and the training which prove a boy's courage, steadfastness and ability to withstand pain before he can claim to be a man. And N'Diongane is early called upon to prove he is a man after the death of his father, while Khary, to hide her inadmissible passion taunts him with her chant of 'Petit-mari' – 'Little husband', attempting to diminish him within the community.

Like 'Sarzan' this is one of the few tales by Birago Diop with a predominantly tragic note, and in which his poetic style is elegiac. Lightly sketched as it is, the psychology of Khary's apparently gratuitous and cruel teasing is convincing, arising as it does from her subconscious need to bring about her brother's death and, by his destruction, free herself from her incestuous desires.

Among the more traditional themes and subjects – to which Diop adds his own originality of expression, form and characterization – are those of virtuous orphans, ill-treated and given impossible tasks by jealous and cruel step-mothers: the African Cinderellas and Snow-Whites and other variants familiar to Western fairy-tale and folk-fable. Virtue, in the form of charity, patience, endurance, courtesy, humility, shown to or demanded from a variety of monsters and goblins, is rewarded by riches and power. The contrary vices, in particular greed, discourtesy to the ugly, aged or infirm, pride, disobedience or even indiscretion, are punished, often by metamorphosis into some natural phenomenon (for example, 'Les Mamelles'), thus linking the moral fables with the cosmogonic myths. The characters and setting are part of the local tradition; the moral and the outlines of the anecdote are usually universal.

Ousmane Socé had briefly introduced the French reader to the fantastic moral tale, of which his best examples are 'Penda' and 'Au temps ou l'homme et la bête se parlaient'. Bernard Dadié draws very fully on this reservoir for the source of his collection of folk-tales (*Légendes africaines*, 1953). This type of tale with human characters, though less common with Diop than the animal fable, is just as original in its detailed treatment and careful composition.

One method of bestowing individuality upon the traditional fable is by varying the setting or introduction. The story of 'Les Mamelles' [The humps] in the first collection of *Tales of Amadou Koumba* is a variation on the theme of sweet good-nature rewarded and envious ill-temper punished. Diop introduces it with a proverb:

When Memory goes a-gathering firewood, she brings back the sticks that strike her fancy. (*Contes d'Amadou Koumba*, p. 28 [p. 2])

Then he passes to a personal note, mingling European experience with African mythology in his imagery:

My eyes are surrounded by closed horizons. When the greens of summer and the russets of autumn have passed, I seek the vast expanses of the Savannah, and find only bare mountains, sombre as ancient giants that the snow refuses to bury because of their misdeeds...(ibid. [p. 1])[11]

[11] The publisher's editor for my translations felt that the staccato style and the apparent *non sequitur* of the introductory sentence and following paragraph, would disconcert the

He reverts to the allegorical style of his *griot* mouthpiece:

Winter is an unskilled weaver who never manages to comb or card his cotton; he spins and weaves nothing but a soft drizzle. (ibid.)

And as the author's own Memory casts about among the dried sticks of his experience to find the firewood to warm his numbed limbs, he is back on the boat bringing him home from France, when a fellow passenger makes disparaging comments on the modest size of the two little hills, mammiform knolls, that mark the most westerly tip of land in Senegal. So he recounts for her the tale that Amadou Koumba told, of the origin of these 'humps', the traditional fable of the man with two hunchbacked wives – one, shrill-voiced, shrewish, spiteful; the other, light-hearted, sweet-natured, friendly. Of course Koumba loses her hump, as a reward for her affability and devotion to her husband, while Khary has the second hump planted on her shoulders to punish her cantankerous jealous spite. When she threw herself into the sea in her chagrin, the waves could not swallow her completely, and it is her two humps which jut out beyond the point of Cape Verde and catch the last rays of the sun as it sets on the soil of Africa.

There is originality in the presentation, the structure and the characterization of this tale. The multiple introduction is designed to hold the reader in suspense, just as the *griot* is accustomed to building with devious digressions his audience's expectations for the actual narrative: but this compound of proverb, apophthegm, personal experience and reminiscence, is Diop's own, as are the picturesque details of the narrative itself. In other tales, after the opening proverb, Diop launches into a long, moralizing introduction before starting the actual narrative which will illustrate the apophthegm. Another time he will combine two stories in one, the first being complete in itself, but also serving as a preface to the other. 'Khary-Gaye' contain most of the stylistic devices by which Birago Diop puts his particular stamp on the folk-tale material which he uses: the introduction of the proverb, axiom or apophthegm at the beginning, usually repeated in a slightly different phraseology at the end to give a nicely rounded construction; the deliberate circumlocution or digression; the story within a story. Most of the tales of this kind have a poetic lyricism of style. To achieve this, Diop has recourse to some of the devices of the *griot*, who has to capture and retain the attention of an audience familiar with the characters, the episodes and the moral of each incident: verbal effects, repetitions, onomatopoeia, rhythmic jingles and litanies are all part of his

English reader, and so introduced the whole story by the words 'Here, far from my home in Senegal', which do not occur in the original, reserving the proverb for the place where Diop repeated it, as a lead-in to the actual anecdote. This does not faithfully reflect the apparently spontaneous musings of the author.

stock-in-trade. In Diop's hands they often given an elegiac note to his fantasies. In 'La Cuiller sale' we find some of the most representative of Diop's carefully harmonized and varied repetitions, with the onomatopoeic refrain *Vey vêt! O! Solitude* given first in Wolof and then in French. In his use of repetitive litanies and rhythmic jingles Diop may be faithful to the *griot* story-teller, whose mouthpiece he claims to be; but in the sophistication of his style he goes beyond the mere spontaneous narrative around the fireside.

There is a second type of moral fable among Diop's collection, which can be said to fall into the category of *contes philosophiques* rather than fairy-tales. The supernatural element is still there, although the elegiac pathos is usually replaced by a more farcical note or by more obscure symbolism. Some of these tales can be compared to those of Aesop, La Fontaine or other familiar Western fabulists. The moral element is similar, but without the economy which is a characteristic of the true fable. Diop's philosophical tales are discursive, often combining many episodes, as was suitable to a story destined to fill a long, dark African evening. One comparison is useful between the European and the African treatment of a similar theme, between, for example, Bürger's *Die Schatzgräber* and Diop's 'L'Héritage' [The inheritance]. The eighteenth-century German poet, who was instrumental in re-introducing the folk element into the literature of most Western European countries affected by the Romantic revival, describes briefly how the sons of a farmer dig and plough and turn every sod in the vineyard, vainly searching for the treasure which their father had told them on his death-bed was buried there. The treasure turns out to be the rich grape-harvest yielded the following year as a result of their labours. Diop's moral is more complex and his symbolism proportionately more abstruse. Before he dies, a wise and wealthy farmer bequeaths to each of his three sons a sack. One contains sand, another string and the third gold-dust. To find the meaning of their unequal legacies they undertake a long journey to consult a man whose wisdom is far-famed. In the course of this journey they see many strange and miraculous happenings, all reversing the normal logic of everyday existence. The sage, when they eventually find him, turns out to be a child who interprets the symbolism of their inheritance and the lessons of the many strange experiences of their journey.

The moral philosophizing of 'The Inheritance' is serious and didactic. In 'Truth and Falsehood', on the other hand, there is a comic irony and worldly cynicism about the lesson that truth has no credit and only falsehood pays. This reversal of the expected moral is in the direct tradition of La Fontaine (was it really the hard-working but ungenerous

Cigale that he offers as a model of virtue?) and is told with an irony worthy of Sacha Guitry's *Roman d'un tricheur*.

One traditional source that Birago Diop never uses directly, in the way that Ousmane Socé and Maximilien Quenum do, is the historical legend. He rather introduces historical allusions, usually to the period of the Islamic conquest, the better to situate his tales, or occasionally to enhance the comic or satirical effects, particularly in the animal fables. The best example is 'Maman-Caïman' [Mother Crocodile]. The story begins as a typical animal fable with the moral that children should always listen to their elders whose wisdom is based on experience. Then, apparently as a tale within the tale – but actually to illustrate the moral by the fate of the little crocodiles who do not listen to their mother – the historical episode is introduced of the battle between the Islamic conqueror Brahim Saloum and the Wolof Prince Yéli. The battle is seen and recounted through the eyes of the animals who make up Diop's bestiary. The first warning is brought by the crows who fly high, singing. When, at twilight, the crows perch on the bank, croaking their omen of streams of blood, Mother Crocodile knows that it is time to depart. But the young crocodiles are tired of the many stories she has told of the human inhabitants of the banks of the Great River. No crocodile is a prophet in her own family. Her offspring are curious to see these new happenings and will not heed the warnings of disaster. The fate of the humans and the animals is ironically fused in the story's conclusion, which is reached in one economical sentence. The young heir to the Mauritanian kingdom is mortally wounded and captured by the Wolof army. All the medicine men are summoned to care for him; in vain, until one wise man prescribes the effective remedy: to apply three times a day, to the wound, the fresh brains of a young crocodile.

Birago Diop was the first to introduce into French literature the rich comic treasure-house of the African animal fable. And no-one since him has used it with greater originality or effectiveness. He never touches the Spider Cycle, which in any case does not belong in Senegal or other Sahelian regions. But he presents what must be the complete range of episodes of the burlesque *geste* of Bouki-the-Hyena, Leuk-the-Hare, Golo-the-Monkey, Thile-the-Jackal. Parallels between Bouki and Renard, *le goupil*, the hero of the *Roman de Renard*, between the despotic king Gayndé-the-Lion and the autocratic king of La Fontaine's fables, and various other characters of the African and European bestiary, are easy and obvious, but not necessary for this account of the development of a literature. Ethnologists can be left to explain the common source for Leuk-the-Hare and Brer Rabbit. What is of interest is the skill with which

Diop has drawn on traditional sources to combine these with original, more sophisticated literary elements in his narratives.

The animal characters themselves are well-known to the *griot*'s audience. The proper names are in fact simply their generic names in Wolof, not, as in the *Roman de Renard*, an attempt to define them by a physical or moral characteristic. Gayndé *is* a lion, *golo* a monkey, *m'bili* a deer, *m'bonatt* a tortoise, *nieye* an elephant, and so on. Their main physical characteristics follow a traditional pattern and are nearly always included in mentioning the animal itself: the monkey's pink, hairless posterior, the jackal's drooping rump, the hare's long, flapping ears, the parrot's curved beak. But Diop usually introduces a miniature fable into the brief sentence containing the physical attributes:

Gayndé-the-Lion with his red eyes, who had borrowed the colour of the sand, in order to surprise his victims... ('La Biche et les deux chasseurs', *Contes*, p. 141 [p. 36])

...the cunning and malicious hare Leuk, whose conscience is as mobile as the pair of old, worn-out slippers which he wears clipped to his head ever since he took them off to run faster, and which he has used as ears ever since... ('Maman Caïman', *Contes*, p. 48 [p. 46])

Bouki-the-Hyena had attended the Koranic school for twenty whole years and all she got was bent and drooping hindquarters from the weight of the bundles of sticks she had carried every day to make fires for the evening classes... ('Bouki sans Leuck', *Contes et lavanes*, p. 73)

Or at the very least, he qualifies the descriptive feature with well-chosen epithet or comparison:

Off went Nagg-the-Cow towards the sparse grass of the veld, swinging her flea-bitten tail and her thin hind-quarters that were as sharp as a sabre's edge... ('Le Salaire', *Contes*, p. 101 [p. 53])

Segue-the-Panther, that dishonourable, two-faced creature, who has the eyes of a master, the soul of a slave, a mottled skin and the gait of a woman. ('La Lance de l'hyène, *Contes*, p. 85 [p. 74])

In his visual artistry Birago Diop inevitably invites comparison with La Fontaine. Both have the same persuasive, apparently easy style, the same economy of expression, the same eye and instinct for the telling image.

Sometimes the physical characteristics are associated with the animal's morals or habits: thus the monkey's black palms indicate his meddling ways; the panther's piebald skin prefigures the murky depths of his heart. For the most part, the moral qualities typified by the animal characters of the fables offer few surprises to the reader familiar with the folk-cycles of West Africa and with those characteristics traditionally associated both with the creatures in their natural state and with their anthropomorphic transference. Correspondences can usually be found in the well-known fables of Europe. The Lion signifies power and majesty, either of the enlightened monarch or the tyrannical despot; the Ass foolishness and indiscretion; the Hare and the Jackal share the prizes for cunning, intelligence, malice; the Panther is sly and untrustworthy; the Parrot a gossip; the Hyena stupid, greedy, ungrateful; the Monkey's greed is allied to deliberate mischief-making and destructiveness; the Elephant is credulous and slow-thinking; the Dog is the symbol of loyalty. Together with these obvious inhabitants of the bushveld and savannah, Birago Diop includes a closely-observed bestiary of lesser fauna: bats, tortoises, and toads, bees and chameleons, hens and tree-frogs complete his tapestry. Here, the author shows more originality in his economical pen-pictures, often betraying the veterinarian's training in quickly seizing the essentials of an animal's behaviour. In this combination of the zoo-psychological with anthropomorphic and totemist attributes,[12] Diop again manifests his skill in composing his story on different levels which are subtly integrated. Diop's animal characters inhabit the world of reality at the same time as they are at ease in the world of fable.

This ability to pass from reality to fantasy makes for the subtle charm and originality of his tales, a gift he shares with that other fabulist, Jules Supervielle. This transference is not limited to animal fables, where Leuk-the-Hare may be the seducer of the King's daughter, and father of her child, or the She-Ass become the King's favourite wife. Sometimes it is overt and deliberate, as in 'Les Mamelles', quoted above, when the memory of a personal experience – conversation with a young woman on the boat returning to Dakar – stimulates the recounting of a cosmogonic legend: sometimes the reader is carried imperceptibly from the world of real life into that of fantasy and fable. One of the best examples is 'Liguidi-Malgam' (*Nouveaux contes*) which opens like 'Sarzan' with an account of one of the author's professional visits into the Volta region. The break-down of his jeep (what more banal aspect of reality!) forces him to spend the night in the village of Liguidi-Malgam. He meets old Nitjema, whose story is translated to him by his driver. This tale, too, starts on the plane of authentic experience – that of Nitjema's journey far into the Sudan to fetch a wife. We are then one stage more removed from the present and more oriented towards an acceptance of the next level of the story, which belongs in a more remote past and a world of fable: the tale of Nitjema's remote ancestor, Nitjema-l'Ancien, who found a treasure of gold and silver buried in an ant-heap and is advised by Leuk-the-Hare of the indiscretions of his wife, Noaga-la-Vieille.

[12] For further comment on this point, see Mohamadou Kane, *Les Contes d'Amadou Coumba*, pp. 135–6.

Diop seems only marginally interested in the moral aspects of his fables, which he takes over, unmodified, from the traditional sources. These are derived for the most part from the homespun wisdom of everyday life, the lessons being those of practical common sense based on the avoidance of excess in all matters, but particularly the social extravagances which can be prejudicial to the individual's happiness and also – possibly more important – upset the equilibrium of the community; undue fastidiousness in the choice of a spouse, or indiscretion in taking an ill-matched spouse ('L'Héritage'); excessive regard for the truth which borders on tactlessness ('Vérité et mensonge'); jealousy and irascibility; disregard for the necessity of like to frequent like ('Mauvaises compagnies'); boasting, pretentiousness, importunity, presumption, escaping one's obligations, are all behavioural excesses which a close-knit community can little tolerate. The lessons of the fables which originally arose from rural communities, were often designed to castigate these aspects of personality and conduct as much as more genuine vices: greed, both cupidity and gluttony, hypocrisy, envy, pride, cowardice, lying, cruelty, imposture. Here, too, Birago Diop treads the middle way, sometimes adopting an ambivalent or opportunist morality of a practical nature, seeming, for example, to condone the Jackal's or Hare's cunning which is allied to intelligence and therefore profitable, but indicating that the ruses of Bouki-the-Hyena, who is stupid, slow-thinking and credulous, will be punished as surely as graver defects. But Birago Diop was not really writing as a moralist. He was both an apostle of Negritude, concerned to resuscitate and preserve his people's heritage of fable and folk-lore, and an original creative writer, whose inspiration, care for composition, personal observation, sense of poetic language and of comedy dictate a variety of tones, of stylistic devices, of narrative technique and a gallery of characters, both animal and human, which make his *Tales of Amadou Koumba* a unique contribution to French-African literature.

Keita Fodeba

KEITA FODEBA: *Poèmes africains*. Paris, Seghers, 1950. o.p. 2nd ed. 1958. Re-issued as *Aube africaine*, Seghers, 1965.

Like Maximilien Quenum, the Guinean Keita Fodeba devoted most of his time to politics rather than literature, but he produced a volume of folk-lore with some literary pretensions.

In the volume, entitled *Poèmes africains*, Fodeba claims to have recreated in French legends which were related, danced, mimed and sung by the *griots* of the villages of Guinea, and which he presents with an indication of the traditional musical accompaniment. Not all of these tales go far back into the past, nor have they equal claim to literary interest, but some of them have a simple unsophisticated charm.

'Minuit', purporting to relate a historical incident, which took place in the Siguiri district of Manding during the Almamy Samory's retreat before the French armies, has more political than legendary overtones. Balaké Camara, who was executed at midnight on 30 September 1892, is presented as much the victim of a miscarriage of colonial justice as the hero of a neo-Romantic tale of love and jealousy. But it is told with an elegiac lyricism that brings it into the category of poetry as much as polemics, as Fodeba deliberately revives a mode and a style associated with older legends to perpetuate a recent anecdote of wrongs and rivet it in the national memory. 'Aube africaine' [African dawn], the story giving its title to the new edition of 1965, replacing the older, non-committal title *Poèmes africains*, also belongs to recent colonial history. Naman is conscripted to fight in the White Man's War and after being wounded and decorated dies, not in action in Europe, but on African soil in the revolt against the White Chiefs at Thiaroye in Senegal. His death at dawn is taken as the symbol of the Dawn of African Liberty. 'Aube africaine' is another interesting example of the incorporation of folk-loric elements into a piece of politically committed writing. The passage of time while Naman's young bride waits in vain for her husband's return is punctuated by the ritual and sacred dances associated with tribal ceremonial.

The other items which make up this collection are more closely associated with the oral heritage in subject as well as in style. 'Sini-Mory', a variation on the orphan and wicked step-mother theme, with the usual supernatural elements and some attempt at visual realism, has not much original interest. 'Moisson à Faraba' [Harvest of Faraba] is a series of brief vignettes (barely more than fifty words each) of scenes of village life on the banks of the Niger, during the harvest season, ending with the moral: 'Soon the granaries will be full, the rejoicings will multiply and Faraba will know that work is the only source of happiness and prosperity.' 'Chanson du Djoliba' is a praise song to the River Niger for fulfilling its mission to bring peace, prosperity and plenty to the inhabitants of Guinea, full of historical references to the past which the River has witnessed. The general tone of the poem is one of sententious moralizing, illustrated by the concluding words:

Flow on beyond your confines across the whole world, quenching the thirst of the parched, satisfying the hunger of the unsatiated, silently teaching Humanity the lesson that only disinterested good deeds have absolute significance.

I entitled this chapter, devoted mainly to pre-Independence writings inspired by traditional elements of oral literature 'Transition from yesterday to today'. Keita Fodeba is the only writer to use the form of the *griot*'s art to spell out a political lesson for the future of his countrymen.

Bernard Dadié

BERNARD DADIÉ: *Légendes africaines*. Paris, Seghers, 1953. o.p. Re-issued with poems, *Afrique debout* and *La Ronde des jours*, under the title *Légendes et poèmes*, Seghers, 1966. *Le Pagne noir*. Paris, Présence Africaine, 1955. o.p. Re-issued Livre de Poche, 1972.

Only one African writer besides Birago Diop has achieved a degree of literary perfection in the recreating of African legends and folk-tales in French. But, whereas Diop's loyalties were divided unequally between his veterinary and literary activities, with a brief interlude after 1960 as a diplomat (by which time he had virtually ceased writing). Bernard Dadié can be considered a full-time professional writer, with a large corpus of publications to his name. Diop is closely and uniquely associated with the *Conte*, whose traditional material was drawn mainly from his homeland, Senegal, with occasional inspiration from his travels in Mauritania and Upper Volta; Dadié has shown himself equally at home in poetry and drama, folk-tale and novel. I shall deal with his contribution to these other genres in later chapters.

For his legends and folk-tales Dadié draws predominantly on the oral heritage of the Ivory Coast where he was born in 1916, in Assinie and where the first school in the Ivory Coast was opened as far back as 1888. He studied at Grand Bassam for seven years before proceeding to the William Ponty School on the Island of Gorée, the nursery for the first generation of Black intellectuals and writers from West Africa. From 1936 to 1947 he worked at I.F.A.N., where his interest in resuscitating and preserving the cultural heritage of Black Africa, first stimulated by his teachers, was given further encouragement and inspiration. After the War he returned to his homeland to work as a primary school teacher; it was at this time that he published his first volume of poetry, whose challenging title, *Afrique debout*! indicates his enrolment under the banner of Negritude. In the same spirit he collected the themes and material for re-telling the tales and legends of his people, the first volume of which, *Légendes africaines*, appeared in 1953. A further collection of folk-tales, *Le Pagne noir*, appeared two years later, in the same year as his autobiographical novel, *Climbié*, after which Dadié's gifts have directed him into literary fields in which he can more fully exploit his creative originality and satiric verve, namely the travel-chronicle and drama. His tales and legends from traditional sources can be roughly divided into four categories: historical legends, cosmogonic legends, moral fables and Spider stories.

Historical legends

In spite of the plural heading, there is in fact only one example of historical legend among Dadié's tales. As an Eburnean he must have felt it more or less his duty to retell the legend of the founding of the Baoulé tribe, which we have already met in Maximilien Quenum's version. Dadié's is much briefer and he makes no attempt to put any personal, literary stamp on the traditional 'facts' of the exodus of a nameless tribe, pursued by its enemies. He gives neither a physical nor moral portrait of the Queen Pokou, nor greater justification for the flight than the superior numbers and extreme ferocity of the enemy. Apart from the absence of local colour, picturesque detail, characterization and psychological motivation of the protagonists, there are other minor differences between the versions adopted by Dadié and by Quenum. Where the latter's victim is a young man who consents to his sacrifice to save his people (an element of traditional African ethos) the former adopts the variant whereby the prince is an infant of only six months, thus making the mother's sacrifice more poignant, and emphasizing her role as the national heroine. The gods of the turbulent river demand the sacrifice, not specifically of a young man, but of whatever the tribe considers its most precious possession. The soothsayer rejects the proffered ivory and gold ornaments, and interprets the demand as being for the tribe's most precious son. It is the Queen herself who casts her infant into the raging waters. Instead of the bridge formed by the baobab trees, Dadié uses the alternative legendary explanation of the miraculous crossing; the school of enormous hippopotami who emerge from the river and range themselves head to tail to allow the tribe to pass over on their backs. The author then adds an explanatory detail omitted by Quenum: that the word 'Baouli', the name subsequently given to the tribe, was the first word spoken by the mother in her grief and meaning 'The child is dead'.

Notwithstanding the extreme concision of the narrative, Dadié shows something of the artist's instinct in selecting the most psychologically poignant and symbolically effective variants of the well-known legend.

Cosmogonic legends

Bernard Dadié included in his 'African Legends' six of these traditional tales giving a mythic explanation of the origin of some of the natural phenomena of the world.

'La Saunerie de la vieille d'Amafi' is an African version of the loss of Eden, the beginning of misery and suffering on Earth. According to this, in a long-past Golden Age, dimly remembered by only a very few old men, Heaven was a low ceiling to Earth and God mixed freely with men, listening to their troubles and settling their disputes. Vice was concentrated in the person of one old woman, so evil that even the Devil would not have her in Hell. The community banished her far to the west of the village, where she lived by crystallizing salt. The inhabitants of Heaven complained of the noxious effluvia from her trade. She defied them, for their part, to live further away and encouraged their removal by continually hurling her pestle against the floor of Heaven whenever she crushed her salt in her gigantic mortar. Gradually Heaven was driven so far away from Earth that God found it impossible to mingle freely with his people. 'La Mort des hommes' is the sequel of this tale, telling of the coming of Death, with her principal ministers, Plague, Typhoid and Smallpox. There is also a myth within the myth: the explanation why men have always hunted the guinea-fowl, to take revenge on her empty-headed stupidity, and why the dog always warns men of the approach of Death.

In these two tales Dadié's own literary personality is completely effaced. He simply reproduces the mythology which was a basic part of his country people's heritage, which he thus saves from oblivion. In four other cosmo-gonic legends we see more traces of the original writer that Bernard Dadié will prove himself to be, in the instinct which guides his choice of the more poetic of the myths, thereby distilling the literary from the simply ethno-logical aspects of the folk-lore, and in the personal additions he makes to the raw material of the tales.

'Attoua, reine des étoiles', tells how a young girl whose beauty was marred by her bad teeth ran away to avoid her companions' malicious remarks. An old sorcerer transformed her thirty-two carious stumps into precious stones, while Attoua herself became a constellation, the 'Queen of the Stars', before these were yet known in the firmament. Dadié ends his story with a characteristic warning that he is not responsible for the legend and that the reader should be careful not to count the stars, charming as they are. It appears that this brings bad luck. 'At least, so they say!'

'La Légende de la fumée' is an 'orphan and wicked step-mother' tale.

Codjo is less successful than some of his fellow orphans in his impossible quest, namely to replace his broken pitcher in the land of Death. He is transformed into smoke to escape from her clutches.

Finally, in 'Nénuphar la reine des eaux' and 'Tawêloro!' Dadié displays his mastery of lyricism at its most moving. 'Nénuphar' is both a cosmogonic legend – from the time before the appearance of man on Earth – and a mythic explanation of the rainbow, the butterfly, the birds and the royal eagle. In poetic imagination this myth is in no way inferior to its Hellenic counterparts. Dadié also displays here his powers of vivid description, particularly in his pictures of the forest, the setting of so many of his legends. There is, to be sure, a certain imitative romanticism in his descriptive prose. But, irrespective of the originality and literary merits of the style, the important thing is that, at this early stage of his literary career, Dadié is not content simply to reproduce the elements of the legend, but recreates it as a piece of original literary composition, with care for the setting, the concept, the characterization, and – important detail for the masterly dramatist he is to become – the dialogue.

The story of 'Tawêloro!', the origin of the tides and the music of the sea, is also lyrical in style and subject. A princess is so beautiful that her parents cannot bear to part with her by giving her in marriage. Finally she runs away from home and becomes a siren. Her mother seeks for her endlessly but in vain, her ghost ever haunting the seashore where her lost daughter disappeared, singing a plaintive elegy at the full moon:

> My child is as beautiful as the Moon.
> Tawêloro! Tawêloro!
> My child is as beautiful as the Day.
> Tawêloro! Tawêloro!
> Tawêloro! ô.ô.ô...!

Moral fables

Dadié includes in his collections of folk-tales and legends a number of moral fables, with either human or animal characters, sometimes both together, and which normally contain a strong element of fantasy and the supernatural. Their tone is usually more serious than those of Birago Diop. It is not that Dadié is not a master of humorous effects, mostly in the form of comic irony – he shows this in his Spider stories, and eventually in his novels and plays – but he rarely calls on it to reinforce the moral lessons of the fables. In fact he tends to dilute the poetic fantasy with a somewhat sententious note, as in the story of the feud between the birds and the animals, which illustrates how a tiny dispute can be inflamed into an affair of state and escalate into a *casus belli*, and prompts the author's comment: 'Ah! these false promises, these perjuries, we humans have not the monopoly of these!'

Most of the stories referred to in this category are variants of well-known themes, different versions of some of which can be found in the *Tales of Amadou Koumba*. For example, 'Le Chien de Coffi' is the traditional tale of the animals' attempts to outwit their enemy, the hunter. It also points the lesson of ingratitude to a faithful servant (the hunter's dog), the latter's unshaken loyalty, and the power of woman's wiles over man. This story is also an example of Dadié's attempts to renew well-known narrative material by care and originality in the composition. In this case he begins at the climax, on the evening of the third day of the siege, when the animals are about to fell the tree. Then he re-traces the preceding events, intriguing the audience, by his skill in bringing the story full circle.

In this group of moral tales are some more variations on the 'orphan' theme, notably 'Le Pagne noir', which gives its name to Dadié's second collection of tales, and refers to the black cloth which Aïwa must wash till it is white as kaolin, and 'Le Cruche', in which Koffi has to replace a broken pitcher and is exposed to innumerable trials of his patience and charity. Both are traditional fables of virtue rewarded and neither shows any outstanding originality of treatment.

In 'Le Chasseur et le boa' we recognize the gentleman who spares his prey and is rewarded by great riches beyond his dreams. (In Western folk-tales he is usually a fisherman, different geographic regions dictating these marginal differences.) But this is more than just a moral fable warning against excessive greed; it is also a philosophical allegory of man's predicament in the face of death. The Hunter is advised that he will die by the time the sun reaches its zenith, unless he returns to the Boa, before noon, the gourd from which all his riches come. The author leaves him, and the reader, with the dilemma: to divest himself of the wealth that has made life sweet, or to embrace death, clinging to his possessions as is the common human instinct.

'L'Homme qui voulait être roi' and 'Crocodile et maître-pêcheur' are two fables where satire is mixed with the moral element. Both emphasize the difficulty of living in harmony and rendering justice, among animals and humans. The parallel is spelled out in the story of the man who wanted to be king. As the animals cannot resolve the quarrel between the chimpanzees and man (the men of the bush and the simian inhabitants of the town), how much more difficult must it be to decide on rights and administer justice between man and man. From a literary point of view, the Crocodile and Kingfisher story is the more effective of the two, rich in a two-edged satire. It includes a delightful portrait of King Lion and a sketch of his role among the beasts, which suggests *Les Animaux malades de la peste*, with a hint of Tartuffe.

Finally, there are two of Dadié's fables which are more in the tradition of the *conte philosophique*. Both are stories of a man who kills out of adulterous lust, and of the subsequent awakening of his conscience. The author varies the theme with skill, so that there is no impression of monotony, but a suggestion that such episodes are common enough occurrences in a community. Both stories contain more elements of realism and psychological authenticity than the majority of the fables but there is a difference in the characterization and in the type of realistic detail in the two episodes. 'La Lueur du soleil couchant', as the title suggests, is more poetical in its treatment and more symbolical. It is the gleam of the setting sun which is the only witness of the murder, and it is on this witness that the victim calls to reveal the crime. 'L'Aveu' is more satirical in its intention, pointing out the difficulty of pinning the blame for a crime on a man who is rich and powerful:

Just try confronting a powerful man and saying that he is a murderer, and see if the other notables do not flay you alive for the affront done to one of their corporation, whose members hide one another's misdeeds.

Spider stories

A few of the tales in Dadié's *Légendes Africaines*, and the majority of those in *Le Pagne noir*, come from the cycle of Kakou-Ananze the Spider. Just as Birago Diop draws on the animal *gestes* of the Sahelian regions, whose popular characters are the Hare and the Hyena, the Jackal, the Monkey and the Deer, so Bernard Dadié quite naturally reproduces elements from the Spider *geste* that belongs to his native forest area. This field of folk-lore has been more thoroughly ploughed by African writers in English than in French, but by all standards Dadié's versions are superior by virtue of his comic verve, his cynicism, the variety of the characterization and his techniques in retelling the traditional episodes. For example, to avoid the danger of monotony, inherent in the Spider's exploits, Dadié sometimes uses the first-person narrative. In the story of how Ananze got his hump, he thereby achieves some subtly comic effects, both in the pastiche of the popular romance and the indirect irony of the self-portrait. He makes free use of dialogue, for which he has the embryo dramatist's gift, to enrich the characterization and to add mock realism to the situation, as in the

encounter between the Hyena and the Spider in 'La Vache de Dieu'. He
even includes a piece of inner monologue as Hyena resolves for once in
his life to get the better of Ananze. Frequently the dialogue both defines
a character and adds to the irony, illustrated in another encounter between
an animal of quick wit – the Hare – and his slower thinking fellow-creatures
who come to him for advice. Another time, the inner monologue develops
into a dialogue between Ananze and the Devil who has infiltrated his mind
with temptation. It is not only by dialogue that Dadié varies the narrative
of the Spider stories and adds a further dimension to the characters, which,
incidentally, have rarely any but the slightest claim to belong to the animal
kingdom: sometimes he introduces brief but picturesque descriptions of
his protagonists – humans in animal disguise, or animals masquerading as
humans. Here is the Pig in 'Le Groin du Porc':

He was going off to the fields with his basket on his head, a stick in his hand, his
pipe in his snout and a fly-swatter under his right arm. He went 'Clouc...clak!'
on his short legs, shod in sandals of *parasolier* wood, and his pipe went 'poum!
poum!', sending out spirals of smoke that were absorbed by the wind. (*Le Pagne
noir*, Présence Africaine, 1955, p. 93)

The comic effect is enhanced by the realism of the details, with only the
use of the word 'snout' and the ambiguous reference to short legs, to remind
us that this is no normal peasant setting off for work in his fields.
    These brief general comments on the Spider stories are applicable to
all Dadié's fables, though his comic gifts are not exploited as thoroughly
in the other types of tales. Throughout he retains the atmosphere of the
spontaneous oral narrative, using all the *griot's* gambits to give variety and
dynamism to his literary style. Yet it is clear that in cutting his literary teeth
on legends and folk-tales, Bernard Dadié, like Birago Diop, has gone
beyond his primary task – dictated by the doctrine of Negritude – of
preserving African traditional lore. While he does little to re-shape the
mythic tales, or to impose his literary personality on his French versions
of these, in the re-creation of the fables and Spider stories he has begun
to forge a precise literary instrument for use in all branches of creative
writing to which he will eventually turn. He already demonstrates a sharp
observation of reality, both external and psychological; although he does
not build up a gallery of animal portraits, as does Diop, their satirical impact
is greater as we recognize the human counterpart through the transparent
disguise. His poetic instinct is demonstrated in a command of lyrical style,
but his sense of fantasy and the supernatural is less strong than Birago
Diop's. Dadié shows his emergent literary talents most strongly in his use
of ironic dialogue and humour generally; this is less bland and urbane than

that of Diop, and already indicates the more trenchant satire of his travel
accounts and his dramatic works.

Fily-Dabo Sissoko

Fily-Dabo Sissoko: *Sagesse noire. Sentences et proverbes malinkés.* Paris, Editions
de la Tour du Guet, 1955. o.p.

The name of the Malian writer Fily-Dabo Sissoko is less well-known than
that of Birago Diop, Bernard Dadié or Ousmane Socé, who all have an
important and well-deserved place in Negro-African literature in French,
or even that of Maximilien Quenum, whose sole contribution to creative
writing was his three African legends. Nevertheless, Sissoko's *Sagesse noire*,
a collection of Sudanese proverbs, axioms and apophthegms is a small but
interesting offering, forming a stepping-stone from the wisdom of Africa's
past to the literature of the present. If the thought is traditional, the merit
for the expression in incisive and often poetical French is Sissoko's.

We owe to the author's own *Crayons et portraits* and memoirs, published
as *La Savane rouge*, what we know of his origins, childhood and inspiration
for his literary activities. Born in 1900, in the village of Dioufoya in the
then French Sudan (Mali), he received his first education in an almost
exclusively matriarchal environment, from his grandmother, so often the
fount of African traditional lore. He was intended to be trained as a
marabout in the Koranic school, but on the death of his last surviving
brother he was sent to the French lay school for his formal education, where
he stayed till the age of fourteen only. During all this formative period
he was deeply sensitive to the mysticism of Africa, the sacred places, the
presence and powers of djinns and spirits, of which he relates several
examples, including his own visionary and prophetic gifts, notably his
premonition of the death of his mother, when in boarding school in
Saint-Louis. At school he was nick-named 'Tom Thumb' because of his
diminutive height; for the same reason he was refused as a volunteer at
the outbreak of the First World War (at the age of fourteen!). Thus, barely
in his teens, he was appointed *moniteur-stagiaire*, that is pupil teacher, at
Ouagadougou, where the local Commandant coached him for his *Certificat
d'Aptitude à l'Enseignement* and then his *Diplôme Supérieur d'Etudes Pri-
maires* which he obtained in 1918.

These details are mentioned to indicate how Sissoko developed outside
the main currents which were influencing the African intellectuals of the
inter-War years, who became the first generation of Negro-African creative
writers. During his youth, adolescence and maturity, he remained in his

own Sudanese territory, except for the few years spent at school in Saint-Louis in Senegal, living and working for the most part in a peasant community from the age of fourteen, and virtually self-taught as he pursued his studies of literature, philosophy and politics. Having become *chef de canton* of the Bafoulabé region of the Sudan after the War, he was elected Deputé de l'Assemblée Nationale in 1945. In Paris he enjoyed the hospitality of a French family who introduced him to Professor Marcel Jousse, incumbent of the Chair of Anthropology (du Mimisme) at the Sorbonne, who encouraged him to publish a book presenting some aspects of the mentality of the Black peasant, as shown in his proverbs and sayings.

Nourished on French seventeenth-century moralists and philosophers, Sissoko takes the opportunity to demonstrate the universality and reality of all things in the Black peasant's milieu. We find the basic premise of the moralist: 'Know thyself' expressed in cogent, concrete terms such as: 'To know how to ride a horse, an ass, to climb, to swim. Nothing equals: To know oneself', which can be compared with Pascal's 'A man must know himself, so be it does not serve to find the truth, it serves at least to regulate one's life, and there is naught more proper'. And to Pascal's 'Man is visibly made for thinking; therein lies all his dignity and all his worth and all his duty is to think correctly', the Malinké echoes: 'The world is what man thinks'.

Sissoko had collected 500 proverbs and axioms during conversations with peasants in the course of his functions as *chef de canton*, and these, translated into French, form the contents of *Sagesse noire*. It is impossible to say how far he was guided in the actual selection of his material by his study of the French moralists, but it seems highly likely that at least his method of classification was influenced by his strong admiration for La Bruyère, whom he was to imitate in his *Crayons et portraits*. The headings which he chooses, under which to range the proverbs and axioms are:

1. The Individual, which he sub-divides as referring to inner life, representative life, affective existence, active life and *Karma*.
2. The Family and Society.
3. Death and God.

The sayings all have the extreme concision and spontaneity of the examples already quoted, and usually contain a concrete image from everyday existence, such as 'Le rônier sort d'un noyau', the obvious parallel to 'Great oaks from little acorns grow'. We do not look for abstruse, metaphysical thought from this simple, practical wisdom of a rural folk, which the author claims only to have translated and classified, but the apology he makes in his introduction, for adding to the vast collection of proverbs from Black

Africa in French, is uncalled-for. Although the sayings themselves are not original, Sissoko's work has a certain literary value in the careful composition and in the incisive language of the translation into French. In this work alone, where he is obviously restrained by the original Malinké linguistic formula, he avoids the tendency to over-flowery style and excessive use of banal epithets which we find in his other freer literary compositions, and even in the introduction to *Sagesse noire*.

THE REAR-GUARD AND THE DECLINE OF THE FOLK-TALE

From the mid-fifties the movement to preserve and re-create the folk-tales and legends of West Africa lost its impetus.[13] Apart from the fact that it was difficult to surpass the work already done in this field, particularly by Birago Diop and Bernard Dadié, politicians and intellectuals were looking to the future and working for Independence. Mysticism, allegory, symbolism, all the appurtenances of fable and myth were somewhat gratuitous and had to give way to a more practical, positivist or unambiguously politically committed form of expression in prose writings. With Independence, the eyes of the political leaders were turned more than ever to the future and to the practical necessities of constructing new nations that must labour to make up some of the lee-way, dividing them from the East as well as from the West, in material productivity and scientific advancement. Creative writers must be enrolled in the service of progress. Story-telling through long African nights is too slow-paced and too indirect a manifestation of African values. Authors were encouraged or inspired to pound their typewriters more directly in the cause of national solidarity, African socialism or the people's revolution.

In many cases it became fashionable to indict folk-lore as being a manifestation of superstition for backward, primitive people and militating against progress. (See the examples quoted on pp. 10 and 12 of the attitudes of the younger generation in Badian's *Sous l'orage* and Olympe Bhêly Quénum's *Chant du lac* – 'We must be careful not to revert to folk-lore'.) Most of the writers who did turn to the past for their inspiration, preferred historico-legendary subjects to fables and folk-tales and glorified warrior-heroes in a deliberate desire to create an epic literature. These themes, usually in dramatic form, are discussed in Chapter 2.

In the sixties, nevertheless, a few African writers formed a small rear-

[13] Birago Diop's *Nouveaux contes d'Amadou Koumba*, 1958, and *Contes et lavanes*, 1963, both published by Présence Africaine, comprise material already collected in previous years and from which the author had been forced to make a first selection in the light of Fasquelle's timidity in making the venture, when other publishing houses had refused the work.

guard, each publishing one volume of traditional tales re-told in his own manner, and with little other purely creative literature to his name. In addition to these, the poet Gérald Tchicaya U Tam'si published in 1969 an anthology under the title, *Légendes africaines*. Tchicaya himself produced one original story for the collection, but the rest of the fourteen contributions were either extracts from longer works in French, which I shall deal with elsewhere (Ousmane Socé Diop's *Karim* and Djibril Niane's historical novel, *Soundjata*) or from Blaise Cendrar's *Anthologie nègre*, mentioned earlier (p. 14), or from works which do not strictly belong within the purview of this study, such as Mofolo's *Chaka* and Frobenius's ethnological writings.

In the following notes on four recent collections of folk-tales I try to give an idea of different conceptions of this genre among African writers of the sixties.

Joseph Brahim Seid

JOSEPH BRAHIM SEID: *Au Tchad, sous les étoiles*. Paris, Présence Africaine, 1962.

Joseph Seid was 35 when he published his collection of folk-tales, fables and legends based on the oral traditions of the regions west and south of Lake Chad. He published only one other work of creative literature, an autobiographical tale called *Un Enfant du Tchad* (Paris, SAGEREP – L'Afrique Actuelle 1967. Dossiers Littéraires de l'Afrique Actuelle, 1).

His tales differ in some respects from those which earlier writers had collected and re-told, not only because they are the first to appear from this region, but more particularly because of the atmosphere which pervades them. The author deliberately sets out to sing a sort of hymn of praise to a utopian existence in a land of plenty, where happiness and love, generosity and harmony reign. 'During all seasons', Seid says in his introduction, 'the children of Chad are the happiest in the world', whether hunting or working in the fields or running wild in the bush. But they are particularly happy when listening to miraculous and legendary tales in the evening. It is this 'pleasure of their simple innocence' that Seid proposes to share with his readers.

Thus he re-tells the local myths and legends of the founding and early history of his native land, as if the memory of this idyllic existence can serve as a raft in the troubled waters which may lie ahead. Of the earliest settlers he tells us that, in the days after the creation of the Earth, there came a great deluge and the tribe of Alifa fled from the waters and settled near a great lake which suddenly appeared one night when the rains ceased. This land was an Eden where man and beast lived in perfect harmony, goodness and innocence. Alifa and his people, received with hospitality by the inhabitants, baptized the lake 'Chad', meaning land of abundance, happiness and mutual love. Seid does not blur this image by including any account of the loss of innocence and the coming of evil, though these must surely have formed part of the traditional mythology.

There follow historico-legendary tales of the early tribes inhabiting the Chad region, which emphasize the utopian atmosphere and desire for peace and goodwill. For example, the story of the twelve tribes founded by twelve young men who removed the spear of contention which was the source of civil war, and went off and founded a new realm. Nearer the present are stories, part history, part legend, of the reign of the sultans, up to the mid-nineteenth century. These are told in a simple, almost biblical style, without any conscious attempt at epic quality, but they have a pleasing dignity in keeping with the author's elevated intention of glorifying the past. Typical is the *geste* of the Sultan Saboun, celebrated in the annals of the people of Chad for his wisdom, goodness and valour, a man of peace and learning who nevertheless overthrew the enemies of his people who sought to destroy their prosperity in covetous wars of aggression.

Apart from this group of more elevating legends, Seid includes a series of fantasy folk-tales, with the usual stock-in-trade of magic horses, capes of invisibility, fairy wands, inexhaustible purses and wicked step-mothers. The familiar ill-treated orphans charm monsters, snakes and evil spirits by their purity and beauty. Then there are some animal fables in which the morals are the usual ones: virtue brings its own reward; Death comes in its own time and not to those who most desire it; and, surprisingly, in view of Seid's idealistic aims and his own career as a magistrate, might seems once again to be right. The apologue of the Lion is original and worth quoting as an example of Seid's animal fables. The Lion and the Hyena decide to form a company into which they put their common capital, a bull and a cow. When it comes to sharing the 'interest' they cannot decide to whom the calf should belong, so they call all the animals to sit in judgement. The tribunal unanimously decides in favour of the Lion, the original owner of the bull, as 'only the bull has the power to procreate'. The Hare arrives late, disconcerted and mournful, a pitiful father who has just given birth to a leveret. He is laughed to scorn by the Lion, who thus disproves his own case, but the moral states categorically: 'in this life only the strongest can win a law-suit' – thus providing a new version and a new illustration of La Fontaine's 'La raison du plus fort est toujours la meilleure'. Like his French predecessor, Seid also has the gift of evoking the behaviour and appearance of the animals in a few lines, sometimes with a happy image, sometimes with no more than common-place characteristics.

To sum up, Joseph Seid's stories in *Au Tchad sous les étoiles* have a distinct interest as a contribution to the literature of folk-lore, as they preserve tales and legends from an area scarcely touched by recent African writers in French. As a creative writer Seid brings a breath of romantic nostalgia for an idealized past, which is somewhat different from the doctrines of Negritude which inspired other Black writers to look at a national heritage as a gesture of cultural solidarity. However, as original writings in French, these tales have few distinguishing characteristics and in a quarrel between 'Ancients' and 'Moderns', they would be only a light weight in the scale of the 'Ancients'.

Benjamin Matip

BENJAMIN MATIP: *A la belle étoile. Contes et nouvelles d'Afrique.* Paris, Présence Africaine, 1962.

In the same year that Joseph Seid's collection of tales and legends was published, there appeared from the same publishers a volume with a similar title, emphasizing the oral origins of its contents, by the slightly younger Cameroonian writer, Benjamin Matip. The author, who had earlier published a novel, *Afrique, nous t'ignorons* (Paris, R. Lacoste, 1957) went on to write a play for the Cameroonian National Theatre in 1963, *Le Jugement dernier*, which does not seem to have been published. Matip has not produced any further creative literature, which is a pity, as he shows original qualities of observation and command of a dry, ironic humour which put a personal cachet on his re-creation of the tales of the chroniclers of old.

In 'Les Dates solennelles', which serves as introduction to the collection of short stories, Matip recalls his youth with nostalgia; the old men sitting round the fire telling stories in the long evenings with, as backdrop, the black mystery of the forest, its cries helping to evoke the world of the traditional tales of ruse, violence and fantasy, of animals and gods who rewarded the good and punished the bad. He sets out deliberately, so he says, to reveal the rich source of wisdom of the past and put it to the service of the Africa of today.

Though he claims, like Birago Diop before him, simply to report some of the ancients' wisdom, the interest of Matip's tales for present and future readers will be found as much in the literary gifts that he has brought to the re-telling of the tales, as in their moral lessons. Two examples will illustrate Matip's power of revitalizing types of traditional story, on the one hand a well-known moral fable, whose lesson might prove tedious, and on the other a *conte* of the Tom Thumb/Frog-Prince type.

'Adieu la guerre, adieu le paradis' is the familiar fable of ingratitude that Birago Diop had told as 'The Reward' in the *Tales of Amadou Koumba*. Here a hunter carries an enormous boa with its young for miles through the forest back to their native lake, only to be threatened with death unless he can get three independent witnesses to prove that a good action should not normally be rewarded by a bad turn. The novelty of Matip's version lies not only in the enrichment of the narrative with a wealth of realistic detail, but more particularly in the colloquial dialogue which he invents to give a lively irony and an *actualité* to his tale. The mixture of fantasy and familiarity, as hunter, serpents, tortoises and other creatures engage in an argument using current French slang, is not without piquancy:

'That's enough', shouted the gigantic snake, aiming an enormous blow a few inches away from the hunter's head. 'No moralizing. You've spent your whole life wiping out every living thing in this forest and you've the cheek to moralize at me. Now you just listen: have you any idea how many of my brothers and sisters you've already bumped off?' ('Adieu la guerre, adieu le paradis', p. 21)

With the dramatist's art, Matip varies the stylistic effects of the speakers, so that we can see and hear each one in character. The wily tortoise, suspecting a trap, and knowing that whatever judgement she gives will offend one of the contestants, either of whom can easily take his revenge on her, plays on her reputation for slowness and for time:

The tortoise pushed her head out a little further, as if the better to see and hear. She considered the poor hunter with indifference, I'd even say with contempt, and said to the boa: 'I beg your pardon, dear brother, but I don't really understand what this is all about. I didn't really take in the question. Would you please be so good as to repeat it, speaking very slowly and distinctly, and explain the whole argument.' (ibid., p. 27)

Differing from other versions of this fable, Matip's does not tell us the outcome of the judgement. Leaving it in the air, he suggests that possibly the hunter did not really deserve to be saved, there being equal wrong and right on both sides.

'Le Drapeau du sourire' is a sophisticated and satirical version of the fairy-tale in which a sterile old couple's dearest desire for a child is rewarded with the birth of . . . a frog, who persuades his father not to drop him in the pond, which would mean his demise, by promising to devote his adult life to working to improve the condition of mankind. He will, he says, fight for Justice, Liberty and Equality, so that men will no longer know the nightmare of hunger and thirst; the shadow of death and slavery will no longer hover over our lands; Liberty will no longer be assassinated; the standard of Glory, Science and Liberty will float for ever everywhere! ('Le Drapeau du sourire', p. 35)

The parody of demagogic tub-thumping and the political satire is enhanced by Matip's solemn quotation of his sources, authenticated apparently by a number of chroniclers: 'One chronicler even reports that the old woman fainted with emotion to hear these words.' (ibid.) Later, this politically-orientated frog, grown to manhood, and exhorted to 'know his place' when he expresses his intention to seek the hand of one of the King's daughters, retorts:

'No! No-one should be condemned to "keep his place". Man must work and struggle to better, not only his own existence, but that of others, especially that of the whole of society. One must never, never stand still. It is our duty, yes, our supreme duty to change things. . . No! A thousand times no! To stay in one place is to shut the door on happiness and progress.' Another [chronicler] reports that 36,000 crocodiles emerged from the River Kongo all together with their fangs bared, to besiege the unfortunate sovereign and express their common indignation. And in this respect a third chronicler had the ingenuity to advance a theory which would make practical men like Darwin and Kipling tremble in their graves: the thesis of the solidarity of animals, in spite of all appearances to the contrary. When these 36,000 crocodiles all emerged simultaneously to spit out their wrath against the scoundrelly king, and perhaps, through him, at the entire human race, who can say that this was not inspired by solidarity for the frog, their kinsman? Naturally, I only report this curious theory of the chroniclers, for what it is worth; I in no wise have to adopt it or contradict it. (ibid., pp. 37, 51)

It is tempting to read 'Blacks' for 'animals' and 'Whites' for the 'human race' and the scoundrel king. But it is up to the reader to adopt or contradict the hypothesis.

Léon-Marie Ayissi

LÉON-MARIE AYISSI: *Contes et berceuses Béti*. Yaoundé, Edit. CLE (Coll. Abbia), 1966.

L.-M. Ayissi, a Cameroonian school-teacher, explains in his introduction to his collection of tales and lullabies his intention to save from oblivion a traditional literary genre which had charmed his childhood, and his approach to his task appears to be one of ponderous reverence. It is somewhat superfluous in the mid-sixties to apologize for the fact that the French versions of African tales will be 're-creations', 'adaptations' and 'renovations' rather than literal translations. The 'renovations' that he proposes consist of dialogue between the narrator and the 'fictional audience' as well as between the characters of the stories, and free verse to make them 'more poetic and more likely to survive'. The use of dialogue will not strike any reader of some of the better-known folk-tales and fables as a greatly original feature. As for the free verse, the poetic lyrical prose of other writers discussed in this chapter is certainly more commanding and more likely to survive on the merits of style alone.

Ayissi gives a useful explanation of the different kinds of traditional Beti tale: the *nlan*, which include myth and moral fable, mnemonics and tales of love and adventure, all of which are recited without musical accompaniment, and the *nkana*, a kind of *chante-fable*, to which the sung refrain was inherent. Four of his six tales are animal fables and two are romantic adventures. The last of these, 'L'Histoire d'Angon Mana et d'Abomo Ngélé', the longest, the most complex and stylistically the most satisfying, tells how the handsome Angon Mana is visited on the death of his mother by the beautiful daughter of the King of the Underworld who has fallen in love with him and asks him to defy her father's powers by seeking her out in her secret haunts. The story of his adventures, vicissitudes, tribulations and impossible tasks fulfilled to win his bride is a cross between the virtuous orphan tale and the labours of Hercules.

Jacques Mariel Nzouankeu

JACQUES MARIEL NZOUANKEU: *Le Souffle des ancêtres*. Yaoundé, Edit. CLE (Coll: Abbia), 1965. Repr., 1971.

J. M. Nzouankeu's literary pretensions are almost as modest as those of Ayissi, but his moral intentions are laudable. In the four tales[14] that form the collection *Le Souffle des ancêtres* [The breath of the ancestors], he sets out to illustrate the conflict of man with the mystic forces that dominate his destiny, according to the traditional Cameroonian metaphysics. In his introduction the author explains, presumably for the White reader, the popular traditionalist belief in the power of the gods, their hierarchy and their intermediaries: the pitiless, uncompromising *devins* (fortune-tellers) who exact an exclusive, immediate, uncalculating obedience to the divine commands. The punishment for disobedience is death from the forces of nature: tornados, earthquakes and thunder-bolts being the favourite weapons wielded by the gods. Human logic and rationalism have no part in this ethos, any more than the pursuit of happiness or the desire to preserve life. The purpose of existence being aspiration to the perfection of the gods,

---

[14] On page 8 of the introduction the author talks of the 'conception of life illustrated in these *six* stories', but the collection only includes four.

only death can bring man near to their perfection: 'the judges of man and the models of perfection are not the living but the dead'. In this spirit Nzouankou sets out to restore the credit of the ancestral gods in his four tales. Each of these ends with a death which is either a sacrifice exacted by a divinity or a punishment for disobeying divine decrees.

The Western critic can only speak with reserve in this matter, but in my view Nzouankeu fails in his intention of inspiring awe or respectful comprehension of these ancestral philosophies and ethics because of the defects in the structure and orientation of his tales. They are recounted in too diffuse a manner, with too much irrelevant detail which, in an attempt to add to the realism, distracts from the atmosphere of mystery in which superhuman powers dominate the destiny of man, and prevents the reader from being deeply concerned with the fate of the main protagonists. The result is that these stories have neither the conviction of realism nor the sense of the awe-ful powers of a menacing, inevitable Fate. The interest of Nzouankeu's tales thus resides less in the literary performance than in the intention to resuscitate a mythology which he feels still has relevance for the people of independent Cameroon. The fact that his book has been found to justify a reprint in 1971 indicates that he is not entirely wrong.

LEGENDS FROM CENTRAL AND WEST AFRICA IN NOVELS AND NOVELLAS

During the colonial period the Senegalese Abdoulaye Sadji, Paul Lomami-Tchibamba and Jean Malonga (from the then Belgian and French Congo respectively) all attempted to treat legendary or fabulous subjects from their home region in the form of short novels. The two Congolese write rather self-consciously of Africa's past and the mysteries hidden in her forests and rivers. Lomami-Tchibamba made no further contribution to creative writing. Malonga made a great impression with his other short realistic novel, *Cœur d'Aryenne*, which is discussed in a later chapter.

Paul Lomami-Tchibamba

PAUL LOMAMI-TCHIBAMBA: *Ngando-Le-Crocodile*. Bruxelles, G. A. Deny, (Coll: Prix annuels de la Littérature de la Foire de Bruxelles), 1948. o.p. Repr. in vol. 1 of *L'Afrique raconte*, Klaus Reprints, 1970.

Ngando-Le-Crocodile is a work of fiction in which the author attempts to explore the mysteries and metaphysics of the daily life of the Congolese and the contingencies of the universe as he conceives it. In the continual presence of death which is often sudden and shocking, always incomprehensible and anguishing, his compatriots have built up a hieratic system of opposing and counteracting forces and powers: the primary life-giving force and a contrary force whose role is to destroy man's existence. This destructive power is in the hands of invisible beings who inhabit a mysterious world hidden from man. To illustrate how the supernatural is an integral part of African daily life, the author mingles the realism of streets, workshops and the banks of Stanley Pool with the mysterious happenings of the river and its islands, inhabited by spirits of all kinds, to whom Ngando is subservient. He sets his scene with care for topographical authenticity, in particular the island of Mbamu, in Stanley Pool, a no-man's-land inhabited solely by spirits and men fleeing from the law. With the detailed description of these spirits, the narrative quits the realm of reality for that of mythology, preparing us for the entirely supernatural journey of Ngando, the emissary of evil powers, bearing the child who has fallen into the river away to the island, the haunt of his maleficent masters.

It would be an easy but completely futile exercise to find logical explanations for the anecdotal elements of this novel and to reduce the supernatural intervention to the level of primitive and foolish superstitions. Not only would this strip the work of its poetry but also of its mythic dimension. It would also blind us to the art of the writer in dominating his material in order to make completely accessible to the Western reader the world in which *ndokis*, evil spirits, and not logic regulate cause and effect, and which forms the reality of the African experience. In this respect the realism of *Ngando* operates on three levels, this sur-reality being completely integrated into a vivid description of the material details of existence – that of Musalinga and his family and playmates – and that of psychological authenticity of the different protagonists of the drama.

Because Lomami-Tchibamba's novel has no political overtones, it has tended to be neglected by Black as well as White readers caught up in the enthusiasm for the doctrine of Negritude. It deserves more attention, not only for its ethnological interest as a link with the traditional past of Central Africa which is rapidly disappearing but also for the inherent poetic qualities of the writing.

Jean Malonga

JEAN MALONGA: *La Légende de M'Pfoumou Ma Mazono.* Paris, Editions Africaines, 1954. o.p.

Jean Malonga's longer and more ambitious *La Légende de M'Pfoumou Ma Mazono* is an exotic novel of African life with mythic elements, followed by the description of the founding of a Utopia. There is a great deal of tedious apologia for the unfamiliar elements of tribal custom, as the author addresses himself directly to the Western reader, and some equally banal moralizing.

The first part of the narrative deals with the marriage of convenience (to ensure the succession) of Hakoula, the eleven-year-old daughter of a powerful and respected chief. The author feels strongly his duty to ensure the social-anthropological interest by detailed descriptions of the spectacular ritual ceremonials of betrothal, the arrival of the bridal party in her husband's village and the listing of the articles of compensation offered to the bride's family. He also has the irritating habit of intervening apologetically between his text and the reader. At one point he puts into the mouth of Hakoula's mother a curious and ponderously expressed defence of the custom of child marriage, along the lines that 'assiduous contact with her husband exalted the notion of conjugal responsibilities and the pride of the awakening woman and developed the feminine faculties linked to the duties of a spouse'. Unfortunately, far from becoming a dutiful spouse, Hakoula had developed into a terrible coquette by the time she was fifteen, with a reputation for sexual promiscuity comparable to that of Messalina (Malonga's comparison). Finally discovered cuckolding her husband with a sixteen-year-old slave she is banished and disappears from the region.

In the first part of the *Legend of M'Pfoumou Ma Mazono* there is great emphasis on the realistic aspect of the narrative, with much enumeration of local flora – banana-palms, mangroves, palmyras – and generous description of tribal custom, the kind of deliberate exoticism and local colour which African intellectuals of the second half of the twentieth century are beginning to deplore, as showing the world of a primitive people, living close to Nature in their unchanged past. With this is integrated a certain dose of the supernatural, including a similar miraculous crossing of a river on the backs of hippopotami, as in the legend of the Baoulé. The author again apologizes for the introduction of the supernatural, which would not disturb the most critical reader. More genuinely unsatisfactory is Malonga's inability to sustain an epic note, in keeping with the miraculous nature of legend. Not only does his deprecatory style militate against this, but the characters and events of the first part of the narrative are not consistently of epic stature.

The second part, entitled 'Redemption or Forgiveness for a Fault', recounts the actual legend which gives the title to the whole book. In her flight, Hakoula falls and loses consciousness; on awakening she realizes with horror the enormity of her conduct and her continuing love for her husband. She has a vision of her dead grandmother who promises to guide her to a place of absolution where she will earn the right one day to rejoin her spouse. This is the beginning of the episode of the strange Utopia in a solitary paradise, in which Hakoula makes her home and where her child is born. After a wealth of practical detail as to how this African female Robinson Crusoe contrives clothes, shelter, eating vessels, tools, the author coyly refrains from a full description of the infancy and early years of her child who is to become the precocious hero of this part of the narrative. He founds a society based on justice, charity and liberal humanitarianism, with his mother considered as a kind of divinity. The new settlement grows as a compromise between African tradition and Western democracy. After another miraculous interlude, Hakoula's husband, overcome by his enemies, arrives seeking asylum, which is granted after a happy scene of recognition and reconciliation. This is the beginning of a long period of prosperity under the leadership of the young 'Patriarch', now enthroned as King M'Pfoumou Ma Mazono.

The weaknesses of this work arise from its being in the form of a novel and it exemplifies the dangers of transposing traditional material into a foreign mould without either the experience of the form's conventions or the mastery to impose on it new structures and the originality of a new vision. The legendary and mythological elements of the narrative would have been better expressed in a more economical folk-tale form, in as much as they stem from a local heritage which had been conserved in this traditional form. In directing his composition to a Western public and extending his narrative to a full-length novel, Malonga has become tediously pedantic with his gratuitously moralizing interpolations. His sense of a suitable style is also at fault. Where a straightforward artlessness or even naïvety would have served him, he fails to hold the reader's interest or impress him by his apostrophes, questions and answers and other self-conscious tricks of rhetoric. In trying to superimpose a collage of a moral tale of sin and redemption, a philosophical account of a Utopian state, a romance of sensual and ideal love, on a background of traditional folk-lore, with its mythic and supernatural elements, Malonga has tried to fuse too many genres and has prejudiced his success in any.

Abdoulaye Sadji

ABDOULAYE SADJI: *Tounka*. Paris, Présence Africaine, 1965 (posth.).

Published four years after Sadji's death, *Tounka* was in fact completed in June 1946. It is thus one of the earliest known treatments of a legendary African theme in the form of a novel in French and one of the most successful as far as narrative style and construction are concerned.

The story, like Malonga's 'Legend', is in two distinct parts. The first and shorter is rather a prologue to the main legend, telling of the exodus of a tribe in search of water from the hot and sandy heart of Senegal, decimated by drought. These nameless people arrive at the shore and, having placated the god of the sea, settle on the Western littoral of Senegal, in the Cape Verde region. They become accustomed to the moods of the ocean, reap its harvest of fishes cast up on the shore, learn to navigate in hollowed-out canoes and manufacture primitive sails from the fibre of the baobab. This semi-legendary account with its grain of truth, explaining the founding of a race of fisherfolk is told with the natural and pleasing simplicity of style which is missing from the self-conscious writings in the novels mentioned above. There is poetry in Sadji's imagery and in the rhythmic phrases and liturgical choruses, which are the natural spontaneous expression of a primitive people. Also the supernatural is less directly described than subtly suggested.

After this prologue comes the legend of N'Galka, a colossal, epic hero who dominates the rest of the narrative (and should logically have given his name to the tale), descended from the patriarch Tyongane, one of the original 'initiates' who led the exodus to the sea-shore. The five generations which had elapsed since then had strengthened his muscles, increased his physical stature, sharpened his intelligence and all his faculties. The best farmer and fisherman, the champion wrestler, N'Galka is the beloved of the gods until he mocks them and incurs their anger and revenge. He boasts that his fishing expeditions have taken him beyond the limits considered too hazardous for the fishermen, where he has been conducted down to submarine palaces and partaken of banquets with the spirits of the deep. One day a disembodied voice warns him to cease boasting of his experiences in the domain of the sea-gods, as he will be wedded to a sea-princess, but the price of this union must be an eternal respect for his bride, everlasting secrecy as to her origin and the promise that their offspring will never wed a mortal. N'Galka brings back his bride from his next expedition, claiming that she comes from the neighbouring Cap Rouge. In spite of a certain apprehension, indeed revulsion, that he feels on contact with the strange, cold being, the marriage is consummated and a son, Tounka, is born – a child of unnatural precocity who soon manifests supernatural powers. Eventually N'Galka wearies of his frigid 'Undine', publicly denounces her and becomes an accomplice in the vendetta which drives her back to her home beneath the waves. The sea-gods are not slow to wreak their revenge on the hero, who is assaulted demoniacally by the sea-naiads to prove to him that they can be as passionate as the daughters of the earth. Exhausted by their brutal, sensual onslaught he loses his wits and drifts back to land.

But the gods of the sea have not completed their vengeance: they unleash a mighty storm that lashes the village and destroys all the fishermen at sea. After an attempt by the master-fetishist to exorcize the evil spirits that possess N'Galka, he dies. Four of the strongest men cannot lift the bier with the corpse, until the son Tounka is placed at the head of the funeral procession.

This brief summary is intended to give an idea of the poetic charm and mystery of this legend, which Sadji tells with economy, mingling realism with supernatural elements to prove that he is at his best in this literary genre.

THE HISTORICAL NOVEL

The critic who attempts to place Negro-African creative writing in categories is sooner or later bedevilled by some work whose nature defies exact definition. So, although this chapter has basically treated prose writings in French whose subject matter stems directly from the oral tradition, I have included a work which the author calls *Poèmes africains*, on the basis that it is the traditional rather than the poetic nature of the composition which is of interest. Similarly, when dealing with novels and *novellas*, I have had to decide to exclude here a number of works of fiction, such as O. Bhêly-Quénum's *Le Chant du lac*, which have incidental references to myth or legend, but where the dominant tone of the narrative is positivist, factual or sceptical. My criterion has been the degree to which the author has drawn on folk-lore for his basic theme and treated his sources with the respect due to a work of exegesis.

I shall apply a similar standard to judge what is a historical novel, for even more works exist in which fictional episodes and characters are situated in an incidental or even endogenous historical framework: to quote two only, Jean Ikelle-Matiba's *Cette Afrique-là* and Benjamin Matip's *Afrique, nous t'ignorons!* But there are very few works of African fiction which can claim to be pure historical novels. For the purposes of this study, I shall take as my definition a serious and reverent attempt to recreate a chronicle of past times and the exploits of authentic or semi-legendary figures. Three works only satisfy this criterion: Paul Hazoumé's *Doguicimi* and Djibril Niane's *Soundjata*, both woven around a great heroic figure, and Nazi Boni's *Crépuscule des temps anciens*, whose protagonists are of more doubtful authenticity but which purports to be a chronicle of pre-colonial Africa.

We have seen how some historical legends have been preserved among the short tales of Maximilien Quenum, Ousmane Socé and Bernard Dadié.

In all these cases the traditional material has been treated respectfully, maintaining the association of historical and mythic elements, but these examples are few compared to the vast number of fables, myths and folk-tales which gave writers like Socé, Dadié, Benjamin Matip and Birago Diop scope to develop their personal literary talents. Historical subjects have been treated extensively in African drama, as we shall see in the next chapter, in large enough numbers to form the corpus of an important literary genre in Negro-African writing in French. The historical novel proper, on the other hand, has not become rooted in French-African literature, for reasons which I shall try to analyse briefly.

Short tales of various types, including the historical legend, were an intrinsic part of the oral literature, part of a shared communal experience. As such, they could readily be translated into dramatic form to be incorporated into the neo-African writing which was motivated by the desire on the part of the first generation of African intellectuals, composing in French, to find and preserve a national identity. It was therefore natural that these tales should be re-created in French, in more or less their traditional form. Indeed we have seen how writers have made a deliberate effort, in composing their French versions, to reproduce the style and structure of the *griot*'s narration. For this reason, folk-tales, myths and fables form an important part of French-African literature of the pre-Independence era. The novel, on the other hand, was a foreign genre, studied and imitated originally by African writers in its late nineteenth- and twentieth-century manifestations, more specifically the French realist and naturalist models and then the novel of social realism, which had no indigenous association with the life and cultural traditions of Africa. When adopted by African writers in the nineteen fifties, when eyes were turned to the future, the novel proved a useful vehicle for the recall of a personal rather than a national past, in the form of autobiographical fiction posing the question 'Whither Africa?', rather than looking to history, or, alternatively, for more militant committed writings, in the form of anti-colonial diatribes. These will be dealt with in a later chapter, devoted to the novel as such. I shall include here the three major historical novels, previously listed, and one slighter work whose subject was drawn from historical or historico-legendary material.

Paul Hazoumé

PAUL HAZOUMÉ: *Doguicimi*. Paris, Larose, 1938, o.p.

In an article in *Présence Africaine* of March 1962 on the Black novel, Olympe Bhêly-Quénum decries what he calls the African regional novel (in which he includes Bernard Dadié's *Climbié*, Socé's *Karim* and Camara Laye's *L'Enfant noir*) as not sufficiently representative of the African continent and its people, and also calls on Black writers of the second half of the twentieth century to purge their literature of 'false exoticism', stories of primaeval forests and their fauna, and primitive tribes in which 'people tired of having invented too much, slaves of their own machines' think to find the true face of Africa. He sees more of the 'eternal Africa' and the inner conscience of the African in Paul Hazoumé's *Doguicimi* than in all the works of Black writers who have merely repeated the formulae of French fiction writers. Bhêly-Quénum's critical judgement is sometimes suspect, but I endorse his statement here, although *Doguicimi* owes more to Flaubert's *Salammbô* than Bhêly-Quénum would care to admit.

Doguicimi, the first full-length prose work of fiction, after René Maran's *Batouala*, written by an African and inspired totally by an African subject, was a pioneering work and still remains unique in its genre. Hazoumé, born in Dahomey in 1890, when the last of the 'Descendants of the Panther' were defending their autocratic rights against the French armies, became a primary school teacher and an ethnologist known for his scholarly study of the Blood Pact in Dahomey,[15] which the Institut d'Ethnologie of the University of Paris published in 1937. He was then inspired to exploit his profound knowledge of the history and customs of his people in this historical novel, which remains his only other published work. A generation older than the African writers of the post-war years, he lent his prestige and support – not his creative talent – to the Negro-African literary renaissance.

Doguicimi is not a legendary story with mythic dimensions, but a carefully documented work of realist-romantic fiction, set in the pre-colonial period of the history of Dahomey during the reign of King Ghêzo which lasted from 1818 in 1858, In his epilogue the author justifies what fictitious elements he has been forced to incorporate in his narrative, in the service of the greater authenticity of the whole work. These inventions, according to him, are purely of a psychological nature intended to motivate more convincingly the actual historical episodes.

The imaginary ingredients being in small proportion, the care for historical accuracy and detail of local colour make of *Doguicimi* an African *Salammbô*; like this work, its interest lies in the study of custom, ceremonial and ritual, the historical background and the portrait of a romantic heroine

---

[15] The name of the Republic of Dahomey was changed in November 1975 to the People's Republic of Benin, reverting to the name of the pre-colonial Kingdom which occupied the north coast of the Gulf of Guinea. For clarity I have retained the more generally known 'Dahomey' and the adjective 'Dahoman' here and in subsequent references to this region.

of noble character. Local colour is conveyed by the minute description of contemporary life, witness every stage of the feast given to the 'Master of the World' and the long passages detailing the customary lay and religious ritual of betrothals, burials and military preparations. In the ceremony of the betrothal of the king's eldest daughter, the role of the *griot* is underlined, who, like the privileged Shakespearean fool is permitted some outrageous and embarrassing commentaries on the ritual. There is historical interest in the councils of war held by the King and the reception of the French emissaries, with Hazoumé using the novelist's prerogative to put into the mouth and mind of the protagonists speeches and thoughts he has imagined for the occasion. There are also vivid descriptions of battles, military campaigns and court life, presented with the painstaking documentation of an eye-witness and memorialist. Indeed the episode when Toffa's presumed death is announced is reminiscent of Saint-Simon's celebrated account of the death of Monsieur, particularly the detail of the slave who turns his back, ostensibly to lament all the more loudly, but secretly rejoicing that one more tyrannical prince has disappeared.

Hazoumé has taken as much care to authenticate the psychological truth of the characters as he has the historical and ethnological framework of his novel, using the device of soliloquy, or long inner musings to expound the thoughts, preoccupations and motivations of his protagonists. He attempts to make his King Ghêzo a not wholly unsympathetic character, with an eye possibly on the Western or 'enlightened' reader's reactions, as well as on the equilibrium of his narrative. Far from being a weak character, as Judith Gleason suggests,[16] he is more far-seeing, less prejudiced than his predecessors, but is caught in the meshes of a system. He is forced to protect his kingdom against the hostile powers of the neighbouring tribes, to envisage the threatened inroads of the French into his territories. But he is concerned as much with the protection of his people's pride and their traditions as with his own and his country's liberty, all of which explains what he considers the 'just wars' undertaken against the advice of his ministers and in spite of the unfavourable auguries. By the same token, although he is personally against the wholesale practice of human sacrifice, he is bound to it by tradition, but attempts where possible to temper the ferocious brutality of his Minister Migan, with a certain amount of magnanimity. In the Polonius-like words of counsel which he gives to the son who will succeed him, he demonstrates the practical wisdom of a subtle and astute sovereign.

The portrait of Doguicimi herself is not drawn with as much care for

---

[16] In the second chapter of her *This Africa. Novels by West Africans in English and French* (see Bibliographical notes, p. 336) which is called 'The Heroic Legacy of Africa', p. 49.

light and shade and as a character she might be thought less convincing on the level of psychological realism. But we must remember that she is intended to be the model of a national heroine, endowed with superhuman qualities of courage and inspired by the most exalted ideals of stoicism, patriotism and conjugal fidelity to endure imprisonment, torture and finally death. Although over-idealized, she does introduce into the composition an indispensable aggrandizement and stature which elevates the whole above the mere chronicle. This epic intention calls for an appropriately elevated style of language, but Hazoumé often offers only the repetition of conventional formulae, such as 'the stinking mountain-beasts' for the enemy Mahi, 'the foul beasts from the sea' for the Whites, 'the seven-ribbed creatures' for women, 'The immense calabash-cover' for the sky. On the other hand, in descriptions of action, such as the panic among the forest creatures at the advance of the Dahoman army, just as in the canvasses of life in market-place and court, his language has a picturesque poetic quality and a precision of epithet and metaphor.

A discordant note is introduced when the author intervenes directly in his narrative, as in the case of Doguicimi's final long soliloquy while in prison, on the respective merits of the different European nations. At this point Hazoumé permits her the prophetic vision of the day when the French will overcome Dahomey, and an apostrophe to these future conquerors as to their duty to her countryfolk. The author himself is speaking with the hindsight of the twentieth-century student, and not as the mouthpiece of his heroine's fierce national pride. His intention is, of course, to end on a moralizing note and the date of this work is relevant here – the nineteen-thirties. This is a period when an African intellectual who has had some success in France would be prepared to whitewash the image of the colonists and present them as having brought a measure of salvation to a primitive people.

Ibrahim Issa

IBRAHIM ISSA: *Grandes Eaux noires*. Paris, Edit. du Scorpion, (Coll: Alternance) 1959. o.p.

Twenty years pass after the publication of *Doguicimi* before another African writer delves into the past of his country, attempting to recreate an episode of its history with even greater imagination. This novel is based on the first White men's exploration of the regions lying south of the Sahara, two centuries before the Christian era, at the time of the Punic Wars. The central anecdote of *Grandes Eaux noires* is very slight, more suitable for a legendary tale than a historical novel.

Continually apologizing for the inadequate sources on which he bases his history, the author tells of the discovery and imprisonment by men of the Garamantes tribe of seven Whites – whether Greeks, Romans, Phoenicians or Carthaginians remains obscure. One of them is condemned to death for having profaned the sacred waters of the Niger (the 'Great Black Waters' of the title) but is saved by a stratagem of the young heir, the son of 'White Beard', the patriarchal Chief. Mansuetude seems a characteristic of this ruling house, for the Chief himself then intervenes to free two more of the seven whom a mysterious old prophetess has said must be sacrificed to save the tribe from disaster. Her prophecy is realized when the two men are found wandering by a band of White soldiers, presumed to be a Roman legion penetrating to the south after the sack of Carthage, and who wipe out the Garamantes during the absence of the young prince.

Issa fills out this rather thin historico-legendary anecdote with some ethnological data on the origins of the Garamantes tribe who are presumed to have discovered the 'Grandes Eaux Noires', a description of their physical characteristics, gastronomic habits, composition of their herds, a note on the flora and fauna of the region, a digression on the introduction of the camel into the desert areas, an account of the legend of the two hyena-men, and numerous, long philosophical moralizings on such subjects as superstitions, and comparative values of Christianity and Islam in the matter of religious tolerance, and different aspects of human nature generally. The weakness of this work is that the author, conscious of an elevated mission to preserve what he calls 'The Song of Africa's Past', has not been able to decide whether to treat it as a subject for serious scientific, historical research, for which in fact he has not the training, or as a fascinating legend with a basis of history, to which he can lend a fiction-writer's imagination. It is a book about which it is easy to adopt a patronizing attitude because of its weaknesses of composition, its self-conscious style, its occasional inaccuracies of French grammar and syntax, the author's ingenuous imprecision about his sources when he constantly refers to his Western reading. On the other hand, Ibrahim Issa has undertaken something of a pioneering study of an era and subject otherwise untouched in African literature. For this he is to be commended.

Djibril Tamsir Niane

Djibril Tamsir Niame: *Soundjata ou l'épopée mandingue*. Paris, Présence Africaine, 1960.
   English translation: *Sundiata. An epic of old Mali*, trans. G. D. Pickett. London, Longmans, 1965 (Forum series).

There are no concessions to poetic imagination in Niane's *Soundjata*, designated in its sub-title as a national epic. There is no romanticism to pad out the chronicle, no attempts to evoke the local historical colour of a picturesque past, no ethnological digressions, but the sober narrative of the semi-legendary Emperor of the Manding of the thirteenth century, whose mythical exploits as told by the oral tradition, need no embroidering on the part of the contemporary, committed historian, writing at the dawn of the Independence of West Africa.

Far from presuming to supply from his own imagination those details on which tradition is silent, or to fill out the characterization or the décor for the sake of a well constructed work of fiction, Niane respects the mysteries of Africa's past, just as did the obscure *griot* of whom he claims only to be the translator. He has been forced, so he tells us, to sacrifice his 'pretensions as an intellectual in Western garb, in the face of the silences of tradition, when overly impertinent questions have aimed at lifting the veil of mystery'. Here we come hard up against an important difference between the intention of Niane's work and that of Hazoumé: Niane is clearly addressing, first and foremost, an African public, albeit a literate, French-speaking one. He is reminding them of the lessons of the glory of their past; he is warning them not to let their new-found Western learning make them deaf to the wisdom of their own traditional scholars, the *griots* whose immemorial task has been 'to teach that which should be taught and leave unsaid that which should be left unsaid'. By this token, he finds it unnecessary to construct his narrative with care for positivist logic and detailed exposition of rationalist cause and effect. Even so, to maintain the balance of history and legend, Niane supplies maps and multiple footnotes to clarify and substantiate the factual part of the narrative, but keeps the epic tone by including all the traditional supernatural elements of the legend. Thus he tells the story of Sogolon, the Buffalo-Woman, given to Maghan Kon Fatta, the father of Soundjata, by the hunters who have captured her but are unable to possess her; of the birth of the ugly, mute, apparently retarded child, and his sudden miraculous awakening at the age of seven or eight, when he rises to his feet for the first time, bends the huge iron bar into a bow and uproots the baobab which he plants before his mother's hut; then his wanderings in exile, until he vanquishes the sorcerer king Soumaoro with a secret weapon, returns in triumph to the capital, Niani, and establishes a powerful empire, based on the rule of Islam in the Western Sudan, where now the independent states are rising again.

In his last chapter, entitled 'Le Manding éternel', the *griot*-historian again explains the lacunae in his chronicle. Then the author adds a footnote to the *griot*'s reported words:

Here Djeli Maoudou Kouyate would add no more. However, several versions are current as to Soundjata's end. Delafosse reports two of these, which he finds convincing: according to one, Soundjata was killed by an arrow in the course of a public ceremony in Niani. The second, very popular in Manding, is made credible by the presence of Soundjata's tomb near the Sankarani: according to this second story, he was drowned in the Sankarani and was buried near the spot where he drowned.

I have heard this second version from the mouths of several traditionalists. But what were the circumstances that caused Soundjata to meet his death in these waters? That is the question to which it would be necessary to find an answer. (p. 150n [p. 95, n. 78])

And so the epic tale ends on as mysterious a note as it began, the hero's end being as much shrouded in legend as his birth.

Nazi Boni

NAZI BONI: *Crépuscule des temps anciens, chronique du Bwamu,*[17] Paris, Présence Africaine, 1962.

Although roughly contemporary with Niane's *Soundjata*, Nazi Boni's *Crépuscule des temps anciens* is nearer to *Doguicimi* in subject and treatment of an historical theme. But the quarter century that separates the composition and publication of these two works is reflected in Boni's consciously didactic approach to his novel. Paul Hazoumé was a scholar who carefully researched the pre-colonial history of Dahomey to produce, for the instruction and edification of a predominantly French readership, an heroic historical romance of love and jealousy with strong emphasis on picturesque realism. Writing in 1961, Nazi Boni claims for his *Chronicle* the purpose of furthering understanding between nations, particularly between the 'Third World' and what he calls the 'Replete World', in the cause of universal peace and the founding of 'the Great Human Community'. Now that the colonial era is over, he feels it imperative to correct many of the prejudices about the Negro's mentality and social institutions, born of the colonists' misconceptions and misunderstanding of the civilization they had usurped. He hopes to show that the Black man was capable of noble passions and elevated principles and that his society was based on excellent principles, without, however, idealizing or 'blurring certain realities which might seem primitive'. On the other hand, he is also directly addressing

[17] Bwamu, region of the Volta, inhabited by Bwawa (singular Bwawii), adjective Bwa.

his own compatriots and independent Africa generally. He will give them a model for their regeneration, by revealing a past of which Africa can be proud and from which she can draw the vital sap for her renaissance and reconstruction. All this is stated explicitedly in the Foreword, a feature of so many West African novels, whose authors feel that their didactic purpose might not emerge clearly enough or who wish to affirm their Negritude.

The method adopted by Nazi Boni to reveal to his White and Black public the truth of Black Africa, will be an attempt to re-live in his imagination the old traditions, the rural life of the Bwa village with its cults, celebrations, wars and personal passions. In the first chapter, the 'Ancestor' of the village, guardian of the traditions of the country of the Bwawa, recalls the time three hundred years ago when the land was a terrestrial paradise, a land of poetry, mystery, and delight, peace and abundance, where Man lived free from care and guile, in symbiosis with Nature. In time wars came and the last remains of the paradise on earth disappeared. Men became less ingenuous, but still the imperturbable Bwawa lived a happy life of sport and flirtations, music and dancing. The story proper takes place at the turn of the present century, finishing with the revolt of the Bwamu tribe against the colonists in 1916, which brought an end to this 'Golden Age' and the independence and equilibrium of the tribes of the Volta region. The author introduces examples of the tales, epic recitals and riddles, the latter usually having lewd innuendo, with which the moonlit evenings were beguiled. He evokes in great detail the life of a typical Bwa village with the routine daily tasks, feasts, celebrations, tom-toms, and the seasonal trials of drought, floods or plagues of locusts. He describes the behaviour of the woman with their salacious talk and their jealousies at the introduction of co-wives. He tells of palavers, funeral-rites for an Elder and the historical or legendary exploits of the *bêro* – the warrior – and his importance to the community. A lot of space is given to the traditional trial of endurance to which the men must submit between the age of twenty-five and thirty (considered the period of adolescence) in order to take their place among the initiated, if they have not meanwhile succumbed to the brutal treatment inflicted on them.

In this framework of sociological and anthropological lore, which occupies four-fifths of the book, Nazi Boni has inserted a double plot, around his two heroes, the rival warriors Kya and Térhé. The ugly, mis-shapen, maleficent Kya hopes to overshadow the handsome, valorous Térhé by his brute strength, but Térhé is eventually acclaimed as the Panther and the Lion, the living example of virtue and courage. Kya is killed by neighbouring villagers whom he has attempted to ambush. His jealous father brews a powerful poison to put an end to Térhé who, he is certain, is responsible for Kya's death. The second plot is the love idyll of Térhé and Hanakki, whom village custom will not allow to wed. They make a blood pact so that they will be joined in death, custom not permitting suicide or the burying alive of the survivor who wishes to die with a loved-one.

As a historical novel, *Crépuscule des temps anciens* is not entirely satisfactory. The author is at pains to give copious footnotes to authenticate the historical happenings and the period, from 1888 when Binger explored the Volta region and visited Bonikuy, Wakara and Ouagadougou up to the uprising and war of 1915–16, which culminated in the defeat of the Bwawa. However, the chronology of the story, as Boni tells it, is rather confused. A footnote tells us that Kya's death did actually occur about 1887, just before the arrival of the first White man (the explorer Binger) in the area. Térhé, on the other hand, is one of the heroes of the war, returning to the sound of trumpets which heralded individual acts of valour, in spite of the sorcery that Lowan had indulged in to try to assure his death in battle. So Lowan would have waited some thirty years for his revenge, and his enemy would already be an old man, which destroys the dramatic tension and the sense of a heroic tragedy. (Even before Kya's death in 1887, Térhé is referred to as a man of forty, which would make him seventy at the time of his heroic exploits in the revolt of 1915!) The mixture of folk-lore and realism with which *Crépuscule* evokes the regional life of the period is less open to question than the historical facts of Kya's and Térhé's rivalry and death. Four-fifths of the book is richly descriptive, to which the frequent use of local terms – not always explained and therefore disconcerting to those readers not familiar with the vernacular – contributes in large measure. When explanations are given, it is sometimes with a clumsy pedantry which interrupts the natural flow of direct speech. The descriptive passages, on the other hand, have a liveliness and colourful exuberance which bring to life the various natural phenomena, the characteristic seasons and activities of the locality, the author using with particular skill the stylistic effects of hyperbole to create an African scene – witness the picture of the fire started by the hunters, full of movement, sound and fury and colour.

For thirty years African writers made a conscious effort to preserve the oral heritage of the old chroniclers and story-tellers, transcribing, translating, re-creating legends, fables, myths and folk-tales and some history with a strong element of legend and myth. Some, in so doing, have not merely served as museum archivists but have made an important contribution to an authentic neo-African literature. Limiting himself to the fable and folk-tale, Birago Diop has proved himself a master of this genre. Bernard

Dadié used traditional subjects from folk-lore for his literary apprentice-ship, becoming later a master of original works of fiction, chronicle and drama. Abdoulaye Sadji on the other hand, began his career with psycho-logical and social romance and then turned to legend in which he was much more successful than in contemporary subjects. Apart from the preserva-tion of folk-lore in folk-tales and *contes*, the form to which it is most suited, mythical references continue to appear in works of fiction of a more realistic nature, although no African writer to date has used the rich reservoir of his traditional mythology as an inspiration for surrealist works of fiction. Novel writing in the second half of the twentieth century, up to the end of the colonial era at least, is a serious business, with little dalliance in the enchanted world of myth and fantasy. Afraid of the accusation of false exoticism (we have seen with what apologies Nazi Boni introduces his evocations of the African past), too concerned with the problems of today and yesterday and their pragmatic solutions, novelists, as opposed to poets and dramatists, have clipped the wings of their imagination which might have taken flight into the supernatural. For this reason the neo-African novel is the least original of all the forms of creative writing in French up to the middle of the nineteen-sixties. Historical subjects have not been popular with African writers of fiction, which is surprising considering the association of national historical themes with literature of a strongly nat-ional bias, as exemplified by the patriotic aspects of nineteenth-century European Romanticism. However, they form the inspiration for nearly all the serious dramatic literature, particularly of the sixties, which I analyse in the next chapter.

2. Dramatic literature

Neo-African dramatic compositions in French grew out of the oral cultural heritage, in a similar way to the works of fiction treated in the previous chapter. Historical, legendary subjects, the repertoire of the *griots*, formed the material for a vast amount of dramatic literature in French from the early thirties to the end of the colonial era. Moreover, the drama of the post-colonial years still continues to find a source of inspiration and an affirmation of principles and ideals for independent African states in the exploits of national heroes and the great events of a historical or semi-legendary past.

According to Ola Balogun, the Nigerian playwright – and, incidentally, the only Nigerian to have written in French – the theatre as such had no place in pre-colonial African society. Popular entertainment and the didactic functions such as dramatic spectacles supplied in Western Europe were provided by music, song and oral narrative, which handed down traditional wisdom, legends, chronicle and mythology. In the preliminary note to his *Shango* Balogun writes: 'There is no theatrical tradition in Africa. . . Contact with Western civilization revealed the theatre to Africa as a means of artistic expression.'[1]

This would imply that there was no attempt to act out any of the primitive lore, and the first dramatic compositions in French had no indigenous stock in Africa on which to be grafted.

Bakary Traoré and Robert Cornevin, on the other hand, in their well-documented studies of Negro-African theatre give some indications of the important place dramatic performances enjoyed in West-African communities from the Middle Ages onwards. According to these two reliable sources, such spectacles were truly social manifestations, with close communion between actors and spectators and participation by the latter in the music and dancing which were an integral part of the shows. These always took place in the open, with no scenery or stage except that provided by nature and the background of village habitations. Costume

---

[1] Published by P. J. Oswald, Honfleur, 1968. Omitted from subsequent printing. Has Balogun had second thoughts?

however, particularly the use of masks, was important, either to create the atmosphere of the past or to symbolize animals, divinities or other mythological aspects of the spectacle. The role of the Chorus was as important as in ancient Greek drama, sometimes establishing the links in the action, sometimes acting as the voice of wisdom to supply a commentary on the events. The action itself was rarely complicated; neither was it dense. A simple incident could be extended over a series of loosely connected tableaux, mixing comic, tragic, dramatic elements interspersed with music and dancing. Western concepts of structured development, with tension, crisis and dénouement were unknown, the public being happy with slow-moving pageantry and repetitious effects, preferring in fact the familiar to the unforeseen.

Many of these early influences are still evident in the Negro-African dramatic works in French, written over the past forty years. However, the dramatists have obviously had at least half an eye on Western audiences and made important concessions to European theatrical conventions and tastes. Since plays were usually to be staged indoors, in conventional Italian-type theatres, that is on a box-stage with proscenium arch separating the actors from the audience, or, alternatively, with increasing frequency in recent years, being produced for radio or television, it became necessary to condense the duration of the performance to reasonable limits, to avoid the repetitions that Western ears find tedious, and consciously or unconsciously to adapt plays to some extent to the traditional forms of French theatre. In this respect Negro-African drama has tended to be unexperimental, conservative, original in theme, but unexciting in form. It is an interesting observation that as contemporary drama in French from Africa has adopted more and more of modern European conventions, including the proscenium-arch stage and a passive public, thus stultifying its own development, so Europe and America have shown tendencies to move away from these limitations towards 'theatre in the round', 'workshop improvisations' and audience participation.

I shall not go into the details of the origins and evolution of what one might call pre-literary drama in the vernacular, which have been adequately dealt with by both Traoré and Cornevin. The subject of this study being the history of literary expression in French by Negro-Africans, I shall take up the story with the first efforts to provide dramatic entertainment in that language, taking into consideration only those works which have been published either in periodicals or in book form. Unlike other literary genres, particularly fiction and lyric poetry whose forcing-house was France, the earliest of these dramatic writings had their beginnings in Africa itself, and it was only some years later that the expatriate Africans turned their attention to writing for the theatre. This was for the obvious reason that the possibility of staging had priority over the openings for the publication of plays for the reading public.

It is a well-known fact that the French educational system and some particularly dedicated educationalists were jointly responsible for the birth in the 1930s of a Negro-African theatre of French expression. This arose out of specific aspects of the academic programme. The first stage was the collection by pupils of folk-tales and legends from their individual home regions, as part of their holiday assignments when they returned to Dahomey or Ivory Coast, Guinea or Mali, from their various boarding schools. These were then transcribed and translated word for word in class, giving the opportunity for a lesson in linguistics. Lastly, groups of boys would undertake to dramatize the legend or tale. The best histrionic talent would be recruited to perform in annual 'entertainments' presented before visiting dignitaries attending prize-givings and Joan of Arc Day celebrations. Sometimes it would be scout-troops which were encouraged to put on such dramatic shows for the entertainment of visitors.

We have detailed records only of the dramatic work done at the Ecole Primaire Supérieure at Bingerville (Ivory Coast) under the direction of Charles Béart and at the William Ponty Normal School at Gorée, which was later moved to Sébikotane on the road to Thies (Senegal) to which Béart was eventually appointed as French master. Bernard Dadié, who was a pupil at Bingerville, includes in his autobiographical novel *Climbié* an account of the spontaneous birth of dramatic activities at the school:

With the arrival of B...[Béart], the school took on a different aspect. By improving the standard of the meals and giving some latitude to the pupils, B... let them begin to enjoy their school life and express themselves freely.

One day, the tailor who supplied the school uniforms replaced the leather buttons with gilt ones. This made the school-boys look like the local militia. They seized on the opportunity to have some fun.

Akabilé, a first-year pupil, took a stick, fastened his belt on top of his jacket, stuck the stick in his belt and acted like a sergeant accompanying the White Commandant to take the census. The Headmaster, attracted by the laughter and interested in the talent of the actors, had a large area of ground cleared behind the refectory which the boys could use in their free time for chatting and discussions. To encourage folk-lorist activities, every Saturday evening was now given up to acting.[2] (In *Légendes et poèmes*, Seghers, 1966, p. 150) [64]

[2] The review *Eburnea* (see Bibliographical notes, p. 331) carries an article entitled 'Quarante ans de théâtre ivoirien' which includes a recent interview with Mme Charles Béart, now living in retirement near Paris; she vividly recalls these activities, the character of the spectacles, the actors and sometimes the authors and corroborates the account of the incident which Dadié gives in his novel.

The first plays, like their European counterparts of the Commedia dell' Arte, were improvised round a given theme. Gradually to the traditional historical or legendary episodes, treated with epic or tragic grandeur, were added incidents of local, tribal life, which could give rise to comedy, burlesque, farce or satire. It is significant that the educational authorities were unwittingly encouraging a Negritude movement *avant la lettre*, as it was their deliberate intention to preserve the African inspiration of the performances and the African mentality of the writers and actors, although the latter used French as their medium of expression. To illustrate this, I reproduce here part of the review which appeared in *L'Education Africaine, Bulletin de l'enseignement en A.O.F.*, 22nd year, no. 84, July–December 1933, pp. 244–5, quoted by R. Cornevin. The occasion was probably the first performance of a local dramatic composition in French for the public of Dakar, written by a Dahoman pupil of William Ponty and acted by his compatriots – *La Dernière Entrevue de Béhanzin et Bayol* – the text of which has not been preserved.

The songs and dances which preceded and closed the performance, the proud, brutal attitudes of the fierce despot, the desperate respect shown him by his subjects, are all rendered with vigour and conviction which deeply impressed all the spectators. The rather long discussion between the Frenchman who defends his rights, wishing to establish the principle of respect for contracts and the Chief who feels his power threatened, maintained nevertheless an atmosphere of tension. This scene, together with the closing songs and dances, a mixture of barbaric gestures and very original music, showed that these young people, while *assimilating our language and our way of thinking, do not abandon either the traditions or characteristics of their race.* [my italics]

In this same year, 1933, Bernard Dadié, a seventeen-year-old schoolboy, composed his first play, *Les Villes*, of which the text has been lost, for the Ecole Primaire Supérieure at Bingerville. After only one other play in 1937, Dadié returned in the sixties to drama, which seems at present to be his favourite medium. The earliest published plays follow, naturally enough, the lines of the improvisations, treating similar themes and subjects: legend, myth and traditional ritual for serious drama; satirical social comment and scenes from village life for burlesque or farce. The year 1935 saw the first two of these publications: *Un Mariage au Dahomey* and *L'Election d'un roi au Dahomey*. In both cases the title indicates the ritual nature of the performances, rather than concern for the originality of the dramatic action or the individuality of the *dramatis personae*. *Un Mariage au Dahomey*, a three-act comedy (acted by the William Ponty pupils on 23 April 1934) is the story of the marriage of Sika. But the title role, that of the traditional consenting bride who claims no say in the choice of her

suitors, is merely a 'walking-on' part. There are some attempts at realism
in the reactions of the parents as to the merits of the rival suitors, some
mild satire at the expense of the local fetishist's enigmatic *abracadabra*, but
the play ends without conflict, simply a pretext for some ceremonial and
the exposition of tribal customs. *L'Election d'un roi au Dahomey*, the first
recorded treatment in French of what was to become a favourite theme,
was a more ambitious composition, more subtle than any of the preceding
efforts of the Ponty pupils. The three acts are three separate dramatic
interludes, loosely connected by the personage of the King. In fact they
constitute three quite distinct spectacles in different genres, giving the
impression that a different author, or group of students might have been
responsible for the different parts. Act I takes the form of an historical
tableau around the ritual associated with the election of the king's successor
in a society which did not have a hereditary monarchy. The other two are
incidents out of his reign, the third, the most original, being the occasion
for some socio-satirical observations on venal justice; 'Le droit du plus riche
est toujours le meilleur', to parody La Fontaine and echo Beaumarchais.

Another popular subject for early dramatic treatment was the African
version of the Andromeda legend. The story of a beautiful maiden who
has to be sacrificed to a monster – usually a serpent – is part of the
fundamental mythology of West Africa, and is deeply rooted in the tribal
life of rural communities which are totally dependent for survival on the
rhythm of the seasons. In a climate where the *hivernage*, the onset of the
rains, is announced by tornados and all the manifestations of choleric
Nature, it was a natural deduction to associate the rains, indispensable for
survival, with the powers of a god manifesting himself in the form of a
water-monster, and that this monster should require an annual tribute in
recognition of which he would send the rain for the crops. According to
the legend, this water-god, usually a river-serpent living in the reeds, had
to be placated with the offering of a virgin, chosen by the elders of the
tribe or the village, One year the lot falls to Sokamé, whereupon her
distraught fiancé decides to kill the serpent to free his bride. He is caught
and is about to be put to death for sacrilege, when a storm miraculously
breaks bringing the long awaited rains.

A dramatic adaptation of the tale was one of the successful William Ponty
productions put on in Paris at the time of the Exposition Internationale
in 1937. The anonymous text is reproduced in *Présence Africaine* no. 4,
1948, pp. 627–41. In spite of the happy dénouement it is called a 'pièce
tragique en 4 tableaux'. Stage directions are included to guide the actors
in their gestures, expression of emotions, etc., and also indications regard-
ing the décor of the various scenes. There is some elementary attempt to

differentiate the characters of the various villagers and their reactions to the drought, their growing impatience that the annual victim has not yet been chosen to placate the water fetish. Sokamé pleads eloquently and poetically with her lover to save her by fleeing with her before the day of the sacrifice. But Egblamakou proves a reluctant hero, fearing the fetish's powers. Sokamé, who seems to have the monopoly of initiative, sends him off to fetch his *gris-gris* to protect himself against the water-god. Meanwhile, Sokamé's flight is discovered and she is carefully guarded until the ritual sacrifice. Egblamakou now obtains from his ancestors a miraculous dagger, which falls from heaven in time for the fine dramatic climax. As the serpent rises up from the reeds to seize its victim, Egblamakou cuts off its head to the horrified cries of 'Sacrilege!'. Just when the fetishist is demanding the death sentence from the king, the rain starts to fall to the accompaniment of thunder and general rejoicing.

This is the stuff of good popular entertainment. The original myth has all the basic elements of dramatic action: pithy unity of structure, central characters caught in a traditional fate, susceptible to arouse our pity and terror, and a *deus ex machina* to solve their dilemma to everyone's satisfaction: a miniature, elementary counterpart of the dramas woven from the legendary themes and mythology of Classical Greece. The originality of the play lies here in the attempt to give some flesh and blood to the hero and heroine of folk-lore. Since there is no psychological conflict, the impending tragedy being purely circumstantial, the author or authors have lighted on the device of making the lover hesitate in the face of danger and the dictates of prudence and tradition, while Sokamé is the dominant personality.

A more sophisticated version of this myth, *Les Fiançailles tragiques* was composed in the fifties by Djibril Tamsir Niane, for performance by the students of the Ecole Normale de Jeunes Filles at Conakry, where Niane was a teacher of history. This play was chosen in 1965 to inaugurate the new Daniel Sorano Theatre in Dakar, and was again presented there in 1968, but has not yet been published. The date being in the 1960s, and Niane's country of birth Guinea, the author introduces a new element of 'engagement' into the traditional situation, as well as enriching the action with more dramatic detail. His play is clearly intended to be a tract against superstition and an encouragement to build a new and vigorous society based on a common, youthful front fighting prejudice and senseless traditions that no-one previously had dared to question.

Niane's heroine, here called Sarata, is at first a willing victim, convinced that her immolation as bride to the Python-God is essential, according to tradition, to preserve the village from the wrath of the spirits and so ensure the crops. Her fiancé, the brave and handsome Séfédoko, a recent convert to Islam (shades of Polyeucte!) is determined to save her against her will, as a gesture of defiance to the superstitious animist practices of the local community. The battle is protracted and bitter, for the monster, like the hydra of Greek antiquity, grows a new head for every decapitation – which must have given occasion for some ingenious and baroque theatrical machinery. When the monster is finally slain, the ensuing tempest is not the sign of forgiveness, but the beginning of a period of disasters – famine, floods and epidemics – which the people interpret as the gods' punishment for the sacrilege. Sarata and Séfédoko, symbolizing the vigour of youth, flee with a few chosen companions from the wrath of their incensed compatriots and found a new society, freed from fears, superstitions, prejudices and taboos, and which grows to greater prosperity than their former home. The didactic message is explicit.

Following the first improvisations in French and subsequent early publications, the anonymous students from the A.O.F. gradually hammered out in the years before the Second World War an authentic, indigenous drama in French with certain well-defined genres: realistic, melodramatic, farcical, burlesque, tragic, epic in turn, but always accompanied by music and dancing. Apart from the traditional themes drawn from legend, history, folk-lore and myth, there were closely observed scenes from daily and tribal life: quarrels between peasants and unfaithful spouses, bargaining over a bride-price, indigenous tribunals, marriage ceremonies, problems of drought and eventually, inevitably, African society confronted by Western influences. Records exist, but not the texts, of the earliest signed plays from the Ivory Coast after Dadié's first youthful effort mentioned above. Coffi Gadeau (born 1913) contributed two comedies of manners between 1939 and 1943: *Nos femmes*, said to be based on his own conjugal difficulties and its counterpart *Nos maris* which he claims to have written in order to placate the outraged ladies of the town, who threatened to lynch the too frank author (Bibliographical notes, Cornevin, p. 330). In both works Gadeau exposed some universal truths of human weakness not peculiar to African society. He also composed the first play with contemporary political implications, an historical drama, *Les Recrutés de M. Maurice*, exploring the evils of recruitment for forced labour. In 1942, with France occupied and under the Vichy government, the French authorities found this exposure too tendentious and the Governor Deschamps banned its performance. It was eventually produced under the more anodyne title *Le Chant de retour*.

It is even more difficult to analyse the evolution of dramatic composition in French from Black Africa than it is for other literary genres because of the rarity of published texts before 1960. If we compare the minimal quantity of French prose and verse by Africans which found its way into print before the end of the Second World War, it is not surprising that only isolated plays appeared in periodicals and none in book form before about the mid 1950s and very little even then until well into the sixties. It is quite clear that such publications could, in the first instance, find a reading public only among Europeans, and mostly in Europe. In France itself only a very small group of White intellectuals had heard of Léopold Sédar Senghor and Aimé Cesaire. In 1958 Bakary Traoré still had to apologize for introducing writers such as Bernard Dadié and Birago Diop to a French reading public. Although such writing was potentially access- ible via the printed page (and some of the poetry was not immediately self-explanatory) dramatic compositions required staging for full apprecia- tion, and these works from Africa demanded some knowledge of the society in which they were rooted. Moreover, compared with the number of people who will attend a theatrical performance, relatively few will buy and read the text of a play. Such performances as these were limited to a few amateur ones in Africa itself (with the exception of the William Ponty productions in the International Exhibition in Paris in 1937). So, paradoxically enough, given the long tradition of drama in African society, and given also the African's undoubted histrionic gifts, particularly for mime, mimicry and dramatic gesture, as evidenced by the untrained talents of the 'Pontins', the rise of a significant Negro-African dramatic literature in French had to wait for the establishment in Africa of con- ventional theatres of European type. With these were associated semi- professional and then purely professional actors. Their companies went on tour in different parts of Africa, then to France, Britain and America. Plays were specially written for performance and some publishing companies, notably P. J. Oswald of Honfleur and Editions CLE of Yaoundé launched series specially devoted to African theatre. (Présence Africaine have still published relatively few plays, with the exception of Bernard Dadié's.) Television has provided a significant vehicle for African dramatic and histrionic talent and has contributed an added stimulus to authors to write.[3] Some film scenarios by Africans exist, but up to the present these are mainly adaptations from works of fiction, which are dealt with elsewhere in this study of African literature, in their original form. It remains to be seen whether these increased facilities for dramatic composition have not sapped some of the authentic sources of African theatrical inspiration, and reduced

[3] In 1967 the O.R.T.F., in collaboration with the O.C.O.R.A. launched the first Inter- African theatrical contest, which has now become an annual event, with the prize-winning plays being published by O.R.T.F.–D.A.E.C.

it to a rather stereotyped imitation of its European or Western counterparts.

In analysing the main contributions to African dramatic literature in French I shall make only a cursory mention of tales or novels which were adapted for the stage, to form the first repertoire for the newly-founded African theatres. None of these gains any new literary dimensions in dramatic form. From among Birago Diop's *Contes* and *Nouveaux contes*, several proved amenable to dramatization, notably 'Sarzan', 'La Légende des mamelles', 'Le Prétexte' (sometimes thought of as Birago's *Tartuffe*) and his superbly comic 'L'Os de Mor Lam'. Olympe Bhêly Quénum's *Chant du lac* made a didactic drama inveighing against superstition. Jean Ikelle-Matiba's *Cette Afrique-là*, a violent melodrama indicting the forced labour era; Ousmane Sembène's *Le Mandat* and *Blanche Genèse*, excellent social and psychological studies, and Mongo Beti's satirical comedy *Mission terminée* have proved successful as drama. Even less space need be accorded here to an African *Tempest* or *Macbeth* or Molière's *Médecin malgré lui*, transmuted into *Le Sorcier malgré lui* and also... *Le Faux Marabout*.

HISTORICAL AND LEGENDARY DRAMA

On the theme of 'The Death of a King'

BERNARD DADIÉ: *Assémien Déhylé, chronique agni*. First production 1936. Published as 'Assémien Déhylé, roi du Sanwi, pièce tirée de la chronique agni', in *L'Avant Scène*, no. 343, 15 Oct. 1965, pp. 37–43.

GERMAIN COFFI GADEAU: *Kondé Yao, étude sur les croyances religieuses et l'histoire des Baoulé*. First production 1939. Published in *Théâtre populaire en République de Côte d'Ivoire*, Cercle culturel et folklorique de Côte d'Ivoire, Abidjan, pp. 131–41.

AMADOU CISSÉ DIA: *La Mort du Damel*. First production (?) between 1936 and 1939. Published in *Présence Africaine*, Nov.–Dec. 1947. Re-issued with *Les Derniers Jours de Lat-Dior*, Paris, Présence Africaine, 1965.[4]

Dramatic treatment of a historical theme or episode has no claim to be an authentic chronicle, a source of accurate documentation. The theatre, in any culture, being rooted in the popular life of the community, has traditionally been a means of preserving the aura attached to great historical events, the lives and exploits of national heroes, rather than a systematic, academic analysis or synthesis of fact. Generations of artists, consciously or unconsciously elaborating an aesthetic of historical drama, form a gangue of legend around the core of historic fact. African drama is no different

---

[4] There are a few very minor textual variants between the two editions, but the only significant difference is the addition by the author of detailed indications for the musical accompaniment to the action.

in this from its European counterpart. I shall therefore discuss both plays based on historical characters and events, dramatic tableaux presenting historical ritual and ceremonial which is falling into desuetude, and dramas woven round pure legend or semi-legendary themes.

As outlined in the introduction to this chapter, these were popular subjects for the first anonymous productions of the students and amateur actors of A.O.F. One of the first signed and published works was a historical fresco by the Eburnean writer, Bernard Dadié, who showed as early as 1936 his command of the eloquent and dramatic resources of the French language in his treatment of a favourite theme, the death of a king and the election of his successor. If we discount the juvenile composition for the Bingerville pupils, *Les Villes*, of which in any case the text has not been preserved, *Assémien Déhylé* was not only Dadié's first true literary composition, written when he was a twenty-year-old student, but the first of a genre to which he was to return with great success more than thirty years later.

Assémien Déhylé, chronique agni[5] was written for production by William Ponty students at Gorée, Senegal, in 1936. In 1937 it was presented in Paris at the Théâtre des Champs-Elysées for the Exposition Internationale. It consists of three separate tableaux linked by the character of Assémien: three incidents in his life with no real dramatic action. The first tableau, entitled 'Peace', shows a typical village genre scene. The local fetishist prophesies the death of a great man and informs Assémien of his mission to depart immediately and save his country from disaster. The second tableau is 'War': Assémien has arrived at the court of the dying king who designates him as his successor and instructs him in his responsibilities as ruler. Assémien dreams of the glory to be won in battle. At the end of the tableau we hear of the approach of the enemy. The final scene is Assémien's election as king after his victorious return.

Assémien has little claim to be considered as drama. There is no action, only an exchange of aphorisms and local wisdom and lore, including an account of the legend of the Baoulé which Dadié included, with a little more detail, in his *Légendes africaines* in 1953. The characterization of the hero is rudimentary, with only a superficial allusion to his war-like ambitions. The dialogue woven around the simple situation has a certain poetic allure. For the next thirty years Dadié neglected drama for poetry and prose, but when he published a series of plays after 1966, he proved that he had mastered satirical drama within a socio-historical framework. I shall return to these plays later.

In 1939, Germain Coffi Gadeau, one of the original participants in the

[5] Agni – one of the main ethnic groups of Ivory Coast.

Ponty shows and who had himself taken part in Dadié's *Assémien*, founded the Indigenous Theatre of the Ivory Coast for which he wrote *Kondé Yao, étude sur les croyances religieuses et l'histoire des Baoulé* [A study of the history and religious beliefs of the Baoulé]. This is again a series of dramatic tableaux, loosely connected by the presence of, or the interest in, the main character Kondé Yao, chief of one of two disputing tribes. The author's intention is to preserve an episode from local history – the origins of war between two Baoulé tribes – and to inform his public (presumably European) on certain aspects of local custom inherited from the past. The first tableau gives an exposition of the situation and the historical setting. In the second, Salé Bona is humiliated by Kondé Yao and vows vengeance. The third tableau shows Kondé Yao falling ill as a result of his enemy's curse and in the next, his death is announced. In the final scene the witch-doctor confirms that Salé Bona's threats are the cause of the chief's death and the whole tribe decides to make war.

Kondé Yao does not have much more pretension to bring a true dramatic creation than Dadié's earlier composition, to which it can be compared. It is a historical and sociological document in rudimentary dramatic form, based on local tradition, and showing tribes determined to pursue certain customs in spite of colonial administration. There is some attention given to the characterization of Kondé Yao, the typical arrogant, impulsive chief and a certain comic realism is introduced in the scene in the court, when a man who has stolen a hen is pursued into the chief's presence and judged without further ceremony.

Slightly more ambitious in dramatic structure and content was Amadou Cissé Dia's *La Mort du Damel* [The death of the king], also written for a Ponty production. The action is set in the nineteenth century, at the time of Faidherbe's campaigns for the unification and conquest of Senegal. It illustrates the internecine tribal wars, born of rivalry, vendetta and the avenging of insults, culminating in this case in patricide. We see the evolution of a tyrant, intoxicated by his own military successes, a theme that will be repeated in many historical dramas, with, to date, Dadié's allegorical *Les Voix dans le vent* the most original and powerful in treatment.

La Mort du Damel has a certain symmetry of structure, opening with the *griot*'s prophecy of the death of a great man (the reigning king) and closing with the assassination of his successor at the hands of his own son. The characters of the different rivals are outlined in a series of rapidly moving scenes. The new Damel, cautious, lacking confidence in his own powers to perform unaided the full charge laid upon him, designates his brother to assist him by taking supreme command of the army; the latter,

Samba Keul, arrogantly and insultingly refuses to head an 'army of hyenas' and 'apes incapable of holding a spear'. The Damel then charges his son, Samba Laobé, to avenge his uncle's insults. Two years later Samba Laobé has justified the faith in his potential, but he in turn has become hot-headed and impulsive. News comes of the Damel's defeat and flight in the face of Faidherbe's advances into the interior. Samba Laobé's inexperienced youth is fertile ground for his uncle's intrigues when Samba Keul incites him to kill his own father, on the pretext that this is the only way to save the kingdom from European conquest. The play ends with the premonition of Samba Laobé's own tyrannical reign.

Slight as this play is, I have discussed it in some detail because Dia was the first playwright to create a realistic period atmosphere and some convincing characterization. The action arises purely out of the historical situation, but there is nevertheless some attempt at motivation and analysis of individual reactions. As such it heralds a line of gradually more complex and more sophisticated historical dramas.

Certain indulgent critics have judged *La Mort du Damel* as a Corneillian tragedy, presumably finding some parallel in the avenging of the insult in *Le Cid*. They also suggest that the fetishist's prophetic vision of an imminent disaster, the death of a great man and the realm tainted with thousands of corpses, is an echo of Pauline's dream in *Polyeucte*. I find these comparisons very superficial. Dreams and prophesies and consulting of omens, a normal part of tribal African life, occur in many African dramas. However, Dia would know his Corneille from his William Ponty days and he may even have intended to compose an African *Cid* with a more melodramatic ending and without any Corneillian conflicts. It is also understandable that Corneille, of all French dramatists, should have a strong appeal to African writers, not for the moral conflicts he depicts but for his presentation of powerful warriors, masters of military strategy and models of unlimited valour: Cinna, the Horatii, the Curiace brothers, as well as the Cid. It is the Roman virtues of the Corneillian heroes that we find paralleled in the protagonists of African historical and legendary drama. These are nowhere better exemplified than in the Zulu king Shaka.

The Shaka theme

LÉOPOLD SÉDAR SENGHOR: *Chaka, poème dramatique à plusieurs voix*, in *Ethiopiques*. Paris, Seuil, 1958. English translation, in *Selected poems*, by John Reed and Clive Wake, London, Oxford University Press, 1964, pp. 67–77.

KONYATÉ SEYDOU BADIAN: *La Mort de Chaka, pièce en cinq tableaux*. Paris, Présence Africaine, 1961. English translation: *The Death of Chaka. A play*

in five tableaux, with intr. by Clive Wake, Nairobi, Oxford University Press
(Coll: New drama from Africa), 1968.
CONDETTO NÉNÉKHALY-CAMARA: *Amazoulou*, précédé de *Continent-Afrique*. Hon-
fleur, P. J. Oswald (Coll: Théâtre africain) 1970.
DJIBRIL TAMSIR NIANE: *Chaka, suivi de Sikasso, la dernière citadelle.* Honfleur,
P. J. Oswald (Coll: Théâtre africain) 1971.
ABDOU ANTA KA: *Les Amazoulous*, in *Théâtre, Quatre Pièces*. Paris, Présence
Africaine, 1972.

The semi-legendary Zulu king, Shaka, a sort of pre-colonial Alexander,
has attracted many Black writers of French. Léopold Sédar Senghor
included his 'Chaka' a dramatic poem for several voices, dedicated to the
'Black martyrs of South Africa', in the collection of poems, *Ethiopiques*.
Three years later Konyaté Seydou Badian published his *La Mort de Chaka*,
pièce en cinq tableaux. The most complete dramatic treatment so far is found
in Abdou Anta Ka's *Les Amazoulous* and Condetto Nénékhaly-Camara's
Amazoulou. In 1971 Oswald also published a *Chaka* by Djibril Tamsir
Niane, the author of the historical novel *Soundjata*.

It is universally accepted that Shaka was a military strategist of great
genius, but the actual historical facts of his life and reign are open to doubt.
The French-African writers in question have all drawn their inspiration
and documentation from Thomas Mofolo's novel, *Chaka*,[6] (trans. F. H.
Dutton, O.U.P., repr. 1971) of which the French translation by V. Ellen-
berger appeared in 1939. According to this version Shaka, the bastard
son of King Senzangakhona, grows up in exile with his mother, Nandi.
On the death of his father, he becomes the leader of the still nameless tribe,
which he calls Amazulu, 'The People of the Sky'. He extends his kingdom
(what is now Natal and Kwazulu) south of the borders of the Transkei
and north to the borders of Swaziland. Ruthless in his military ambition
and single-minded in his desire for the greatness of his people, he was
responsible for the death of countless disobedient courtiers and generals.
He was himself eventually assassinated by his half-brothers, plotting with
the generals who were either jealous of his power or tired of the incessant
military expeditions.

The final judgement on Shaka's character and psychological motivation
is not easy to establish. But an assessment of his personality and the
violent episodes of his life and reign have all the essential ingredients for a
drama in the Classical, Shakespearean or even Romantic traditions (following the model of Musset's *Lorenzaccio*). Ray Autra, in the preface of Niane's
Chaka, claims that the Zulu drama has close affinities with Greco-Latin

---

[6] I have adopted the generally accepted English spelling *Shaka*, based on the Zulu form.
Mofolo naturally used the Sotho version, *Chaka*. The French works cited here adopt
Mofolo's spelling, all the more understandably in that 'ch' in French is pronounced 'sh'.

mythology and that Shaka, like the Mandingo hero of Niane's novel *Soundjata*, has his counterparts among the legendary heroes of Greek and Roman antiquity. I would deny, however, that any contemporary African dramatist writing in French, has succeeded in producing a masterpiece comparable with those of the great European dramatic traditions, probably because none has been able to distance himself from the political aspects of his subject. They have all, to a greater or lesser degree, succumbed to the temptation to draw parallels with the present day and point lessons in Negritude or political commitment.

According to the legend perpetuated by Thomas Mofolo, the dying king's last words were: 'You assassinate me in the hope of taking my place when I am dead. This will not be so, for the White Man is on the march and it will be he who will rule over you and you will become his subjects'. This is the text of both Senghor's and Badian's works. Senghor's Shaka is a great hero of mythical, tragic dimensions, a responsible ruler haunted by the fear of the White Man's conquest of his people. His sole preoccupation is to forge a great nation capable of confronting the Boers as they spread north and east in their trek from the Cape. He sacrifices his beloved, Noliwe, to protect himself from human weakness, as no tenderness must deflect him from his ambition and his duty. The first Canto (there is no attempt to give normal dramatic form to the composition) is a dialogue between Shaka, in the hour of his passion, and the White Man speaking the reproaches of future generations for the king's infamies. Shaka defies the charges laid upon him exulting in the ravages he has wrought, comparing them with the burning of the sterile veld before the sowing, or the cutting down of dead wood from the forest. He has no regrets, for only evil must be regretted and for him the only evil is weakness and cowardice. Of this he has never been guilty. He bursts into a lyrical song of love and praise for Noliwe which is like a reprise of Senghor's celebrated poem 'Femme noire' in *Chants d'ombre* (1945). Shaka claims that he had to free himself from his love for Noliwe in order to give himself wholeheartedly to his people. In Senghor's *Chaka*, we can also catch echoes of another conflict: that of the statesman torn between his love for Europe and his loyalty to Africa. He denies ever having hated the White Man – the 'pink-eared' invaders who taught him the use of the canon. The second part of the short work, Canto Two, is a lyrical, elegiac plainsong between the dying Shaka, the Coryphée (leader of the Chorus) and the Chorus itself.

This *Chaka* is not a dramatic work in the true sense of the term – it has no action and only alternating voices – although it has been staged and produced for radio performance (staged at Toulouse as an Oratorio-Ballet in 1968 and again in Senegal; and in 1972 performed by Artistes de l'Université d'Ife). It is more of a cantata, in which we forget the crimes of the unrepentant murderer, forget the political motivations, and are carried along by the exultant love-song addressed to Noliwe and by the tide of images, rich harmonies and surging rhythms of Senghorian chant.

While belonging more strictly to the category of dramatic literature, Badian's *Death of Shaka* misses tragic dimension altogether. In fact he has sacrificed all the noble or epic potential of Africa's greatest if most ruthless military genius, to a frankly partisan treatment of his subject. At the time Badian was writing, Mali had just separated from federation with Senegal to form a new socialist republic. Badian concentrates on Shaka's last military exploit before his assassination. The major part of his play is taken up with the parleying of the generals, which causes an imbalance in the action and in the title role. The central core of the play is provided, not by any dramatic action or tension, or by the presence of Shaka himself, but by his mouth-piece N'Dlebe who comes to announce the king's decision to attack at dawn. N'Dlebe then spells out the moral lesson of the piece: it is to follow the example of the ruler who has sacrificed his own ease and pleasure, as he has sacrificed even his own kith and kin, to be wholly at the service of the people and to build them into a powerful nation. So must they too sacrifice themselves for the sake of the state. Badian even succeeds in placing some uplifting words on women's part in the cause of African socialism. In the fourth tableau Shaka leaves the rebellious generals to retreat while he advances to victory with N'Dlebe's support. The fifth and final tableau shows the counting of the losses after the battle and the king's prophetic exhortation to the young people come to do him homage.

A play in form and in theory, Badian's treatment does not have the merit of Senghor's eloquence and dignity: the language is trite; there is no attempt at characterization nor synthesis of action; there is no historical colour and little heroism. All the epic potential of the subject has been sacrificed by Badian in favour of a moral lesson in political commitment.

Ideologists and sociologists (and particularly the ideological sociologists) are equally unsuccessful in their efforts to infuse new life into the historical subjects that they aim to turn to use in the cause of the people's revolution. Condetto Nénékhaly-Camara's *Amazoulou* is, in many ways, even less adequate in its dramatic treatment of a personage who, as the author himself admits, was one of the two historical figures (the sixth century Arab warrior-poet Antar was the other) to symbolize the historical evolution of Africa and what he calls 'its *élan* and its revolutionary vocation'. Because he is a sociologist by training it is understandable that he adopts a realistic basis for a drama of which the hero is, in his own words, 'the first founder of a modern African nation'. What is not understandable is that he has in fact so diminished his hero in the cause of realism and to make him 'accessible to the African masses' that, far from inspiring the latter with any enthusiasm, we doubt if he would, to use the French expression, 'pass the footlights'. Nénékhaly-Camara expresses his concern for the two roles of the writer which he aimed to perform in this work: as leader in a cultural revolution and as producer of 'works which may transcend and so outlast those present contingencies which limit the creativity of a writer'. If he had looked more closely at the models of Ancient Greece and particularly the great Classical tragedies, which provided popular education, while making no concessions to popular limitations, he might have succeeded better.

Mario de Anrade, in his preface to *Amazoulou*, reminds us of Bakary Traoré's words: 'African theatre must be epic or nothing'. But we look in vain for epic qualities in Nénékhaly-Camara's treatment of the Shaka theme, although he could have found these in abundance in Thomas Mofolo's *Chaka*, which he presumably took as his source. The Sotho writer, who, as a product of Christian missionary training, saw the Zulu chief as a savage and terrifying matricide, receiving from the sorcerer Issanoussi the secret of omnipotence in exchange for the promise of utter ruthlessness, described the King's death as the just retribution for his paganism. With Nénékhaly-Camara, gone is the superhuman stature of the hero, like Milton's Satan, as haughtily confident of his destiny in error as in right; gone is the grandeur of his exploits, inspiring equal terror and admiration; gone is the supernatural that lifts the facts of history to the domain of myth; gone, too, is the noble eloquence of language that charms the ear and uplifts the passions. In his deliberate effort to 'demystify' his hero, and so offer to his compatriots (the people of Guinea), a figure with whom they can identify their own revolutionary efforts, the author has forgotten that a great national hero must of necessity be surrounded by a mystic, mythic aura – that he must possess qualities that inspire the common man to transcend his own limitations, his own mortality even – whence the necessity for the insistence on the divine, the miraculous or the supernatural element in the true epic.

The Shaka of *Amazoulou* is indeed a poor creature, who shows no evidence of either grandeur of exploits, divine mission or tragic fate. In the Prologue he is found hiding in the forest when first Issanoussi (reduced to the role of an itinerant pedlar, whose reputation as a soothsayer is gained from the knowledge he accumulates in the course of his travels) and then Malonga and N'Dlebe seek him out to announce the death of his father and his ascension to the throne. The two conspiring generals then drug Shaka to make him more surely their tool. Shaka's appearances and pronouncements do little to paint the portrait of a great leader, called to head a tribe and build it into a nation. One has only to compare the episode of the baptizing of the new nation in Mofolo's novel and in Nénékhaly-Camara's play. Mofolo's Shaka, an eloquent, heroic figure, cries triumphantly like Jupiter:

'Amazulu. Because I am great. I am even as this cloud that has thundered, that is irresistible. I, too, look upon these tribes and they tremble. If I fall upon any they die...Zulu. Amazulu!' (Mofolo *Shaka*, p. 125)

And, now, this Shaka, in response to Malonga's and N'Dlebe's sarcasms that he reigns over an anonymous people, who do not even know who they are:

Shaka: Then learn their name, for they possess one. They will be distinguished from all other peoples of the earth, because they are the chosen people of the heavens. (*To Mohlomi*) It is a name you said which combines the storm and the tempest. It is a sign which reigns high in the heaven and over the earth. It will reign henceforth over the hearts and consciousness of men. Henceforward, you are the chosen people of the heavens. You are the fire from the heavens...Amazulu! (*Amazoulou* pp. 74–5)

Finally, instead of the tragic or melodramatic end of a warrior struck down by his enemies at the height of his victorious campaigns, Nénékhaly-Camara's hero flickers out of the drama, like a burnt-out candle, complaining to Issanoussi of his utter weariness, a man afraid of shadows, downcast with the premonitions of the overthrow of his empire, and happy to hand over the responsibility for repelling the White invaders to the Sotho king, Moshesh. The play thus ends on a speech combining the incongruous elements of Shaka's instructions for the welcoming of Moshesh with celebrations and games, and his announcement that the Zulu people must prepare for a new struggle to 'defend their patrimony and their blood'.

The historian Djibril Tamsir Niane is not much more successful than his compatriot Nénékhaly-Camara in his attempt to inject new life into the Zulu epic, or to give a new vision to the title role. In his *Chaka*, Niane too fails to give dramatic form, historic verisimilitude, psychological conviction, superhuman dimension or supernatural aura to the action or the hero.

The first Tableau, comprising one-third of the play, is devoted to Shaka's childhood. It is a pity, however, that the episode of the lion-killing, which would justify the young Shaka's being accepted as a leader, is not included in this part of the action. The structure of the second Tableau, forming the other two-thirds of the play and devoted to the end of Shaka's reign, is equally unconvincing. There are a few references to his campaigns, but little idea of his military genius can be gleaned. There are indications of the plots against him, but these do not contribute to a feeling of tension and the imminence of his end. There are examples of his summary justice, but these are couched in such colloquial language that they arouse little horror or awe at a monster of ruthlessless. If this use of twentieth-century colloquialisms is surprising even in the opening scene with the herd-boys, it is quite incongruous in an action which lays claim to heroic inspiration or tragic dignity. I would not hold any brief for archaisms or artificial local colour to evoke historical authenticity or atmosphere; but if Niane has a serious intent in treating the Shaka theme – and with his proven talents as historian and writer, I cannot doubt this – then he must be aware of the need for a consistent and appropriate language register to give his protagonists and action their required stature. In his preface to the 1971 edition of the play, Ray Autra claims 'one of the least of Niane's merits' was to have been able to give:

a greater breadth and a sharper vision to our meditation – to have widened it to the dimensions of the whole world in which, from time immemorial, the custodians of Power – temporal, spiritual power, power over material possessions – in a word OPPRESSORS and OPPRESSED have been locked in struggle (Niane, *Chaka*, p. 22, his capitals)

Meritorious as such an aim may be, I found it hard to agree that Niane has realized it by his dramatization of the Shaka epic, which far from having enlarged, he seems to have impoverished.

Abdou Anta Ka also admits the debt he owes to the translation into French of the Sotho novel. In his foreword he claims that his excuse for adding one more dramatization to the Shaka literature is that he wishes to speak as the 'common man', to present Shaka as the man of the people he was in his youth: the bastard, the rejected son, condemned to death by his father, reviled by his half-brothers, brutalized by his fellow herds-men, until finally recognized as the leader of the people. If this aspect is not abundantly clear from Ka's drama, what is appreciable is the original, imaginary, visionary dimension that he infuses into the historical and legendary material. He sets his action in the mysterious island of Sangomar, which Senegalese mythology claims as the home of the dead, haunted by gods, djinns and spirits of all kinds. Three masked men (the gods) preside over a kind of tribunal before which Shaka appears to answer his accusers. Noliwe, who has been a willing sacrifice, because to consent to sacrifice exacted in the cause of the people was part of Negro-African ethics, insists on taking her place at his side. But Shaka is nevertheless tormented by his conscience. His half-brother Latyr (replacing the Dingane of history), his counsellors, his enemies and his allies, each in turn act out their part in the rise and fall of the Conqueror. The people, too, have their say, but not entirely in Shaka's favour. They have brought a troupe of mummers with them as their mouthpiece, as actors are privileged to speak truths others dare not say. This gives rise to a burlesque interlude in which the mummers mimic and ridicule Shaka and his dignitaries at court. Finally Shaka re-enacts the murder of Noliwe and then prophesies the fall of his empire in spite of her sacrifice. Past and present are now combined in a final vision of the future. The whole company is seen in the dress of present-day South Africa, and to the accompaniment of guns, police whistles and Miriam Makeba's singing, Shaka foretells the pass laws, influx control and all the martyrdom of apartheid. In spite of some confusion in placing the Zulu epic in a Senegalese mythical situation, and of some association of this work with a psychodrama, Abdou Anta Ka's *Les Amazoulous* is the most original of the Shaka dramas, with a strong poetic appeal, bringing to life the conflict of the king, torn between his desire for earthly happiness and the welfare of his people.

Two warrior princes on trial: Lat Dior and El Hadj Omar

AMADOU CISSÉ DIA: *Les Derniers Jours de Lat Dior*, preceded by *La Mort du Damel*. Paris, Présence Africaine, 1965.
MAMADOU SEYNI M'BENGUÉ: *Le Procès de Lat Dior*. Dakar, Grande Imprimerie Africaine, 1971. Also Paris, O.R.T.F.–D.A.E.C., 1972.
GÉRARD CHENET: *El Hadj Omar*, Honfleur, P. J. Oswald (Coll. Théâtre Africain) 1969.

We have noted how the African writers who attempted to present the drama of the Zulu king Shaka somehow failed to transcend the historical facts or the political implications of their subject. Except for Senghor, who has not composed a true play, they have had neither the artist's vision, the moralist's insight, nor the poet's tongue to achieve a work of literary quality or dramatic impact. On the other hand, the parallel historical situation in West Africa, when great warrior princes – Lat Dior, the 'Damel' of Cayor and El Hadj Omar, the hero of the Islamization of Senegal – pursued their conquests preceding the incursions of the French, has inspired some dramatic work of originality and quality. In each case, though in differing proportions, the dramatists have suggested a certain dichotomy between a theoretical idealism and its practical realization; between high-minded principles and the infliction of human suffering; between the role of the patriot and the subjacent personal ambitions of the individual. The higher the dramatist elevates his central character to the role of a superman, the greater is his zeal to clear him of charges of human weakness, and the less striking is the impact of the drama. This is particularly the case with the story of Lat Dior.

Stripped of even the vestiges of an intrigue, such as exists in *La Mort du Damel*, Amadou Cissé Dia's second drama in his diptych in honour of the last of the Senegalese paladins to resist the forces of Faidherbe, *Les Derniers Jours de Lat Dior*, is a pure historical pageant accompanied by all the attributes of traditional African ceremonial. Making the minimum concessions to the exigencies of external action or inner conflict, it is rather a dramatization of the *griot*'s song of praise to the Damel Teigne Lat Dior of Cayor. In fact the importance of the role of the *griot*, who opens the first tableau, is clearly indicated.

The correct historical setting is first suggested by the references to the Damel's battles against his weaker neighbours, this is reinforced by the arrival of an envoy from the Almamy Amadou Cheikhou, successor to the redoubtable El Hadj Omar Tall, and the only one of Lat Dior's adversaries, besides the French, to equal him in courage and military strength. Amadou Cheikhou proposes an alliance against the 'Toubabs', which the Damel's proud and suspicious nature rejects, because he both fears a ruse and desires to assert his faith in the strength and militancy of his own armies. The scene at Saint-Louis, in Faidherbe's camp, although imaginary, seals the historical authenticity by clarifying the French general's strategy of dividing the indigenous rulers of Senegal, confirming the success of his campaign and sketching his policy for the unification and pacification of the country – the building up of educational and agricultural services and the introduction of the indispensable railway from Saint-Louis to Dakar. The vanity of Lat Dior's solitary resistance to the last is commented upon by Faidherbe, but the psychological importance of the scene is to consolidate the portrait of the Damel, by showing the great respect that he inspires in the French general, who recognizes him as a worthy adversary. This scene, enjoying as it does the central place in the structure of the darama, also motivates the decline of the Damel, which is presented in the two final tableaux.

The composition and language of this work are worth careful study and show it to be the creation of a conscious artist. The overall tone is one of epic nobility, with a lyrical and archaic grandeur. But, although the general impression is of a *griot*'s chant, Cissé Dia has obviously borne in mind the need to avoid monotony in presentation. To this end he has varied his dialogue, as well as insisting on the importance of the musical accompaniment. The first tableau is realistic in setting, familiar in subject and generally colloquial in style. For Western tastes, the insertion of the episode of the importunate and greedy *griot* may seem incongruous, contradicting the solemn role of the *griot* in the drama. I suggest that its purpose may be to serve as a 'curtain raiser' while the audience settles down for the main spectacle which opens in the next tableau at the court of Lat Dior. Here the tone is of a ceremonious, ritual chant, building up to a crescendo in the festival of the tom-toms, which corresponds to the peak of the Damel's glory. In Tableau III, the decline is announced; the language of the French officers is dignified, but without rising to the lyric heights of that at the court. Tableau IV shows the Damel betrayed, his confidence lost, aware of the imminence of his final failure, coming humbly to consult the most holy marabout, Sheik Mamadou Bamba, and wishing for conversion. In this penultimate act, the language is that of prayer and meditation, the majority of the dialogue being the quotations from the Koran with which the marabout replies to the king's pleas for guidance. This is the *largo* of the symphony ending with the marabout's song of praise to the Lord of the World, which forms the counterpart to the exaltation of the temporal ruler of men in the second tableau. The play closes, soberly, after a duel of words between the envoy of Faidherbe, offering peace, the intransigent Lat Dior still finding honour in resisting the railway, the wise counsellor Demba War, accepting that present concessions will avoid future shameful defeats and the voice of the hot-headed *tiédos* who call for war and conquest without calculating the cost. Lat Dior speaks the final words, resuming the battle with the French, knowing that this one will be his last, but unable to divest himself of his pride.

Mamadou Seyni M'Bengué's *Trial of Lat Dior* was a prize-winning play in the O.R.T.F. Inter-African drama contest in 1971 and may have qualities more suitable for broadcasting than for the stage. M'Bengué imagines the Damel called before the Tribunal of Posterity, which will decide whether he was a blood-thirsty, bellicose tyrant, bleeding his country to death by incessant military campaigns, or a great patriot, unifying West Africa to stem the inroads of the colonial powers; a sincere convert to Islam or a Tartuffe playing lip-service to religious observance for personal ambition. The weaknesses of the play stem from the question-begging nature of the assumptions, the imbalance in the presentation of the problem, a dramatic form which too slavishly follows the language and procedure of the judiciary, and the lack of centralization of the hero, Lat Dior himself. The Damel appears briefly as a haughty monarch in the opening scene, then for five-sixths of the argument he has no speaking part, even in the final scene of his acquittal and rehabilitation in a triumphant apotheosis.

Gérard Chenet's *El Hadj Omar* is a much more subtle and successful attempt at historical, heroic drama. As conscious as M'Bengué of his responsibility as a historian, as conscientious a chronicler in assembling the documentary raw material of his subject, he has far more of the artist's gifts for synthesizing these into a compelling, dense drama of tragic dimensions. He does not fall into the trap of providing facile answers as to the true personality and psychological motivations of his complex hero. Without diminishing El Hadj's superhuman stature, he nevertheless presents his concomitant human characteristics quite consistent with the Islamic ethos: his sensuality combined with mysticism, the ascetic with carnal instincts. Chenet contrasts the fervour of the fanatical Muslim prophet with the aggressive vitality of the liberating warrior; the superman high above the moral and material preoccupations of daily existence is presented simultaneously as the simple believer who mingles with the crowds who flock to evening prayer. The dichotomy of Omar's personality and his inner conflicts are presented dramatically by the device of contrasting protagonists, each symbolizing profound and inseparable aspects of the central character. Just as one ideal or principle must be immolated to another stronger or more immediate urge, so one by one the characters that personify them are the victims of El Hadj's own crusade: a pilgrimage and a Holy War, in which he sheds the dispensable baggage of his humanitarian ideals.

The factual foundation of Chenet's play is the campaign which Sheikh Omar Fall, originally a simple Toucouleur (Fulani) marabout, waged through Western Africa during the last third of the nineteenth century. His exploits exemplify the last attempts of the flourishing centres of Islamic culture to survive the crises provoked by slave-trading and the progressive insinuation of European influences. Each episode in this ably constructed drama contributes an important detail to the vast historical fresco; each character, however minor, in the relatively large cast, adds some important perspective to the total impression of Omar's campaigns, his complex character or contradictory ideals. In this way the large canvas is reduced to manageable proportions and a unity of action and structure is ensured. For example, the Slave symbolizes first the exploitation of the ignorant people by the marabout masters who ignore the true state of the world and deliberately perpetuate obscurantism and servility; liberated by Omar and appointed as a *sofa* chief (the fugitive slaves who become members of the prophet's convent) he illustrates the leader's ideals of freedom and democratic equality of all in the sight of God. Yimba, Chief of Dinguiraye, typifies the hostility of the fetishists. The envoys from the chiefs of Fouta express the hostility of those rulers who derive material benefits from the European traders in human flesh, guns and other goods.

They also serve as a Chorus, as the voice of prophecy, with insight into the mixed motives of El Hadj. Aissata also speaks with the prophetic voice that warns the warrior that he is no longer the leader of men, but their slave; no longer the holy man but the servant of baser passions. As he abandons the peaceful persuasion of the Word, she typifies the pity he no longer feels. She represents the Future, standing for life itself, the source of generation and regeneration when life is destroyed by Omar's pride and ambition. Samba the Transfuge represents the majority of the 'faithful' for whom creed is a matter of convenience or the repetition of a meaningless formula by way of a password to safety. The two young men who come to join El Hadj in the early scenes of the play, symbolize the ambivalent nature of the hero and the dual aspects of his campaign: the Warrior, armed with his bow and the Disciple, the Koran under his arm. The *griot* prophesies that the day will come when Omar will have to choose which servant will prove more faithful: the Sword or the Book.

The central character who shares the stage with El Hadj, and is equally important to the inner psychological action of the play is the *griot*, Salif. His role seems to be a compound of the privileged Shakespearean Fool, the confidant of Classical drama, the community and Chorus of antiquity and the element of humour and music which is traditional to African spectacle. In fact he is much more: by his flashes of clear-sighted wisdom he is the personification of El Hadj Omar's conscience and temptations; by the gifts of prophecy linked with the *griot*'s role, by his vocational power to link past, present and future, he is the symbol of what will remain of the Pilgrim's spiritual conquests and temporal rule. He is, in fact, the only one of Omar's followers left alive at the end of the action, to transmit to posterity the message of his master. When the *griot* is left alone, after the final disappearance of El Hadj, he sums up the message of the tragedy and the final judgement on the Warrior Prophet:

His place is in heaven rather than on earth. He was said to be a scourge. The fact is that on earth he surpassed the dimensions of a man. And yet the memory of him will call men to order again. They will be reminded of what it costs if man is diverted from the paths of mankind. (*El Hadj Omar*, p. 113)

But this is only a partial interpretation of the drama: while justifying his choice of a protagonist 'surpassing the dimensions of a man', Chenet nevertheless refrains from pronouncing final, arbitrary conclusions on his hero. He leaves the tragic dilemma of his inner conflicts unsolved. The final message is not that he should have chosen the Word without the Sword, the power of persuasion rather than of force; there is no final answer as to the dominant factors of good or evil in his character, but a simple, universal moral, or morals. In the words of the *griot*:

Hatred always remains hatred. It is as contagious as leprosy. It starts as a tiny spot; then the fingers fall off; then the whole hand. That is what hatred is. It erodes into the very heart of man. (ibid., p. 111)

More broadly applied to all the passions: 'It is easier to combat others than oneself.'

These universal truths, couched in a simple biblical style, enriched with symbolic imagery, make of this densely constructed drama woven around a complex hero of African history, one of the few really successful contemporary tragedies inspired by traditional lore.

The 'Geste' of the rulers of Mali: Soundjata and Da Monzon

SORY KONADE: *Le Grand Destin de Soundjata.* Paris, roneoed text no. R/18 554, O.R.T.F. Library.

EUGÈNE DERVAIN: *Saran, ou la reine scélérate,* suivi de *La Langue et le scorpion.* Yaoundé, Edit. CLE, 1968.

A full dramatic version of the Soundjata epic has still to be written. Given the possibilities for strong characterization of the protagonists, the opposition of the rival wives and heirs to the Manding kingdom, the supernatural elements associated with Soundjata's birth and childhood, and the miraculous exploits of his youth and manhood, this should be a rich field to exploit in African drama. Meanwhile for the student interested in the return to historico-legendary sources in neo-African writing, I mention Sory Konade's entry for the O.R.T.F. contest in 1971, which has no claim to dramatic form, nor any presentation of character or action, only the descriptive commentary of the *griot* with some dialogue distributed between the main protagonists.

Da Monzon, the semi-historical, semi-legendary ruler of the kingdom of Ségou which dominated central Mali from the last quarter of the eighteenth century until El Hadj Omar's conquests in 1861, is much better served dramatically by Eugène Dervain. He makes it quite clear that it is his intention to draw on the rich reservoir of African legends just as French authors have turned for inspiration to the myths of Ancient Greece. The Prologue in *Saran, ou la reine scélérate* [Saran, or the villainous queen] speaks as follows:

The company that plays for you this evening wanted an African play to be written for them. And the author followed the Classical example. He drew on legend, but instead of seeing Ismene, Antigone or Creon debating Attic problems, you will see Queen Saran in love with a handsome prince, as only the women of Ségou know how to love. It is only a first attempt, but the store of legend is rich: we have our Cid, our Ruy Blas, our Curiace...(pp. 13–14)

Saran and the play that follows it in the same volume, *La Langue et le scorpion*, are both dramatizations of incidents from an African *chanson de geste*, woven around the exploits of Da Monzon. The hero of both episodes was, according to popular opinion, a most remarkable sovereign. He combined great military skill with unusual wisdom and statesmanship, and finally succeeded in extending his empire south to what is now Ivory Coast, north to Timbuktu and east to Gao.

Dervain, using the same literary device as Birago Diop in his *Tales of Amadou Koumba*, and Niane in his *Soundjata*, claims merely to be reproducing in dramatic form the Bambara epic as told by the *griots*, transcribed and translated by the scholar Amadou Hampate Ba. Lilyan Kesteloot explains in her preface to the two plays, that this is the reason for the different language and style of the two dramas – the *griots* who originally recounted them being of different talents.

As Dervain suggests the possibility of a parallel with classical Greek mythology, I would see his Saran as the African Medea, so engulfed in her passion that she will stop at no crimes, but eventually the victim of her own machinations. Married when little more than a child to the king Douga of Koré, who is old enough to be her father, Saran frets, and pines in boredom. In spite of her husband's generous gifts she feels neglected and dreams of a powerful romantic love. There are echoes of Musset's Fantasio, too, in her ennui. And when her confidante upraids her for her discontent, Saran replies: 'I have everything, in truth. The only thing I lack is love, and love is everything. I shine like a sun in the sky, but I would prefer to be the smallest star, lost in the velvet night' (p. 25). Meanwhile she thinks that only the *griot* Tiécoura, who had been sent on a mission to her husband by the powerful Monzon, ruler of the neighbouring kingdom of Ségou, can dispel her melancholy by his music and tales, particularly by recounting the charms of the son of Monzon, the young prince Da Monzon. We then hear the rumour that Tiécoura is in fact on his way back to Douga's court having left Monzon with the contemptuous declaration that he would play no more for the sons of slaves. Douga, in his wisdom, fears that this is a trap to lead his peaceful, prosperous realm into war with his powerful neighbour.

The turning point in the tragedy is in the second act, in the epic confrontation between the older, wiser Douga, intent on maintaining peace, and the headstrong, arrogant Da Monzon, come under the pretext of claiming back his father's *griot* Tiécoura, but in fact determined to provoke Douga into war. The dramatic tension is enhanced by the device, which follows traditional custom, of making the two warrior rulers speak through the mouthpiece of their respective *griots*, who are themselves father and son. Tiécoura, now become the personal *griot* of Douga, thereby forced to insult and challenge his own father, becomes the instrument of the Fate which brings the play to its tragic climax. In a subsequent scene Saran bribes one of her serving women to accompany her at night to Da Monzon's camp. From a petulant child she has developed into a ruthless woman, carried away by passion. She defies all the proprieties, all the duties she owes her husband and her position as, in passionate bravado, she throws herself at Da's feet flaunting her adulterous love. Da and Saran recognize a common destiny in their youth, beauty, strength and ruthlessness. But Da's pride forbids a clandestine, adulterous affair in which he would share a mistress with her lawful husband. He vows that he will win her by conquering Koré, which seems impregnable even to a long siege. Saran then promises to destroy her husband's reserves of gunpowder and to betray the secrets of his fetishes, on which Douga relies for magic invulnerability.

As the outcome of the action is as well-known to readers and public as the dramas of Roman history or Attic legend, the dramatic tension is ensured by the rapidity of the messengers' accounts of the final events: the betrayal, Tiécoura's suicide, the entry of the invading army into the palace. Douga, taken prisoner, realizing Saran's treachery, curses her and stabs himself. Da, in fury, orders his soldiers to pillage, destroy and ravage the whole city and massacre all prisoners in the palace. In this way Saran meets her death and she and Da are deprived of the fruits of her betrayal. Da realizes the futility of the whole campaign. He made war for a *griot* who will not return to Ségou, succumbed to passion for a treacherous woman whose death he himself unwittingly caused. Will his whole existence follow this pattern of destruction? Will all his campaigns be equally vain? *Saran, la reine scélérate* has dramatic density, a convincing unity of structure and action, a noble eloquence of language and an authenticity of characterization, particularly of Saran herself who matures under the influence of passion from a restless child into an unscrupulous woman. If the language is that of the *griot*, as Dervain would lead us to understand, the dramatic talent to construct from his raw material a piece of rich French African theatre must be the author's own.

The second play of the Da Monzon *geste*, 'The Tongue and the Scorpion', is much shorter, its action less rich and less convincingly architectured. In place of a classical, epic tragedy of passion and fatality, this is a baroque morality woven round the Bambara proverb: 'Before a man puts a scorpion in his mouth he must be sure that his tongue is in a safe place'; that is, before taking a great risk, see that you take adequate precautions. The young Da Monzon of *Saran*, the ambitious, ruthless military strategist of indomitable will-power, has become the wise, middle-aged ruler of

Ségou, a wild Prince Hal transmuted into an African Henry V. The language of the play is lively and full of popular imagery suited to both text and theme. When the anecdote which illustrates the homespun wisdom of the proverb is played out, a modern *griot* has the last word, ending ironically with the suggestion that 'Ingratitude is forever banished from among all rulers'.

The fall of the Sudanese Empire: Ba Bemba, Samory and Alboury

MASSA M. DIABATE: *Une Si Belle Leçon de patience*. Paris, O.R.T.F.–D.A.E.C., 1972.

DJIBRIL TAMSIR NIANE: *Sikasso, la dernière citadelle*. Honfleur, P. J. Oswald, 1971.

CHEIK SIDI AHMED NDAO: *L'Exil d'Albouri*. Honfleur, P. J. Oswald, 1967. *Le fils de l'Almamy*. Honfleur, P. J. Oswald, 1973.

I include, for reference only, Massa Diabate's prize-winning play, based on an episode during the wars between the rival rulers of Sudan, the Almamy Samory and Ba Bemba Traoré, at the end of the last century, when the French were pushing further and further inland with their conquests. The theme has also been the subject of dramatic works by more experienced authors.

D. T. Niane's *Sikasso, la dernière citadelle* is the work of a professional historian who is also a conscientious Marxist. I have already mentioned how, in the unpublished 'Fiançailles tragiques', he turned a traditional myth to the service of the people's cause. In telling the drama of the siege of Sikasso and the fall of this seemingly impregnable citadel to the French in 1898, Niane offers a serious, documented chronicle, in which the elements of a heroic tragedy are interspersed with proof that he has his Negritude commitment and the workers' cause at heart.

The action takes place alternately at Ba Bemba's court, on the ramparts and in the streets of the besieged capital and in the French camp, opening at the moment of crisis when the king must decide on the final strategy to break the siege and closing with his defeat and death at his own hand, rather than surrender. The Narrator closes the play with an exhortation to the people of Africa who are on their knees to rise up and remember the example of the heroes of Sikasso.

The scenes among the soldiers and citizens of Sikasso, attempting to show the sacrifices and suffering of the people, are far less telling than those at the court. Possibly influenced by the 'popular' scenes of Shakespeare's *Julius Caesar*, Niane has nevertheless not succeeded with this genre and is patently happier in the dignified dialogue of the court and in rendering the noble pathos of his main protagonists. Especially moving is the character, Sogana, the wife of Ba Bemba's elder brother, a very Roman heroine. (Again we are reminded of *Julius Caesar*, both of Calpurnia and Brutus's Portia.) She shows a noble and calm stoicism in her example to the women of Sikasso who must encourage their men-folk in the unequal fight, but yields to despair when she has to bid farewell to her husband with her child in her arms. In Ba Bemba, Niane draws a portrait of a wise, moderate, courageous ruler, convinced of the justice of his cause, having offered friendship and free trading to the French, who then betrayed his hospitality, and determined in his devotion to his people and his country to stand up to the superior forces.

Sikasso clearly shows that Niane's creative talents, his sense of tragic destiny, his command of noble eloquence, his sensitivity to the conflict between human and heroic sentiments, are all sufficient to achieve a great African heroic drama. But his artistry is at variance with his political commitment; in obedience to the charge to put culture at the service of the people's cause, he has interrupted the tragic unity of his drama. The lesson of the courage of the defenders of Sikasso is clear enough and theme enough for one action. The call to the workers of the world to unite, the arguments put in the mouth of the unwilling French soldier, of the inequality of rich and poor, the capitalists' exploitation of the proletariat, could well have been kept for another time and place.

A much more original historical drama, more compactly classical in its action, more human in the dilemma presented, is the story of *L'Exil d'Albouri* by the Senegalese Sheikh Sidi Ahmed Ndao. Ndao, also takes his inspiration from real characters and an authentic episode in the nineteenth-century history of the Empire of Mali. The author, an English teacher at the William Ponty Normal School, has succeeded in composing an epic drama, free of any contemporary political inferences, somewhat in the Corneille tradition, with realistic elements. The language is elevated, the characters well opposed, the king's moral dilemma clearly and convincingly stated and the action economically conducted to its inevitable historical climax.

Alboury, differing from the ruthless Shaka, and without the proselytizing mysticism of El Hadj Omar, is caught in a conflict between his sense of responsibility to his people and the traditional concept of honour and courage. The situation is rapidly presented of the Djoloff Empire of Mali – which included present-day Senegal – on the dawn of invasion by the Spahi troops, armed by the French general, Faidherbe. Alboury decides on a strategic withdrawal to Ségou, the home of a friendly prince. The basic moral dilemma is then revealed in the confrontation between Alboury and the Queen Mother. To the challenge that retreat signifies lack of courage he argues prudence, the superior arms of the enemy and the necessity to save his people from slavery.

Another concept of the dictates of responsibility is expressed by the King's sister, the dignified Linguère Madjiguène, who is in charge of his household. To her, this means selfless dedication to a task of duty, an ideal she tries to instil into Alboury's young Queen Sêb Fal, a restless, bored, discontented child, desiring only her husband's attentions. In a confrontation between the two royal women, the Queen vaunts her youth, beauty and femininity, taunting the older woman that she is deluding herself about the importance of her tasks to compensate for growing old and losing her grip on life. The third confrontation is between Alboury and his brother, Prince Laobé Penda. The Prince advances reasonable arguments against accompanying the King into exile, but the latter, his confidence shaken in the face of so much opposition, suspects the Prince of conspiring with his enemies in the hope of usurping his throne, and tries to have him arrested. From now on Alboury is alone, save for the women of the court who all decide to accompany him for different reasons: the old Queen Mother refuses to fall into the hands of the Spahis; the Linguère knows that it is her duty to the King; the young Queen petulantly refuses to be left behind, the abandoned spouse of an exiled sovereign. Eventually, in a moving scene, Sêb Fal convinces her husband that her irritation and impatience are caused by her genuine love for him. He persuades her that his love too is sincere, but that grave problems of state have caused his apparent neglect.

The last two tableaux are movements in *rallentando*. It is the twilight of the Empire and the King's belief in the wisdom of his decision is gradually weakening. The Queen Mother's strength is declining with the hardships of the flight. The royal cortège is reaching unknown country and is unsure of the welcome awaiting them in Ségou. Now the young Queen, having lost her arrogant impulsiveness, is ready to give a lesson in endurance. But the King is finally crushed by the realization that far from saving his people he is the cause of their final defeat.

Samba, a *griot*, in traditional fashion, speaks the epilogue, telling of the King's death from a poisoned arrow, his son's capture by the Mauritanians during the retreat before the Spahis, the final dispersal in the face of the colonial invasion of all the people who had accompanied Alboury into exile. The final words are a feeble afterthought – an attempt to infuse a committed message into a play that is rich with tragic conflicts and elements of fatality. Without them, *L'Exil d'Albouri* has all the essential criteria for good theatre: by probing into the hidden motives of the King's actions, by not clearing him of the charges of human error, Ndao has achieved a work of tragic dimensions and psychological authenticity.

When Sheikh Ndao published *Le Fils de l'Almamy* in 1973, his second historical tragedy which he had written about 1967, he took up the promise of Samba's reincarnation, making the *griot* Maliba speak a short prologue, in which he repeats Samba's final words of the epilogue to *Albouri*: 'The Word does not die.' But this device adds nothing to the force of his new tragedy, for the message of the destiny of Karamoko, son of the Almamy Samory, and of Samory himself, is not a message of hope, but the conflict of two intransigent characters at the beginning of the twilight of the Samorian Empire.

Le Fils de l'Almamy more than confirms that Ndao is a tragic writer of impressive stature and originality, whose works have an universal, moving appeal. This second work is even richer in characterization, more consistent in action, and economical in structure than the earlier play. It has a classic concision, a disturbing complexity of personalities caught in a critical moment of history, which makes them victims of circumstances, of interested ill-wishers, and of the clash of their own inflexible characters, in which one is doomed to destroy that which he loves, and at the same time shatter his own existence. It is the tragedy of the honour of a son pitted against the honour of a father.

The Almamy Samory Souré, the last warrior king of the Sudan to be subjugated by Faidherbe's armies, is painted as proud, uncompromising, intolerant, sombre and suspicious, but at the same time a great and courageous patriot, with his own concept of honour, which is synonymous with the glorification of his country and his people. Neither his limited experience nor his unlimited arrogance can allow him to conceive of his country's defeat by any but mysterious, supernatural forces. He is, by his very nature, receptive to the plots woven at court for the destruction of his son, Karamoko.

The play, as the title suggests, is the tragedy of Karamoko, a man born before his time, the only one to understand that Africa had not the means to confront the powerful war machine of Europe and to believe sincerely in the possibility of peace with Europe, when the tradition was one of uncompromising belligerency. He is the victim of his own vision as well as of the plots and machinations that his unconciliatory nature inspires at the court. It is also the tragedy of Sendi, his devoted wife who goes mad with grief at his terrible fate. Samory, persuaded that his son is a traitor, has his hut walled up for him to die Antigone's death. But it is first and foremost the tragedy of Samory himself, shown here not as the legendary conqueror, nor as the defeated Emperor, but like his son, the victim of his own times and his own intractable, proud and suspicious character. After carrying out the cruel judgement on his son, on whom he has laid such hopes for the continuance of his own glory and that of his dynasty, Samory gives orders to raise camp for the attack on the French and to quit the place of accursed associations: it is with the sense that his personal greatness, like that of his empire, is irrevocably doomed.

Folk-lore, historical fiction and legend

OLA BALOGUN: *Shango*, suivi de *Le Roi-Eléphant*. Honfleur, P. J. Oswald, 1968.
EUGÈNE DERVAIN: *Abra Pokou*, Yaoundé, Edit. CLE, 1969.
CHARLES NOKAN: *Abraha Pokou, une grande Africaine*. Honfleur, P. J. Oswald, 1970.
RAPHAËL ATTA KOFFI: *Le Trône d'or*. Paris, O.R.T.F.–D.A.E.C., 1969.
MBAYE GANA KEBE: *L'Afrique a parlé*. Paris, O.R.T.F.–D.A.E.C., 1972.
JEAN PLIYA: *Kondo le requin*. Paris, O.R.T.F.–D.A.E.C., 1969.
FRANZ KAYOR: *Les Dieux trancheront, ou la farce inhumaine*. Honfleur, P. J. Oswald, 1971.

Many African writers in recent years have attempted to dramatize semi-historical, semi-mythical aspects of local lore, with the mixed aims of preserving a cultural heritage, presenting the picturesque in African traditions and, often, pointing a lesson in the political and moral responsibilities of the citizens of newly independent communities towards the forging of a national personality, particularly in the case of the socialist democratic states. (When the latter intention dominates, it is usually at the expense of the dramatic impact and also of the treasury of myth and legend, which is impoverished and de-sacralized.)

A Yoruba tyrannical monarch and a Baoulé heroine queen both belong to the mythical period of African history. The Pokou legend has been a favourite subject with contemporary Eburneans and other writers in French from West African territories. The Yoruba tale would probably have no place in a study of French-African writing had it not been for the association of the Nigerian Ola Balogun with the Institut des Hautes Etudes Cinématographiques in France and his consequent incentive to write in French for the stage and screen. In his dramatic treatment of the Shango legend, Balogun tells us that he combines two apparently contradictory versions. In both Shango is depicted as a bloodthirsty tyrant: in one case, driven from his throne by an uprising of the people, he commits suicide to escape from their wrath; in the other version, having tried in his megalomania to domesticate the thunder he only succeeds in setting fire to his own palace, and takes his own life in despair and rage at his failure. By adding the mythological and symbolic elements of the second version to the core of probable historical fact, Balogun has produced a drama with some of the poetic tragic dimensions of a classical hero overtaken by the retribution of the gods.

The story of Shango's rise to power and his subsequent downfall is told in a series of brief scenes, with a prologue and epilogue entrusted to a Narrator. The first scene establishes Shango's character as the ruthless despot, not brooking any criticism of his actions, and putting to death the wise chief of his council of elders, who attempts to warn him of the outcome of his policies. In Act II, Shango's exiled brother, whose throne he has usurped, regrets the pacifism and idealism which led to his overthrow and decides to return his brother's aggression, to prove himself an energetic ruler, capable of binding the country together against its enemies. Shango learns of the plot to overthrow him and, aiming to rid himself of his generals who are siding with his brother, consults a sorcerer as to the means of gaining power over the elements. He is given a charm to make him master of the thunderbolts, but with the warning that 'No man can become equal of the gods and remain a man'. When Shango wields his magic powers against his rebel brother, the charm escapes from his hand and the thunderbolt consumes his own palace. The symbolism up to this point is clear. But then, Balogun's attitude towards his protagonist becomes somewhat ambivalent. The King and Queen are shown in flight into the forest where they take their own lives with dignity.

According to conventional Western criteria of unity of structure, theme and moral tone, this would have been a satisfying conclusion, but Balogun prolongs the action into the future, where Shango seems to have realized the sorcerer's prophecy that by commanding the weapons of the gods, one enters their realm, leaving us with doubts as to whether Shango should be revered as the divinity he seems to have become, or reviled as the sanguinary despot he was. In any case there is not the clear-cut attitude of poetic retribution that would be traditional in a Western drama of tyranny and ambition to rival the gods. The only positive lesson is that there are powers beyond the comprehension of man, and wherever and however these powers manifest themselves, man must do them homage.

If the moral of Balogun's *Shango* seems a little ambiguous, we at least appreciate that he has recognized and attempted to perpetuate, in a lyrical drama half-way between legend and history, something of the superhuman quality and mythic grandeur of Shango's legendary fate.

The more admirable mythical heroine, Queen Abra Pokou, has been less well served by her dramatic exponents than by those writers who have related in simple narrative form the legendary explanation of the founding of the Baoulé tribe.

Eugène Dervain's *Abra Pokou*, a short one-act play, is merely a dramatization of Dadié's better-known version of the legend. Charles Nokan's *Abraha Pokou, une grande Africaine* is a freer interpretation. A series of tableaux present the major incidents in the Queen's life and reign, the founding of a new country for the Baoulé after their exodus, Pokou's accession to the thone and the democratic designation of her successor in her old age.

I have no quarrel with Nokan's aim to assume a new perspective with regard to his traditional subject. But it seems a pity that in his desire to give it a topicality, to illuminate it with a partisan interpretation, by rationalizing the miraculous aspect of the crossing of the river, by omitting the voluntary sacrifice of Pokou's child, he has stripped the legend of all its poetic quality, all its symbolic attributes. The lessons he gives in civic responsibilities, the militant exhortations, the political commitments, are so clearly spelt out, that this work belongs to the field of doctrinaire pamphlets and not to the domain of imaginative, creative literature. Nokan may well have succeeded in composing a militant manifesto for social revolution and popular liberation. In so doing he has sacrificed a popular, poetic, heroic myth and impoverished his country's literary heritage. His series of tableaux, are not constructed round any organic dramatic unity. There is no tension, no climax, no transition between the brief statements of each isolated episode.

The piece opens with the hope of some dramatic, romantic conflict, with the young heir to the throne expressing his desire to marry a slave girl, with whom he is in love. His sister, Abraha Pokou, speaks in his favour, so anticipating her role as the people's mouthpiece and defender. However, the prince Dakou very easily renounces his chosen bride, in deference to the wishes of the elders. When the old king dies, he is poisoned by the rival claimant to the throne and Abraha Pokou leads the traditional exodus of her supporters, mostly slaves who fear the tyranny and oppression of the new ruler. During the flight, a treacherous slave tries to kill Pokou, but his arrow strikes the child she carries on her back. Thus the episode which is the keystone in the Pokou myth is completely glossed over and all elements of miracle and of heroic sacrifice are omitted. When she has wiped away one tear of regret for her dead child the march is resumed until they reach the angry waters of the river. Here the story of the crossing is completely demythified, the virtue of the tribe's salvation being vested in the fifteen strong young men who swim across the river to fetch help from a friendly community on the other bank. The rationalistic explanation is obviously easily acceptable, making no call on symbolic interpretation. In the final episodes, the Queen, now growing old, explains her intention to abdicate and leave her people to choose a successor by democratic vote. This introduces a pedestrian announcement of the results of the election, more in keeping with a radio bulletin than the climax of an historical or mythical drama, and offering the most extreme example of obedience to the demands of social realism. The epilogue proclaims the victory of the international proletariat.

The eras of tribal conflict and conquest have inspired several entries to the O.R.T.F. competitions. None of these is a striking contribution to dramatic literature, but they do show that there is a rich reservoir of material to be drawn on.

Raphaël Atta Koffi's play about the golden throne of the Abrou king is a fictional treatment of the wars between the Abrou and the Ashanti. It purports to laud the military virtues of the Amazonian queen Yangoumar of the Abrou whose forces are powerless before the European rifles of the Ashanti. In spite of the melodramatic incidents of the last act, the play is slow-moving, the language pedestrian and it does not move one to horror or pity.

M'baye Gana Kebe's *L'Afrique a párlé* is a post-Independence plea for harmony and understanding between Black and White. The story is in the nature of a symbol. Paulin, the European confidant, counsellor and familiar of the King of a mythical African realm, is accused of having stolen a sacred mask. Paulin, deeply in love with Africa, is ready to shed his blood on her soil rather than accept repatriation. After some rather unconvincing dialectic Paulin stays to cement a future of reconciliation and peace between Europe and Africa. The play has much eloquence and some lyric grandeur, but is a little too reminiscent of Senghor for true originality. Lacking economy of structure and being inconsistent in the presentation of the character of the king, the play falls somewhat short of its intentions.

Kondo le requin, a historical drama in three acts by Jean Pliya, is another example of the popularity of the historical subject among aspiring African dramatists. The action, which takes place in the kingdom of Abomey (Dahomey) between 1889 and 1894, is claimed by the author to be founded on fact. In the opening scene we see the arrival of a French mission at the court of King Glélé, determined to put a stop to the atrocious practice of human sacrifice. The play moves slowly through scenes of incomparable cruelty and bloodshed, over the five years of the French advances, showing attempts at negotiation with the uncompromising king Gbêhanzin, known as The Shark, the hardening attitudes of the Europeans, culminating in the seizure of the capital. Kondo the Shark burns his palace to save it falling into the hands of the conquerors. Finally, called upon to abdicate, he gives himself up freely to the victorious General Dodds.

Franz Kayor's play, *Les Dieux trancheront, ou la farce inhumaine*, purports to take place in Bamoun, the Western province of Cameroon, at the court of Sultan Njoya-Moluh, the ruler over a warlike people who waged victorious campaigns against the neighbouring tribes. At the beginning of the action Bamoun is about to be invaded by the Germans. Njoya-Moluh is a composite of several authentic sovereigns, including one whose watchword was: 'War is not won by force or weakness, but by guile'. The climate in which the action advances is at the same time one of jealousy and intrigue amongst two of the sultan's co-spouses and their two sons (both heirs designate) and a carefully cultivated respect for the history and prestige of the royal line. This respect for tradition is emphasized by the important roles of the chief *griot*, the tutor to the young princes and the Sultan's official historiographer, as well as that of the Sultan himself.

The situation and the plot are quite ingeniously managed, but the play suffers by its inability to inspire any real interest in the fates of the protagonists, who include no truly tragic figures. The young princes, dutifully repeating their lessons in history and traditional lore are cardboard puppets manipulated by their tutor. Although we are given hints of Seidou's uxorious nature there is no indication of more than a passing flirtation with the young queen, no hint of a deep, incestuous, tragic passion; nor is there any preparation or motivation for his sudden emergence as a traitor at the end. The fact that at court he is referred to as the son of the 'foreigner', that is, a woman from another tribe, does not seem sufficient justification for his selling out his father's kingdom to the Europeans. The Sultan himself impresses for his bonhomie rather than his sense of tragic destiny, this impression being maintained throughout the play by the bantering quality of the dialogue: a frivolity which relieves the rather tedious repetition of extracts from the chronicles that slows down the movement of the action.

With one exception, even the best of the fictional or semi-fictional dramas in an historical setting are less successful than the more historical tragedies: notably *El Hadj Omar*, *L'Exil d'Albouri* and *Le Fils de l'Almamy*. This exception is Bernard Dadié's *Les Voix dans le vent*, which really falls into a category all of its own, and his equally original *Béatrice du Congo*.

An original historical tragi-comedy

BERNARD DADIÉ: *Béatrice du Congo*. Paris, Présence Africaine, 1970.

Two of Dadié's post-colonial era plays are hybrids which refuse to fit into water-tight compartments: *Les Voix dans le vent* and *Béatrice du Congo*, both published in 1970, but written in that order. *Les Voix dans le vent* is a variation on the theme of the African king's successor – often the subject of the early improvised historical spectacles – but the characters and situations are completely imaginary and the fundamental interest is not the study of an historical or even legendary episode but the analysis of the complex psychology of a fictional tyrant. I have decided for this reason to discuss it in the section of this chapter devoted to political satire, rather than historical drama. In the case of *Béatrice du Congo*, Dadié fuses an anti-colonial diatribe into recognizable periods of colonial history, with authentic characters, although many of the key episodes are obviously invented. It seems logical, to consider this work as an historical tragi-comedy, in which we no more expect every detail to be authentic than in Shakespeare's *Richard III*.

Béatrice du Congo is a pageant of symbolic events, covering the history of the colonization of West Africa by the Portuguese. The episodes range from Henry the Navigator's victory over the Infidel Moors at Ceuta, through the Portuguese voyages of discovery down the West African coast which led to Diogo Cão's discovery of the mouth of the River Congo in 1483, to the emergence of the prophetess Beatrice of the title towards the end of the seventeenth century. The original Dona Beatriz, on whom Dadié's character is based, was a member of the Antonin sect who was burned for heresy by the Portuguese in 1706.[7] As Dadié is more concerned with portraying the loss of national identity of indigenous peoples, following the growing inroads of European colonization he makes his Beatrice a martyr to her patriotic zeal – half Cassandra, half Joan of Arc – rather than to her religious beliefs.

Although the action of the play ranges over two and a half centuries and two continents – set now in Portugal (Bitanda), now in Africa, the work has a clear unity of structure, underlined by the irony of the opening scene, which anticipates the climax – the revolt of the colonized Africans. The play opens at the court of King Henry with the celebrations of the victory over the Infidel invaders, whom the Portuguese have finally driven from their land. The King, in a dialogue with his chief counsellor, Diogo Cão,

---

[7] For more details on Dona Beatriz and this period of the history of Angola, see Georges Balandier, *La Vie quotidienne au royaume du Congo, du XVIe au XVIIIe siècles*, Paris, Hachette, 1953.

points out the lessons to be drawn from the victory at Ceuta: barbarians who have sucked the country dry for centuries must be driven out finally. No tyrant can continue to oppress a whole people indefinitely. Henry and Diogo, in a triumphant litany, exult in their new-found freedom, with obvious analogies to a later period in history. Henry declares that it is his mission to evangelize the rest of the world, sending his caravels across the ocean, his envoys to spread the message of Christ and the glory of the kingdom of Bitanda. The King eloquently enlarges on his ambitions, to the sounds of the ocean growing in volume to symbolize the Portuguese explorations and crusades.

Gradually the King is shown to be as much the slave of his territorial and imperial ambitions as he was of the Infidels who occupied his country. The original high-minded intentions of his crusades are lost to view under the more and more questionable means employed to realize them. If professional sailors refuse to embark on the dangerous voyage into uncharted seas, then jails must be emptied, thugs and criminals conscripted. To finance the ventures merchants must be bribed with promises of untold riches, gold and diamonds, rivers flowing with gold nuggets; promises also of the monopoly of slaves, and that all these benefits will be tax-free and all expenses re-imbursed if the ventures fail.

By this time the satirical implications of the play are clear: to point out the self-interest that lies beneath so many apparently idealistic schemes; to underline the permanent and universal lesson of the corrupting power of ambition; to confront the so-called benefits of 'civilization' (i.e. Western concepts) with those of backward 'savages'; to indicate the dangers of accepting one limited experience as being the only guide to happiness and wisdom; and finally, bringing the play full circle, to return to the theme of liberty and the rejection of a conqueror's yoke, with which the play opened.

The action progresses fast, after the arrival at the court of the King M'Banza Congo, of the Envoy Diogo and the Algaves, emisaries of Dom João, who has succeeded Henry, bringing gifts and offering friendship and alliance, but actually in search of Prester John's fabulous kingdom. The comic element is still dominant, in a scene of mordant satire, where the Bitandese faith in the superiority of their preconceived ideas begins to be shaken. To Diogo's extreme embarrassment he is offered two 'wives' in return for his gifts, and as an earnest of M'Banza's cordial reception of their mission. The notables of the Court of Zaïre, astonished and bewildered at hearing of the European custom of monogamy, exclaim that with them a man who has braved the fury of the oceans and tempests would deserve a hundred wives as a reward, and in another comic litany they explain the undoubted benefits of polygamy. Diogo plants the Bitandese cross, as an ostensible sign of friendship and alliance. While the Congolese king's autonomy is gradually sapped, no-one heeds the prophetic warnings of the old woman, Beatrice's mother. When Mani Congo, King of Zaïre, leaves his thumb-print on the document proffered by his guests, we know that he is signing away his kingdom.

The third tableau shows Diogo's return home, his first mission accomplished, bringing news of the discovery of a vast territory of unsuspected wealth, and Mani Congo's gifts of gold and ivory, skins and slaves. These blackamoors arouse contemptuous laughter from the courtiers, amused that a king of such complexion could presume to ask to be considered as their sovereign's royal cousin. This successor to Henry the Navigator has no truck with his predecessor's evangelizing mission. His sole ambition is to add this terrestrial paradise as the richest jewel to his crown, and he vows to wage pitiless war, both to civilize these savages and to repel other Christian states who might venture near Africa's shores.

In the second act, the civilizing process of Zaïre is progressing, under the control of the various Bitandese specialists sent to exploit the country's resources and solve the many problems of health, education, agriculture, economy, etc., of which the inhabitants and their rulers were originally unaware. The capital is renamed San Salvador; the King christened Dom Carlos the First, after the formality of renouncing Satan and burning the sundry fetishes, masks, statues and the inconvenient old prophetess of misfortune. However, when Carlos hesitates to renounce all his wives but one, for fear that this will cause an insurrection and bring about the downfall of his kingdom, Diogo reassures him that he will bring in White troops to protect him. The king accepts monogamy and exacts from his courtiers the promise that they will follow his example. Eventually his country has all the attributes of its European model: a rich capital with sumptuous palaces, cathedrals, roads and the protection of troops and forts against the conspiracies which continually threaten the King's power and his life. Famine and misery are rife throughout the land where joy and simple contentment used to reign. Slaves toil ceaselessly for the rich and privileged, who all now have one wife and several mistresses, and the era of slave-trading is born. But Dona Beatrice, the daughter of the old prophetess, begins to arouse the people to revolt.

Before the action finally changes into tragedy, the comic element is again dominant in a scene in which the new counsellors, sent by the King of Bitanda to manage the affairs of Mani Congo, try to teach him the ways of Europe, and in particular table manners and court etiquette, to prepare him – a Black Monsieur Jourdain – for a state visit to his royal Bitandese cousin.

Finally the King realizes that he has been caught in a trap, that he has become the helpless tool of the Bitandese who have destroyed his kingdom, and that he should have listened to the prophetess Dona Beatrice, whose voices told her that she must save her country. He decides, too late, to forbid slave-trading, rally his people and return to the traditional beliefs and ways of life. But Dona Beatrice has already been arrested by the Bitandese, and the King himself is assassinated by the 'counsellors' sent to run his country, as in his fury he seeks to tear down all the emblems of his own subjugation and the destruction of his kingdom. Beatrice is subjected to a parody of Joan of Arc's trial, before being burnt at the stake, prophesying the liberation of her country and the return of peace for her countrymen.

Béatrice du Congo is Dadie's greatest play and also the most successful and original of all the satirical drama, if not all the drama that Black Africa has produced in French. It is a baroque masterpiece, successfully mingling allegory and unrestrained humour – from verbal wit, through savage irony to black comedy – leading through fast-moving action to a tragic climax. The construction is faultless in its symmetry and economy: each scene has its own almost classic architecture, building up to its own climax, with its own *coup de théâtre*, propelling the action on its inevitable way to the tragic conclusion. Dadié has achieved a truly African play, but with implications beyond a limited geographical setting. It has a Voltairian power to shake preconceived ideas and shatter prejudice.

COMEDY, SATIRE AND MORALITY PLAYS

There is not always a clear distinction in contemporary French-African drama between historical and satirical plays. Many writers, as we have already seen, are particularly attracted by an historical subject (for example, Shaka) because of the possibility of drawing from it a political lesson or affirming an ideological alignment. In the first part of this chapter, I have treated as historical those plays concerned with fidelity to chronicle or oral tradition, or those in an historical setting in which the poetic, epic, tragic or mythic element is dominant, even when the subject is less purely historical than legendary or semi-fictional. Plays which may have some historical background, but with predominantly didactic, polemical or satirical intentions will be treated as political satire. I shall also deal here with works of social satire, which may have little or no comic element, and also with pure comedy of manners; the intentions of the authors of works in this genre are similar, only their dramatic mode of expression differs and, usually, the success of their message.

Differences of genre had already been noted by Charles Béart in his report on the dramatic activities of the William Ponty students. He pointed out that the Sudanese and the Senegalese preferred historical pageantry, which he found to correspond to their personality and culture: students from Ivory Coast, Dahomey, Guinea and the more southern regions of A.O.F. generally produced only comedies and contemporary plays. This distinction still applies *grosso modo* to French-African dramatic literature, and certainly to the most successful efforts. I have already pointed out (p. 118) that the most outstanding of the historical plays are those of Ndao from Senegal, together with Chenet's tragedy *El Hadj Omar*, whose subject is at least inspired from the same region; the most original and most successful dramatists in the satirico-comic vein are the Eburnean Bernard Dadié and Guillaume Oyônô-Mbia from the Cameroon.

No texts survive of the earliest comedies. I have mentioned how the first improvised spectacles were often inspired by everyday situations and types. From these arose what one might call the popular theatre of West Africa, as opposed to the 'aristocratic' genre of heroic drama, dealt with above. This includes didactic, moral and allegorical scenes – somewhat comparable to medieval mystery and miracle plays – satires and plays with social and political implications, comedies of manners and comedies of character and some rather elementary *comédies larmoyantes*. These can again be classified according to theme; the most popular being expositions of the evils of the colonial régime (for example, the forced labour system) with a few attempts to deal with the continuing fight against colonial domination outside the French-speaking territories. There are also attacks on the inherent suffering caused in primitive communities by superstition and tribal justice: studies in the transition from tribal society to the realities of the modern world of westernized Africa and some analyses of the endogenous social foibles of the newly-independent African states.

The anti-colonial theme: some minor works

Considering the large number of Negro-African novels in French dealing with the evils of the colonial régime, it might at first be thought surprising that this theme did not provide inspiration for more plays. But publication of a novel in France was one thing and the performance of a public spectacle in the colonies, denouncing local conditions, was quite another. We have already seen (p. 90) how Coffi Gadeau's attack on the forced labour system, *Les Recrutés de M. Maurice*, was banned in Ivory Coast in 1942. Nevertheless, it is worth mentioning that several prize-winning plays in the O.R.T.F. annual competitions from 1969 to 1972 have dealt with the sufferings of the colonial period or the anti-colonial struggle. None of these has very great merit if judged by objective literary standards; some are frankly simplistic in subject and elementary in structure. But these plays were to be broadcast in Africa where the radio is taking over the functions of the *griot* in providing popular diversion and instruction and the aspiring playwrights doubtless felt that an anti-colonial subject was a sure formula for success among their compatriots.[8]

CONDETTO NÉNÉKHALY-CAMARA: *Continent-Afrique*, suivi de *Amazoulou*. Honfleur, P. J. Oswald, 1970.

The only skilful theatrical treatment of the evils of the colonial period is Nénékhaly-Camara's tragi-comic satire, *Continent-Afrique*. The deeply committed Guinean writer, whose *Amazoulou* was discussed in the first part of this chapter, here sets out to glorify the historical evolution of Africa and the ability of her culture and civilization to survive and be regenerated after the colonial repression. He uses Antar, the Arab warrior–poet of the sixth century A.D., as the key to his allegorical pageant and the symbol of Afro–Arabic unity on the continent. A wounded soldier who announces Antar's death in the Prologue has a series of prophetic visions before he dies. The first 'Vision', as the author calls his tableaux, presents the farcical session of an 'Academy of Scholars' who represents the colonists of Africa, intent on compiling a brief history of the civilizations of the world. This is a pretext for castigating the deliberate obscurantism of historians in respect of the part played by Africa and the so-called 'sub-civilizations'. They exclude from the records such discordant notes as the contribution brought by the specialist in pre-history, the egyptologist and the pre-Columbian historian. Even the Greco-Roman scholar is rejected for his discovery that Aesop was a Negro. The toast that they offer him in honour is Socrates's cup. In similar ways they are able to dispose of all audacious attempts to submit dangerous, subversive 'hypotheses and conjectures', 'non-scientific aberrations' on the equality of human races and civilizations. The second Vision shows the imprisonment and death of Patrice Lumumba and closes with a chorus of praise for all freedom fighters – the symbols of the future greatness of *Africa resurgens*.

Irrespective of the impact of the message of *Continent–Afrique* – and Nénékhaly-Camara's ideological commitment allows no compromising light and shade in his representation of his situation – there is great interest in the care with which he has managed the scenic effects and

---

[8] The student of sociology may be interested to pursue this further, so here are details of plays not analysed here (all published by O.R.T.F.–D.A.E.C., Paris): Pierre Dabire: *Sansoa*, 1969; Antoine Letembet-Ambily: *L'Europe inculpée*, 1970; Martial Malinda: *L'Enfer c'est Orféo*, 1970; Jean-Baptiste Obama; *Assimilados*, 1972.

staging. The mock academicians' session, played on a basically farcial note, is particularly succcessful, making use of masks, disguises, a trap-door through which importunate visitors can be dropped after an invitation to occupy the vacant chair placed ready for the new 'Member'; the symbolic clock whose figures represent the scientific contributions made to the world by different civilizations (hieroglyphics, zero, pi, the compass, arabic figures, etc.); the huge hour-glass marking the passing of the centuries, all bear witness to the author's sense of what is required to compose a living theatre. In the second scene or Vision, with the transition from burlesque to a sombre note, the effects are more restrained, achieved by a variety of lighting, rather than of *jeux de scène*. Use is made of films and slides to illustrate the recital of two narrators, and finally the lighting, and thereby the action, is concentrated on three sections of the stage in turn, with stylized scenery representing Lumumba's prison-cell, his wife and children's home, and a diplomat's residence in Brussels. This is the only dramatic work considered here in which the author, in the basic composition and structure of his play, has taken into account staging requirements as well as the basic text.

Indictment of tribalism

Some aspiring African dramatists did not wait for the coming of Independence to assume their responsibilities for educating their less emancipated compatriots, particularly in pointing out the evils of superstition, the dangers of charlatanism and the sufferings caused by some tribal customs. Unleavened by comedy or satire which makes didacticism more digestible, these earnest moralizings have little claim to literary or dramatic merit. The objective critic can only wonder at the choice of a European language for their expression, as the naiveté of conception and unpretentiousness of composition of the majority of these works would make them more suitable for presentation in the vernacular to a rural community, as part of an educative programme.[9]

GUY MENGA: *La Marmite de Koka-Mbala*, Monaco, Edit. Regain (Coll: Le Pied à l'Etrier.), 1966. Also: O.R.T.F.–D.A.E.C., 1969.

The most satisfactory dramatic treatment of superstitition and obscurantism serving to perpetuate cruelty and injustice, is by Guy Menga, a young

---

[9] Examples of these can be found in François-Joseph Amon D'Aby's *Kwao Adjoba* (1955) and *La Couronne aux enchères* (1956, both published by Les Paragraphes littéraires de Paris and in the undated roneoed texts of CLE, Yaoundé. Jean Laforest Afana: *La Coutume qui tue*; Joseph Kengni: *Un Père aux abois*; Lui Chindji: *Le Choix irrévocable*. See also Antoine Epassy: *Les Asticots*, Paris, O.R.T.F., 1972 (roneoed text).

Congolese novelist and dramatist. *La Marmite de Koka-Mbala* is a politico-social satire and a symbolical philosophical drama. The cauldron of the title is the symbol of the superstition by which the head fetishist and chief counsellor holds his power over the king, the other ministers and the people of the typical little kingdom of Koka-Mbala. It is the concrete image of repression and tyranny. It gives a unity and meaning to the action, and the possibility of a splendid *coup de théâtre* in the climax. The head fetishist has had the idea of confirming his autocracy by spreading the belief that the cauldron contains the ancestral spirits and by its presence alone prevents any movement of revolt or reaction against the iniquities of tradition. One night the king has a dream that is interpreted as meaning that the ancestors are tired of bloodshed. Encouraged by his wise and strong-minded wife, but in the face of frightened opposition from his ministers, and the threats of the fetishist, he decides to spare the life of the next young man who is brought before him, charged with the capital crime of having gazed on a woman. The king himself is eventually condemned to death, but saved by the opportune return from exile of the young man whom he has spared. The latter had profited by his freedom to enlighten others of his generation about the oppressive powers of the fetishist, under whose authority, strengthened by the belief in the authority of the cauldron, they daily risked a cruel death. The rebels smash the symbolic object, demonstrating the emptiness of the fears it had fomented, and overthrow the reign of terror.

Guy Menga's *Marmite de Koka-Mbala* is a good example of how unnecessary it is for African writers to compromise the fundamental Africanness of their inspiration to produce dramatic material that can have a universal appeal. Here the mythology, the protagonists, the historical situation are rooted in the author's own birthplace: but by the clarity of his expression, the firmness of his dramatic structure, which progresses rapidly on the stepping-stones of African conventions (dreams, fetishist objects, superstitious prejudices) from the premonitions of the opening scenes to the explosive climax and, above all, by condensing his message into a symbolic form, the author has written a play that transcends geographic or temporal boundaries.

The marriage market

GUY MENGA: L'Oracle, Paris, O.R.T.F.–D.A.E.C. 1969, repr. 1973.
GUILLAUME OYÔNÔ-MBIA: *Trois Préténdants...un mari.* Yaoundé, Edit. CLE, 1964, 2nd ed. 1969. *Notre Fille ne se mariera pas.* Paris, O.R.T.F.–D.A.E.C., 1969. 2nd ed. 1971. English version by the author: *Three Suitors, One*

Husband, with *Until Further Notice* (see p. 131). London. Methuen, 1968. Repr. 1975.

One aspect of traditional tribal society that has not disappeared from Africa under the impact of Westernization, is the dowry or bride-price offered to a girl's family by her suitor. There are serious inherent problems in the system: apart from the whole question of polygamy, there is the common situation of the girl being given to the highest bidder, irrespective of his suitability or her personal wishes and not unfrequently the suitor faces impoverishment in his efforts to meet the exorbitant demands of his prospective parents-in-law. Nevertheless, it is the comic potential of the theme of the marriage market that has been exploited most successfully by African writers to produce an original and popular comedy of manners.

The subject of the rival suitors and the bargaining parents was the source of one of the early William Ponty productions, a farce entitled *Les Préten-dants rivaux* [Rival suitors] which was presented in Paris in 1937 at the Théâtre des Champs Elysées. This is the theme that Guillaume Oyônô-Mbia took for his first play, *Trois Prétendants. . . un mari*, [Three suitors, one husband], written, according to the author's note to the published text, when he was a twenty-year-old student in 1956, to divert his class-mates, and thank them for having helped him with his maths assignments. This is also the subject of Guy Menga's *L'Oracle* [The oracle], while Oyônô-Mbia gives it a fresh and paradoxical twist in his second play, *Notre Fille ne se mariera pas* [Our daughter shall not marry].

In all three of these comedies, the conventional problem of the marriage is complicated by the fact that the daughter in question is not only the local beauty, but the only 'college girl' of the community – which makes for involved financial transactions in view of the need to recoup the expenses of her education.

In Oyônô-Mbia's plays the plot is fairly straightforward, but logically developed; the humour is mainly verbal, with some good fun at the expense of village types – characters recurring in his plays and stories. He is a master also of good comic situations, and a basic element of his satire is the confrontation of the rural African with the benefits of modern consumer society and his westernized city cousin. The 'country mouse', though momentarily disconcerted by the complexities of new-fangled ideas and institutions, is not necessarily worsted by his experiences nor over-whelmed by the superiority of the 'town mouse'.

Guy Menga's *Oracle* is less sophisticated in its ironical situations, less fundamentally comic in the gallery of village types, but nevertheless derives much of its humour from the character of the avaricious father, torn between the two possible ways of realizing his investments. He has agreed to let his pretty Louaka go to high school, very much against the mother's wishes, not at all for the girl's satisfaction or welfare, but because he has the foresight to see her education as an investment which would bring good returns on her eventual marriage. But he is faced with a dilemma when a rich, elderly polygamist offers an astronomical dowry for sixteen-year-old Louaka, on condition the wedding take place without delay before Louaka has completed her schooling. For the miserly Biyoki the only argument is the *dot* [dowry], and this gives rise to one of the richest comic scenes of the play as he enters into some anguished calculations over the exact financial rating of his daughter, according to whether she obtains her school certificate or not. He finally decides that the precious diploma can be compensated for by a couple more enamel basins and some aluminium saucepans. The determined Louaka wins over to her side a surprising ally in the person of her old grandfather, no conservative traditionalist, but in favour of the right of a young woman to an education and to choose a congenial spouse. The parents are persuaded to consult the oracle, the local fetishist. This is an excuse for some sly digs at the villagers' superstitious deference to his prophetic powers and at his charlatanism. By dint of suitable remuneration, the fetishist allows the grandfather in hiding to pronounce his judgement of Solomon: that Louaka shall remain at school and marry her young school-teacher sweetheart who happens to be a patrilineal cousin, thus satisfying local custom that encourages inter-marriage. As *deus ex machina*, the 'oracle' goes further. Emerging from hiding, he argues the evils of the heavy bride-price system and insists that Louaka marry *sans dot*. This makes a good dramatic climax and satisfies the demands of the younger generation to break the shackles of a tradition which they find increasingly unacceptable. It is clear that Guy Menga's main preoccupation is not to compose a comedy of character, concentrated on the miserly father and the quack fetishist, but a social satire, questioning the situation of the marriageable girl in a society in transition.

This is basically the inspiration of Guillaume Oyônô-Mbia's first successful play, the village comedy of *Trois Prétendants...un mari*. The bargaining of the father with the three suitors is over his daughter Juliette – the most desirable match of the village, the local beauty and the 'college girl' to boot. But Juliette has learnt unheard-of emancipated ways with her higher education and not only claims the right to have a say in the choice of her husband, but has jumped the gun by bringing him back into the bosom of her family, divided over the claims of the rivals of their choice. Each of the uncles, as well as the parents and grandparents, is looking for some personal advantages in the match, whether in the form of cash, the concomitant gifts or the association with an influential personality. There are obvious elements of social satire, directed mainly against traditional nepotism, superstition and the subjection of women. But Oyônô-Mbia's moralizing is lighthearted and it is clear, in what becomes a riotous farce, that his first intention is to exploit to the full the comic potential of the situation and the characters.

There is plenty of scope for his particular gift for drawing burlesque portraits of village types, a characteristic of all his works, as he continually returns to the inspiration of his native village, Mvoutessi. The names vary, but the caricatured portraits are always recognizable. He introduces the drunken illicitly-brewing uncle; the self-important, protocol-conscious chief; the pretentious *grand fonctionnaire* intent on impressing the yokels; his chauffeur, in the tradition of the comic valet; the prudish, teetotal catechist, the grandfather, lamenting the good old days and the deterioration of modern youth; the witch-doctor called to smell out the thief, who, like Dr Knock eliciting his patient's symptoms, gets his credulous client to furnish him with all the necessary information for an adequate 'diagnosis' of the case.

There is irony of situation in the confrontations of superstition with the benefits of modern progress. There is, too, good handling of the comedy of misunderstanding (the *quiproquo* dear to Molière and reminiscent here of Harpagon with his lost *cassette*) in the scene where the grandfather's laments over the viper which the young people have eaten up, 'only leaving three quarters for the elders' are confused with the father's outcries over the loss of the 300,000 francs which the suitors have left as a deposit on their bride and which must be refunded to the unsuccessful claimant. The touches of verbal irony are discreet but telling. The happy *dénouement* is achieved by the device of the fiancé Okô, whom Juliette has herself chosen from amongst her college mates, being presented to the family as the most eligible suitor. Not only has he exactly 300,000 francs to offer as the bride-price (by a happy coincidence the precise amount required to reimburse the other three unsuccessful suitors, being in fact the same money 'stolen' by Juliette from her father), but he also holds the ace of a superior education with which to dazzle the simple villagers. It takes a little time for them to be convinced of this advantage, but with some persuasion from Juliette's cousin, the battle is won for youth and women's rights.

If some of the situations of Oyônô-Mbia's comedy seem reminiscent of better-known scenes in French dramatic literature, let it not be forgotten that Molière himself was a famous snapper-up of others' unconsidered trifles. The peculiar qualities of Mbia as a comic writer are his ironic verve, his spontaneity, his command of scenic situation and verbal humour, and above all, his ability to infuse into his gallery of village types and his caricature of an African society sufficiently universal aspects to give his work a wide appeal. If he has succeeded at the same time in combining a grain of moralizing with uninhibited laughter at the burlesque or farcical elements, then he is also following an excellent precedent.

In his later and maturer comedy of village life in Mvoutessi, the didactic element is a little more evident, though not at the expense of opportunities for comedy. One important difference between the earlier play and *Notre Fille ne se mariera pas* is in the form: the latter was written specifically as a radio play. Mbia is proficient enough not to have confused the techniques needed to convey the comedy to his listeners, with the different ones of staged action. Thus, although there is still a good deal of farcical movement, the author has relied firmly on verbal humour and sound effects, and has been less limited in the actual setting of the action. The other difference is in Mbia's making one of the characters the voice of moderation and common sense between the two exaggerated extremes of obstinate rural ignorance and pretentious city contempt for tradition: he thus suggests some possibility of compromise for a society still in a transitional stage.

The opposition of the two elements of contemporary African society is nicely expressed in the symmetrical structure of the play. The first act takes place again in Mvoutessi, in and around Chief Mbarga's hut, to the cacophonous accompaniment which is characteristic of village life in the Cameroon backwoods, or in the local bus on the road to Yaoundé. The second act is set in the city of Yaoundé, either in the select apartment inhabited by Mme Colette Atangana and her spouse, Monsieur le Conseiller Technique, representing the intellectual élite (to the accompaniment of Beethoven's Fifth Symphony on the hi-fi), in the Antangana's Citroën DS19 in the streets of Yaoundé, or in the offices of the local police station, where city bureaucracy reigns.

The problem of the marriageable daughter is given a new dimension by Charlotte's family having decided that after all the expense they have incurred in giving her a university education she must remain unmarried, so they can rely on her assisting them, both in kind and in influence, in view of the good job she can now command. After all, argues Mbarga, 'Would she be able to order everyone around at the big Ministry in Yaoundé, if I hadn't killed myself sending her to college?'

A family expedition, consisting of father Mbarga, selected wives, children, bags of provisions, goats and sheep, sets off in the local bus to visit Charlotte, to request the 150,000 francs needed to pay the dowry for Mbarga's most recent young wife, and to remind her of her obligation not to marry now that she has her job at the Ministry, lest her salary go to her husband, her children and herself, instead of her deserving parents, uncles and cousins: 'Notre fille ne se mariera pas'. Unfortunately, the emancipated Charlotte is already endowed with a legitimate husband, whose existence she has kept secret from them for fear of the storm this would let loose on her head. The solution this time lies in the hands of Charlotte's young sister, Maria, who has come to the city in the hope of obtaining a clerical job. She compensates in time-honoured fashion for her relative illiteracy and complete ignorance of the art of typing, and succeeds in getting the post of secretary to – the Commissioner of Police himself. Thus Mbarga can envisage a rosy future for himself and his family, with the best possible insurance policy for his old age, and is reconciled to Charlotte's misalliance with a mere specialist in agronomy.

The humour of Mbia's play ranges from the frank farce and burlesque that is found mainly in the first act, to the satire of emancipated Africans, and especially the 'prétentieuses ridicules', of the second. But it is here that the author submits his plea for understanding the Mbargas of Africa. It is clear that in spite of certain exaggerations of the family's claims on Charlotte, they have some degree of justification. He puts the voice of moderation and good sense into the mouth of Monsieur le Conseiller Technique, André Atangana, who, unlike his snobbish wife, has not forgotten his village origins. In a long and quite serious discussion, in which there is no grain of irony. Atangana points out to Colette the difference between well-to-do parents who can afford the luxury of disinterested generosity to their children, paying the expenses of an education without expecting anything in return, and the sacrifices that his and Charlotte's families made for their children. The discussion finishes on a note of compromise, with Atangana agreeing with his wife that there is room for a change of attitudes.

The play ends with a pirouette in the form of a touch of literary irony, as Atangana-Mbia informs us that it has all been a radio play and it is time to go home – presumably leaving the audience to sort out the lesson for themselves.

Some minor comedy of manners

GUILLAUME OYÔNÔ-MBIA: *Jusqu'à nouvel avis.* Yaoundé, Edit. CLE, 1970. *Le Train spécial de son Excellence.* Paris, O.R.T.F. Library (roneoed text).
PATRICE NDEDI-PENDA: *Le Fusil.* Paris, O.R.T.F.–D.A.E.C., 1970.
BERNARD DADIÉ: *Sidi, Maître Escroc.* Yaoundé, Edit. CLE (roneoed text) 1969.

Comedy of manners, comedy of character, comedy *tout court*, is obviously
the field in which Guillaume Oyônô-Mbia displays to the full his dramatic
talents. After the success of *Trois Prétendants . . . un mari*, he wrote a radio
play in English, *Until Further Notice*; the B.B.C. awarded it a prize, and
a stage adaptation was produced at the Edinburgh Festival of 1967. A
French stage version, *Jusqu'à nouvel avis*, was published by Editions CLE
in 1970, the original English version having been published by Methuen
(see p. 127 above).

The setting and the basic characters remain those of *Trois Prétendants*,
namely the village of Mvoutessi in Eastern Cameroon and its inhabitants.
The plot is of the slightest, being a pretext for some good-humoured
ridicule, ostensibly of the 'ignorant' villagers who do not understand the
benefits of the new civilization (pre-packed and imported food, female
cosmetics, air-conditioned offices, European wigs for Black women, etc.):
but the main target of the satire is obviously the sedulous city imitators
of everything Western, including the artificialities of an over-sophisticated
consumer society and the superstitious awe in which village communities
today hold Black bureaucrats, who seem to have usurped the prestige of
the sorcerer.

The same theme and the same mild satire are evident in the latest of
the Mvoutessi cycle, *Le Train spécial de son Excellence* [His Excellency's
special train]. The whole scene takes place at a little rural railway-siding
where the local station-master dreams of promotion to a real station and
the possibility of wielding unlimited powers over rolling-stock and human
freight (including the live-stock which frequently accompany the latter's
displacements). The opportunity to impress his superiors and have a word
put in for his promotion comes with the announcement that a Great Official
(His Excellency) is taking the train from his siding that very afternoon.
After much amusing stage business preparing for the ceremonious departure
of the special train, the station master discovers that 'His Excellency' is
not an Excellency at all, and that the train of the real 'Excellency' will be
passing non-stop through the siding. The text of *Le Train spécial de son
Excellence* at present exists only in roneoed form at the library of the
O.R.T.F. in Paris, but it is announced for early publication by Editions
CLE in Yaoundé. It should be noted that this play is a dramatized version
of the short story appearing under the title *La Petite Gare* in *Chroniques
de Mvoutessi I* (Edit. CLE, Coll: 'Pour tous', 1971). The narrative has
been expanded and more characters added, but I think the dramatized
version adds little to the spontaneous humour and economical effects of
the original tale.

Another Cameroonian writer, Patrice Ndedi-Penda has produced a lively comedy on an episode of village life, in *Le Fusil* [The gun]. We recognize some of the typical inhabitants of a Cameroon village to whom Oyônô-Mbia has already introduced us: in particular the self-important Chief, jealous of his authority and position; the Catechist, anxious to safeguard his reputation for learning, piety and temperance; and with these, a new comic character, the veteran of the European war, boasting of his universal sexual conquests rather than his military exploits. The action turns on the visit to Douala of Ndo, the most successful of the local cocoa farmers, to sell his crop and buy the gun he has long coveted. There is the usual fun at the expense of two yokels at large in the big city, and some digs at venal officials. Inevitably Ndo loses all his money at the hands of city tricksters and returns discomfited to his village without the long-awaited gun. However, an improbable *deus ex machina* assures a happy ending.

Before he turned to more serious politico-satirical drama, Bernard Dadié also composed an amusing and completely light-hearted farce, *Sidi, Maître Escroc* [Sidi, master swindler], about a charlatan who exploits human greed and credulity in a way not necessarily confined to Black Africa. He makes people believe that he can make them rich by means of a miraculous suitcase which has the power of producing money, like the goose laying golden eggs – with, of course, adequate remuneration for Papa Sidi.

The importance of these little comedies, however slight, should not be underestimated. They are not only the proof of a flourishing and genuinely indigenous African comedy in French, but they are also indications of a healthy literary climate. The writers I have particularly commented on, Guy Menga, Guillaume Oyônô-Mbia, and the newcomer, Patrice Ndedi-Penda, are no longer looking to the past for their inspiration. They are firmly rooted in the present world and in the soil of their own origins. They can look lucidly at their own society, their own contemporaries in town and country and find there enormous comic resources. They spare neither human foibles nor weaknesses in the system. Bureaucracy, parasitism, nepotism and even the milder forms of corruption, come under their ironical scrutiny. But instead of using a tone of acerbity, they succeed by raising a hearty belly laugh – this has always been a satirical dramatist's most efficacious weapon: a pinch of humour is worth a peck of moralizing. This is certainly true of the best of the political satirists, Bernard Dadié.

Political satire and polemics

MAXIME N'DÉBÉKA: *Le Président*. Honfleur, P. J. Oswald, 1970.
BERNARD DADIÉ: *Les Voix dans le vent*. Yaoundé, Edit. CLE, 1970. *Monsieur Thôgô-Gnini*. Paris, Présence Africaine, 1970.

Bernard Dadié has made the biggest contribution, both in quantity and quality, to French-African satirical drama. The main theme of *Monsieur Thôgô-Gnini*, as of the historical tragi-comedy, *Béatrice du Congo*, is still the nefarious influence of White colonization in Africa, treated here with trenchant wit and in burlesque situations. His *Voix dans le vent* [Voices in the wind] is an allegorical tragedy of universal implications, not limited to either a colonial or specifically African situation; the study of the corrupting influence of power and an indictment of totalitarian régimes and all dictators.

The lesser-known writer Maxime N'Débéka uses a similar theme for a successful satirical comedy, *Le Président*, with the political scene in a fictional independent republic of the New Africa, as his target. The newly-elected President symbolizes corruption and the power of evil. In a most effective opening scene, demonstrating the author's mastery of theatrical effects, the President has his servants strip the palace of all its furnishings, leaving one single chair on the stage. In this way he can make a display of poverty and impress his people with the fiction that he has inherited from his predecessors a state with empty coffers, and so extract riches from sycophantic courtiers hoping for advancement. He is confronted by his son who symbolizes the spirit of purity, and who tries to sabotage his evil designs. However, the President has his son assassinated with as few scruples as he has sacrificing all principles in the way of his ambitions. He gains pleasure from the humiliating manoeuvrings of the boot-licking courtiers, as they try to ingratiate themselves with him, share his present power, and possibly displace him. There is comic business at the expense of the miser, whose ambition to be the Chief of State's right-hand man is in conflict with his tight purse, and satire directed at belief in the power of magicians in an age of enlightenment. The ambitious Colonel Osse, representing the military power responsible for many a twentieth-century *coup d'état*, has his desire for promotion realized by being appointed as the President's personal bodyguard, armed with a flit-spray and the special assignment of protecting him from mosquitoes. Meanwhile, he has to look on while his wife is seduced by the Chief of State arrogating his *droit de seigneur*. The infuriated colonel eventually perpetrates his *coup d'état* and the President is sent to join his son in the next world, where the two sycophants continue to fulfil their role of President's doormat into eternity.

We are told that the 'People' are now in power; they have supplanted the tyrannical dictator, and have chosen their new President, General Osse, to represent them democratically. Yet it seems doubtful if anything has really changed. In the Preface, Henri Lopes claims that N'Débéka's play is a war-cry against imperialism; but is surely more of a universal satire on the intoxication of sudden power and the destructive contagion of tyranny and corruption. Without suggesting any alternative régime, the author shows that he can compose an eminently theatrical work on a political theme without necessarily adopting a partisan stand and can attack a political situation that is not limited to independent African states. Nevertheless, the abuse of power by African rulers, whether traditionally-elected kings or presidents of contemporary republics, is a common enough phenomenon to have inspired Dadié to treat this subject in his poetic tragedy, *Les Voix dans le vent*, an African allegory with universal application.

The play is carefully constructed on a circular plan. It opens with King Nahoubou in his decline, a prey to insomnia, tormented by the 'voices in the wind', which taunt him with his manifold crimes, including matricide and fratricide. Among the voices of the many victims who haunt him can be distinguished that of Truth – even the vigilance of his guards cannot exclude this from the palace. As he restlessly seeks sleep as a refuge from the persecuting voices, he is confronted with a vision of his early childhood. The flash-back presents the homely scene of the village hut, whose realism contrasts with the imaginative atmosphere of the palace with its ghostly voices. Nahoubou's mother marks him already as a child of ill omen, callous, brutal, respecting neither laws nor rights of property. Then comes an episode from his manhood and married life: victimized and despoiled by the King's men, despised and finally abandoned by his wife, his desire for vengeance is translated into a lust for power and ambition to become king himself one day. At first he deludes himself – and the sorcerer Bacoulou whose assistance he solicits – that his ambition arises purely out of the altruistic desire to avenge the wrongs done by the present tyrannical king and to introduce a new era of security and respect for all men. Finally the admission escapes him: he wants to be a god. Bacoulou is not the traditional sorcerer, relying on hocus-pocus, but a man of wisdom and insight, who reads Nahoubou's heart, analysing his true motives and exposing the dangers of his ambition. When he agrees to grant Nahoubou's request and sets a price on his accession to the throne, we know that the sacrifices that the sorcerer exacts are in fact the crimes that the tyrant will have to commit in order to eliminate the obstacles in his path; like Macbeth he must find the means to obey the supernatural prophesies which are the voices of his own ambitions.

Then we see Nahoubou as the autocratic tyrant, well advanced in his career of war and pillage, but unable to buy or conquer the one thing he still covets: the beautiful, sensitive, intelligent Losy, who prefers the love of a simple man to the riches and power with which a ruthless monarch would endow her. She counters his wooing with cautious, evasive answers, beguiling him into believing that she accepts him, but playing for time in order to escape with her lover. When, after days of waiting for her return, the King realizes that she has deluded him, he becomes completely paranoiac and, in his thwarted fury, declares universal war, calling on his guards to assassinate the taunting voices, massacre the wind and annihilate the tom-toms that prevent his peace. Finally, goaded by all the wives and mothers of his victims, the whole country rises up in revolt against the ceaseless wars and perpetual famine. Surrounded by a host of phantoms, the crescendo of voices calling on him to join them, Nahoubou must finally explore the kingdom of the dead, to see if his tyrannical reign will have sway over that final unconquered territory.

From this survey, it is difficult to appreciate the full dramatic potential of Dadié's allegory. Within the limits of theatrical conventions of time and space he shows the birth, the evolution and eventual downfall of a ruthless dictator. Basically, the subject is not original, but the treatment is richly imaginative, the psychology of the characters is everywhere convincing, even the ones who make the briefest of appearances, for example the Mother, the Witch-doctor, the girl Losy. The dramatic effects are sure, and the dialogue, from the colloquial speech of Nahoubou's mother and his first wife, to the eloquent, ghostly voices or the ranting of the distraught king, persecuted by his conscience, is flexible and dramatically appropriate.

In *Monsieur Thôgô-Gnini* Dadié returns to the subject of the evils of the colonial past which he had treated in *Béatrice du Congo*. Again he exposes the responsibility of the White man for these evils, owing to the geographic, economic, moral and cultural inroads he made into a society that had its own traditional and stable foundations; but at the same time he does not exonerate the African society itself, in whose midst the universal time-server could be found to exploit his own compatriots for his own profit. In place of the militant symbolism and melodrama of *Béatrice*, that culminates in tragedy, Dadié now concentrates his ferocious sense of the comic in scenes of burlesque and pure farce.

Monsieur Thôgô-Gnini was written in 1966 and was performed in 1967 at the first Pan-African Cultural Festival in Algiers, where it was most enthusiastically acclaimed. In a series of tableaux Dadié presents a carica-ture of the extortionist, profiteer, self-made man, seducer and suborner, Monsieur Thôgô-Gnini who combines in one well-upholstered person all the evils accompanying the White man to Africa. The intention of the play may well have been militant as befitted the occasion for which it was written, but Dadié's sure sense of theatrical effects, particularly of comic writing, often gets the better of his didactic motives, and the scenes in which he gives full rein to his verbal humour, irony and farcical burlesque are some of the funniest on any stage.

The play opens in an African village in 1840. The first White traders arrive bringing gifts as earnest of their desire to assist their benighted Black brethren to a better life. To the local king they offer ridiculous moth-eaten military uniforms for his guards, and obsolete rifles to help him to wipe out war – in return for plenty of palm-oil. The lesson is inculcated: the more palm-oil the natives can produce, the more prosperous will be their country. In fact the White people will do them the great service of teaching them to build prisons, so that they can keep sufficient free labour to exploit the palm plantations more profitably. To combine the social and economic lessons with a little elementary introduction to metaphysics, the trader also suggests that as the invisible Almighty is a little difficult for the mere mortal to apprehend, it is a distinct advantage to have some visible, tangible manifestation of divinity on earth to worship. This the White men have realized in the form of bank-notes, which they are prepared in their generosity to disperse among their Black friends, in return for their planting more palm-trees and ground-nuts and producing more oil which Europe needs. He ends his exhortation with an eloquent echo of Louis-Philippe: 'Enrichissez-vous!'

In the succeeding tableaux we see Thôgô-Gnini's rise to riches and power as he sedulously follows the lessons of his White friends and becomes the overseer of forced labour and the middle-man for the White traders. In one night of uneasy sleep he has an allegorical vision in which all the barriers to advancement – Loyalty, Gratitude, Age, Respect for Age, Women and Children, Love – are systematically executed without trial. The skeletal plot advances in some rather more tedious scenes involving one N'Zékou, who represents the victims of Thôgô-Gnini's unscrupulous dealings. Then burlesque takes over with the return of the White men bringing more trashy gifts, including a 'jute-suit', which they declare is the latest fashion in Europe. This fires Thôgô-Gnini with the ambition to visit Europe, to show off his finery and be acclaimed for the powerful man he is. He would also like – for the usual price, naturally – a street in Europe named after him to crown his fame. The Whites warn him that this is extremely costly, even for a man as important as Thôgô, but think that they will be able to have his name affixed to...a provincial *vespacienne*, thus usurping a Roman emperor himself for this privilege.[10]

[10] It is impossible to translate into English the rather bawdy joke on the French name for a public urinal, derived from the Emperor Vespasien, to whom is attributed the establishment of these conveniences in Rome.

The climax of this extremely funny scene is the finding of a suitable *titre de noblesse* for Thôgô, in order for the ceremony of the naming of the edifice to be carried out 'with a minimum of decency, so that people won't think that it has been an arbitrary decision', a title, in brief, that will be in keeping with his new-found dignity. They settle on 'Monsieur de Thôgô-Gnini de la Panthère des Afriques des Trafics du Benin'.

After this, the final *dénouement* of the plot seems arbitrary and anti-climatic. Three young thugs set upon Thôgô and rob him. N'Zékou is subjected to a parody of a trial, which nevertheless results in the judge being persuaded of his innocence and consequently acquitting him. *Thôgô-Gnini* is uneven in structure, Dadié obviously being torn between his desire to write a fierce satirical comedy, an allegory and a morality play. The allegorical elements and the shreds of plot are less convincing and make less good theatre than the frank burlesque of the comic scenes, in which the author makes his political satire unequivocal and exploits his dramatic gifts to the best advantage.

CONCLUSION

In the preceding pages we have traced the growth of Negro-African drama of African inspiration and French expression from the Bingerville and William Ponty improvisations of the early nineteen-thirties to the sophisticated compositions of the sixties and early seventies. Dramatic literature was slower to develop than poetry or prose fiction, but this is not surprising as it could only grow in direct ratio to the available public. The establishment of radio and television networks and the building of theatres in African cities have been major factors in stimulating writers to try their hand at dramatic composition, particularly with the encouragement of the annual O.R.T.F. competitions.

Of the large number of entrants to these, there are naturally very few, even among the prize-winners, whose work deserves more than an indulgent pat on the back, but they are important for the indication they give of the increasing interest in African drama and the trends in inspiration, theme, and form. Only two writers of significant dramatic talent have emerged from these contests: Guy Menga and Guillaume Oyônô-Mbia, the latter writing as easily in English as in French and adapting his work or writing direct for the B.B.C. The only one of the pre-independence established writers to turn with success to writing for the theatre is Bernard Dadié. Having proved himself as a poet, story-teller, novelist and essayist, he has shown since the middle sixties that he is an undoubted master of satirical drama as a vehicle for his polemics, amply fulfilling the promise he showed while still a pupil at William Ponty Normal School when he composed his

Assémien Déhylé for their annual theatrical production. His humour is more discomforting than Oyônô-Mbia's, his irony more trenchant. He combines moments of pure farce or burlesque with tragi-comic effects or scenes of near tragedy. His *Monsieur Thôgô-Gnini* recalls Le Sage's Turcaret, while we might see in his *Béatrice du Congo* a Voltaire who had decided to give dramatic form to a subject similar to *Candide*, with a political rather than philosophical message. In the field of historical drama three names are paramount: those of Dervain, Gérard Chenet and Sheikh Ndao.

Although I have classed the plays studied in this chapter as historical dramas or social and political satires, the categories are far from water-tight, of course. It would be more accurate to see the divisions as stylistic or generic than thematic; the first section being more noble and poetic, and generally tragic in scope, the second more popular and with the emphasis on the comic element. The drama of the first category could be said to belong to an aristocratic didacticism, aiming at preserving a heroic past, perpetuating the exploits or relating the tragedies of semi-mythical figures. Some of the criteria of French classicism are met, in as much as the protagonists are usually of superhuman stature, great warriors or princes, and the plays respect the unity of action, if not of place and time. In the second more popular drama, the instructive element is associated with the realities of the present day, not with the historical models of a semi-legendary past. The moral and didactic purpose is often disguised by comedy: the better the pill is sugared, the more effective the medicine. The human frailties attacked with some degree of indulgence for their comic potential are universal ones of avarice, self-importance, greed, credulity, hypocrisy, and snobbery; the social and political diseases exposed are superstition, corruption, venality, parasitism, nepotism, ignorance, exploitation, injustice. Even in the most farcical of situations, the public is invited to question some weakness of human nature or the social system. Sometimes these are associated with a colonial régime, sometimes with a contemporary independent society.

Elements of fantasy, imagination and fable are rarely present in this dramatic literature, except in an effort to evoke the historical past, or in an occasional vision, prophetic dream, or allegorical passage. The rich vein of mystery and magic which is so great a part of traditional African life and folk-lore has barely been exploited in drama in French. Insistance on the necessity to combat superstition, which is so frequent a theme in satirical and moral plays, would indicate that this is deliberate; that mystery and magic are now associated, not with the power of poetic vision, but with a primitive, animist past that must give way to the practical realities of the present day, fighting to hold its own in the face of economic pressures. The impoverishment of some of the traditional or poetic myths, for example that of Abra Pokou and Sokamé, by offering a rationalist explanation of miracles, would bear out this thesis. It is also important to remember that the Islamization of Western Africa, from the middle of the nineteenth century, with its crusade against fetishism and animistic beliefs, has clearly left its mark on a literature whose purpose is strongly diadactic. For what it is worth, I would add the comment that the work in this category which gives the most evidence of the writer's power to evoke a mysterious, supernatural world, is *Les Amazoulous*, by Abdou Anta Ka, a writer whose existence is largely spent in mental hospitals.

A limited gamut of human emotions is introduced. In only one play is the tragic action associated with a passionate love – that of Saran, and there, though her machinations to consummate her adulterous love lead to the betrayal of her husband and her country, her own death is a circumstancial one, due to a twist of fate, a trick of dramatic irony. In few plays do we find exposed noble, generous passions, except for an excess of patriotism, which is usually associated with personal ambition rather than with heroic sacrifice. The austere sense of duty of the dignified Linguere in *L'Exil d'Albouri* is too self-righteous and intolerant to win our sympathies. There is a hint of maternal love in the minor character of Aissata in *El Hadj Omar*, the indications of tender emotions linking Alboury to his young bride, the anguished grief of Sendi in *Le Fils de l'Almamy*, Shaka's remorse at the sacrifice of his gentle Noliwe; but for the most part we are faced with hatred, jealousy for power, pride and ambition leading to cruel tyranny, unassociated with personal, human relationships. Where the protagonists are shown to be prey to conflicts, the dilemma is mainly occasioned by historical circumstance or tradition, and not by opposing loyalties, antagonistic duties or responsibilities, or inner psychological struggles. Africa has not yet achieved its Golden Age, when stability, prosperity and self-confidence can inspire its writers to explore the full spectrum of human passion. This is understandable in view of the political climate in which this literary form has grown: because drama is a public art, the play relying on the theatre and the presence of the public to reach its full dimension, it has been put to the service of political or social causes. In some cases the partisan has over-ruled the artist; instilled with the idea that the writer who does not put his talents to the service of revolution is a parasite on the community, he has painstakingly spelled out a lesson in doctrinaire politics in the simplistic, monosyllabic sentences of social realism. But the whole range of human feeling is there for future dramatic treatment.

As far as the form and structure of the plays is concerned, there is little of either characteristic African traditions, classical European influences or original innovations. Music and dance is still occasionally integrated into the action, but in small proportions as plays have been written for production in an enclosed theatre or an Italian-type three-wall stage. Some of the works are divided into acts and scenes, though rarely following the careful architecture of the classic three- or five-act European play. The pattern of the traditional indigenous spectacle is often evident in a pageant-style presentation, or a series of loosely-connected tableaux, particularly in the heroic, historical works. The best of the comedies, on the other hand, show a certain attention to composition and the advancement of the action to a dramatic climax, with a comic or melodramatic or ironic *coup de théâtre*. The lack of innovations in style or originality in form may paradoxically be attributed to the lack of a long tradition of written drama, and not to too great a subservience to existing models. In Raymond Queneau's definition, 'Originality always feasts on a knowledge of tradition and the works of the past.' In other words, there is no betrayal of the present by building on the past, and true originality consists in renewing the best in the past, so ensuring a continuity of artistic creativity. In the case of African dramatists, the only existing indigenous tradition was an oral one, with limited application to contemporary needs, particularly for a French-language theatre. On the other hand, there existed the great models of European drama, which they had been shy of following, in case they were accused of trying to produce a Black Racine, Corneille, Euripides, or even Shakespeare.

If in the preceding pages I have occasionally made comparisons with French writers, I have not deliberately been tracking down literary influences, nor had I any intention of trying to fit French-African theatre into the pattern of French dramatic literature. Such comparisons arose quite spontaneously out of evident and incontrovertible literary echoes of the French culture to which African writers have been exposed. To close on this note I would say that the drama that Africa has produced in French in the past forty years is most closely associated with the Middle Ages and eighteenth century of Europe, by its attachment to the didactic and popular intentions of the first and the democratic rationalism of the second. Something of what De Tocqueville says must be apposite to sum up:

literature in democratic ages can never present, as it does in periods of aristocracy, an aspect of order, regularity, science and art. . . Style will frequently be fantastic, incorrect, overburdened and loose – almost vehement and bold. Authors will aim at rapidity of execution more than at perfection of detail. . . There will be more wit than erudition, more imagination than profundity; and literary performances will bear marks of an untutored and rude vigour of thought – frequently of great variety and singular fecundity.

This quotation is interesting in as much as it describes *grosso modo* many of the characteristics of the drama dealt with here. Although the historical works usually give evidence of erudition, and imagination is not a dominant element, with some rare exceptions, where the authors are poets as well as dramatists, it is true to say that the dramatic literature of this period is exuberant and bold with much vigour of thought, showing variety and fecundity of inspiration, but associated with a certain disregard for style, structure and presentation. A twentieth-century theatre, making use of the innovations of the past two decades in the West, is not yet in existence.

3. Negro-African poetry: from Negritude to 'disengagement'

It is a generally accepted fact that no strict division could be made between poetry and prose in the traditional oral literature of Black Africa and that, as Senghor wrote in his preface to Birago Diop's *Nouveaux Contes d'Amadou Koumba*, such a distinction often remains tenuous in neo-African creative writing. Nevertheless, it was mainly in recognizable poetic compositions, ranging from the most conventional to the most liberated verse structures, from Parnassian to Claudelian influences, from Mallarmé to Surrealism, that Negro-African literature first manifested itself in French: and it was essentially as poets that the founders of the Negritude movement made their literary reputations and illustrated their literary manifesto in the immediate post-war years. They were helped by the publication in 1948 of L. S. Senghor's *Anthologie de la nouvelle poésie nègre et malgache*, with the now celebrated introductory essay by Jean-Paul Sartre. 'Negritude is essentially poetry', wrote Sartre. He goes on to explain:

Because it expresses this tension between a nostalgic past, to which a Black man can never completely return, and a future when it will give way to new values, Negritude wears a tragic beauty which can only find its expression in poetry... For once at least the most authentic revolutionary project and the purest poetry spring from the same source... (Preface to L. S. Senghor's *Anthology*, 1969 edition, p. xliii)

In discussing the birth and evolution of Negro-African poetry in French, it is impossible to adhere to the strict definition of an African writer adopted for the purposes of this study. The poetry of Black Africa was so linked to that of the Caribbean writers in the early years, that mention will have to be made of the West Indian poets who so deeply influenced the Black Renaissance in Africa itself as they made common cause with fellow poets from Senegal or Ivory Coast, even North America and Madagascar, on the basis of their common black complexion. It was more particularly poetry that these young intellectuals of the years between the Wars, on the Left Bank of Paris, used as the literary expression for the doctrines of Negritude: poetry was primarily to be the means of exploring all the dimensions of their Black personality and the expression of Black values. The reasons for this are not hard to find. In the first place, poetry is the most economical vehicle for subjective writing, for sublimating into dense, literary imagery a whole range of personal experience, associations, emotions and sentiments. There is also the important fact that a form of poetic expression existed against which the disciples of the new doctrine could react, as indeed they felt it their mission to do. Long before Negritude became a war-cry among the Black intellectuals of the Left Bank, Caribbean writers had been composing verses in French that were purely derivative, evoking the Parnassian and neo-Romantic influences of the end of the last century. At a time when French-African drama was finding its first expression in the improvised spectacles at Bingerville and William Ponty Schools, inspired by purely African subjects and situations; while the African novel still in its infancy (René Maran's *Batouala*, Bakary Diallo's *Force Bonté*, Ousmane Socé's *Karim*) bore the unmistakable stamp of its African origins, such poetry as had been published by Black writers was clearly the fruit of a grafted Western culture. We have already seen how the first manifestations of rudimentary poetic talent among freed slaves in North America, at the end of the eighteenth century, took the form of portentous odes or sentimental lyrics inspired by the modes popular in Britain at the time. A hundred years later, and well into the first third of the twentieth century, writers from the French-speaking islands of the Caribbean were still composing verses lacking in originality of form and sentiment. They had evolved no individual idiom and no Negro personality had emerged from what was frankly a literary exercise of little intrinsic merit or lasting interest. The best were inspired imitations, conscious or subconscious pastiches of French models.[1] None indicate by poetic form or expression the writer's ethnic origins. However, one little poem by one of the earliest Creole poets is worthy of attention. Here is a translation of 'Moonlight' by Louis Borno, President of the Republic of Haiti from 1922–30:

> the silent goddess on her pillar throned
> commands my heart with all her beauty brown.
> With her soft eyes, black as a starless heaven,
> with her black eyes, soft as a moonlit sky,
> yet sad and ever soft. As if the light
> of a black moon.[2]

[1] A most striking example is a poem, irresistibly recalling Leconte de Lisle and significantly entitled *Midi*, by the Guadaloupan Gilbert de Chambertrand, who was awarded the poetry prize 'Ceux d'Outre-mer' in 1936 for his collection of verse *Images guadaloupéennes* (included in *Poètes d'expression française 1900–1945*, ed. L. Damas, Edits du Seuil, 1947, p. 43). It illustrates the best of the work from the Caribbean poets.

[2] Original title 'Clair de lune', in *Panorama de la poésie haïtienne*, ed. Carlos Saint-Louis & Maurice A. Lubin, Port-au-Prince, Edits. Henri Deschamps, 1950, Kraus Reprints,

In spite of the triteness of the subject and the rather contrived nature of the treatment, the imagery is interesting, discarding the traditionally accepted symbol of white as the colour of light, purity and beauty, deliberately accentuating blacks and browns and fostering a sort of literary colour-consciousness, which ante-dates the doctrines of Negritude and shows Louis Borno as the forerunner of what Sartre later calls the 'Annunciation of quintessential blackness'.

The first clearly expressed revolt against continued imitations of French models in verse, accompanied by a positive programme for a poetry that would be Negro-centric in origin, inspiration and expression (while maintaining the use of the French language), came from Etienne Lero, a brilliant young student who had left his native Martinique at the end of the twenties to study English at the Sorbonne. In 1932, together with his compatriots Jules Monnerot and René Ménil, he founded *Légitime Défense* as an organ for his political and literary doctrines. His aim was to mobilize young Black poets under the banner of Marxism to create a *littérature de combat* amanating from the Islands of the Caribbean.

From this date, which marks the birth of Negritude even before it had become conscious of its own existence and been baptized, Lero affirms the association between politics and poetics, which was long to remain one of its primary characteristics. He denounces at one and the same time the bourgeois society of his homeland for being both intellectually and physically bastardized, for being 'fed on White decadence for its literary fodder', and he urges them to 'think Black'. These descendants of two hundred years of slavery and expatriation could not speak properly of 'cultural alienation' or of the 'ethnocide' which is now a fashionable term; they had never had the chance to translate their own indigenous cultures, traditions, history, mythologies or even language with which to transmit tribal memories, as tribes and even families were separated in slave-ships, slave-markets and slave-gangs. (This situation, with its breakdown of communication between the different tribal units of this Black cargo, is described with imaginative acuity by Simon Schwarz-Bart in his novel, *La Mulâtresse Solitude.*) The conscious stimulation of a Black Renaissance had to be associated with a search for common cultural origins in Black Africa. Hence Lero's command to his compatriots to 'think black', to re-affiliate themselves with Africa as the source of their lyricism, their subjects and themes, and to find deep in their subconscious what Roger Bastide called: 'the profound vegetal soul, the hidden source of the barbarian gods, the

1970, p. 119. It also appears in *Anthologie d'un siècle de poésie haïtienne 1817–1925*, compiled by Louis Morpeau, Paris, Edits. Bossard, 1925, Kraus Reprints, 1970, p. 145.

hallucinatory music of the tom-toms and the strange flowers of the Black libido'.[3]

Nevertheless, be he Martiniquan, Senegalese or Haitian, the Black poet writing in a Western tongue, in turning his back on the literary heritage of Europe had no leaders in Africa for his crusade to win his cultural autonomy. These leaders were found in North America, in the Afro-American revolutionary poets whom Lero so enthusiastically admired: Langston Hughes, Claude MacKay, Countee Cullen. He declares that:

The wind that arises from Black America will speedily sweep away from our West Indian Islands the abortive fruit of a decadent culture.

and goes on to add that the American poets have brought

marinated in red wine, the African love of life, the African joy in love, the African dream of death. And already the young Haitian poets are producing verses bursting with a future dynamism.[4]

Lero himself was not only a theorist: he also set the example for poetic composition, bursting with a new Black vitalism and expressing Black aesthetics. In his poem 'For a Black Virgin', for example, we find a frank sensuality of subject and treatment, with colours, rhythms and images that are fundamentally African.[5] After Lero, French-African poetry is to owe its originality and its authenticity, and thus its durable contribution to the poetry of this age, to a return to tribal origins, deliberately flaunting its African roots.

Nevertheless, certain compromises were made right from the beginning of the campaign against cultural colonization or cultural assimilation, either from practical necessity or from literary instinct. There was, for the most part, no rejection of the French language as the medium of poetic expression (we are not concerned here with writing in Creole). Moreover, the Marxist analysis which Lero applied to the Island societies, and which he took to express literary as well as social emancipation of the proletariat, was un-arguably of European inspiration if of universal application; and finally the techniques of Surrealism, on which much of the Negro-African

---

[3] In an article entitled 'Naissance de la poésie nègre au Brésil', *Présence Africaine*, no. 7, 1949, p. 223. To put the quotation in its full context, Bastide is, in fact, commenting that these are the African elements which at the time (till the end of the nineteenth century) were still absent from Brazilian poetry, for which Africa constituted a poetic theme but not an original source of lyricism.

[4] There are no copies of *Légitime Défense* in the Bibliothèque Nationale or other libraries in Paris, but Lero's Manifesto is included in L. Kesteloot's *Anthologie négro-africaine (panorama critique des prosateurs, poètes et dramaturges noirs du XXe siècle)* Verviers, Marabout University, 1976, pp. 76–8. The extract quoted above can be found p. 78.

[5] In Damas's anthology, *Poètes d'expression française* pp. 114–15. An English version by the present author can be found in *Contrast*, South African Quarterly, no. 3, Winter 1961, pp. 40–1.

poetry in French of this first period of protestation was modelled, were elaborated in France. The choice of French was largely a matter of expediency and is not surprising: it was the only *lingua franca* by which the intellectuals of Africa, Madagascar and the Caribbean could communicate (the Black people from the English colonies not associating themselves with the Negritude movement), and even within the African continent these were separated by a multiplicity of vernaculars, complicated by dialects and with no formulated grammars, let alone written literatures. From this necessity the Black poets made a virtue. Both the adoption of the French language and the Marxist doctrines contributed to a certain degree to the great attraction that Surrealist poetry had for the Black writers of the thirties. Bakary Diallo explains this by the liberation that Surrealism offered from the rigorous discipline of formal French syntax: the ellipsis and syntactic licence which the Surrealists made use of in the service of economical poetic expressivity was particularly seductive to a writer composing in a language foreign to his own culture, all the more so when this language has been acquired relatively late, as in Bakary Diallo's own case.

Lero was introduced simultaneously to Marxism and to French Surrealist writing of the twenties. He was convinced that Surrealism alone, and automatic writing in particular, had the power to liberate the Black writer from the taboos imposed by Western cultural traditions and social *mores*, so allowing him to explore his own unconscious, return to his own origins and express the totality of his Black personality, by stripping poetry down to its essentials. Lero is more important as a theorist, as a catalyst even, for the flourishing poetry of the Negritude movement of the thirties and forties than for the application of his own doctrines to his own compositions. In any case, dying at the age of thirty and leaving a very slender body of verse, he did not have the chance to show how his talents might have developed. As far as themes are concerned, the majority of his poems betray more solidarity with suffering and victimized humanity as a whole than with the descendants of Black slaves and all the sons of Africa. This is why Senghor felt it necessary to apologize for Lero's lack of Negro-centricity in his introduction to the ten poems which he included in the 1948 *Anthology*. He writes: 'I do not doubt that, had he lived, he [Lero] would have given us works that would have been more personal, more "Negro", at least more West Indian'.[6]

---

[6] The adjective used by Senghor and the writers quoted above, Damas and Bakary Diallo, is *nègre*. The adoption of the more uncompromising '*noir*' was not yet common among Black intellectuals as it now is. The poems by Lero included in Senghor's *Anthology* will give a good idea of the discrepancy between his theories and his practice of what was to be known as Negritude.

Senghor had no need to make any apology in his introduction to the poetry of Aimé Césaire, Lero's compatriot and junior by four years, the true apostle of Negritude who gave a name to the new gospel and who was amongst its first great exponents. The 'great Black poet', discovered by André Breton in 1943, possessed the mastery of an original poetic expression equal to his dedicated mission and uncompromising message. Surrealism proved that 'miraculous weapon'[7] announced by Damas, ready made for the militant poet. With it he explored new realms of inspiration, making it the normal mode for the poetics of aggressive Negritude for more than a quarter of a century. Although Europe taught Césaire the techniques of Surrealism, he used these to probe the depths of a Black subconscious, a Black experience, pouring forth a torrent of strange, disconcerting, shocking images of an unlimited richness of association. If Césaire's Marxist doctrines also originated in Europe, his total commitment is that of a Black man making common cause with all men of Black complexion and African origins, in poetry of combat that militates against all the wrongs done to their contemporaries and to their forbears. From the beginning of his literary career, that is, from the composition of *Cahier d'un retour au pays natal*, which dates from 1935, although it was not published in France in volume form until 1947, and in his plays and collections of verse which followed, Aimé Césaire affirms his Negritude, his confidence in African values and expresses a vigorous rejection of European cultural assimilation. But he does not reject Europe entirely, nor does he separate men into Black and White, but rather victims and victimizers; innocent and guilty; prisoners and jailer: 'My mouth shall be mouth of the misfortunes that have no mouth my voice the liberty of those who have sunk down in the dungeons of despair...' This is not basically very different from the call of Paul Eluard to poets at the time of the occupation of France: 'The time has come when all poets have the right and the duty to maintain that they are deeply involved in the life of other men, in the life of all men.' Associating himself closely with his contemporary from Senegal, the young Léopold Sédar Senghor, with whom he founded *L'Etudiant Noir* in 1934, Césaire formed the bridge between an existing mediocre poetry from the Caribbean Islands and the new school of poets from Africa proper, who imposed a vigorous, original, Negro-centric expression on their compositions. He is the apostle of their committed Negritude, and this remains the orthodox doctrine of at least one generation of poets from French West and Equatorial Africa before Independence.

The themes adopted by different poets, disciples of this orthodoxy, range

---

[7] *Les Armes miraculeuses* was the title of Aimé Césaire's first volume of poems, published in France in 1946 by Gallimard.

from the aggressively polemical and revolutionary to the subtler intimations of areas of subjectivity supposedly more accessible to Bantu sensitivities than to artists of other origins. We hear in the first instance many voices of Angry Young Men, denouncing the violence, the humiliations, the injustices suffered under colonization in Africa and sometimes in the Mother Country. We also find evocations of a common ancestral past and the expression of pride in the physical attributes of the Negro, including the celebration of the beauty of the Black woman. There is also the manifestation, considered to be peculiar to Black poets, that Peter Guberina calls 'The expression of the concept of a link between things and the interaction of people and things'.[8] However, this perception, this sensitivity to the relationship between the visible and the invisible, the animate and the inanimate, the material and the spiritual, which in any case is characteristic of the Surrealist vision, is part of the gift of many poets and cannot be arrogated to those of one cultural heritage or ethnic origin. One has only to think of Baudelaire aspiring to 'hover over life' and 'effortlessly to understand the language of flowers and voiceless things' or Jules Supervielle, whose ambition was to be able to speak of a horse as a horse would itself in its own language ('parler d'un cheval en cheval'). In fact, the concept of a kinship between man and objects, an invisible link that unites the poet to all forms of nature in the mineral world – rocks, stones, stars, metals – is so basic that he assimilates man into the world of things.

The deliberate effort of the Black poets to liberate their verse from the cultural prescriptions of the colonial West, is extended to language and style as well as to the themes and circumstances of its conception. The rhythms often echo the cadences of the African dance or the beat of the tom-tom, with the almost universal use of free or liberated verse patterns, rather than regular, classical prosody. They adapt the language of Boileau and Mallarmé to the expression of their passionate impulses and imagery, making small use of the French language's traditional facility for abstract expression. Like Hugo, they are more given to hyperbole – which best suggests the vast proportions, the *démesure* of Africa – than to sobriety and precision, and eschew the monochrome in favour of vibrant, variegated colours. The imagery often betrays a strong sensuality and an obsessive sexuality, although this is not the eroticism of the West, but rather, a preoccupation with the sources of life. Imagery is, moreover, often deliberately African in source: in a poetry imbued with animist beliefs and a strong telluric spirit, all the elements have special powers of association, but particularly the earth and all the aspects of the West African and Equatorial landscape,

[8] In 'Structure de la poésie noire d'expression française', an article in *Présence Africaine*, Dec. 1955–Jan. 1956.

from savannah to forest. The forest, especially, is rich in symbolic significance, as the home of spirits and genii of all sorts, while the great rivers are often closely associated with myth and legend, history and an ancestral way of life that has been lost. The referential role of Africa, with its new range of colours, images and sensory impressions, was not introduced into poetry to make concessions to the Western readers' curiosity or taste for exoticism. The poet is not deliberately painting what is alien to the European, but rather expressing a range of experience in which the White man and his civilization are the misplaced elements.

The grammatical and syntactical anarchy which the Black poets inherited from Surrealism also serve to emphasize their divorce from Western values, by cocking a snook at Classical clarity and Cartesian logic. To the best of these Black poets, who thus revitalize the French language, may still be applied the words by which André Breton first evaluated the impact of Aimé Césaire's work in 1941. He spoke of a Black man who 'guides us today into new unexplored territories, establishing new contacts for us as he goes, making us advance as if on flashes of light'.[9] It is to Césaire's example and influence that Negro-African poetry in French owes its new vitality, the expression of lucid faculties in a lyricism that is not hide-bound by any of the conventions of traditional poetic forms. The main criterion is usually musicality – the music of the tom-toms, of the *balafong*, the *kôra*, the rhythms of African dance. 'To sing or not to sing, that is the question', again writes André Breton in his appraisal of the work of Césaire. 'There can be no salvation in poetry that does not sing, although we must ask more of a poet than merely to sing...'

The 'something more' that Breton demands of the true poet was, in the case of Césaire and the Negro-African poets of his generation, the expression of the experiences and emotions of their people, to make the Black poet the deliberate mirror and interpreter of his land, his environment, his people, Black *qua* Black. The Black poet must not reject the indignities, the shame, the misery and degradation of his people's past history of colonization and slavery, but distil out of memories of slave-ship or forced marches a new pride of race and colour, to find its expression in the explicit statement: 'It is a fine and good and legitimate thing to be a Black man.' *Nigra sum et formosa.* In his *Return to my Native Land*, Césaire flung the challenge of the new poetic doctrine into the face of the West and also of his contemporaries who had been content with their literary slavery as with their social subservience.

[9] Preface to *Cahier d'un retour au pays natal*, Bordas, 1947, p. 12. This work is now available in a bilingual edition, with the English title *Return to my Native Land*, Paris, Présence Africaine, 1971. (English version by Emile Snyden.) The above quotation will be found on facing pages 14–15.

To this intellectual and artistic awakening that began in the Antilles, poets of West Africa added their voices. Few of Césaire's African contemporaries or disciples forged as original a verbal instrument, as obedient to all the shades of emotion of a people seething with the unexpressed and suppressed passions of hundreds of years. But, without ever giving way to pure effusions of the heart, their verse continues to express, with greater or lesser success, the gamut of human emotions, from vengeful hatred to *caritas*, from haughty rancour to compassion. Their poetic register ranges from the war-cry to the cry of anguish, from exultation to pity: at the one extreme we have the virulent polemics of David Diop and at the other the persuasive, conciliatory Negritude of Léopold Sédar Senghor. In the following pages I shall comment only on those African poets whose published work can be considered, by as objective standards as possible, to contribute something of recognizable literary value.

LÉOPOLD SÉDAR SENGHOR

LÉOPOLD SÉDAR SENGHOR: *Chants d'ombre*. Paris, Seuil, 1945, o.p. *Hosties noires*. Paris, Seuil, 1948, o.p. *Chants pour Naëtt*. Paris, Seghers, 1948, o.p. *Ethiopiques*. Paris, Seuil, 1954. o.p. *Nocturnes*. Paris, Seuil, 1961 (includes the poems of 'Chants pour Naëtt' now entitled 'Chants pour Signare', but with one of the original poems omitted). *Poèmes*. Paris, Seuil, 1964. (This is the collected works of Senghor, containing all the above, as well as a few unpublished poems and some translations.) *Lettres d'hivernage*. Dakar, Nouvelles Editions Africaines, 1972; Paris, Seuil, 1973, with illustrations by Marc Chagall, limited edition. *Poèmes*. Paris, Seuil, 1973. (New, paperback edition of 1961 collected verse, taking in *Lettres d'hivernage*.)
English translations: *Selected Poems*, Trans. and intr. by John Reed and Clive Wake. London, Ibadan, Accra, O.U.P. 1964. *Nocturnes*, intr. by John Reed and Clive Wake. London, Ibadan, Nairobi, Heinemann, 1969 (African Writers Series) including eight poems first appearing in the *Selected Poems*.

The greatest of Césaire's partners in elaborating the literary creed of Negritude and forging original verse illustrating its principles, was Léopold Sédar Senghor, linguist, classical scholar, statesman as well as poet. While Aimé Césaire expressed the exaltation and militant qualities of Negritude, Senghor's was the voice of gravity and reflection. The one, the descendant of slaves, deliberately aspired to repudiate a tradition of servility; the other, the direct descendant of independent rulers of Africa, was conscious of origins firmly rooted in African soil. Their literary paths converge in a common aim, to be the mouthpiece of their people's ideals: one's is the accent of revolt, the other's, a deep maturer acquiescence in the forces of nature. They complement each other as they both deliberately cultivate a conscious pride in race and colour expressed in poetry that is profoundly African in subject, inspiration and imagery, using supple free verse and the flowing Biblical rhythms that Paul Claudel had introduced into twentieth-century French poetry.

The first Black *agrégé* of France, the first Black poet to see his published work acclaimed unreservedly in France, the first President of the Republic of Senegal, this elder statesman of Independent Africa and the Apostle of Negritude is now less a prophet in his own continent than in Europe and the West. For the average French scholar or cultivated reader, even at the beginning of the seventies, Senghor symbolizes the whole of Negro-African poetry in French. The younger generation of African intellectuals, on the other hand, is beginning to question his poetic reputation, primarily because they contest his political authority. Typical of his critical attitude is Daniel Ewandé's *Vive le Président*, published in 1968. In this satire of 'our decolonized Africas', whose tone ranges from burlesque to vituperation, Ewandé directs most of his barbs against anonymous 'good presidents' (there being no 'bad presidents, only bad tyrants and dictators'). Nevertheless, it is significant that he names Senghor and devotes a whole chapter to him. He attacks with equal virulence his policy of African *Francophonie* – the old Imperial wolf in sheep's clothing – his pedantry and his poetry, this being unrepresentative of Africa and incomprehensible to the masses. If they understand and read French at all, affirms Ewandé, the autochtones prefer La Fontaine and Victor Hugo.

While it is not given to all poets to be Victor Hugo (*hélas*! or *Dieu merci*!?), it must be admitted that Senghor is caviar to the general. But this need be no condemnation: we might compare the popular appeal of a Gerard Manley Hopkins or of a Claudel. Political considerations and ephemeral polemics apart, Senghor is undisputably Africa's greatest French-speaking poet of the twentieth century, to whom numbers of young African scholars are devoting critical studies, their doctoral theses and other publications, adding to the works of exegesis in which European critics had already recognized his original creativity.

Senghor's poetic register ranges from the lyrical to the epic, while the short dramatic poem 'Chaka' indicates that, had he been tempted to follow Claudel in genre as well as in versification, he might have produced great poetic drama. Although from the very first he dedicated himself to the doctrines of the Negritude movement, he is aware that no artist creates in a vacuum and must have literary predecessors. In the 'Post-face' to *Ethiopiques*, he admits the debts he, in common with the other poets of his 1948 anthology, owes to France. Far from denying these, he states that the Black poets should glory in them. For himself, if his allegiance to Africa is visceral, his attachment to France is certainly more than merely cerebral. He remains a 'Bi-Continental', like Jules Supervielle, who coined the term, and it is this divided love that his political enemies cannot forgive.

Senghor's first poems, *Chants d'ombre* [Songs of the shadow], were composed before his mobilization and belong to the period when he was closest to the birth of the Negritude movement and the formulation of its creed. Most of the verse is circumstantial, the inspiration arising from an immediate, personal experience during his life in France, but nourished by the emotional links that he maintains with his homeland. We feel the ambiguity of his situation in France in these pre-War years, and the ambivalence of his sentiments towards his country of adoption. (He had taken French nationality in order to be eligible for the *agrégation* examination.) Expatriated, lonely, often humiliated, eaten up by the desire to impose his Black personality on his writing, and be the mouth-piece of his compatriots, he nevertheless feels a profound empathy for his 'White brothers' and strong ties with the country whose culture he has espoused. The poems of *Chants d'ombre* betray these two currents: resentment and affection; revolt and attraction; nostalgia for the robust, violent aspects of the African landscape and the poet's eye for the discreet luminosity of the French countryside. The poet recognizes his 'Manicheism', his ambivalent attitude towards Europe and France, which runs like a *leitmotiv* through many of the poems of *Chants d'ombre*. We find constantly his efforts, throughout his voluntary expatriation, to fix permanently the images of his birthplace. It is not a question of the normal nostalgia of exile, but the anguish of a Black man torn between loyalty to the new doctrine of Negritude, of which he was one of the main architects, and the irresistible attraction of France and her culture, against which he has consciously to arm himself. Some of the poems are inspired by the threat of war and the first months after mobilization. The autumn of 1939 is associated with the menace of universal carnage and the destruction of a civilization in which Senghor had long believed. But this is at variance with his feeling of having betrayed his origins by having become so perfect an adept of a foreign culture and language. He invokes his native land to wash him clean of all the 'contagion of a civilized man', calls on his 'pagan sap' and ironizes over the incongruity of his situation as a teacher of French in France. The epitome of Senghor's dichotomy can be found in the poem 'Neige sur Paris', written on Christmas Day 1939, and betraying the double inspiration of the date and scene.

In 'Femme noire' there is no ambivalence. This poem, one of the finest that Senghor ever composed, best illustrates what Sartre calls 'the

Annunciation of quintessential Blackness'. It is both a love poem – a paean of praise to a universal mistress – and a glorification of Black Africa herself. The vision is Africa, the symbolism African. Each line presents a wealth of rich, evocative imagery that seems the fruit of a tropical earth. The music is the music of Africa, its indigenous rhythms beat with the thrumming of the tom-toms. Yet all the interlinked themes – love for a woman, love of one's native-land, the passing of beauty and the inevitability of death – have a universality that transcends any committed writing, dedicated only to a transient cause.

Senghor's second volume of poems, *Hosties noires* [Black sacrifices], were composed during the Second World War, mostly as a prisoner of war in Stalag 230. He now assumes his role as the voice of his people, not so much expressing the Black personality as expressing his solidarity with the humblest of the Senegalese riflemen, his brothers-in-arms, whose lot he is sharing as a private soldier and prisoner-of-war. Yet, even so, he is divided between bitterness against the White oppressor and compassion for the sufferings of Europe. His fellow prisoners in the Stalag are French peasants as well as Blacks. He cannot encapsulate himself in an enclave of purely Black victims of White aggression. Moreover, he cannot deny his debt to France. He appreciates the virtues of the French cultural traditions, the love of liberty, the proclamation of equality and fraternity, even if these are not always applied, and the qualities of the women of France particularly, to whom he addresses a panegyric. *Hosties noires* which opens with a proclamation of solidarity with the Senegalese soldiers, and continues to celebrate their endurance and their virtues, also honours the common people of France and the whole of Europe in distress, to end with the moving 'Prayer for Peace'.

After the Liberation Senghor is no longer an exile in France, nor a prisoner sharing the privations of the common soldier, no longer subject to nostalgia or humiliations, but an honoured member of the National Assembly, representing his native Senegal. His sojourn in Paris is now in his capacity as 'Ambassador of the Black races'. The poems of his third volume, *Ethiopiques*, are consequently less personal in theme and inspiration, more rhetorical in style, more deeply impregnated with the colours, the images, the rhythms, the eloquence of Africa. The qualities are best exemplified in the exultant ode to the River Congo, which is the epitome of non-militant Negritude, the model of Negro-centric aesthetics. It is the positive assertion of aggressive pride in Africa and a passionate, visceral attachment to her waters, forests and plains, her flora and fauna. Through the pulsing drum-beat of the verse he expresses sentiments that are at the same time telluric, sensual, erotic, and pious. The great river is queen, mistress, mother, goddess, sorceress. She has life-giving and aphrodisiac powers; she can soothe and invigorate and instil wisdom. Above all, she is the symbol of the immutability of Africa and the permanence of the poet's attachment to his native continent, and the constant counter-force to the lure of Europe, from whose 'spongy soil and smooth, insidious songs' he asks to be delivered.

Ethiopiques also includes the dramatic poem, 'Chaka', commented on in the preceding chapter, and the series entitled 'Epîtres à la Princesse' which invites comparison with Saint-John Perse's 'Anabase', rather than a search for the influence of the French poet, which Senghor has denied. Although the 'Letters to the Princess' are undeniably inspired by a personal relationship – a private friendship – they are not out of harmony with the rest of the works in a volume whose main theme is the author's responsibility as leader of his people and his attachment to his origins. The poet here still speaks unequivocally as 'Ambassador of the Black people' to a sovereign of the North. He expresses his wish to understand her country better so that their two lands may have some link.

As a 'Postface' to *Ethiopiques*, Senghor answers certain criticisms and reproaches, as well as objective questions put by critics and friends about his poetry. He explains the force and 'multivalence' that he attributes to his imagery, the importance of the musicality of his verse, the significance of the so-called exoticism of language and the use of certain figures of speech which he adopts instinctively. He defends his use of French as a poetic medium and expresses his ambition, shared with contemporary Black poets, 'To be the forerunners, those who show the way for an authentic negro poetry, which never abandons its intention to be French.'

Senghor's next volume of poetry was *Nocturnes*. This consists of twenty-four 'Chants pour Signare' originally published in 1949 as *Chants pour Naëtt* and five 'Elegies'.[10] While the inspiration for all the poems of *Nocturnes* is more personal than *Ethiopiques*, they are all firmly rooted in the soil of Africa. The original 'Songs for Naëtt' were love poems addressed to Senghor's first wife, Ginette Eboué. In changing the dedication to the more general 'Signare' (the Creole women of Senegal), he also makes it possible to interpret this cycle of love-poems as addressed to the personification of Africa, in the form of the gracious Senegalese woman (although in doing so he is forced to omit one poem specifically addressed to Naëtt, 'Je veux dire ton nom Naëtt').

The 'Songs for Signare' are among the most moving and beautiful of Senghor's verse and can be ranked with the best of French love poetry.

[10] In fact two of the elegies had already appeared in the review *Présence Africaine* before he became President.

Indeed there are few poets who have succeeded in expressing the depth of a lover's passion with such discretion and sobriety (there is far less sensuality or eroticism in these poems than in many of the other verses, particularly the 'Elegies') and in giving to a personal attachment a universal significance.

The 'Elégies' that complete *Nocturnes* are really odes, intensely personal reflections on the role of the poet, the act of creativity, the desire to reconcile his position as statesman, his responsibilities as a leader with his search for private peace and his need for human relationships. The tone of these poems is elevated as befits the ode, oratorical as befits the voice of the leader, lyrical as befits the subjectivity. They are as rich in African imagery, symbolism and sensuality as any of the poems of *Ethiopiques*, whose rhetorical quality they also share. Many of these elegies suggest echoes of Claudel's *Cinq grandes odes*, similar cadenced litanies, whose rhythm follows faithfully the natural measure of respiration, and whose assonances betray a discreet sensuality. Just as Senghor's 'Congo' can be compared to Claudel's 'Cantique du Rhône', so there are affinities between 'L'Elégie de minuit' and 'Cantique des parfums' from the *Cantique à trois voix*, between 'L'Elégie des eaux' and 'L'Esprit et l'eau' of the Second Ode. While the comparisons with Claudel are compelling,[11] Wake and Reed also suggest correspondences between Senghor's love poems and those of the Renaissance, especially the *dizains* of Maurice Scève and Ronsard's sonnets to Hélène. However, I find more than a hint of the magic of Rimbaud's *Illuminations*, his musicality and richness of evocative associations, in some of Senghor's lines and some striking affinities between his poetic vision and that of Jules Supervielle. These are not limited to the Manicheism of the 'Bi-Continental', already mentioned. Both poets have a preoccupation with the Greco-Latin civilization and a similar spontaneous exoticism enriches the verses of both, born of their close contact with the soil of their birthplace and its flora. Both feel a similar disorientation in the face of time, Senghor's 'I do not know what period it was, I always confuse the present and the past' ('D'autres chants' from *Ethiopiques*, *Poèmes*, p. 149) recalling Supervielle's 'man who has lost his way in the centuries.[12] Both poets

[11] For an extensive study of this subject, I cannot do better than refer the reader to Senghor himself, to the paper that he presented at the Rencontre internationale de la Société Paul Claudel held at Brangues in July 1972. This study entitled 'La Parole chez Paul Claudel et chez les Négro-Africains' was the first text published by the newly-established Nouvelles Editions Africaines, Dakar, in 1972. See also *Nocturnes*, trans. by J. Reed and C. Wake, Heinemann, 1969, their introduction pp. viiff.

[12] In an unpublished dissertation for the degree of Master of Arts, presented in 1959 at the University of Manchester – The function of poetry and primitive psychology in the work of Jules Supervielle' – Louis Allen sees the poet's identity with the primitive mind, as analysed by Lévy-Bruhl. He does not make the comparison with Senghor which I suggest,

published a volume of poems entitled *Nocturnes*, night being a time of special vision for both, when the inner and outer worlds fuse and man can become aware of the secret soul of things; a time of peace too, or a time of insomnia, to be peopled with mythic life. There are also resemblances between the war poems of Senghor and Supervielle, both those inspired in the older poet by the 1914–18 holocaust, and his *Poèmes de la France malheureuse* of 1939–45. In both we find the expression of personal suffering, compassion for the suffering of their fellow-men and fears for the death of a civilization.[13]

BIRAGO DIOP

BIRAGO DIOP: *Leurres et lueurs*. Paris, Présence Africaine, 1960.

When Senghor compiled his *Anthologie de la nouvelle poésie nègre et malgache de langue française*, which appeared in Paris in 1948, he could find only two poets besides himself to represent 'Black Africa' as opposed to ten writers from the Caribbean and three from Madagascar. Neither of these, Birago Diop or his namesake David (no relation), had as yet published a volume of poetry, but the work of both was known to Senghor. Some verses of his friend Birago had appeared in the first numbers of *Présence Africaine* and the first *Tales of Amadou Koumba* had recently been accepted by Fasquelle, but all the verse was not collected for publication until 1960, then with the punning title *Leurres et lueurs* [Snares and gleams].

It must be admitted that the real poetic talent of Birago Diop is best manifested in his short stories, rather than in compositions adopting a conventional poetic form. Most of the verses of *Leurres et lueurs* were written in his youth and are fairly classical in form and derivative in expression. They have a pleasing musicality but do not contribute any striking enrichment to French poetry or Negro-African writing. The best of his poems can be found in the story 'Sarzan' from the *Contes*: the well-known 'Souffles' [Breaths] often quoted for its quintessential expression of African animist communion of all things and all forms of life, and the sinister haunting song of Sarzan-the-Madman, who loses his wits because he despises the traditional beliefs of the community and defies the spirits of the Ancestors. The mad song 'Black Night' has an authentic poetic expressivity as memorable as some of Shakespeare's songs. It would be hard to find verse which evokes so compellingly the atmosphere of

but he sees in Supervielle's concept of the normality of metamorphosis, his sense of the magic inherent in animate and inanimate things, his awareness of the secret soul of things, proofs of his affinity with an African, animist interpretation of the universe.

[13] See page 179, where, in the Conclusion to this chapter, I add a post-script on Senghor's *Letters d'hivernage*, which appeared after this work was completed originally.

powerful supernatural forces abroad. In 'Breaths', Diop expresses the same spirit of non-militant Negritude as in his tales, that is the permanence of Black values and the validity of traditional beliefs to maintain the vigour of an African community in the face of Western logic and pragmatism. Whether a younger generation of Africans will continue to subscribe to this traditionalism is a matter of doubt, but there is no doubt that the haunting music of Birago Diop's cadences will be accepted as an important contribution to the African lyric heritage which for him, like his Tales, is uniformly rooted in the past.

DAVID DIOP

DAVID DIOP: *Coups de pilon*. Paris, Présence Africaine, 1956. o.p. Repr. 1961. Re-issued as Livre de poche, 1973.
  English translation: *Hammerblows and Other Writings*, trans. and ed. by Simon Mpondo and Frank Jones. Bloomington and London, Indiana University Press, 1973. As *Hammer Blows*, trans. S. Mpondo, Heinemann, 1975.

The only other poet whom Senghor could find in 1948 to represent the French colonies of Black Africa was a young man, half Senegalese, half Cameroonian, who had just reached the age of twenty, but whose poems composed since the age of fifteen had been recently appearing in *Présence Africaine*. Nearly a decade later another seventeen short poems, were published in a *plaquette*, entitled *Coups de Pilon* [The pounding of the pestle]. In 1960, four months after he had turned thirty-three, Diop was killed in a plane crash and with him were lost the manuscripts of his unpublished work. We have thus no means of judging how he would have matured from his early promise, as indicated by less than two dozen short poems.

In introducing the five poems of the young Diop which he included in his anthology, Senghor reproaches him for his 'violent expression of an acute racial conscience' and adds

We have no doubt that with age David Diop will understand that what makes the Negritude of a poem is less the theme than the style, the emotional warmth that gives life to words and which transmutes the spoken word into the act of creation [*qui transmue la parole en verbe*]. (*Anthologie de la nouvelle poésie nègre et malgache de la langue française*, p. 173)

From his earliest published works, through the short span of his creative career, Diop showed himself an uncompromising disciple of Aimé Césaire, committed to the most dynamic expression of militant Negritude in poems of combat. Although born in France and partly educated there, he never became a Black Frenchman like René Maran, even less the 'cultural half-caste' that Senghor admitted to being. He reacted violently against his French environment and the French culture to which he had been exposed, with deep hatred for all things European. To him, more than to any other of the West African poets, do Caliban's words apply: 'You taught me language: and my profit on't Is, I know how to curse...' He never saw the 'Suns of Independence' and we cannot tell what inspiration he would have drawn from the more conciliatory climate of decolonized Africa, when his bitter resentments would have had no more to feed on.

In the five poems over which Senghor expressed reproach, Diop calls down Caliban's 'red plague' to rid those who wielded the overseer's lash, those who insulted, raped and killed. Not all of this is poetry, but some of it is very good poetry. It is a passionate attempt to articulate the centuries of pent-up grievances of his fellow-men who have been brutalized and trampled underfoot. This is the 'Cry Rage!' of impotent, seminal desperation, whose only weapon is language, his aim to be, in Césaire's words, 'the mouth of those who have no mouth'. We find similar accents a quarter of a century later in the verse of young South African Black poets.[14] Diop never whimpers his woe; he bellows with rage in his searing agony; he spits out vituperation. This is no 'emotion recollected in tranquility' but the red-hot expression of an unbridled passion. The themes of his poems are now stereotyped in Black prose and poetry, but when David Diop was writing only René Maran's *Batouala* had appeared. Ferdinand Oyono had still to publish his 'Houseboy' and Mongo Beti his *Ville cruelle*.

It is undoubtedly easier to write a novel of protest than protest poetry. The question remains as to whether 'poetry' and 'protest' are not self-negating terms. Is poetry a medium for polemics? The more dialectical the theme, the more the verse must be endowed with some special magic to lift it above pamphleteering, to evoke in the reader a range of emotions and reactions that are beyond the power of the same message expressed in prose. Even the clarity which is essential to the success of literature of combat, however ironical the mode, is the enemy of pure poetry, to which some shreds of mystery must adhere. It is not enough to understand, to share the agony; it is not enough to be convinced that the cause is just. Poetry is not functional, as Sartre claimed in his 'Black Orpheus' essay. A newspaper editorial is functional, and may be more use in immediately

---

[14] *Cry Rage!* is the title of a collection of poems by the South African Cape Coloured writers James Matthews and Gladys Thomas, published by Spro-Cas, Johannesburg, in 1972. It is banned in South Africa. Matthews writes: 'I record the anguish of the persecuted/ whose words are whimpers of woe/ wrung from them by bestial laws./ They stand one chained band/ silently asking one of the other/ will it never be the fire next time?'

combatting an evil than a poem. Anything that is purely functional has a built-in destructive element, since functions change with changing times. To-day's functions are tomorrow's redundancies. To lift his protest poem above the immediacy of the present, or the historical interest of the past, the poet must offer an aesthetic experience, in the best sense of the word. He must extend the reader's vision, enrich his inner being. The heart of the poem must go on beating when the last echoes of the call to action have died down.

Some of these first poems of Diop read twenty-five years later seem nothing more than a safety-valve for letting off the steam of indignation. But in some lines (rarely the whole poem), he achieves this extra dimension, as in 'The Time of Martyrdom', where the stark simplicity of language does conjure up a race's anguish. The poem that begins unpromisingly with 'You're only a nigger' has a greater poetic impact still. Here, the economy of expression has the power to suggest larger vistas of association. The irony has a multifaceted quality. We realize after the brutal opening lines that the perspective is continually changing, like a film shot from several angles. Gradually Diop the Black poet has intercepted the White man's words and is gradually, subtly, turning the invective into an apologia. The origin of each assertion ricochets backwards and forwards between denunciation and self-identification, leading up to the final ambiguity of: 'And let my pity fall away/ Before the horror of the sight of you.'

These few glimpses of promising, original talent were substantiated by *Coups de pilon*, on which David Diop's reputation as the most striking new voice in poetry of the fifties rests. Here shows a mastery of the crescendo effect, more musicality of rhythms, wider, subtle revelations in his imagery. The themes, too, are more varied with a greater gamut of tonalities, the 'cry pierced through with violence' alternating with 'the song guided by love alone'. The emotions expressed are more varied, transcending the nihilism of hate to assume a greater human appeal, as in the poem 'Hours' which paraphrases Ecclesiasticus. There is also a greater variety of rhythms which often have a robust vitality, manifesting the very Negritude of style that Senghor reproached his work with lacking. In 'To a Black Dancer', which seems of all David Diop's poems to bear the greatest imprint of Senghor's own work, we find dance-like cadences, repetitions which recall the litanic sequences of oral literature, sonorous effects based on warm, round vowels and long, sibilant and fricative consonants, which insidiously evoke the luxuriant life of tropical Africa.

Nevertheless the tender notes and the sensual lyricism are still rarer than the urgent militancy of the call to action. The essential message pounded out by the pestle, like the beat of the talking drums, is an admonishment not to forgive or forget the past of the slave-gang, forced-labour gang, rapine, lynchings and brutal murder. In 'The Vultures', Diop recalls the wrongs done in the name of 'civilization' by colonizers and missionaries, raptorial creatures who battened on the 'mutilated body of Africa'. 'The True Path' is typical of his expression of the 'Them and Us' attitude and his solidarity with the struggle of his African brothers for liberation and fulfilment. The poem 'Listen Comrades...' celebrates one of the martyrs of colonialism, based on the death of Mamba, a venerable, white-headed man, the symbol of all the victims of blind brutality, whose memory should be an inspiration to young African revolutionaries. The two most striking of the militant poems of *Coups de pilon* are 'Africa' and 'Nigger Tramp'. In the first he asks what is the true identity of this Africa he has known so little; is it the old submissive victim of wrongs and injustices? The poem ends on a positive note, a reasoned dialogue, with hope for the future having the last word.

'Nigger Tramp', the longest of all the poems, is dedicated to Aimé Césaire and its flow of violent imagery recalls the Martiniquan's 'Return to my Native Land'. This poem is a fitting climax and conclusion to the little volume. Its themes sum up all the preceding verses; its allusions range over the whole panorama of Black history, from the great warrior kings of Bantu tribes through the Calvary of slaving days and the indignities and ignominy of the colonial present to the hopes of a future, which David Diop will not live to see, when

> we shall rebuild Ghana and Timbuktu
> And refashion guitars inhabited by pounding hoofs
> Echoing the sonorous pounding of the pestles
> Of pestles
> Resounding
> From hut to hut
> In the promise of dawn.

Although still conscious of the urgency of his message, the poet now lends to its expression a mythic aggrandizement which brings his poetry to the frontiers of universal significance. Then the militant voice of the revolutionary does not stifle the accents of the true poet. But the examples are rare in the work that his short life allowed him to realize.

BERNARD BINLIN DADIÉ

BERNARD BINLIN DADIE: *Afrique debout!* Paris, Seghers, (Coll. P.S.) 1950. o.p. *La Ronde des jours.* Paris, Seghers, 1956 (Cahiers P.S., publiés par 'Poésie 56', no. 476) o.p. Both the above collections are included in: *Légendes et poèmes*. Paris, Seghers, 1966. *Hommes de tous les continents*. Paris, Présence Africaine, 1967.

Bernard Dadié whom we have met as a narrator of folk-tales and as a dramatist, actually began his serious literary career as a poet, if we discount his experiment with drama for the William Ponty productions.

Ten years Senghor's junior, Dadié still belonged to the first aggressive period of the Negritude movement to which the title of these poems bears witness. He differed, however, from his near contemporaries – Senghor, Birago Diop, the Caribbean poets – in that he never frequented the milieux of the young Black intellectuals and artists in Paris who formulated the theories of the movement. His link with the architects of Negritude came when he met Alioune Diop, the founder of the review *Présence Africaine* soon after the Liberation of France. But while fellow West Africans talked in Paris of a literary emancipation from cultural colonization, Dadié was active in his homeland in the fight against oppression. He had joined the Democratic Party of Ivory Coast after the War, and in a series of articles rallied his compatriots to struggle for Independence. In 1949 he was arrested and imprisoned for his political activities. *Afrique debout!* appeared soon after his release.

Dadié's formative years were spent solely in Africa and France is never present in his poetry, as in Senghor's, vying with Africa for part of his allegiance. But he is always objectively fair in his recognition of the virtues of France – *la France généreuse* – whom he exonerates from the crimes committed in her name by the colonists. 'How can people exercise oppression', he asks, 'in the name of a nation which was the first to take up arms against tyrants and oppressors?' His first poems formed a long litany of protest against colonial domination and a call to arms to his people: 'Africa arise!' But, committed poet that he was, he eventually took as his profession of faith the axiom of Marshal Lyautey whom he much admired:

The man who is solely a soldier is a bad soldier; the man who is solely a teacher is a bad teacher; if he is solely a manufacturer, he is a bad manufacturer. The whole man must shine his lamp on all that is the honour of the human race.

This can be interpreted as: If a man is solely a committed poet, he runs the risk of being a bad poet.

Dadié, who aspires to being a whole man, a whole poet, saves his talent from being engulfed in anger and bitterness like David Diop's. The message of his commitment is positive, but in the last resort he remembers Lyautey's lesson and in the best of his poems we find the accents of the complete man, an echo of something that transcends Black chauvinism, a fraternity that realizes that it knows no national frontiers.

This maturer philosophy, this greater serenity is not present in the first volume of poems; nor is Dadié's full command of poetic expression. There is much truculence and not overmuch poetry in verses where it is a question of 'seizing the warmongers [the colonists] by the scruff of the neck' or of 'telling our torturers what we think of them' (Fidélité à l'Afrique'). This may be good demagogy, a stirring call to action in the cause of patriotism and liberty, but Eluard did it in much better poetry. Although in his prefatory poem he advocates 'following the rhythm of your blood', he does not succeed in bringing new accents, new rhythms or the imperative voice of suffering to these first verses.

Four years later, in the poems of *La Ronde des jours*, we perceive the poet through the chinks in the armour of the militant. This volume contains one of the most moving and dignified of the protest poems of Negritude, 'I thank you, O Lord, for having created me Black'. In a mixture of defiance before men and humility before God, without the earlier truculence, Dadié flaunts those physical aspects of the Negro which are traditionally despised according to Western aesthetics: round head, flat nose, thick lips. But this is more than a variation on the theme 'black is beautiful'. With haunting rhythms and a mastery of verbal music, with a range of imagery that extends the scope of the theme in ever-widening circles, Dadié brings to all readers the sense of the suffering and forebearance of a race that can be considered the 'sum of all man's sorrows'. Dadié's poem is also a prayer in an accent of sincere piety that is rare in his work: not an entreaty or a supplication, but the expression of pious resignation. He accepts that the creation of the Black people and their sufferings must have some part in God's design for the world. Was this purpose, he asks, only to be the accursed scape-goat, the sacrificial lamb? Was the Black man's destiny to be a permanent martyr, a Saint Sebastian pierced with arrows of hatred, a new Christ whose Calvary will bring redemption to the world? It is interesting that nowhere in the poetry of Senghor, the Classical scholar and deeply pious Catholic, do we find such a concentration of Greek mythological allusions and Christian imagery as in this poem of Dadié's: the centaur, half-man, half-horse, doomed to extermination (was not the Negro-slave treated worse than a beast of burden?); the god Atlas, condemned to carry the world on his shoulders; old Testament allusion, too, to the Creation of the world. The emphasis is, through Hebraic, Greek or Christian symbolism, on the Black man's inextricable part in the destiny of universal man.

One other poem of *La Ronde des jours* will illustrate the development of Dadié's poetic expression, his accession to a universal tonality – the one with the first line, 'We are the ones who meet cold stares'. In this poem

there is no epithet, no allusion, no image that specifically applies to the
Black man. Until the last stanza, with the association of Night and
Mystery, there is not a single indication of sable hue or reference to the
Dark Continent. A reader faced with this text for the first time would have
no means of identifying the voice of the Negro amongst the chorus of the
rejected, the have-nots, the anonymous outcasts of society: cripples and
beggars, the embarrassments of the privileged. Dadié again expresses the
sober challenge of 'We thank Thee, O Lord', once more inviting the White
reader to a new vision of the human condition, compassionate and devoid
of prejudice. He now uses little imagery, next to no abstractions and the
rhythm of the verse is almost imperceptible, needing the support from time
to time of an irregular rhyme pattern. The result is that the poem is a harsh
litany of suffering and ignominy, expressed in terms of concrete reality that
increases the immediacy of the message. We find in this poem, which
finished on an optimistic note, echoes of a Villon, speaking in the name
of all beggars, vagabonds and outcasts.

Bernard Dadié's poetic talent is uneven. He never achieves the sonorous
eloquence of a Senghor, but he avoids that poet's pedantry, his message
being more directly accessible to the literate African who might read
French. Since the publication of *La Ronde des jours* in 1956, he seems to
have felt that prose, specifically travel chronicles and drama offer him a
greater scope and a greater range of expressivity, although one of his plays,
Les Voix dans le vent, betrays the voice of the poet. In 1967 he published
a new volume of verse, *Hommes de tous les continents*, [Men of all the
continents], mostly written since the dawn of Independence. These poems
exemplify the maturing of his philosophy, his humanism, and illustrate
his command of subtler poetic effects. The title alone indicates that the
author is now liberated from the necessity to militate in the name of Africa
alone. The poem which gives its title to the volume (written in May 1960)
sums up the universal fraternity which Dadié can now envisage. Gone is
the barrier between 'Them and Us'. The poet speaks for all men, from
the beginning of time and from all corners of the earth, but particularly
for those who have known the purification and regeneration of toil, hunger,
fire and bloodshed.

In the 'Dialogue with the Poet', which Quillateau published in 1967 in
his study of Dadié, we have the poet's own explanation of how he came
to the first poetic forms adopted in *Afrique debout!* He also explains the
inspiration he received from the publication in a Dakar periodical in 1942
of the poem entitled 'Coups de pilon' by David Issa (David Diop, then
aged fifteen). It was this poem that gave him the impetus to start composing
in free verse the poems that comprise his first volume, for which he did

not find a publisher until 1950. He deliberately attempts in his verses to capture the pounding of the pestles, the stamping feet, the clapping hands of an African community, by staccato effects, accumulation of monosyllables, a preference for harsh plosive or palatal consonants, sharp, closed vowels. If we then compare the later poems of *Hommes de tous les continents*, we find at the same time an expression of wider fraternity, and the maturing of his poetic talent with his human warmth. His versification takes on a greater suavity; the conciliatory mood is translated by more whispering sibilants, the polyphonic harmonies of round and nasal vowels and discreet alliterations replace the staccato monosyllables and the lack of resonance of the earlier verses. He still uses anaphora to emphasize the liturgical, litanic dignity of his message. He takes up the themes of the two poems we have quoted above, 'I thank you, O Lord, for having created me Black' and 'We are the ones. . .'. It is the history of centuries of suffering and the role of the Black man in the design of the universe, and the universal fraternity of humankind. The sober nudity, almost prosaic expression of 'Nous sommes de ceux' devoid of any imaginative effects, is now replaced by a far-reaching play of highly-charged images, which give a wider range to the vision, while retaining a great economy of form.

Although he took his first inspiration from David Diop, and he was often moved by righteous indignation at the ignominies suffered by colonized Black Africa, his verse never borrowed the accents of hate and anger of the younger man. His humanism, which owed much to his sincere piety, has matured along the lines of Senghor's. Like the statesman–poet, he does not deny the debt he owed to France; he has a poem entitled 'What France has given to me' which ends with 'She has awakened in my heart the love of mankind'. He is never blind to injustice or continued wrongs, but inspired by Christian beliefs, he expresses an inherent faith in human nature and the possibility of understanding, indeed of love, uniting people of different races. Dadié's poetic talent is infinitely more limited than Senghor's as is the compass of his poetic compositions. His verse has not the musicality, the compulsive rhythmic force, the command of compelling imagery, all Africa-based, nor the deep mysticism which forms the link between a pragmatic present and an animist past. On the other hand Dadié's verse is more realist, more accessible to the average reader. No Ewandé could reproach him with being incomprehensible even to the masses – provided that they read French. The best of his verses have a moving quality, based on their sincerity and simple persuasive lyricism which makes it a matter of regret that he has not written more poetry.

PAULIN JOACHIM

PAULIN JOACHIM: *Un Nègre raconte*. Paris, Edition des poètes, 1954. o.p. *Anti-grâce*.
Paris, Présence Africaine, 1967.

Paulin Joachim also takes some inspiration from David Diop, dedicating
one of the poems of his second volume to his memory, but although some
of Joachim's poems are tinged with bitterness, there is more melancholic
nostalgia than acerbity. Indeed Sartre's definition of Negritude as expressing a tension between a nostalgic past and a future giving way to new values
(see p. 143 above) aptly describes the verse of Paulin Joachim at his best.
So strongly do the poems of *Anti-grâce* reconstitute what is considered to
be the essence of Africa's past identity that they seem to belong (though
the date of composition of all but one clearly belies this) more to the
pre-Independence period than to the second half of the 1960s.

After his early collection, *Un Nègre raconte*, which never took full flight,
Joachim devoted himself to journalism. His second volume shows a much
surer lyric vein, clothing a message, half-nostalgic, half-challenging, in free
verse that evokes in its heavy cadences the burden of being Black and a
yearning for the simple spontaneity of an evanescent Africa. The poem
'Femme noire, ma mère', written in Paris in 1953, best sums up the
ambivalence of the Black expatriate poet who takes as his mission to
constitute himself the memory of Africa, the witness to his continent and
his people's existence, and who is penetrated with a sense of guilt for having
abandoned his birthplace and his people. Not only is the title reminiscent
of Senghor: there is a similar though more elusive sensuality, the similar
insistent affirmation of the anaphora, woven into the intermittence of the
beat and echoing the pulsating life-blood of Africa.

> I see you Mother felinely soft and supple
>
> . . . .
>
> O Mother I see you dressed like your sisters in brief loin-cloth
> drawing telluric strength from the baptismal waters
> I see you at the evening mass
> I see you Mother lost in mystic algebraic contortions
> I see you splendid breaking into the dance
> with ceaselessly swaying hips
> you are a blazing ripple at the foot of the *houngan*
> and seemingly bonelessly supple beneath strong spices...
>
> (*Anti-grâce*, pp. 51–2)

There is more suggestion of bitterness at his exile, more poignancy and
more original expressivity in the imagery when he celebrates the dawn of
Independence in 'Pour saluer l'Afrique à l'envol rendu libre' [Salute to
Africa, freed and on the wing].

they thought themselves cunning the architects of my absence
believing they had buried me forever in distant suburbs
on the periphery of life but the tunnel of death
soon became for me a summit and I found to my hand
a torch which lit up my flailing arms
as I painfully swam through those waters
condemned as I was to anihilation

.   .   .   .

and I say that this torch of salvation
that this sensuous incandescence of affliction

.   .   .   .

I say that this torch was a defiance to ashes
the resurrection already the victory held out to a people

.   .   .   .

(ibid., pp. 16–17)

The title poem of the collection, dated Paris 1965, suggests the hesitancies
and disillusionments of a poet's hyper-sensitive and solitary essence, exacerbated by his Black inferiority in a White-orientated society. If the
message seems curiously archaic in the mid-60s, it shows that a life-time's
experience has left deep furrows of melancholy on a poet's mind and soul
which the reversion of a political régime cannot efface. A quotation from
this poem will best sum up Joachim's inspiration and his art:

...I call this anti-grace
this life of crumbs and little words
which dredge up doubt to the skin's surface at the moment of leaping
I dreamed of a locomotive
drawing headlong a train of stars

but I did not count on this anti-grace
which condemns me to a long dying solitude
on the straw of an agricultural show ·
I had had pre-natal dreams of becoming a prince not a yokel

I call this anti-grace
my face infernal unwanted on the Broadway of pleasures
like suddenly recognized shame
the typhoon of loving rivetted to the slow toil of the miner
and the world around which insists on itemizing my infamy
while I make frantic eyes till I lose my sight.

(ibid., pp. 22–3)

MALICK FALL

MALICK FALL: *Reliefs* (Poèmes), Paris, Présence Africaine, 1964. Preface by Léopold Sédar Senghor.

Some of what are presumably earlier poems in Malick Fall's only published volume to date also show that indignation and rebellion associated with the disciples of the short lived David Diop. But the majority of the verses of *Reliefs* anticipate the existential conflicts, the themes and ideals contained in Fall's novel *La Plaie* [The wound], that appeared three years later.

The first part of *Reliefs*, headed *Soi-même* [Oneself] expresses the search for identity and self-affirmation – a search for authenticity, too – which was not only a feature of the Negritude doctrine, but, on a more universal level, a characteristic of Fall's hero Magamou Seck. These poems reaffirm the very principles of Negritude while, at the same time, lending poetic form and accents to that passionate devotion to freedom and obedience to the imperatives of human dignity that are basic to his 'Man-with-the-ulcerated-wound'. Reflecting as he does the twilight before the dawn of Independence (notwithstanding the publication date of 1964), the poet rejects specious exoticism, rejects the role-playing imposed on the Black man under colonial domination and, in verses more austere, less rich in evocative imagery than Paulin Joachim's, proclaims the right of every man to his personal dignity and the control of his own destiny.

If, as we can reasonably presume, the four parts of *Reliefs* correspond roughly to the chronological order of composition, then Malick Fall's poetic inspiration evolved from the defiance of Negritude to a more objective representational portrayal of African life in Part II (more neutrally subtitled *Touches*), which is still, however, consistent with the earlier Negritude commitments. The next section, *Sentiments*, betrays an awareness of changing times and new contingencies, presented in many cases with wry irony. The last part, aptly entitled *Communion*, sings of universal emotions, jealousy, pity, dreams of love, occasional nostalgia, reactions to simple things and human miseries. These are grouped around a key poem, 'Toute la Terre' (pp. 81–2), which expresses the poet's ultimate panphilia, when the whole world invites him to its 'feast of darkness' and he accepts to love all things in their own way.

The title poem of Part III, 'Sentiments' (p. 68) forms the bridge between the poems of compassion and those of indignation at social evils and the suffering caused to man by man. The scene could be the market-place that is to be Magamou Seck's haunt, where he scrabbles for scraps in dust-bins with beggars who knot rags about their naked limbs chapped with cold. The poet is revolted at the inhuman humiliating sight, concluding:

> I know nothing more atrocious
> Than Truth silent at bay
> Than Justice denied
> Swollen Pride
> And Love rejected.

Even at his most deeply committed, when his soul is seared by suffering and injustice, Fall refuses himself the indulgence of hyperbole or hysteria. A conscious and controlled artist, he gains his effects by irony, by rare and economical images, by one strident note in a monochord melody, by one loaded word as a climax to a sober litany or by the deliberate anticlimax of a bathetic understatement. He uses for the most part regular rythmic patterns, bare rhymes interspersed with assonance, much imitative harmony, and those devices loved by African poets – alliterations, particularly of dentals and plosive consonants which reproduce the beating of the African drums, combined with the insistence of anaphora to drive home the urgency of the message.

The following quotations, in which I have tried to render the stylistic effects, as well as a translation can permit, are typical of Malick Fall's themes and his austere poetics. 'Experience', from Part 1, expresses the proud dignity of a man arrogating to himself the right to choose his own humility, but not to be patronizingly exploited or humiliated:

> I shall not be a watchman,
> Nor a junior clerk,
> I shall be no man's chauffeur
> No man's messenger
> I shall not be a slave nor a factotum
> Nor overseer to a convict gang of rebels
>
> I am worker
> If I choose
> A peasant
> If I please
> Opprobrium in my entrails
> Jeering at your royalties...

> > > (*Reliefs*, pp. 28–9)

Then Fall can be lyrical, either to express his personal emotions, as in the song of disillusion called 'Distress' (p. 35) or to underline the irony of 'Plus Rien' [Nothing left] which sings of the destructiveness of periods of transition, in a dirge to lost innocence:

> I shall no longer offer to the wheedling breeze
> My modest breasts of a barbarian woman
> They say it is indecent

I shall no longer offer my sepia skin
To April's kindly sun
They say it is absurd

I shall no longer offer my ebony arm
To my companions in the tom-tom dance
They say it is unseemly

I shall no longer offer my amber songs
To the night torpor presaging the storm
They say it is eccentric

I shall no longer offer cascades of laughter
To the tenacious silence of tormented hours
They say it is improper.

(ibid., p. 63)

SOME SECONDARY VOICES

KEITA FODEBA: *Poèmes africains.* Paris, Seghers, 1950. Repr. 1958. *Aube africaine.*
    Paris, Seghers, 1952.
MARTIAL SINDA: *Premier chant du départ.* Paris, Seghers, 1955.
JOSEPH MIEZAN BOGNINI: *Ce dur appel de l'espoir.* Paris, Présence Africaine, 1960.[15]
FRANCIS BEBEY: *Embarras & Cie, nouvelles et poèmes.* Yaoundé, Edit. CLE, 1970.

Of the minor voices added to the small band of African poets writing in French in the fifties and sixties, we have already mentioned Keita Fodeba in the chapter dealing with folk-lore. He revived in French the poetry of the oral tradition in which a chanted narrative and chorus was combined with dancing. His themes are simple, usually recounting the charms of a tranquil rural existence, expressed in a rather facile lyricism. Prolonging a traditional form of oral expression which he translated into French, he does not bring innovations of theme or poetic form into his verses.

Martial Sinda, from the Republic of Congo-Brazzaville, has published only one small volume of poetry, also rooted in rural life, tribal traditions, beliefs and local lore, in which an extreme simplicity of expression is combined with a spontaneity which gives the impression of a ritual incantation, translated from the vernacular.

Joseph Bognini is a young poet of promise from Ivory Coast whose verses have a more sophisticated expression and his themes a deeper significance than Sinda's. He draws his primary inspiration from his native land, exalting the beauty of nature and the grandeur of cosmic forces; but he adds a personal, melancholy note – an introverted subjectivity rare in French African poetry, which tends to eschew what Sartre had called

---

[15] Bognini published another volume, *Herbe féconde*, P. J. Oswald, 1974, too late for comment
to be included in this work.

'effusions of the heart'. His images are fresh and his rhythms lightly musical. His expression of personal emotions sung in a minor key and his appreciation of the sensual appeal of nature make Bognini one of the few neo-Romantic poets, of French-speaking Africa.

Francis Bebey is known as a poet, musician, musicologist, novelist and short-story writer. His poems have appeared in periodicals since the late fifties, but he has not published any single volume in verse. Each of the short stories in the collection entitled *Embarras & Cie* is followed by a poem which echoes the theme, sometimes personal, sometimes traditional, in which fantasy, humour, reverie and serious reflections all meet. Bebey is a very articulate artist, completely at home in a Western cultural environment in which he mainly lives. But he retains a deep loyalty to the artistic traditions of his origins in the Cameroon. The humour, the fantasy and the light-hearted irony of much of his writing belie his seriousness as a disciple of an enlightened neo-Negritude school, less portentous than its predecessors and stripped of all militancy, which the situation in any case no longer demands.

GÉRALD FÉLIX TCHICAYA U TAM'SI

GÉRALD FÉLIX TCHICAYA U TAM'SI: *Le Mauvais Sang.* Paris, Edit. Caractères, 1955. o.p. *Feu de brousse.* Paris, Edit. Caractères, 1957. o.p. *A triche-cœur.* Paris, Edit. Hautefeuille (Caractères), 1958. Re-issued P. J. Oswald (Coll: J'exige la parole) 1960. o.p.

(All three above titles reprinted in one volume by P. J. Oswald, 1970. Coll. 'L'Aube dissout les monstres'.)

Epitomé. Les mots de tête pour le sommaire d'une Passion. Tunis, Société Nationale d'Edition et de Diffusion (Coll: L'Aube dissout les monstres) 1962. *Le Ventre.* Paris, Présence Africaine, 1964. o.p. *Arc musical*, preceded by *Epitomé.* Honfleur, P. J. Oswald (Coll: P. J. O. Poche) 1970.

English translations: *Brush fire*, by Sangadore Akanji. Ibadan, Mbari publ., 1964. *Selected poems*, trans. and intr. by Gerald Moore. London, Ibadan, Nairobi, Heinemann Educational Books (African Writers Series), 1970.

With Tchicaya U Tam'si we find a poet who stands alone and high above all his contemporaries and elders in the field of French-African verse, by the sheer quantity of his poetic output, the incontestible superiority of his talents to all except Senghor's and by the great originality of his themes and expression. An extremely independent personality, Tchicaya has denied conscious allegiance to the positive doctrines of the Negritude movement enunciated by Senghor and Césaire, and which provided the motor force for the resurgence of Black poetry in the years before and immediately following the Second World War. At the Dakar Conference on African literature, in March 1963, his answer to the question about his attitude to Negritude, in relation to what he says in his poetry, is unambiguous:

That [the question] implies that Negritude can be discerned in my poetry. I have said before that my Negritude was unconscious, or at least involuntary . . . The way to analyse African writing nowadays is perhaps to follow a method of literary criticism very common in the nineteenth century, which involved defining a man's position first by reference to his works and only afterwards by reference to other criteria. This may suggest something to my questioners. And now let us have done with this question of Negritude once and for all. (*African Literature and the Universities*, ed. G. Moore, Ibadan University Press, 1965, p. 62)

Four years later, at the African–Scandinavian Writer's Conference held in Stockholm, he disavowed quite categorically any association with militant movements, partisan activities, or the writer's responsibility to a cause.

In 1946 the fifteen-year-old Gérald Félix Tchicaya accompanied his father to Paris, when the latter was elected as the first Deputy to represent Congo-Brazzaville at the National Assembly. He has made his permanent home there ever since, as a voluntary exile from Africa, adopting the name of Tchicaya U Tam'si. In spite of his protestations of 'disengagement', he has been by no means indifferent to the fate of his homeland. On the contrary, his verse shows a deep concern for past exploitations and the dissensions that were rending both Congos during most of the period that he was writing his six collections of poems. He is thus associated with neo-Negritude ideals on the basis of solidarity with the country of his origins and the Africanity of his style. But again this does not encapsulate him in a Black world. He shows himself a disciple of Senghor in the universality of his basic message which, once it has been deciphered – and the Surrealist techniques which he uses, like Césaire, make his work even more hermetic than the latter's – will be found not to be addressed solely to men of black complexion. He adds, moreover, an element unknown before in Black poetry, although less rare in the folk-tale and the novel: humour – from puns to Rabelaisian, insolent farce (Bebey's humour is more ironic, more urbane). Senghor, in his preface to the collection *Epitomé*,[16] speaks of 'Negro laughter, Negro humour', by means of which 'the poet has reached forgiveness'. These positive, regenerative, redeeming powers accorded to laughter remind us of Dadié's 'And my laughter over the World, in the night, creates the day'. But this is not specifically an African prerogative. In the case of Tchicaya, his particular form of humour,

---

[16] This preface is only found in the 1968 Oswald edition which is out of print. It is unfortunately not included in the re-edition of *Epitomé* together with *Arc musical* in the 1970 Oswald edition.

together with his frank sexuality, which sometimes borders on obscenity, gives us some pure Rabelais, whose humour is also therapeutic. This is especially the case in *Le Ventre*, a sort of tragi-comedy in verse, with the Belly as the main protagonist. But the main objection against Senghor's judgement, apart from the fact that he has a facile habit of pigeon-holing characteristics as 'African' to suit his thesis, is that in Tchicaya's case the humour, the laughter, is not so much an instrument for forgiveness as an armour for his own protection.

With the exception of the first volume, *Le Mauvais Sang*, and the last, *Arc musical*, Tchicaya's works are not collections of independent poems, united under a more or less arbitrary title, but sequences of verses developing the one unifying theme of the title, sometimes having an elementary narrative line – somewhat like Césaire's *Return to my Native Land*, to which the Surrealist techniques also ally U Tam'si's work. His first two volumes date from the end of the colonial era – 1955 and 1957 respectively. The appearance of this third volume, *A triche-cœur*, coincided with the Independence of the Congo in 1960. The last three belong to the first post-Independence decade, with nothing new since 1969. The titles indicate neither an indictment, nor a cry for vengeance. Only one, *Feu de brousse* [Bush fire], owes any semantic association with the continent of Africa. *Epitomé* is subtitled 'The synopsis of a passion' which is the Calvary of the Congo. The title of *Le Ventre* betrays the visceral aspects of its contents: that of *Arc musical* the more purely lyrical character of this latest collection to date of Tchicaya's poetry.

The title of his first volume of poetry, published when he was twenty-four, betrays the inspiration that he drew from Rimbaud. In this respect his own testimony adds to the clear evidence offered by his work.[17] Twenty-eight of the thirty-five poems are rhymed sonnets, mostly classical in form. The final piece which sums up the volume under the title 'Le Signe du mauvais sang', a longish prose poem, brings us back to Rimbaud by its form – that of the *Illuminations* – as well as by the theme. (It is of interest to remember that Rimbaud gave his work the provisional titles of 'Livre païen' or, alternatively, 'Livre nègre', eventually abandoned in favour of 'Mauvais Sang'.) It can be said that almost a century before Tchicaya, Rimbaud had been responsible for a kind of 'Negritude in reverse', calling himself a representative of 'the inferior race', a 'Nigger', and invoking his 'pagan blood'. There is also to be found in Rimbaud this same preoccupation with racial memory which characterizes the first generation of Black poets writing in French. We shall see that Tchicaya returns to this Rimbaldian

[17] See U Tam'si's statement at the Dakar Conference, *African Literature and the Universities*, p. 63.

inspiration in *A triche-cœur*, where we find a struggle between Christianity and paganism comparable to that expressed in Rimbaud's 'Mauvais Sang'.

This conflict is not yet apparent in Tchicaya's *Le Mauvais Sang*. These verses explore the personal experience of the poet as he opens his heart, practising a kind of vivisection of the soul and putting the whole of his existence to question. The major themes are *ennui*, oblivion, love, solitude, twilight – a compound of Baudelaire and Verlaine as well as echoes of Rimbaud, but always saved from pastiche by the very personal irony and the original Surrealist imagery. He also clearly has started on the first stage of a *voyage en soi*, an inner Odyssey, which he will continue throughout all his subsequent verse. Only occasionally, in this volume, does he allow us a discreet glimpse of the humiliations peculiar to the Black Man's condition, among the areas of distress of any sensitive young poet, particularly in the frequent image of the bastard, the universal symbol of the pariah. However, nowhere in this volume do we find any cry of revolt, only the urgent need to understand his own condition which he announces in the prefatory poem. Finally, he arrogates to himself, the Black man, born with the curse of this bad strain of blood, the right to pride, the vice of 'men of honest fortunes'.

For his next volume, *Feu de brousse*, Tchicaya takes as his inspiration and key theme a mythic journey to his native land, 'Across time and river'. exploring an Africa which is a reservoir of metamorphoses, with a fabulous fauna, where everything is part of a continually shifting pattern of evolution. And the poet inevitably finds his place in the changing landscape with its inhabitants who undergo a constant mutation. From this landscape of tropical Africa the poet distils the characteristic symbols which will recur from poem to poem and link this volume with his subsequent works. Foremost among these are the basic elements of fire and water: not only rivers, cascades, torrents and dew, but also tears, sweat, sperm and briny water crystallized into salt. The fire of the title is the source of life, of purification and of destruction, and also a barrier between man and man. There is still much of Rimbaud in these poems which express the anguish of a man torn between despair and a desire to love (love being, as with Rimbaud, still to be re-invented) but this is a long step from the spleen and neo-Romantic melancholy with echoes of Verlaine of the first volume.

The next one, *A triche-cœur*, comprises six poems loosely connected by recurring images, themes and echoing lines, to form one long, mystic legend. The main motif is the personal isolation of the poet, the man who has lost his way, taking up again the pilgrimage of *Le Mauvais Sang*, but expressed in greater depth, in a surer, more precise style in which the versification is at once freer and more illusive. The key themes, which lend the mythic scope to these poems are exile, hunger, thirst, doubt, searching, the orphan (replacing the bastard of the earlier poems), death-throes. The key-images are either physiological (sometimes sexual): flesh, blood, mouth, carious teeth, thighs, penis, childbirth – or cosmogonical, often with sexual associations: rocks, earth (often ploughed soil), sun and moon, wind, and once more fire. There is much reference to fauna: buffaloes, crocodiles, wild boars and even ladybirds, parrots, nightingales, quails, seagulls and crows, But the symbolism is dominated by water – the sea, the tide, rivers (sometimes 'sister-river' or 'mother-river') – and the tree, in effect, the Tree of the Passion.

Carnal existence is explored from birth to death. The search is for love, for deliverance and for the resurrection. The fundamental dilemma exposed is that of the Black man who cannot reconcile himself to the Christian idea of salvation. The central poem of this collection, 'The Strange Agony', opens with an allusion to the Stations of the Cross, the Crucifixion and the Resurrection. Then, after one of the many passages of violent sexuality, in which the poet becomes convinced that carnal love cannot bring him relief, he states his refusal of Christian love, which brings us back to Rimbaud.

Tchicaya develops the theme of the Passion still further in *Epitomé* (whose full sub-title is 'Mots de tête pour le sommaire d'une passion'), lending it a greater scope and a more explicit expression. He is no longer exploring his own existence, nor his condition as a Black man: he is a Congolese poet identifying himself with his country's martyrdom, pouring forth the soul of his people. This Passion is the story of the violent history, the Calvary of the Congo. The poems of *Epitomé* embrace a series of antitheses: death and resurrection; disease and regeneration; corruption and purification. The main symbols are again water and the tree: rivers leading to the sea, with salt again the purifying element; the tree, signifying life and growth, but also the Tree of the Crucifixion and, at the same time, the poet's own genealogical tree which he cannot trace. But he finally recognizes himself in the tortured land of the Congo. Then he launches into an attack on the saints who belong to Europe and so are indifferent to the fate of Africa (here again there is a hint of a punning echo of the familiar *ne pas savoir à quel saint se vouer*) and on the angels ('fratricidal or angels of peace'), but above all on Christ, who is not a Messiah for Africa, but the source of false hopes. Nevertheless there is everywhere a certain ambiguity in the confused emotions of the poet. He curses Christ for having betrayed him – again an echo of Rimbaud who is not *embarqué pour une noce avec Jésus-Christ pour beau-père* – but he cannot deny him. He even identifies himself with him in his Passion. Then, contronted with his crucified country, he assimilates himself to both the redeemer and the contemptor, summing up this double identity in the line: 'He who is worthy of love is worthy of a slow death'. In the final stage of his vision his gaze goes out from himself, the incarnation of all the sufferings of the Black man; from the Congo in its martyrdom, to the whole of Africa, and then the whole world. The word 'Nègre' becomes the symbol for all who suffer. In this phase U Tam'si recovers his powers of laughter: 'laughter which kills' has now become the laughter that delivers, that leads to forgiveness – that 'laughter of the Negro' referred to by Senghor in the preface to *Epitomé* mentioned above.

The laughter that comes to the surface in *Epitomé* and suggests a means of salvation, is evoked in *Le Ventre* by what I must call 'black comedy' without any punning intention. Tchicaya himself, fortunately, gives his authority for the expression, saying in a discussion in 1969, in the course of the Conference of the Association for African Studies in Montreal:

There is one permanent characteristic in what I write, and that's a sort of black humour, a hidden grin, like a chuckle. I'm laughing at myself when I write, and this is apparent in my work. It's true that there is in my work this universe, all this solitude, the melancholy of man, of man everywhere, whether he be black or white or yellow...

Le Ventre is the most disconcerting of Tchicaya's works. It is part baroque drama, enacted for the most part without dialogue but to the accompaniment of the author's commentary. It is part allegory – a burlesque *Pilgrim's Progress*, with the voice of a Surrealist Gargantua breaking in. Sometimes the farcical note is drowned in ferocious satire. Sometimes the scene could be a Brueghel Kermesse. But always, in the heart of the humour, the burlesque and the farce, the poet's personal anguish lurks and solitude and death are ever present. The setting for the action is the city of Kin (Kinshasa?) a city of bloodshed over which the ghost of Lumumba hovers in June 1960. The last canto but one is entitled *Les Corps et les biens* [roughly 'Persons and property'] and is a dialogue between the Soothsayer, the Surveyor, the Builder, the Poet and the Soldier, all those who presumably have a stake in the city. The Soothsayer does not know under what earth to protect his dead. The Surveyor has measured out miles of hearts which it is difficult to step over. The builder knows the value of fire. The poet goes from song to song and from heart to heart, from hell to hell, from mourning to mourning. As each contributes his experience or submits his dilemma, the repetition of the verbs *Je sais...* *Je vais...Je fais...* with their internal rhyme, gives a litanic effect to this exchange, which has allusions to an ambiguous quest, for the Sangreal, or for gold and precious minerals (of Katanga?). The epilogue gives the sybilline reply to the riddle.

> He who lives
> Will see the Congo
> Astride the Congo
> or floating amidst the water-hyacinths.

The final short chapter, 'Le Ventre reste', finishes the work on a serio-comic note:

> Praise be to God seers fall
> more often than not on their backs
> more often than not with open arms
> more often than not
> belly uppermost to the heavens!

Just as the poems in each of Tchicaya's volumes are linked to a central theme, so from volume to volume we can trace a certain unity of idea, symbol, preoccupation. *Le Ventre* can be read as a sequel to *Epitomé*: after the quintessential agony, the resurrection to physical life and force; after the fever, the lysis; it is the scenario of a convalescence. It has a very positive moral, summed up in the motto to 'Les Corps et les biens':

> I condemn man
> to losing the contempt
> for himself and the folly
> of women which is his undoing.

In this work, more than any of his others, we are reminded of Tchicaya's axiom that the writer must be a whole man speaking into the intimate heart of men.

Arc musical, whose gestation took another six years after *Le Ventre*, is another story of a voyage, a quest, a progression through life with all the sign-posts pointing in the wrong direction. The poet returns to the more personal preoccupations of his earlier verse, expressed in isolated poems, linked by the themes of solitude and fraternity, nostalgia for past childhood and despair for present suffering, cries of pain, revolt, despair, love, the threats of death. But the outside world crowds in on him and at no time can he be indifferent to the crises of any people whom he assimilates to the Negro, *nègre-juif, juif-nègre-errant*. The tone of *Arc musical* is often sombre, but once again the poet is saved by his humour and by his music.

U Tam'si is a poet of astonishing virtuosity. He progresses from the more regular rhymed stanzas of *Le Mauvais Sang*, which are never derivative, although showing the influences of the French symbolist masters, to a skilful, assured manipulation of free verse. He has as much, if not more command of subtle rhythmic and musical effects in his liberated versification as in his early pieces. He is at once an intensely personal writer, expressing the whole gamut of emotions of a unique passionate and solitary being, the representative of the Congolese people, and the poet assuming the burden of Everyman. His reservoir of imagery seems inexhaustible, although he continually returns to certain, basic, elemental symbols which make of his Negro-African Surrealist verse both the voice of a private anguish and the expression of a collective soul.

CONCLUSION

The first original Black poets writing in French between the Wars, or in the immediate post-War years, whether from the Caribbean, West African territories or Madagascar, were mobilized under the banner of Negritude. At the time this was a war-cry for writers committed to the cause of Black solidarity and liberation from colonial oppression. The accents of anger and bitterness were frequently present. Under the circumstances the voices could not be that of universal man, the 'complete man' of Lyautey, the 'total man' that Tchicaya U Tam'si is to advocate. This uncompromising commitment is a phenomenon associated with, born of, a period of crisis, The generation of Senghor, Césaire, Dadié, and even the younger David Diop, were facing a political struggle which would lead to Independence. This struggle was inevitably reflected in creative literature, the dominant note of which was revolt; since poetry is more amenable than prose to the expression of national as well as personal passions, it is understandable that the earlier poets used their verses as a vehicle for a whole gamut of emotions inspired by their commitment – from indignation and anger to bitterest hatred.

Very few of the writers of this generation, who are still alive in the years that follow Independence, are in fact still writing poetry, if they are writing at all. Since 1960, Césaire has devoted himself almost completely to theatre and has simply re-edited his poetry of the 1945–50 period. Dadié and Senghor are the only important representatives of the generation of Angry Black Writers, who have produced new, unpublished poetry in recent years. The title of Dadié's latest collection, mostly written since 1960, is very significant: *Men of all the Continents*. This indicates that he is now clearly disengaged from his former standpoint and from the necessity to militate solely in the name of Africa and Black values. As for Senghor, I had completed this chapter and commented on the fact that he had published only one volume of verse since his election as President of Senegal in 1960. I was referring to *Nocturnes* which appeared one year later, but of which the whole of the longer first part consisted of poems written before 1949 for his first wife, re-edited under a new title as *Songs for Signare*. Then *Lettres d'hivernage* appeared in Dakar in 1972, followed a year later by the Seuil edition with Chagall's illustrations. These new poems, which include some of the most moving, and certainly the most personal that Senghor has written, do not however invalidate the point that I had previously made: namely that if the president is impelled from time to time to launch a rallying cry to the old Negritude colours, the poet has clearly recognized that the moment of 'engagement' has long passed. The title again is significant: *l'hivernage*, the rainy season in Senegal, was the season when the colonial armies took respite from fighting and, like those of ancient Rome, retired to winter quarters. It is also the West African equivalent of the European Autumn, the season for meditation, for taking stock, conducive to melancholy, 'season of mists and mellow fruitfulness'. This is the tone which pervades these deeply subjective verses, many of them love poems, the counterpart of the earlier *Chants pour Naëtt*, the tribute that the poet pays to the *Signare* of his later years. Earlier in this chapter (p. 152) I quoted D. Ewande's condemnation of Senghor's poetry as being too esoteric for his own compatriots, who preferred Hugo. A comparison with the French master nevertheless presents itself, for Senghor too, with advancing years, progresses from *Les Châtiments* to *Les Contemplations*. Be that as it may, Senghor, who was the Apostle of the committed Black poets, has not achieved the role of Guru of the period of disengagement. When political issues are finally divorced from poetic values, posterity will doubtless reinstate him.

Of the new generation, only one voice can be distinguished which can be compared with those of the 'Golden Age' of Negro-African poetry – that of Gérald Tchicaya U Tam'si. Now that the need has passed to contribute to a 'Defence and Illustration of Black Civilization' and Negro-African poets are liberated from their commitment to party or cause, from the need to *use* literature and especially poetry, they must dredge up their inspiration from the depths of their personal experience or from their share in a common humanity. From the world outside Africa, writers are expressing their sense of despair in the future of humanity as faith in the old values diminishes – social, political as well as spiritual values. Since Independence, since the holocaust of the Congo, from which U Tam'si drew much of his inspiration, Africa is no longer isolated from the dilemmas and the anguish of the rest of the world. Yet there is a dearth of intense, vital talent among the mass of African poets, whose themes and expression now span the whole range from the insignificant to the banal. Will the final distinguishing feature of Negro-African poetry be that it can only flourish in periods of a nation's immolation, or will one day the voice of the African poet be joined to that of a world chorus to mourn its universal distress or celebrate universal values?

4. The African novelist and the Negro-African novel in French

TOWARDS A DEFINITION OF THE AFRICAN NOVEL

Since the nineteenth century, the novel has proved the most amorphous of all literary genres, the most easily adaptable to continually changing social and political climates, as well as more personal and purely literary exigencies. Because of its treacherous facility, moreover, a vast number of embryo writers are tempted to use it for their literary apprenticeship, some of whom never develop beyond this stage. On the consumer level, with the growth of literacy this century throughout the world, the novel has proved the most easily accessible of all literary forms for readers whose mental and imaginative faculties are adequate to follow a writer into the escapist world of fiction, or to deduce his didactic or polemical message, but who have not been trained to respond to poetry. As a result of these and other factors, of the thousands and thousands of works of fiction in all languages dumped on the markets of Europe yearly (not even including so-called 'pulp fiction'), only a small proportion will make any contribution to the cultural patrimony of the world, or even of their own country of origin. Why then should the objective critic be expected to greet with unbounded enthusiasm (at the worst) of cautious praise (at the best) all the works of fiction that have emerged from Black Africa, in French and in English, in a steady and ever-growing stream since the mid-century? The fact which has resolutely to be faced is that the Negro-African novel in French, for all its pioneering efforts and proliferation, has proved on the whole a disappointing literary phenomenon, lacking the vigour, originality and imperative voice of African poetry. The acclaim that has greeted many works could be attributed to the exotic novelty of the subject, or the situations with which the market became eventually glutted, or to the militant ideological commitment which later lost its urgency with the remedying of the evils it sought to expose. The fact that many *romans à thèse* proclaimed important truths and unveiled areas of human suffering unknown or ignored by the West, is not grounds for hailing with benevolent paternalism every Negro-African novel as an important contribution to a national literary heritage.

If we discount narratives inspired by folk-lore, legend or history, we find that the novel proper appeared relatively late in the evolution of Negro-

African literature in French – that is, after the first tentative works of Bakary Diallo and René Maran, mentioned earlier. It is true that the novel was not indigenous to the literature of Africa, although the oral tradition included some semi-legendary chronicles of the pre-colonial past which can be compared to historical fiction. The pioneers of Negritude made it their duty to resuscitate this pride in the past; from historical and legendary tales it was but a step to more original works of fiction, leading to the great *essor* of the French-African novel of the nineteen-fifties. The majority of these first novels were more or less autobiographical, sometimes with mention of recent, contemporary or historical events. They frequently tell of a personal dilemma, an individual experience which is the mirror of a national experience and dilemma: the intelligent, ambitious young Negro at the cross-roads of his own existence, reflecting the confrontation of two cultures, two traditions; in short, the conflict between Black and White and the struggle against colonial domination. With few exceptions, this first generation of novelists produced a number of variations on the theme of a disrupted society, forced to abandon its own foundations and follow the lead of twentieth-century Europe. Very conscious of the necessity to remain close to reality, in order that their message should be clearly accessible to the biggest possible readership, these writers mostly follow the traditions of the realist, or social realist, or naturalist novel, including the latter's determinist philosophy, now mainly discredited. The characters are thus the product of their milieux, their social origins and their time. Contrary to the poetry of the same period, which bears the imprint of Surrealist influences, it is rare to find traces of contemporary European innovations in the structure and style of this African novel in French: no suggestion of a Proust, of a James Joyce, not to mention a Robbe-Grillet or a Claude Simon. By setting out to be the faithful mirror of the African condition of the first half of the twentieth century, the French-African novel remains obstinately based on the French novel of the second half of the nineteenth century. In the following pages we shall see what some thirty years of novel-writing by French-speaking Africans has produced.

The question still remains to be settled whether there is a definable African novel, or are there just African novelists; that is, writers from Black Africa who have adopted the novel as an apparently easy form of expression and one capable of reaching the largest readership, in Europe, America and Africa itself?[1] Just as the novel has tempted the creativity of the largest proportion of African writers, so has the desire to analyse it

[1] On the still vexed question of at whom the African writer directs his attention, I refer the reader to an article by Mohamadou Kane, 'L'Ecrivain africain et son public', in *Présence Africaine*, no. 58, 2nd quarter, 1966, pp. 8–31.

attracted the largest number of critics and scholars (until very recent years, predominantly non-African) to devote articles, papers and various works of exegesis to attempting to define the phenomenon of African fiction. Their common line of approach has been to establish affinities between writers in English and French, based primarily on common themes and situations. Works have been classified as pre- and post-Independence; they have been categorized for treatment of City Life, Village Life, Family Life, 'Inner Life'; they have been dissected to expose the nerves of Nostalgia, Religious Faith, Death, Anguish, Solitude, and even Existential Absurdity; the portrayal of the White Man in Africa (usually the missionary or the Colonial officer) depicted, not as the expatriate, but as the personification or tool of European authority, as opposed to the dilemmas of the Black Man in Europe. At least one critic has attempted a national or regional approach to the classification of the African novel: Jarmila Ortová, in her *Etude sur le roman au Cameroun*, sets out to demonstrate that Cameroon is 'an important centre in the heart of Francophone Africa'. Although it is true that Cameroon literature is among the richest in fiction of French-speaking Africa, this study does not do it justice by either throwing any new light on the works she mentions or drawing any significant conclusions about the specific character of the Cameroon novel and its possible common elements.

I have discounted any of these approaches as invalid for a study of the history of the Black novel in French. Many of them are redolent of the academic thesis, for which almost any subject can be selected and suitable works found to illustrate it, without ever revealing the anatomy of the whole. Moreover, the corpus of work to be treated cannot be categorized, because statistically the amount of material is too small. Even the broadest chronological division into pre- and post-Independence is only useful when dealing with a few representative authors or works, mainly in the light of the associated political and sociological context. It is impractical if we want to survey the works of novelists whose literary career stands astride the watershed of 1960, for example, Ousmane Sembène, whose *Docker noir* was published in 1956 and his most recent novel in 1973. Where, too, would we situate chronologically writers such as René Philombé, who even in the late sixties are still returning for inspiration to the themes of colonial Africa, as in *Un Sorcier blanc à Zangali*, set in Cameroon in 1915? The common denominators that can be established are of limited usefulness. In the topographical field the action never ranges further than France (when it is not situated exclusively in Africa), and there, those quarters of Paris, Bordeaux or Marseilles familiar to the expatriate writer. Chronologically, if we exclude the very few historical novels mentioned in chapter 1, these works, with the exception of Ouologuem's *Devoir de violence*, are all concerned exclusively with the twentieth century, usually the decades within the writer's own experience. Ethnologically, when the novels are peopled with other than Africans, these characters are very conventional representatives of one or other of the supposedly typical European colonists or settlers. Again, with the exception of the works inspired by folk-lore or legend, and the notable exception of all Camara Laye's novels, there is little intervention of fantasy, mystery, the supernatural or the mythical. It is paradoxical that the literature which was conceived in the conscious desire to assert African values and preserve African traditions, has so completely adapted the novel to the service of its commitment that positivist expressions of the physical world and social realist manifestations have banished the mythic and symbolic elements which so enrich many contemporary works of European fiction. Given the reservoir of African myths, which share the great universal themes with Greco-Hebraic mythology, these form a notable omission from the French-African novel, whose authors have not transcended the mundane, the concrete, the factual events of a fictional narrative. They deal with personal, social, or political situations in a recognizable geographical and temporal context. Many have thinly disguised autobiographical elements. The fact that they are rarely presented in the first person is the only concession made by the writer to the necessity to give a certain universality to the experiences recounted, so that they cannot be accused of gratuitous individual soul-searching, in the tradition of the Romantic *roman-confession*.

On the question of style and structure, the most striking common features are negative ones. Until the appearance of Malick Fall's *La Plaie* (1967) and Ahmadou Kourouma's *Les Soleils des Indépendances* (1968), there was a complete absence of any experimentation in narrative techniques, even the most timid attempt to break away from the solid tradition of the linear, realist or naturalist fiction. The best are soundly if unexcitingly architectured and the plot convincingly developed. With rare exceptions the language and style adopted ranges from the pedestrian to the pretentious; only very few novelists use dialogue with any flexibility of modulation, adapted to the characters and social and psychological situation. This is too easily explained away on the grounds that the language of expression – French – is foreign to the African protagonists and a language of adoption of the author, but this is no serious limitation in the hands of a master: to take the most extreme example, when Birago Diop puts dialogue into the mouths of his animals, not only does each one speak *in character* but, without the French being in any way stilted, he gives the subtle impression that they are in fact speaking *Wolof*. Even fewer of the

African novelists have a gift for stylistic irony which lifts their writing above that of a laudable literary exercise, adds impact to their polemics and lends their work a personal, original stamp. Notable in this minority is the Cameroonian, Mongo Beti, in his three major pre-Independence novels (see p. 206).

Nevertheless, even when the level of achievement is low, the authors' intentions are consistently elevated. We find here no escapist fiction, no adventures recounted for the pleasure of unravelling a good plot, just as there is no gratuitous experimentation in form, such as characterizes the work of the New Novelists in France. Many of the novels I am about to discuss are overtly partisan or consciously committed; the overwhelming majority serve some cause directly or indirectly. There is a minimal preoccupation with purely philosophical, moral, metaphysical or personal, psychological dilemmas. When these occur they are treated in the framework of a political or sociological situation, for example, the emotional and sentimental difficulties born of the stigma associated with sterility, problems of polygamy, the tradition of the bride-price, tribal and caste antagonisms, alienation and assimilation in a changing society. In this respect it is easy to understand why the African novel has attracted to its study and exegesis primarily the disciples of Georg Lucász and Lucien Goldmann. My approach will be elementary, to the point of being simplistic: eschewing any rigid categories, classifications or comparisons – except those which suggest themselves incidentally in the course of discussion – I have established three major periods which slightly overlap, corresponding to the evolving social and political situation during the forty years under review, and which, to a greater or lesser degree, form the back-drop to all the novels. In the case of novelists with numerous and chronologically widely-spaced publications, I have found it helpful to make certain compromises with chronology, and group together such works of any one writer as fall within a given period, although this will involve returning to the discussion of certain authors in a later section. By so doing, I hope to offer a broader spectrum of the development of the French-African novel as a whole than if I had treated each writer separately, or proceeded according to the dates of all publications.

My first period goes from 1935 – the date of the appearance of Ousmane Socé's first novel and the composition of Abdoulaye Sadji's *Nini* – to 1955, but within which most of the novels discussed appeared in the immediate post-war decade. Apart from any proximity of publication dates (which do not always accurately reflect the dates of composition) none of these works shows any deep involvement with the doctrines of Negritude, insofar as these were to become the rallying cry for a literature of combat.

This can be explained by the need that a work of fiction has for a longer gestation period than poetry, so that a time-lag will frequently be seen between political events or topical ideologies and their expression in the novel. My second period covers the years leading up to and those immediately following Independence, namely 1954–65. Among the large number of important as well as lesser novels of these ten years, two distinct trends can be discerned, not necessarily divided by the watershed that 1960 was to be, in respect of the political re-organization of the then French colonies. I have thus dealt with the novels of this period in two sub-sections. The first of these is devoted to works of deeply committed writers, who used their fiction-writing as a weapon in the anti-colonial struggle, including some whose post-Independence publications were partisan or polemical. Then I come to those works which reflect the relaxation of tensions in a clearly transitional period, and which announce an era when the evils of colonialism will be part of history. My third period, 1964–74, shows how novelists reacted to the changed climate of Independent Africa. Of these, I shall examine first the new works of authors who had already acquired a reputation for their novels written under the colonial régime, and in so doing point out their ventures into new themes or styles of writing. Finally I shall treat the new voices of French African novelists, appearing in the second lustrum of the post-Independence decade and their explorations of a wider field of fictional subjects.

1935–55: Authors and works in the margin of commitment

Ousmane Socé Diop

Ousmane Socé Diop: *Karim, roman sénégalais*. Paris, Nouvelles Editions Latines, 1935. Preface by Robert Delavignette. 2nd edit. 1948 followed by *Contes et légendes d'Afrique noire*. *Mirages de Paris*. Paris, Nouvelles Editions Latines, 1937. 2nd edit. 1948, followed by *Rythmes du Khalam*, poèmes. Re-issued 1956 and 1964.

Excluding René Maran's *Batouala* and its sequel *Chien de brousse*, to which I referred in an earlier chapter, and Bakary Diallo's *Force Bonté* which, literary values apart, is an autobiography and not a novel in the true sense of the word, Ousmane Socé's *Karim* is the first work of fiction in French published by an author who is unequivocably African, according to the definition I have adopted. As a pioneering work and for its intrinsic interest, it deserves more praise than it is usually given. The original limited acclaim can be partly explained by the unfortunate timing of its first appearance: in the tense political and social climate of the mid-thirties in Europe, the dilemmas of a young Senegalese brought into contact for the first time with French culture in the city life of Senegal and caught in the toils of the profit-making machine of Western civilization, did not seem to have great relevance. Also the discretion and sobriety of tone adopted by Socé in recounting his hero's vicissitudes were guarantee against any *succès de scandale* such as had greeted *Batouala*, and the descriptions of life in Saint-Louis, Senegal, though closely observed and authentic enough, were not sufficiently coloured with the mystery of 'primitive' African life to arouse the enthusiasm of the public which acclaimed Camara Laye's *L'Enfant noir* twenty years later. It is true that *Karim* lacks the poetry and the nostalgic lyricism of *L'Enfant noir*, too, but in many respects it is a more original novel – that is, a work of imagination, based on personal observation and experience, but transmuted into a structured and motivated series of situations to form a co-ordinated literary entity with a certain universality of application, so that one is not forced to identify the author with his hero.

Karim introduces into the African novel a situation and theme which will be taken up and inspire many variations in subsequent decades of fiction-writing: the African at the cross-roads where two civilizations meet; the attempt and failure of the Black man to reconcile two conflicting systems of values in a rapidly changing urban African situation. What characterizes Socé's novel is his lack of aggression and emotional involvement. This may be explained by the author's inability to analyse the emotional reactions of his chief characters (particularly Karim himself and Marie N'Diaye), or by the fact that neither of these is capable of very deep sentiments. Be this as it may, no matter what difficulties and misfortunes Karim encounters, there is no hint of deep moral suffering, even less of the permanent psychological scarring that often marks the heroes of similar novels or autobiographical works. This is because Socé does not attribute Karim's setbacks to anything but his hero's own character: his insouciance, his extravagance and grass-hopper mentality which is incapable of making provision for the harder morrows, combined with his Senegalese pride and quickness to take umbrage. The first crisis in his life, which brings to an end the Saint-Louis episode – the most coherent of the whole novel – is not caused by ill-treatment or racial prejudice, injustice or any of the overt themes of the colonial novel, but is endogenous to the whole social situation of the time, with which Karim's personality is in conflict. It is his ambition to live up to the standards of the *Samba Linguère* (the aristocrate of Senegal in pre-colonial times) on the monthly pittance of a clerk, which causes his downfall. If he is nearly ruined financially and meets with failure in his sentimental ventures, it is not the fault of race discrimination or the colonists' victimization, but simply his own inability to make the necessary adjustments, to evolve and change his standards with the changing social pattern in which he exists. The only wrongs that the Whites have done to Karim and his generation, suggests Socé, is to change the world into which they were born: in this new world the traditional qualities which they admire most – the extravagant generosity, rich display, noble sentiments, heroic actions of an epic past cannot be accommodated.

Although set in the colonial period, this novel is not an indictment of colonialism. Although it is a story of the clash of two cultures, Socé does not set out to prove the superiority of one over the other; if he has any thesis to prove, it is simply the inherent incompatibility of two sets of values. It is a chronicle of an age, the testimony of an era, presenting, with a gift for wry and ironic humour, a series of boldly drawn characters who live for us, with the details of their physique and personality, as do the towns in which the episodes unfold: Old Saint-Louis, slow-moving, symbolizing the life of the past, and the new city of Dakar, brash and uncompromisingly dedicated to the gods of modernity and speed and money-making.

Ousmane Socé's second novel is greatly inferior to *Karim*, but has, like the first, the merit of being a pioneering work, the first indeed of its kind to appear before the 1939–45 war. Though the plot is tenuous and largely predictable, the characterization shallow and the descriptions of life in Paris in the early thirties lacking in the vigour which marks the social milieu portrayed in *Karim*, *Mirages de Paris* did introduce a new theme into the Negro-African novel in French; one which was to be over-exploited by his successors. It proved the progenitor of a long line of fictional or thinly disguised autobiographical accounts of the 'Negro in Paris', the emotional involvements of the *déraciné* with a White girl, the social rebuffs he encounters and his final failure to make the necessary adjustments which, in the case of Socé's hero, leads to tragedy.

The more ambitious *Mirages de Paris* fails, where the simpler, more coherent *Karim*, more closely observed, more richly described, succeeds. Socé had leavened his first novel with humour and recounted it with a certain airy detachment: in his second he introduces long passages of philosophical or moralizing discussion which add nothing to the central conflicts and militate against involvement in a personal tragedy, by reducing the protagonists to marionettes acting out a *roman à thèse*.

Abdoulaye Sadji

ABDOULAYE SADJI: *Maïmouna, la petite fille noire.* Dakar, Les Lectures Faciles, 1953, o.p. Paris, Présence Africaine, 1958, 1965, o.p. Re-issued Livre de Poche, 1972. *Nini, mulâtresse de Sénégal.* In 'Trois écrivains noirs', Paris, Présence Africaine, 1954. Re-issued Présence Africaine, 1965.

The above citation lists Abdoulaye's two novels in order of publication dates, according to the principle which I have adopted throughout, within the relevant sections. However, *Nini* was written in 1935, although only published in 1954, as a serial forming four special numbers of Alioune Diop's literary periodical, *Présence Africaine.* I shall therefore discuss this work before *Maïmouna*, which appeared a year earlier, in order to illustrate the development of Sadji's command over the novel form in the interval separating the composition of the two works.

In *Cœur d'Aryenne*, another of the three novels which made up this special number of *Présence Africaine* (see p. 205 below), Jean Malonga hints at the social problems created in Africa by a too literal interpretation of the Biblican injunction 'Love one another'. In *Nini, mulâtresse du Sénégal* [Nini, Mulatto from Senegal], the subject is the marginal existence of that intermediary class, the product of inter-racial *amours*. In this, Sadji breaks new ground, as he also does in making the central character of each of his two novels a woman.

Although concerned with preserving and perpetuating African values, which he best does in recounting the *Leuk-le-Lièvre* [Leuk the Hare] fables, in collaboration with Senghor, and in his legend of *Tounka*, discussed in an earlier chapter (pp. 71–3), Sadji's two novels do not show any involvement in an anti-colonial conflict, nor any positive Negritude doctrine. He aims rather at painting a realist picture of the Senegalese society of the time and at drawing certain moral conclusions. In both cases, this seems to be the rather negative message that there is value in accepting one's place and misery accrues from any aspiration to a sort of Barrèsian *déracinement* or uprootal.

The case of Nini, the half-cast heroine of Sadji's first novel, is however, by no means as clear-cut as the author evidently intended it to be. In presenting his savage, satirical portrait, without the slightest compassion, he clearly intends to demonstrate that Nini's failure in life is due to her rejection of her African heritage and her desire for complete assimilation with the 'best' society of Saint-Louis, that of the White colonists. But though the representatives of the latter are not particularly admirable, he does not show how she could find her place in the fast evolving social system of Africa. Moreover, he makes his heroine a blue-eyed blonde, with minimal physical features betraying her African blood. She would really have lived in a twilight social and racial world, but Sadji has no conception of the mental anguish that such a situation could produce. Forced to choose between Black and White, at the time of racial oppression at the worst, or victimization and indignities at the best, his heroine might have been forgiven for 'trying for White', particularly if she had been capable of deep affection for her European lover (or lovers). But Nini is a caricature of the most incredibly stupid, vapid, sensual, pretentious little snob, despising everything Negro as savage, uneducated, uncivilized, and claiming to prize the 'allure' and 'good taste' of Western culture.

The portraits of Nini and her Eurafrican friends are so obviously burlesque in nature that it is difficult to accept Sadji's claims, set out in his introduction to the novel, to paint 'the eternal moral portrait of the mulatto woman, be she from Senegal, the Caribbean or the two Americas'. He suggests, too, that far from blaming or even pitying this hybrid being, the charitable action is to offer her a mirror to see her true image. We may not agree with this definition of philanthropy, but experience shows that the object of such 'charity' would be the last to learn from the satire. In any case Sadji does not follow his own precepts. By the cruelty and exaggeration of the portraits of the Ninis, the Madous, Nénés and Riris there is inherent censure and contempt for the class they represent. He admits, too, that the problem of the Eurafrican half-caste woman is a vital one (though why does he specifically allude only to the *mulâtresse*?) as more and more light-brown offspring of mixed unions can be expected to people a wished-for world in which barriers of race and colour are broken down. How are these to apply in practice Sadji's injunctions to stay in the society to which they belong? To which traditions do they belong? If the Ninis and her like are born of stable, or at least legal unions, and are not the product of promiscuous wenching of migrant colonists, then who can deny them a right to a White as much as a Black heritage? Ideologically and morally ambiguous, *Nini* is also stylistically an unsatisfactory work, undecided as the author was as to its genre; was it to be unadulteratedly burlesque satire or a realistic portrait of Saint-Louis society in the nineteen thirties?

Maïmouna has the makings of a better novel than *Nini*: better constructed, better written in the first part at least, and bearing witness to a greater understanding of human weakness. However, it too suffers from many unconvincing elements and melodramatic features that mar the development of the work. The theme of *Maïmouna*, as in *Nini*, is the social *déracinement*, in this case the downfall of the simple village girl who loses herself in the vice of the big city.

In the early scenes Sadji paints with sympathy and understanding a delightful portrait of the child Maïmouna, growing up in the village of Louga, with her widowed mother Yaye Daro, in the company of her doll 'dome Nabou'. There is a universality and delicacy in his suggestions of the psychological unrest of her puberty and her growing coquetry, as the loving, obedient little girl develops into a moody, rebellious young woman. We understand her vague dissatisfactions and her desire to join her sister Rihanna, married, and enjoying the fuller life of the city. Similar touches of psychological authenticity are lent to the slighter portrait of the mother, particularly in the description of her loneliness after Maïmouna has left. The Dakar characters are, on the other hand, two-dimensional, unsubtle: the sister calculating, ambitious with little human warmth, finally treating Maïmouna with exceptional harshness after the young girl's seduction; her husband, Boumouna, while a more sympathetic character, still shown mainly as the typical successful city opportunist; the jealous maid, Yacine, a figure of melodrama. It is into this category that all the latter part of the novel descends. Jilted by her lover, disgraced by her pregnancy, disfigured by smallpox, she is told by her mother that she can now only choose between starving to death or the life of a market-woman like herself. In spite, then, of some promising touches, *Maïmouna* fails like *Nini* as a psychological novel, because the configurations are not consistent throughout. Basically, Sadji shows himself incapable of understanding the subtler motivations behind human conduct, or any but the crudest of human emotions. For similar reasons this is also an unsatisfactory love-story, although it patently intends to operate on this level too. Maïmouna is, in part, all innocent naïvety, and partly a restless Bovary looking for the excitement of a great passion to relieve the tedium of an empty existence. But when the opportunity does occur for the overwhelming love which will prove her downfall, we are hardly moved as her lover is so shadowy a figure and the occasion for the love at first sight so improbable. Sadji briefly exploits the possibilities of environmental realism, both in descriptions of village life and some compellingly vivid pictures of Dakar, particularly a feast in Bouhouma's house, and finally the passages describing the outbreak of smallpox and its ravages in the Louga district. But these are inadequate and not consistent enough to give the novel a unity of tone on the level of a document of social realism.

Maïmouna, like *Nini*, is the exposition of a severe punitive, negative morality, stated with the same lack of compassion. The girl Maïmouna must be punished by fate and censured by society, not so much for her human error, but for her disobedience to traditional *mores*. Her basic fault was not to be content to stay in her native village, marry the local suitor and continue the traditional cycle of existence, or at least let her sister and husband choose a suitable husband and accept her fate as a submissive Muslim wife. The conflict is stated in terms of the woman's role and the moral is ambiguous because the alternatives offered are so unsatisfactory. Yaye Daro may be a model of virtue by African Muslim standards but the rewards for her obedience to tradition are meagre. The example she offers to her daughter is not inviting and to imitate her fate is in fact Maïmouna's punishment: to scratch out a bare subsistence as a market-woman – or starve completely.

Saverio Naigiziki

SAVERIO NAIGIZIKI: *Escapade ruandaise, Journal d'un clerc en sa trentième année.* Bruxelles, Deny, 1949. *Mes transes à trente ans, de mal en pis, histoire vécue, mêlée de roman.* Astrida, (Congo) Groupe Scolaire, 1955. (The second publication is a re-edition of the first with a short sequel.)

Creative writing from Equatorial Africa was much slower to develop than in the other French-speaking territories. By 1950 only two full-length works of fiction had been published. The first was Paul Lomani-Tchibamba's legend of *Ngando-le Crocodile*, discussed in a previous chapter (pp. 68–9). The year after Lomani-Tchibamba was awarded the Brussel's Colonial Fair Prize, this honour fell to a young Ruandese, Savario Naigiziki, for his autobiographical novel, *Escapade ruandaise*. The sequence of the awards is interesting, for it illustrates the progression from the inspiration of myth and legend to that of the practical and moral problems of contemporary day-to-day existence.

Unlike *Karim*, in which the theme of the clash of cultures is fundamental, here it is only ancillary, a catalyst as it were for a personal dilemma. On the surface it is the difference attached to the meaning of money by the African and the European that makes for the downfall of Justin, the hero. It is suggested that money has not acquired the European values, remaining a means, not an end; not to be accumulated nor treated with respect, but to be used, particularly to help a brother Bantu in distress. But in Justin, an ex-pupil of a seminary, destined for the priesthood, a Christian sense of values and an understanding of sin have been inculcated, and he is dogged by his sense of guilt. With the opening lines of Dante's *Inferno* as motto, Justin introduces himself in this journal as having reached his thirtieth year and the turning-point in his life. Married, his ambitions for the priesthood abandoned, he has taken a job as clerk-manager-salesman in a trading store in Nyanza, to keep his family. By his own confession 'of doubtful morals', he is also clearly a man of weak personality torn between a sense of duty to his legitimate wife and the attractions of his mistress; harassed by the imminent necessity to find the large sums of money which he has 'borrowed' from the till in order to help some needy friends, and by involvement in doubtful expedients to try to recoup the missing funds defrauded by the said friends when he applies to them in turn. The whole of Justin's existence has now crashed around him: his career ruined by his own loose morals and by abuse of confidence, he decides to flee into British territory before being caught in the toils of the law.

Escapade ruandaise is written in an easy, flexible, sober language, which keeps the reader mindful of the fact that this is the diary of a literate man. Justin's mental distress does not blind him to the world around him: on the contrary, seeking desperately some escape from his dilemma, people and landscapes alike being potentially hostile or helpful to the fugitive, he needs all his acuity of observation, to which we owe some pages of strikingly vivid description. However, for the work of a Black writer to be successful in the fifties it had either to satisfy European readers' taste for African exoticism (as with *L'Enfant noir*) or be swept by the tide of Negritude into the haven of his fellow Africans' acclaim. *Escapade ruandaise* satisfied neither of these criteria. The descriptions of life in the town of Nyanza and the surrounding country during Justin's flight, the characters who people the chronicle, are vividly enough observed but are not painted with a sufficiently rich colour to attract with any startling novelty. Naigiziki can by no means be considered a disciple of Negritude doctrines either; on the contrary, his book shows a deep integration with the humanism of the West and the imprint of the universal conscience of Christianity, with some hint of a Villon, a Gorki and a Dostoievsky. Now that the urgency of the Negritude issue has receded somewhat, Naigiziki's talent and the originality of his 'Escapade in Ruanda' should be given more recognition.

Camara Laye

CAMARA LAYE:[2] *L'Enfant noir*. Paris, Plon, 1953. New illustrated edition (Coll: 'Super') 1967. Re-issued Livre de Poche, 1967. *Le Regard du Roi*. Paris, Plon, 1954. Re-issued 1965.

English translations: *The Dark Child*, trans. James Kirkup. London, Collins, 1955, o.p.; as *The African Child*, Collins and Fontana, 1959; as *The Dark*

[2] *Camara* is a common West African patronymic and *Laye*, the diminutive of 'Abdoulaye' – a given name. As often occurs with African names in European context, there has been some confusion as to which is the surname in the case of this author. It would be pedantic to attempt to restore the names to their true attribution, so the commonly accepted form – even if erroneous, is retained.

Child, trans. J. Kirkup, E. Jones Gottlieb, New York, Noonday Press, 1954, o.p. *The Radiance of the King*, trans. J. Kirkup. London, Collins, 1956, o.p. Re-issued 1965. Re-issued Fontana Books.

No French African novelist has inspired more controversy amongst Black critics and intellectuals than Camara Laye. What is more, there has been a clear-cut divergence of opinion as to the merits of his work, between Black and White critics. The Guinean writer was long considered in Europe as the most talented of African novelists, on the merits of his first two works, published in the fifties. By the same token he has been denigrated by his contemporary compatriots, more interested in a positive contribution to the literature of Negritude than an expression of poetic and subjective nostalgia. So they attacked his first autobiographical novel for its Flaubertian influences and for its portrayal of an Africa which was related to neither the reality of today nor the promise of tomorrow. The second work, the Kafkaesque *Regard du Roi*, more fundamentally original in theme, concept and composition, did nothing to reconcile Camara with his Black detractors: breaking with folk-lore, regionalism, politics, the battle for the emancipation of the Black people, the affirmation of Black personality – all the acceptable justifications for Negro-African literary creativity in the fifties – this allegorical novel of quest and redemption seemed a gratuitous literary exercise to the exponents of commitment. Finally, after a long silence, he published *Dramouss*, to the White critic a mediocre novel, doing nothing to enhance his reputation as a writer, lacking the poetry, the symbolism, the sensitivity of the two former works, giving the impression of having been written under duress, without inspiration, to answer his Black critics, even if, as is clear, he cannot restore himself to favour with Sékou Touré's régime.

Now that the heat of the Negritude debate has cooled, there is little questioning of *L'Enfant noir's* place as a classic of Black literature, the most remarkable of the autobiographical novels emanating from Black Africa. It differs from the majority of its counterparts in not presenting the difficulties of the Black man in coming to terms with a new set of basic values with which to guide his existence in a Western-European situation or in an Africa in which the old system is crumbling. Camara Laye neither indicts the Africa of his childhood for its colonial régime, nor the Europe of his later years for racial discrimination. And yet, in its own individual way, this book makes an unconscious contribution to the substance of the Negritude doctrine, in so far as this sets out to preserve purely African values, threatened by Western materialism and determinism. This Laye does when, from the remembered facts of his own experiences, he attempts to distil the quintessence of Africa.

He himself described at the Seminar on African Literature in Dakar, in March 1963, how his first book was written almost accidentally, with neither a creative mission nor a polemical intent, simply to dispel his fatigue, his spleen as a poor expatriate in Paris, by peopling his nostalgia with the still sharp memories of his country and its people. An unnamed friend to whom he submitted the first rough drafts, encouraged him to persevere, to improve the style, suggesting that he study Flaubert's *Education sentimentale* for the authentic subjectivity of the inspiration, allied to a careful, deliberate objectivity in choice of expression– particularly in the use of tenses.

The resultant account of life in an unsophisticated but prosperous Guinean village, where the Musulman religion maintained strong ties with animist beliefs, combines a realistic description of everyday activities with a strong dose of nostalgic, partly euphoric, subjectivity. On the level of realism, the author evokes in flexible, lyrical prose, the harvests, the feasts and dancing of his school-days, his father's forge, the initiation classes, the circumcision ceremonies. The language of the tom-tom and the practice of his father's craft as a goldsmith form the bridge between objective realism and the supernatural: the secrets of the fetishists, the magic powers of the smith, the ancestor rites and worship, the divinations of his mother. We feel that Laye has rejected all but the happy memories of a childhood in which the basic elements were love and mystery, and his only dilemma was whether to continue his studies in a Western institution and a technological discipline, and so associate himself irrevocably with an alien civilization, or to join his father in the goldsmith's workshop and become an initiate into the sacred mysteries of his craft. We know that he made the former choice, which introduces a certain dichotomy into his dealing with the supernatural. Following upon his technological training, he often feels impelled to attempt a logical or psychological explanation of a custom, belief, tradition, or the mysteries of Africa, for the benefit of the sceptical, Western reader and one is reminded of D. H. Lawrence's view that modern education is an obstacle to a proper understanding of the symbol – the message of the serpent.

For the Western public *L'Enfant noir* was the first revelation of the rites and cults, customs and traditions of an African, rural society, with its spiritualization of craftsmanship, its totemic and fetishist beliefs, exposed with lyricism and a certain amount of idealization from within that society, not from the standpoint of the European-based ethnologist or social anthropologist. For the majority of the African intellectuals of the time, as we have mentioned, the author's vision was too rose-tinted, his attitudes too optimistic and could only diminish the force of their struggle against colonial repression. With a certain hind-sight, the author claims in 1963 (at the Dakar Seminar quoted above) that he was deliberately setting out to rehabilitate an African civilization that dated from the fourteenth century and to high-light the dominant characteristics of that civilization – namely Mystery and Love – which had allowed it to know a brief renaissance during the Samorian Empire, and to remain dormant, but not dead during the colonial period. Now he defends strongly the emphasis put upon the supernatural, the mystery of the life he led in his village of Kouroussa, in Upper Guinea where 'genies' peopled the air, the water and the savannah. Nevertheless, the arguments that he propounds in defence of his thesis are not those of orthodox Negritude, or of a specifically African civilization, but of an universal aspiration to spirituality and a transcendence of rationalism and positivist values with a certain Rousseauesque rejection of the appurtenancies of a mechanized age. Because he succeeds in his evocation of a mythic, universal super-reality that gives meaning to existence, even when it is only half comprehended, *L'Enfant noir* deserves to be included in the outstanding works of fiction of the twentieth century. In respect of the mythic content, it would be interesting to see some future researcher undertake an analysis of the importance in this novel of the two basic elements of fire and water: the life-maintaining water, usually of the Niger, and the blacksmith's fire which purifies and creates.

In his next novel, following hard upon the publication of *L'Enfant noir*, Camara Laye presented a much more sophisticated allegory of man's voyage through life in quest of the ineffable. In the talk, given at the Dakar Conference in 1963 Laye explained the process by which his father, a sculptor as well as a goldsmith, transposed reality in the figurines which he carved. These two books show the same creative evolution of the writer. Starting from the representation of reality, of an experience of life in *L'Enfant noir*, Camara Laye arrived at the abstraction of *Le Regard du Roi*, with the resultant even greater universality of its theme and setting. The theme is again an attempt to penetrate to the hidden meaning of man's existence, but presented as pure allegory. The setting is symbolic – an undefined region of Africa, removed from geographical as from temporal limitations. *Le Regard du Roi* presents, moreover, a set of original protagonists who reflect in their equivocal and paradoxical character, a similar suspension of the laws of reality that apply to time and place. Except that he has lost all his money at poker, we know nothing of the main character, Clarence, the penniless flotsam of Europe in a Black territory: of undefined class, origins, profession, he is rejected by his fellow Whites and despised and ill-treated by the Blacks. Second in importance to Clarence are the beggar and the ambiguous, identical twins. The former, symbolic of a marginal existence and no social identity, lives on charity but dispenses it also at times; he proves a helpful guide and mentor to Clarence in his wanderings, but is also his Mephistopheles, selling him to the Naba to serve as a stud. The twins with the anagrammatic names, Nagoa and Noago, are two aspects of an individual identity, that of Clarence himself, manifested on the one hand in his quest for the 'radiance of the King' – his aspiration towards the ineffable, and on the other, his sinking into the lowest degradation of lasciviousness. There is Samba Baloun, the eunuch with the enigmatic smile, symbolizing an ambiguous sexuality; and Akissi, the 'wife' accorded to Clarence, who adopts a different form in his bed each night, and who personifies the faceless protean temptation of lust.

Le Regard du Roi is as remarkable for the variety and originality of the anecdotic element as for the invention of this series of *dramatis personae*: his journey to the south, in search of the King, the momentary vision of whom has given a meaning to his existence and a hope of redemption, is at once a Pilgrim's Progress and a Season in Hell. His adventures combine absurdity and nightmare, Surrealist fantasy and eroticism, echoes of Le Sage, Kafka, Beckett and André Breton in the vicissitudes at the hands of the rascally inn-keeper; the accusation of his having stolen his own jacket; the parody of justice at his trial; his flight through the labyrinth of the courtrooms; the endless journeyings through tropical forests, with viscous flora and tentacular vegetation, the descent into erotic bestiality with the fish-women; and, ensnared by Dioki and her serpents, his final degeneration as he involuntarily services the impotent sultan's harem.

The Kafkaesque quality of the narrative – the sense of being trapped in an absurd dilemma – has been sufficiently commented upon. The quotation from *The Trial* that appears on the title page of the Plon edition[3] (omitted from the English version) leaves me in no doubt as to the direct influence that reading of Kafka exerted on Camara Laye at the time he was writing *Le Regard du Roi*[4]. The author nevertheless discounted the extent of this influence in an article entitled 'Kafka et moi', which appeared in *Dimanche Matin* on 2 January 1955. He limited it to one of technique, denying that his theme itself was associated with any Kafkaesque dilemma.

In his *Afrique des Africains* (p. 73), Claude Wauthier comments on 'the differences in tone, style and probably the intentions of the two books by

---

[3] 'The master will pass by in the corridor, he will look at the prisoner and say: "This one must not be shut up again; he is coming to me".' F. Kafka.

[4] A curious misprint, which seems an example of Freudian association, occurs in Eustace Palmer's *Introduction to the African Novel*, which offers one of the most pertinent and percipient studies of *La Regard du roi*. In the Contents, the title of the English translation by Kirkup figures as *The Radiance of the K*.

Camara Laye' which suggests to him some doubt as to their being by the same hand. To me, as to Janheinz Jahn (*Muntu*, p. 218 [Bibliographical notes, p. 325]), there is no doubt about these being the works of the same writer, even if, as the author himself suggests, the first manuscript underwent a certain amount of stylistic editing. The insistence on the importance of the spiritual world and the attainment of happiness, together with the arguments we have mentioned earlier, is further evidence that *Le Regard du Roi* is a kind of allegorical continuation of *l'Enfant noir*. For Sunday Anozie (*Sociologie du roman africain*, ch. VII) *Le Regard de Roi* is the 'interlude' between the two autobiographical works; in *cette aventure intérieure au symbolisme obscur et allégorique* ['this spiritual adventure with its obscure and allegorical symbolism'] the vicissitudes of Clarence – and his name means 'light' – express in parable the aspirations after grace and love of the author himself. (It is worth noting in passing the importance that the sociologist Anozie attaches to Camara's literary production, which is an indication of the author's rehabilitation in the eyes of the more objective African critics of recent years.)

In some respects, in spite of the undefined character of the topography, in spite of the reproaches made to the author for the non-Africanness of his second novel, it possesses a very strong poetic African climate, to my mind more impressive, more original, more transcending reality than the setting of some of the contemporary works of fiction that I shall be discussing later. In the description of the crowd scenes, in the forests where Clarence is submerged, we feel the pervasive colour, smells, luxurious vegetation, as truly redolent of African impressionism as Senghor's rhythms, imagery and verbal music.

Fily-Dabo Sissoko

FILY-DABO SISSOKO: *Crayons et portraits*. Mulhouse, Impr. Union, 1953. *La Passion de Djimé*. Paris, Edits. de La Tour du Guet, 1956. *La Savane rouge*. Avignon, Presses Universelles, 1962.

Sissoko's *Crayons et portraits* is listed as poetry in Jahnheinz Jahn's *Bibliography of Creative African Writing*. Senghor is right to remind us in his preface to Birago Diop's *Nouveaux Contes d'Amadou Koumba* that there was no fundamental distinction between poetry and prose in the old oral narratives of Negro-Africa, the poetic recital being simply more strongly and more regularly rhythmic than those in prose. Fily-Dabo's work is certainly difficult to classify neatly as to genre, either by content or style. *Crayons et portraits* [Sketches and portraits], his first published work, could be considered stylistically as poetic prose, but it is certainly not in the same category of lyric poetry as the works of poets considered in the preceding chapter. From the point of view of content, there is an autobiographical narrative, which can as justifiably be considered as autobiographical fiction as Camara Laye's *l'Enfant noir*, with which, indeed, it has much in common. The second part of the work consists of character sketches, for which the author acknowledges his debt to La Bruyère, who himself was one of the important influences on the evolution of the eighteenth-century novel in France.

Like Camara Laye, Sissoko describes a happy childhood: a calm, even idyllic, rural existence in his native Sudan, where, as in Laye's Guinea, traditional rites went hand in hand with a deep mystical Mohammedanism. Fily-Dabo was brought up by his grandmother – he lost his mother at the age of fourteen – in a matriarchal society. His visionary nature, which manifested itself early, is apparent in the respectful awe with which he described the sacred sites, the residences and rendezvous of *djinns* and spirits of all sorts, with whom he was familiar. He recounts two experiences of his childhood, first-hand encounters with the supernatural: the first when he glimpsed a shining being, dressed all in white, and the second when he became aware of a hunter without a gun who suddenly disappeared – patently a *gôté*, a spirit-hunter on good relations with men. He accepts unquestioningly mythic explanations for natural phenomena such as whirlwinds. He is as convinced as any villager that supernatural causes are responsible for the sudden death of a young girl on the eve of her marriage.

Although the supernatural is a commonplace in his existence, Sissoko makes little attempt to embroider on reality in his simple account of his childhood and adolescence, immersed in Nature, where the only events that marked the even tenor of the years was the coming of the missionaries, apart from the normal births and deaths, with occasional crimes as the result of local enmities. The child Fily-Dabo listens to the accounts of war and adventure, told by the elders; he watches the hunters train, to the accompaniment of the guitars. He describes his games with the other village children; his chief play-mate (for slavery had not been abolished *de facto*) was a little slave-boy, until the latter's master took him away to the East. They hunt grey lizards and palm-squirrels and catch fish by poisoning the water-holes. He describes the hazards met by the young shepherd boys taking the goats to pasture: poisonous insects and snakes, grasses that cut and sting, thorns that tear the flesh. But he fails to communicate any real shiver of alarm, or any shared torment, leaving the reader with the impression of a period when life in Mali seems to have been one long uneventful bucolic.

The 'Portraits' that make up the second half of the book are, for the most part, frustratingly brief notes on the external features and character of Whites and Blacks who peopled the author's Sudan. Even the best of them from a literary point of view are little better than good stylistic exercises from a baccalauréat pupil, composed in the style of La Bruyère on the observation of types which he knows.

As *La Savane rouge* was a re-handling of the author's reminiscences, presented in the earlier *Crayons*, and written between 1936 and the date of eventual publication in 1962, I shall discuss it before *La Passion de Djimi* (1956), which belongs more truly to the realms of fiction. The style of *La Savane rouge* [The red savanna] is more personal and, at the same time, more incisively economical and more poetic than the *Crayons*, and does in fact more merit being classified as poetry. Sissoko often deliberately uses stylistic procedures of prosody, particularly anaphora and refrains, while the rhythm is more emphasized and the presentation in places in actual 'versets' is that of the prose poem. There is a poignant simplicity in some of the descriptions of the author's experiences that is absent from the memories of his childhood of the *Crayons*, when he seeks more deliberate literary effects. In the account of his journey to Ouagadougou, to take up his post as student-teacher, the reader enters into all the discomforts of the train and boat: the smoke, the cinders, the smells, the promiscuities; then on through the bush on foot, through villages ravaged by famine, his feet either pierced by the nails of his heavy school-boots or, when these are abandoned, by the pitiless thorns called 'old women's teeth'. There are more brief 'Portraits', and some anecdotes, showing his interest in his country's immediate past, and dialogues to enliven the narrative. In all this Sissoko gives evidence of a novelist's potential that is never quite realized. In 1956 he published a work of prose fiction, *La Passion de Djimé* [Djimé's passion]. This is a slight romance, set in an undefined period of Sudanese history; it is not an historical novel, but a story of intrigue and passion. Prince Djimé, married to the Princess Kani, is in love with the captive Sanou. The King Diapora, Djimé's uncle, sends him away on a military mission, to avoid scandal, since Sanou, already four months pregnant by the Prince's child, is to be married hurriedly to her destined husband, a cousin of Djimé. After eight years of happy marriage, Kani's household has become a hornets' nest; she is abandoned by her husband and her *griotes* and captives are all jealously fighting among themselves. Sanou is known to have been responsible for the unrest, but she is also thought to be responsible for the death of any man who is involved with her, three previous husbands having already died. Djimé plots to kidnap Sanou on her wedding night having first sent his repudiated wife back to her family. The bridegroom, true to the tradition, is bitten by a deadly snake when searching for his bride. The book finishes with war declared and Djimé's death in battle.

Kani is a dignified, tragic figure. But disappointingly the gifts for sketching a realistic portrait and catching the psychological essentials that Sissoko showed in his 'Portraits' are little in evidence here, where they would help the reader's involvement with the drama of the action. This seems proof that the author undoubtedly had gifts for observation of reality and a talent for narration, but inadequate imagination to make a successful novelist, particularly in a field where observation of his own experience could not be put to immediate use. The structure of the novel, too, is rather unsatisfactory, the economy of the narrative verging on the incoherent. The style is uneven; at times it rises to the nobility of tone of the epic, at others it is abrupt and jerky, as if also the result of a desire for terseness and rapidity of movement, which is not completely successful.

David Ananou

DAVID ANANOU: *Le Fils du fétiche*. Paris, Nouvelles Editions Latines, 1955.

David Ananou's only novel appeared one year after Mongo Beti's first full-length work of fiction, but in spite of my intention to present the novelists chronologically, according to their first published work, I shall deal with it here, to give greater coherence to the study of those novels which have a more clearly colonial situation and anti-colonial orientation. Published in 1955, *Le Fils du fétiche* [The son of the fetish] makes no reference to the fact that the action takes place under colonial domination. The author's only direct allusion to the European colonists occurs in his introduction, and then in brief terms of gratitude to the 'civilizing powers' who have brought enlightenment to the dark continent and particularly those areas, including his native Togoland, still under the nefarious influence of fetishists and charlatans. He also makes it clear that the main aim of his novel is to counter the 'indifference, the coldness and the contempt with which the Black man is treated by his brothers of another race', so that after this unbiassed, objective study of the Black African's private life, 'it is likely that his foibles would be forgiven and he would be viewed with greater indulgence for his basic humanity'.

Le Fils du fétiche operates on this level as an ethnological text book, with the specific aim of combating racism by offering a better understanding of tribal life and custom, as well as a portrait of a typical Togolese family.

Ananou presents as his hero one Sodji, who respects unquestioningly every belief and tradition of the fetishist community of Seva in Southern Togoland, where he belongs. The author endows him with two shrewish wives, whom he repudiates, to marry his childhood friend Avlessi, apparently sterile, but who eventually bears his eponymous son and several daughters. Tracing the life cycle of this family, presented as a microcosm of tribal existence, Ananou manages to describe all the troubles and vicissitudes which can befall an individual (in the course of his 'basic, common humanity') and all the rites and ceremonies which traditionally punctuate the community existence. There are the problems of polygamy, child marriages, everyday conjugal relationships, the economy of the home, upbringing of children, treatment of illness. There are the rituals associated with normal birth and that of twins, betrothal, different marriage customs, bride-kidnapping, a trial for same, burial rites, funeral celebrations, mourning for widows, reconciliation after quarrels and a blood pact. And over all this hovers the power of the fetishist, who must be consulted at every eventuality of life and death.

However the author is ambivalent about his subject. While calling on the White reader's indulgence for his heroes, once their private lives are revealed, he condemns – presumably for his African readers – the superstitions which cloud and complicate their very existence. Thus, on the second level, *Le Fils du fétiche* is an indictment of traditional pagan beliefs, 'grotesque fetishist practices' and a call for acceptance of the message of the Gospels. The novel ends after Sodji's death, with Dansou (the son of the fetish), his wife, cousin and twin sons emigrating to the neighbouring Gold Coast where they come under the influence of an old catechist and accept baptism.

From Ananou's explicit statement in his epilogue, it is clear that he intends his novel to be a treatise on social anthropology, combined with an evangelizing tract, the whole thinly disguised as fiction. How far does it actually succeed as such? The didactic purpose is far too obvious, lacking the subtlety which would make its message palatable. The action is of the most tenuous, being confined to the normal vicissitudes of a fairly typical family in the Southern Togolese fetishist community of the period. By and large the incidents of the various chapters are mundane and disconnected. Here and there a little drama is introduced, rather unconvincingly, as in the case of the disappearance of Dansou's sweetheart, Afiavi, and his subsequent trial for kidnapping; but it is clear that this, as in other aspects of the narrative, is a pretext for more folk-lore. The characters themselves are two-dimensional and stereotyped with here and there a little attempt to give some individual features (for example Dansou's up-to-date cousin). Dansou himself is something of an anti-hero, particularly before the birth of his twin sons and the death of his father combine to invest him with a sense of responsibility. Previously he had been impulsive, quarrelsome, not particularly courageous, selfish and after the main chance. There is little consistency in the character of the father Sodji and the women never come to life at all.

Le Fils du fétiche is thus a mediocre novel as far as construction of action and presentation of character are concerned, as well as in its didactic purpose. It suffers, moreover, from being heavily over-written and its stylistic devices are exaggeratedly artificial. The author indulges in a ponderous and pedantic facetiousness or, seemingly uncertain of the force and level of the language, crams his text with every cliché, every idiom, every preciosity or circumlocution that he has ever read or heard, as if revelling in his own virtuosity. His linguistic prestidigitations have frequently grotesque results, particularly in his attempts to render African peasant speech in pedantic French. This verbal incongruity may well stem from the author's didactic and satirical intentions. The strong linguistic flavour of eighteenth-century French suggests that Ananou has steeped himself in Voltairian prose. Indeed there are clear parallels between the former's attacks on superstition and obscurantism and those of the Enlightenment: for anti-clericalism read anti-fetishism. *Le Fils du fétiche* has the makings of good comic satire in the tradition of the *conte philosophique*, but the effects are diminished by the author's heavy facetiousness and constant interventions. He rarely lets a burlesque situation speak for itself, as if underestimating the power of his readers to appreciate the joke and interpret the irony: this even goes to the extent of adding a footnote, for clarity, as when he wishes to expose the charlatan Afo's prophetic powers.

1954–64: AROUND THE ANTI-COLONIALIST CAUSE: 'ROMANS À THÈSE'

With the end of the fight against Hitler in Europe, with the realization of the vast task to be undertaken in introducing a new social and political order in a France that had been torn asunder by the Occupation and stood on the brink of revolution after Liberation, the movement of *engagement* in literature gained an increasing number of adherents. Writers who had been adjured to eschew creativity during the years when their very existence and the foundations of a whole civilization were in peril, now in large numbers turned their gifts to the defence of political ideologies with which it was hoped to build a new and better world. The fifties thus saw a notable production of committed writings, particularly in the field of drama and fiction. This was particularly true of African writers, whose fight for liberation from the yoke of colonial domination was now at its height. Very few African authors – the most outstanding being Ousmane Sembène, of whom more later – put their pen to the defence of workers' movements, condemning monopolistic practices of a capitalist society (White dominated to boot) and expressing solidarity with the syndicalists. The majority of the novelists of Africa of this period writing in French are concerned with condemning the evils of a colonial régime pure and simple. This had been one of the themes of the poetry of Negritude of the earlier decade, prompting Jean-Paul Sartre to write in his essay 'Orphée noir', prefacing Senghor's *Anthologie de la nouvelle poésie nègre et malgache*, in 1948: 'Black poetry has nothing in common with effusions of the heart: it is functional...' This is re-echoed more categorically by Senghor himself in 1956, stating at the first Congress of Black writers and artists, held at the Sorbonne: 'African literature is a committed literature.' The gestation of a novel is however necessarily slower than that of a poem and it was somewhat longer before anti-colonial works of fiction began to appear in important numbers.

As shown in an earlier chapter (p. 18), René Maran had given the lead over thirty years earlier, in works of great audacity at the time, which cost him his post with the French colonial administration. His *Batouala* and *Djouma, chien de brousse* were undoubted revelations to his White readers (and he could scarcely have counted on many others) who either lived in complete ignorance of the evils of the colonial system in Central Africa, or complacently accepted them as necessary, impugning Maran's picture as biassed, exaggerated or untrue, if they were deeply involved in the system themselves. Those Black writers, on the other hand, who took up the attack in the fifties, had need of much less courage and certainly had little to lose. At the worst their work might be banned, as was the case with Mongo Beti's *Le Pauvre Christ de Bomba* when it first appeared in 1956, but this was more a question of morals and of the alleged offence to the Church than because of the aspersions cast at the colonial administration. (We should compare the banning of Coffi Gadeau's play, *Les Recrutés des M. Maurice*, by the Governor of Ivory Coast, because of its attack on the recruitment of forced labour.) By the mid-fifties it was no longer an act of *lèse-blancheur* to condemn colonial officials for stupidity, ignorance or even brutality, nor complete blasphemy to suggest that Christian missionaries had not necessarily brought a new Jerusalem to the Dark Continent.

Now that the system and its inherent evils had given way to Independence, now that the 'functional' aspects of these works have been served and the conditions they decried belong to history, from the relative distance of between twenty to twelve years from publication, if not from procreation, one can begin to try to assess the literary merits of these works of anti-colonial inspiration and theme.

Jean Malonga

JEAN MALONGA: *Cœur d'Aryenne*. In 'Trois écrivains noirs', Paris, Présence Africaine, 1954.

Jean Malonga wrote his novel, *Cœur d'Aryenne*, towards the end of the forties, probably 1948, but it was not published until 1954 when the review *Présence Africaine* issued a special number entitled 'Trois écrivains noirs', in which it appeared with Mongo Béti's *Ville cruelle* (under his first pseudonym of Eza Boto) and Abdoulaye Sadji's *Nini*. Unsatisfactory as the two latter works are, they have some redeeming features, and in both cases the authors followed up these first tentative compositions with novels of greater maturity in which their undoubted talents are manifest. *Cœur d'Aryenne*, on the other hand, is such a thoroughly bad novel that there are only two possible reasons for discussing it at all. It might be taken as the *terminus a quo*, by which the phenomenal strides made by the West African novel over the last twenty years or so may be judged. But this is invalidated by the fact that in the thirties and forties even the weakest of the published writings showed much greater professionalism and originality and the best demonstrated outstanding talent, as witness some mentioned earlier in this chapter. The other justification, then, would be the importance attached to it at the time of its appearance and for some time afterwards. In other words, it must be considered as a sociological or even political rather than as a literary phenomenon.

Malonga attempts a realistic, romantic novel on the theme of racial prejudice and love across the colour bar, set in the French colony of Congo-Brazzaville. The love affair between the two adolescents, White Solange and Black Mambeké, develops from a simpering, sentimental idyll (shades of Bernardin de Saint-Pierre) to a torrid romance in which the near-salacious eroticism of the cheap novelette is interspersed with the crude melodrama of the penny-dreadful. The characters are improbable burlesques, without even the consistency of a caricature. The exaggeratedly precious style is often unconsciously funny... For further analysis I would recommend the chapter that A. C. Brench devotes to it in his study, *The Novelists' Inheritance in French Africa* (pp. 75–83). Literary merits apart, I suggested above that the interest of Malonga's novel is the light it throws on certain sociological and political attitudes of the fifties and early sixties.

In spite of some contradictions in the general principles implicit in the work – resulting from the author's own ambivalence – it is easy to see how *Cœur d'Aryenne* achieved its success in the pre-Independence era. Ideologically cautious as it is, it nevertheless includes homeopathic doses of the popular ingredients of the anti-colonial novel and some of the minor literature of Negritude, including the usual indictment of White colonials (un-Christian clerics, inhuman administrators, debauched settlers) and the exhortation to reject Western values and return to the wisdom of the Ancestors (couched in vague terms in Mambeké's final speech). The hint of denigration of bourgeois materialism would also be a concession to the partisan commitment of the time. Fortunately for the future of the African novel, other writers achieved better results in the field of committed literature.

Mongo Beti

MONGO BETI (Pseud. of Alexandre Biyidi, early work published under pseud. Eza Boto): *Ville cruelle*. In 'Trois écrivains noirs', Paris, Présence Africaine, 1954 (under name of Eza Boto). Re-issued Paris, Les Éditions Africaines, 1964. o.p. Re-issued Livre de Poche, 1972. *Le Pauvre Christ de Bomba*. Paris, Laffont, 1956. o.p. Liechtenstein, Kraus Reprint, 1970. *Mission terminée*. Paris, Corrêa, Buchet/Chastel, 1957. o.p. Re-issued Livre de Poche, 1972. *Le Roi miraculé*. Paris, Corrêa, Buchet/Chastel, 1958. o.p. Re-issued Livre de Poche, 1972.

English translations: *The Poor Christ of Bomba*, trans. by Gerald Moore. London, Ibadan, Nairobi, Heinemann Educational Books, 1971. *Mission accomplished*, trans. Peter Green. New York, Macmillan, 1958. o.p.; as *Mission to Kala*, London, Muller, 1958. o.p. London etc., Heinemann Educational Books, 1964. African Writers Series, repr. 1966. *King Lazarus*, trans. anon. London, Muller, 1960. Repr. 1969. London etc., Heinemann Educational Books, 1970.

In 1954, a twenty-four-year-old Cameroonian, Alexandre Biyidi, studying at the University of Aix-en-Provence, published his first novel, *Ville cruelle*, after a novella, *Ville sans haine et sans amour*, which had appeared in *Présence Africaine*. His literary début thus coincided approximately with that of Camara Laye. By 1958 he had published three more novels in rapid succession, since when his literary output apparently ceased abruptly, as far as fiction at least was concerned. In the five to six years which formed the transition between the pre- and post-Independence eras for the majority of West and Central African states, there was a notable decline in creative literature. Most of the established writers were, in the first instance, engaged in anti-colonial conflicts; after 1960 some were channelled into diplomatic posts and a few were occupied in political opposition to the new régimes. Then, by the mid-sixties, some of the more important poets, novelists and dramatists, who had gained a reputation in the fifties – Bernard Dadié, Ousmane Sembène, Aimé Césaire, Tchicaya U Tam'si, found new inspiration and joined the growing ranks of the younger generation of post-Independence writers. Mongo Beti remained apparently a notable exception, until he broke his sixteen year silence by publishing two new novels in 1974. (See page 281.) If the works of his first period had been limited to a denunciation of colonialism, his long silence would have been explained by the removal of his main target. Then his virulent attack on the régime of President Ahidjo, *Main basse sur le Cameroun* [The Rape of Cameroon] (Paris, F. Maspero, 1972)[5] suggested that he might also be preparing these works of fiction, into which he would incorporate, like other recent Black novelists, his indictment of local, post-Independence politics.

Mongo Beti, though a satirist of the first water, was never at first entirely a polemical novelist. He was concerned not only with politico-social institutions or people engaged in political activities, but also with the human conflicts that result from such institutions and activities: no totally political preoccupation guides the themes or forms the setting for his novels of this first period. Even in the still clumsy fictional experiment, *Ville cruelle* [Cruel city], we see the attempt to deal with a human situation, although the vicissitudes of the protagonists are in large measure due to adverse economic circumstances resultant from the colonial régime and to the brutality and corruption of the White colonists themselves. The three next novels, when Beti has a surer mastery of his literary medium, are tragi-comedies resulting from human weaknesses, false illusions, the tricks that fate plays on man's ambitions and ideals. The colonial situation, the educational system and particularly the missionary influences that it had fostered in Cameroon, more especially in the inter-war years, are only incidental to the interplay of conflicting principles and ideals which operate on a completely different level from assertion of purely nationalist principles.

For the novelist Olympe Bhêly-Quénum, writing in 1962, Mongo Beti was the most talented and the most intelligent of young African writers, superior to his compatriot Oyono and far surpassing Camara Laye. This judgement is based on Beti's avoidance of 'false exoticism' which Bhêly-Quénum holds in horror, together with the mysticism which permeates *Le Regard du Roi*, regionalism and all the *niaiseries* which have been expressed about Black races. This is correct enough although I cannot altogether agree with the conclusion that Beti best 'poses the problem of the African and hence the problem of man in constant evolution', what

---

[5] He calls him 'nothing but a puppet, placed in power by France, with the intention of maintaining her economic interests behind the screen of an artificial independence'. This publication was banned in France.

Bhêly-Quénum calls elsewhere in this same article 'the universalist [sic] vision of the African'; even less that *Ville cruelle* 'already revealed his talent, his mastery, his solid imagination'.

Other over-indulgent critics have tended to exaggerate the literary merits of this first novel, perhaps dazzled by the prestige attached to the author after the success of his later works, perhaps influenced by the acerbity of his criticism of the colonial milieu. It is, however, an interesting indication of the author's own assessment of this work, that it has never appeared under the pseudonym which he eventually adopted and by which his literary production is widely known. With the republication of *Ville cruelle* in 1972 in the Livre de Poche collection, it is still attributed to 'Eza Boto', while the jacket notes to *Perpétue* (1974) accredit him with being the author of only *three* previous novels.

In common with a long line of heroes of West African fiction, the central figure of this novel, Banda, is a young peasant, ambitious but unarmed against greed and corruption, who is driven by the backward conditions of the bush to try his fortune in the 'cruel city'. The period is the mid-thirties. The realistic if melodramatic treatment of Banda's miseries and disillusionment in the town of Tanga adds another page to the chapter of satirical, anti-colonial fiction opened by *Batouala* in 1923, and illustrates conditions in the town as bad, if not worse, as Maran had depicted for the rural areas, with the peasant shown at the mercy of greedy, unscrupulous traders as well as vicious and corrupt officials.

The twenty-four-year-old Biyidi does touch on the 'problem of the African in constant evolution' as Bhêly-Quénum suggests, but does not come seriously to grips with this in a convincing anecdote nor with characters whose fate deeply concerns us. Banda is too arrogant, too opportunist, too given to violence himself to be the true 'naïf' of the archetype of a lost generation. Nevertheless he is trapped between the economic depression of the bush and the menace of city life; similarly he is suspended in a psychic vacuum, in revolt against the authority of the elders, cynical about their traditional beliefs and disillusioned with the civilization and religion of the West, based respectively on the cult of money and a devalorized Christianity. Here his denunciation of the Whites, and in particular of the Catholic missionaries, anticipates the more corrosive satire tempered with burlesque humour of *Le Pauvre Christ de Bomba* and *Le Roi miraculé*. However, he is equally cynical about the prestige and powers of the witch-doctors in the village society of his origins.

The author shows some powers of vivid description – suggesting not only the appearance but also the spirit of the setting against which the action is played, particularly in the opening paragraphs, describing the two faces of the town of Tanga – on its hill, overlooking the equatorial forest, the south slope occupied by the rich commercial and administrative buildings and the comfortable White residences; the north side, unlit, swallowed up by the sordid slums of the native population – suggesting, from the beginning of the narrative, but without great subtlety, the dichotomy of life in the colonies. The quality of the writing is uneven; at the best 'Eza Boto' already shows evidence of his descriptive powers, here dashing off a caricatural portrait; there, evoking briefly and realistically the noisy activity of the city scene. The greatest weakness, besides the melodramatic nature of the anecdote is the sketchy psychological characterization of the three main protagonists, and the consequent shallow emotional relationship that links them. Odilia and her brother Koumé are very slightly drawn and we are hardly touched by the latter's death. Even Banda's main regret at the loss of his friend is that he never had the chance to ask him for a useful tip on how to rob a Greek trader; so he pockets without a qualm the wad of notes from the corpse, which Koumé had himself stolen from his boss. Banda is in fact neither a true naïf, nor a frankly picaresque rogue. The author experiments with the first person singular narrative, in an attempt to penetrate into the inner workings of his hero's mind; though here and there the dialogue is lively and realistic, the style tends to be repetitive and stilted.

When Mongo Beti published his next novel in 1956, he had made astonishing progress in the originality of his subject, in the mastery of his fictional composition and style, in the deeper understanding and greater subtlety of his character drawing, of Blacks and Whites.

Le Pauvre Christ de Bomba is the most cynical of Mongo Beti's satires of the colonial régime of the pre-war period, equalling in virulence *Batouala*. But the threshold of tolerance of political out-spokenness had lowered since Maran's novel caused such a furore more than thirty years earlier; and so it was most probably its attack on the missions and consequent implications of corruption within Church-sponsored organizations, that caused its banning by the Governor of Cameroon when it first appeared. By now Beti had brought an important new weapon into his armoury: a ferocious irony and that brand of bawdy humour known as *gauloiserie*. He continued to perfect these in his next two novels. His own humanism had also broadened and matured so that he was sensitive to the tragedy inherent in the White missionary's disillusionment, while he denounced the missions as being the corruptors of a rural society and the minions of an interested political authority. This is a subtle novel, whose construction revolves around two apparently antagonistic axes, thus increasing the impact of the irony; these, like the negative and positive poles of a magnet are responsible for the movement and pattern of the magnetic field between them. At the one pole we have the young Black boy, Denis, scarcely more than a child, ignorant and virginal in every sense, acolyte and sedulous admirer of his master the priest, whose every word is literally his gospel: the true innocent, whose education in corruption, and advancement into incredulity and final disillusionment forms one of the two main threads of the narrative. At the other pole we have the austere Reverend Father Superior Drumont, who in spite of his years still remains an innocent, too, in his credulity, believing in his proselytizing powers and incapable of seeing either that his mission is a school for lubricity and lechery rather than of Christian conduct, or that he himself is a tool of the colonial administration.

The story is told by the ingenuous Denis, thus deliberately distorting the angle of vision in the interests of irony. Drumont was completely unaware that his *Sixa* had become a brothel, that his catechists are pimps, his African staff corrupt opportunists, his converts simply fugitives from forced labour. Denis, on the other hand, who narrates the discovery of this shocking state of affairs, was quite simply ignorant of their true implications. Instead of either an omniscient author relating a series of events and Drumont's reactions, or, as might have been possible, a first person account by the Reverend Father himself, similar to the narrative process of *Le Roi miraculé*, using diaries and letters, here the child tells what he scarce comprehendingly observes, both of what goes on behind Father Drumont's back and how the latter reacts in his growing frustration, anger and disillusionment with the failure of twenty-five years' dedication to an ideal.

At the time of its publication *Le Pauvre Christ de Bomba* was mainly praised for its audacity and courage in laying bare the antagonism between, on the one hand this 'imported Christianity, the corollary, in the eyes of the natives, to colonialism and all its coercive forces, and, on the other, the spirit of independence and customs and traditions firmly rooted in the land of the Bantu' (Chas. Bodzinski, *Lettres françaises*, 26.5.56).[6] Now that all this has become a part of history, we can see that the novel has a merit beyond the temporary impact of the polemics, that will almost certainly cause it to survive when the social problems it castigates have become curiosities. This is mainly the vision of Father Drumont's calvary. Not for nothing does Mongo Beti call him the 'Poor Christ'. It is not only, and perhaps not primarily, the Bantu people whom he shows as the victims of the system, and the sordid intrigues that it encourages. Nevertheless

---

[6] A. Biyidi's first pseudonym, Eza Boto, means *les gens aliénés*–the alienated people; the one he finally adopted, Mongo Beti, signifies 'the child of free men'.

I would treat with great reserve and caution Leonard Sainville's statement in the introduction to his anthology, *Romanciers et conteurs négro-africains*, that the 'dominant theme of Mongo Beti's novels is not social and nationalist revendication' but these can be 'divined under the humour and irony which is characteristic'. The latter are not gratuitous, but the deliberate weapons of the practised satirist, handled with remarkable skill by such a young writer. It is worth noting that it took Bernard Dadié another ten years before he achieved such successful effects of burleque irony in his satirical plays of the late sixties. (I also note Sainville's incomprehensible suggestion that Beti, like Camara Laye, 'practises serenity' in his 'attempt to bring to life the men and women of the Cameroon, that is an African humanity'! Serenity is incompatible with any satire, and those of Mongo Beti have the nature of a Philippic.)

In his next work, *Mission terminée*, Beti adopts as the basic mode of expression Rabelaisian comedy with which he relieves the truculence and savage irony of *Le Pauvre Christ*. Again, I am struck by the misinterpretations to which this most transparent of novels has been subject on the part of critics of good will but bad judgement. It seems that it was imperative to find *engagement* and autobiography in all Negro-African novels prior to Independence, as if it were to indict a Black writer for *lèse-négritude* to suggest that his work might have universal implications. As examples: Judith Gleason in *This Africa*, a study of novels by West Africans in French and English, analyses it in a chapter entitled 'Inner Life', as a 'satirical study of the effects of the French educational system', thus promoting to the level of the author's main subject and intention, what is patently only an incidental theme and an ancillary target at which Mongo Beti cannot refrain from launching a few barbs *en passant*. Wilfred Cartey, even less justifiably, includes *Mission terminée* in his chapter on autobiographical novels, together with *l'Enfant noir* and Cheikh Hamidou Kane's *Aventure ambiguë*, and with particular reference to the 'mother and child' theme – so much for the imperative search for themes and categories in the Black novel! The 'autobiographical' element and the 'satirical study' above mentioned, (but no 'mother and child theme'), can indeed be be found in the one personal note of bitterness that Mongo Beti allows to intrude into the narration that proceeds for the most part as a mixture of farce and joyous *fabliau*. I have already quoted, in an earlier chapter, the author's acrimonious reminiscences of his schooldays in the Cameroon in the forties. But this is by no means the subject of the novel and might even be considered stylistically as introducing a false note, destroying the unity of the work, as it is the only place in the novel where Beti dips his pen in acid.

Edouard Eliet, whose *Panorama de la littérature négro-africaine* is intended as a 'manual for the reader wishing to be informed of tendencies in the modern world dominated by the accession to independence of the former colonies', and is based, according to his introduction, on 'littérature de combat', has no hesitation in including *Mission terminée* in this category. Indeed he interprets it as a 'drama of a double conscience', the confrontation of the young student Medza who has lost contact with traditional Bantu village life with 'the image of Negritude' in the person of his cousin Zambo, and the ancestral voice of his race which his Westernized education has made him incapable of understanding. Eliet even interprets the true symbol of the 'mission' of the title as a 'search for something common to the West and to Negritude', which is realized by the sympathies and affinities linking Medza to his village cousins and the qualities by which they complement their respective deficiencies. Now, interesting as such a thesis may be, this is surely to be haunted with the ghosts of Negritude and to push the necessity for proving militancy too far. What is more, such limited interpretations give no credit to the true originality of Mongo Beti's third novel which transcends preoccupation with a transient social situation.

It is true that *Mission terminée* is as determinedly satirical as the preceding works, but the target here is more universal. It is not simply an attack on African urban life and the superimposition of a foreign educational system, nor a plea for a return to village life and traditional African values. It is a brilliantly comic verbal cudgelling of self-sufficiency born of mythomania and exaggerated enthusiasms for the foreign, the unfamiliar, the imported product. It is also, and primarily, a clever piece of literary satire and comic pastiche. In the first place, the vicissitudes of Medza in the course of his 'mission' are a direct reversal of the misadventures of the peasant at the mercy of the city slicker and rogues of all sorts, a common theme in Western literature from the eighteenth century onwards, and abundantly exploited in negro-African fiction and drama. Here, on the contrary, it is the apparently sophisticated urban youth who is dispossessed with ease by his canny rural kin, in Kala. Like any innocent abroad, Medza learns not to trust appearances, nor his pre-conceived ideas, and in spite of his inadequate education, he acquires a certain amount of horse-sense, in the end, after some chastening and disconcerting experiences.

On the second level of parody, we have in *Mission terminée*, from the title itself, through the long *résumés* that introduce each chapter's contents, in the portentous manner of the eighteenth-century picaresque and some nineteenth-century Romantic novels, a mock epic, a burlesque heroic romance. It combines the tale of the knight adventurer setting forth on a difficult and dangerous mission with a send-up of the quest, and with loss of innocence which is supposed to be the basic common factor (Harry Levin *oblige*) of the modern novel, as opposed to the earlier romance. As Professor Levin only published his *Gates of Horn* in 1963, Mongo Beti could not have been aware of his theory, nor that he was parodying two opposing genres with instinctive awareness of the danger of too great trust in categories. But he leaves no doubt that he intends his novel to be read as a literary satire, as the chapter summaries and particularly the beginning of Medza's adventures illustrate, where elements of pastiche are everywhere apparent.

Finally, more cautiously, I would suggest that a parody of the philosophical novel can be discerned. At the end of his adventures, Medza has seen fail all the criteria by which he had thought previously to measure success in life; in their place he has learned to prize one thing only, namely freedom. But this is not political freedom – not a hint of this here – but a Gidian *disponibilité*. He forfeited this freedom by setting his sights on an education for which he was not intellectually equipped; and, in the final resort, he rejects the possibility of romantic love, together with the rest of his earlier ideals, in order to enjoy this new-found freedom in the company of his athletic cousin.

With *Le Roi miraculé*, Mongo Beti returns to the theme and situation of *Le Pauvre Christ de Bomba*: the conflict between native shibboleth and Christian doctrine, with the French colonial authorities holding the uneasy balance between the theological and the ideological. It is now the post-war period – 1948 – and Father Le Guen, whom we knew as *vicaire* to the Reverend Father Drumont, becomes responsible, like his predecessor, for a crisis in tribal life. As complacent and convinced of the efficacy of his mission, he is just as doomed to failure by his inability to come to terms with the African situation and to realize that there is only one guiding principle – expediency.

Although the central idea of the amateur baptism *in extremis* and the subsequent miraculous recovery of the bibulous, gluttonous, polygamous Chief Essomba is rich in comic and dramatic possibilities, which Mongo Beti exploits to the full, this last novel is less satisfying than either of the two preceding works. It lacks the unity of the *Pauvre Christ* and gives the impression of having been padded out to the required length for a novel. Moreover, it suffers from the diversity of angles from which the main theme is viewed, as well as the multiplicity of subsidiary themes which distract from the main episode. It would probably have been more satisfactory artistically if it had been limited to the dimensions of a novella and some of the vissicitudes of the secondary characters reserved for future short stories.

The characters of *Le Roi miraculé* can be divided into actors and observers, the latter being too numerous. Because the drama of *Le Pauvre Christ* is seen and narrated solely by the ingenuous acolyte Denis, his naïveté adds to the irony, and his admiration for the Reverend Father increases the reader's involvement with his fate. Denis's counterpart, the twelve-year-old Gustave, Le Guen's prize pupil, is a minor onlooker at the illness and recovery of the chief and adds no dimension to the understanding of the events. These are narrated by the traditional omniscient author, except for two brief extracts from the priest's letters to his mother. (It is a pity that this formula, which gives too fleeting an insight into Le Guen's character and motives, is not further exploited.) Apart from young Gustave, the other onlooker is the rather unlikable Kris, a rebellious student who has fallen into disgrace at school and who has the makings of a wide boy. The nephew of one of Essombo's wives, Kris is sent to Essazem to look after his aunt's interests and takes advantage of the opportunity to consolidate his shaky finances by brewing illicit liquor for the improvised camp. He is not a narrator, as Judith Gleason states in her study *This Africa*, and he never actually intervenes in the action. His sole function, shared with his school-friend Bitama, is to suggest that the future lies neither with the chief, his harem and his village elders, nor with the colonial powers, but with the young generation who are equally lacking in respect for tribal tradition and European authority. Among the other observers of the drama are a young colonial officer and a Negro doctor, who reverts to his Ongola back-street accent and manners after several glasses of wine. They leave the impression that they have been filled out from walk-on parts and given their lines to prove the author's virtuosity in painting a diversity of portraits. This is unnecessary as there are enough main and secondary characters to give Mongo Beti ample opportunity to display his undoubted descriptive gifts. In the event, the degree of visual detail bestowed on portrayals is not necessarily proportionate to their importance to the action. The two protagonists, the chief and the missionary, are scarcely described. The most vividly depicted is the very minor character of the Elder Ndibidi. The care with which this buffoon is drawn, taken in conjunction with equally grotesque descriptions of the old crone Yosifa – the chief's aunt who is responsible for the amateur baptism – of the elderly first wife, Makrita, and the concentration on the skeletal, the obese and the verbose, makes it clear that Beti's chief talent as a portraitist is for caricature and that the main features he is interested in are the burlesque, the ludicrous, the exaggerated. Although the author shows his observation of the minutest physical detail in these cases, he is often satisfied to suggest a stock type, rather than to draw an individual in depth.

Ezoun, the catechist, never in fact confirms his reputation as 'the village Tartuffe'; the charms of the favourite young wife, Anaba, frequently alluded to, are never described, while those of her young sister are; the chief's offspring, Maurice, the pimp, and Cecilia, the tart, are scarcely visualized but Raphael, 'the hero of Koufra' and the local mechanic, and a picturesque hunter who has the briefest of appearances, are described in detail. This all adds up to a series of pages out of a talented caricaturist's note-book, jottings of unequal observation which the artist cannot decide to jettison.

The ambiguity of tone, tragi-comic but more burlesque than tragic for the major part of the story, also detracts from the final impact and militates against the author's serious intentions: namely, to show the failure of mission work in Cameroon, and to paint a society about to disintegrate, refusing Western values as symbolized by Christianity and monogamy, but not yet ready to propose alternatives. Although the futility of the mission work is amply suggested, we are not as concerned with the disillusionment of the missionary, a less absolute character than his predecessor Drumont. In spite of his hubris and violence Father Drumont was a fundamentally tragic character, both the forger of his own downfall and the victim of circumstance. So, too, is Le Guen, but because he is more worldly-wise, less austere and single-minded, we are less moved by his fate.

Even when account is taken of the weakness of his first published novel and some inconsistencies in *Le Roi*, Mongo Beti must be considered as one of the most noteworthy of the French African novelists. As far as his plots are concerned, there are hardly any false notes: everywhere the situations are original and peculiar to Cameroonian society of the pre-Independence era. The action, when at its best, is lively, compelling and convincingly developed, in accordance with the situation and the characters presented. In some of the epic crises the stage is filled with motley, raggle-taggle hordes which lend a Breughel quality to the narration, in which fantasy and robust realism mingle with violence. Although not a master of psychological analysis in depth, Beti has a gift for acute observation which he translates by a pungent phrase of witty comparison, thereby high-lighting ironic associations and idiosyncrasies of appearance, character and language. He has a particular gift for rendering peculiarities of speech, in a highly flexible dialogue, adapted to age, social position, race and character: he can range from the jovial to the pedantic, the familiar *faubourien* to the bureaucratic and the semi-facetious. This aptitude for dialogue, together with his skill in depicting burlesque and dramatic situations, suggests that he might have rivalled Bernard Dadié as a successful, satirical dramatist. Beneath the mockery and the irony, usually less astringent, and less inventive than Dadié's, the serious intention of *Le Pauvre Christ* and *Le Roi miraculé* is equally present: to show a society at a period of imminent crisis, when the delicately achieved balance of powers can be upset by the intrusion of a disturbing element. In any case, it is evident that the traditional past is on its way out, giving way to a new era, which cannot fail to be marked by the reaction to colonialism.

Benjamin Matip

BENJAMIN MATIP: *Afrique, nous t'ignorons*. Paris, R. Lacoste, 1956.

Matip's *Afrique, nous t'ignorons*, first published in 1954, in no. XIII of *Présence Africaine*, contributed to the explosion of anti-colonial fiction from West Africa in the fifties. As in *Ville cruelle*, by his compatriot Mongo Beti, with which it is contemporaneous, Matip's book refers to the exploitation of the Cameroonian planters and attempts a portrait of the unscrupulous, bullying European trader. But this aspect of colonial life is neither the whole nor the fundamental issue of the novel. The key is in the title: *Afrique, nous t'ignorons*. The first person plural pronoun embraces the whole generation of young, university-trained Negroes, reaching maturity in the fifties and responsible for the future of Black Africa. They contemplate the past of their country, from which their Western education has to a certain extent divorced them, and with which Hitler's war has made an irreparable break. This past, not only of the colonial era, but also of the pre-colonial period, is embodied in the patriarchs of Bidoé, and the other notables of the village, including the evangelist and the catechist, for both Protestant and Catholic missions have left their mark on African society. All these are convened for a palaver in times of crisis, in this case the outbreak of the war in Europe. The patriarchs are unable to decide how the war will affect the village community; the younger men, led by the patriarch Guimous's son, Samuel, wish to use the opportunity to revolt and break the authority of the colonists.

Presented in fictional form, with elements of the *conte philosophique*, *Afrique, nous t'ignorons* is not a very satisfactory novel. The characters, Black and White, are sketchy and unconvincing, from the lying opportunist missionary to the chief patriarch Guimous. The latter is neither ignorant nor illiterate. He went to secondary school under the Germans and is stated to have liked city life at that time, but to have been unable to acclimatize himself to French-orientated colonial existence. He claims to have the wisdom and percipience of age but is completely blind to the true character of the despicable Robert, whom he calls a *chic type*, adding that such a quality is rare in the most honest of traders, which his son finds improbable. Robert himself is a bundle of inconsistencies and melodramatic traits. He is partly the stereotyped bullying White trader, intimidating his Black customers and thrashing his houseboy. He is also shown as a coward, a political turncoat, a deserter and a would-be murderer. He had been secretary to a Communist cell before joining a right-wing party and then emigrating to Cameroon just after the 1918 Armistice, when he loses all political commitment. He despises all Blacks, but is prepared to spend over three hours in a deep political discussion with Guimous, to the fury of his wife who is waiting to serve lunch, and even at 2.30, when he has shut up the store for the afternoon siesta, he is disappointed that Guimous has not waited to prolong the conversation. He considers shooting his wife (who seems prepared to return the compliment) but changes his mind. When he is about to depart in the middle of the night, to avoid mobilization, he decides instead to have the lady despatched by hired murderers from among the villagers of Bidoé, where he intends to hide.

The young Samuel is presumably meant to act as the mouth-piece of the author and in fact that is all he is, a voice without a personality. He never seems a character in flesh and blood. He is the pretext and the vehicle for a certain amount of philosophizing and discussion on the situation and future of Africa, which is, of course, the main subject of the book.

The action is of the slightest, with dramatic titles given to the three parts in an effort to highlight the inherent tension of the historical situation. The first part is called 'Alarm': the young Samuel returns from school but the chronology is a little vague as it is stated to be late in September 1939, not the normal end of the school year or the beginning of the holidays. He takes his father's bananas and cocoa to the market in Kézzaé together with personal presents for the trader from Guimous, who considers him his friend. Sam brings back news of the outbreak of war. Part two is inexplicably entitled 'Hell', but there is little indication of the hell that has already or is about to break loose, either in Europe or in Africa. The council of elders is convened, the messengers are designated and sent to Pastor William, Robert and the witch-doctor. Guimous gives his son a lesson on the wisdom of the Ancestors and they have a philosophical discussion. In part three, called 'The Patriarchs', Robert receives his call-up papers and disappears into the night after having previously sent all the stock from his store to his friend Guimous for safe-keeping for the duration of the war. The villagers hold their palaver. And that is all.

In an article on the literature of Cameroon, appearing in *Le Monde* of 25–6 January 1970, Philippe Decraene wrote of *Afrique, nous t'ignorons*,

as 'the story of the break between emancipated individualism and traditional mimesis, an absorbing work misunderstood in Europe at the time
of publication, in spite of its qualities'. I would suggest that one of the
reasons why it was not understood is a certain timidity on Matip's part
in stating his theme, and that the qualities are certainly not those of a master
of the fictional form. He is happier when recounting traditional legends
and the folk-tales of his native land, discussed in a previous chapter. I
referred above to the potential of *Afrique, nous t'ignorons* as a *conte philosophique*; there is certainly an eighteenth-century element about the role that
discussion and moralizing dialogue play in the narrative. What an opportunity Matip missed here of presenting his Africa, with the portraits of
the representatives of the different generations, in the form of a philosophical dialogue in the manner of Diderot!

Bernard Binlin Dadié

BERNARD BINLIN DADIÉ: *Climbié*. Paris, Seghers, 1956. o.p. In *Légendes et poèmes*.
  Paris, Seghers, 1966, o.p.
  English translation: *Climbié*, trans. Karen Chapman. New York, Africana
    Publishing House, 1971. London, Ibadan, Nairobi, Heinemann Educational
    Books, 1971.

Bernard Dadié has never claimed to be a novelist and none of his prose
works can strictly be considered as fiction. On his own admission,[7] there
is little invention of character in *Climbié* and of neither character nor action
in *Un Nègre à Paris*.[8] While there is some justification for treating *Climbié*
as autobiographical 'fiction', I shall not discuss *Un Nègre à Paris* here. As
there is not sufficient material in the form of *belles lettres* from French-
speaking Africa, I add a brief study of Dadié's travel chronicles in an
appendix (see p. 320).

   After having published in volume form his first poems and the African
folk-tales and legends which he had collected and retold as his contribution
to the conservation of Africa's cultural heritage. Bernard Dadié selected
the most poignant memories, the most meaningful episodes and impressions of his own life and assembled these under the title of *Climbié*, the
fictional name for his *alter ego*.[9] Climbié's experiences do not diverge to
any appreciable extent from those of his creator.

   In the interview with C. Quillateau quoted above, Dadié comments on

---

[7] See 'Dialogue with a work and a poet', in C. Quillateau's *Bernard Binlin Dadié: l'homme
   et l'œuvre*, Présence Africaine, part IV, p. 152.
[8] Cf. A. C. Brench: *The Novelists' Inheritance in French Africa*, ch. 5, pp. 84–91 and Jahn
   & Dressler's categories in their *Bibliography of Creative African Writing*, item 282.
[9] In *Un Nègre à Paris* Dadié tells us that the name Climbié means *un jour* [one day].

the lessons he drew from his reading of Guy de Maupassant's *Contes*, whose form and structure he much admired. In spite of the apparently episodic nature of *Climbié*, the narrative has a latent symmetry of structure which betrays already a concern with form and composition. The book consists of two nearly equal parts, corresponding to the two periods of the life which it recounts. The first part is devoted to Climbié-Dadié's first twenty years: his childhood, schooldays and studies. The second tells of the period from his leaving William Ponty School in 1936, to take up a clerical post with the colonial administration in Dakar, to his discharge from prison in 1950. The thread that links the apparently random collection of memories and anecdotes that form the first part is Climbié's thirst for knowledge and his progress through the various stages of his formal education. Some incidents, such as the arrival of the conjuror and the yellow-fever epidemic, are clearly introduced to mark the passage of time in an otherwise uneventful existence, and to indicate of what stuff this small-town African society was made. With this is associated the rural setting, the life of the planters, the importance of retaining the attachment to the soil and one's origins and, lastly, the gradual awakening of Climbié's political awareness. Part two is the story of his political education and the formulation of his philosophies, principles and ideologies. There is no sentimental education; only a brief mention in part one of the girls at the neighbouring school in Grand-Bassam, with whom the boys frolicked innocently, and the Nalba whom Climbié has shyly singled out and whose last words to him, as he leaves for William Ponty School in Senegal are: 'Don't be like all the others who don't recognize us any more when they come home'.

We are plunged into the first theme from the dramatic opening paragraph which describes the seven-year-old Climbié fleeing desperately to escape the brutal beating which will be his punishment for having practised his letters on the primary school walls. Already we appreciate the problems and share the anguish of a little Black boy who does not understand the reasoning of an alien, adult world, and is only anxious to master the mysterious hieroglyphics which are the key to knowledge. The next stage in his education is his initiation into rural existence, to learn the problems of the planter's life, the seasons for sowing rice, bananas, sugar-cane, the care of the coffee and cocoa plantation, exposed to the vagaries of the weather and the depredations of animals. There is no deliberate search for local colour, but economical reference to a regional way of life to which Dadié is deeply attached. Then it is school again – the struggle for the good marks that are the open-sesame to the future effaces the memories of the rice-fields and the legends recounted by his uncle and the days spent chasing birds and insects.

In Dadié's memories of the school in Grand Bassam, the episode of the 'symbol', the wooden cube, stands out, indicating the pressure put on these primary school pupils from A.O.F. to acquire a mastery of French, which we have referred to earlier (p. 11). Dadié achieves the feat of writing on two levels simultaneously: on that of the child Climbié, in whose pocket the little wooden cube weighs so heavily, preventing him playing, eating, a lonely pariah until he can find another miscreant speaking dialect; and on that of the African writer who, twenty-five years later, can exploit the infinite expressivity of French, and while satirizing the Frenchman's horror at the 'cavalier treatment of the language of Vaugelas', has a sneaking respect for this reaction.

On the whole it is in a narrative tinged with melancholy that Dadié re-lives the loneliness and ardours of his youth, cut off from his family and his rural origins and dedicated to acquiring a new language and mastering examination syllabuses. Two small episodes that barely fill a page significantly point to his eventual destiny. Young Climbié's passion for reading leads him and a friend to rifle the schoolroom cupboard and remove two books each, on the pretext that they were intended for the pupils, but for two years no-one had bothered to distribute them. But the child is conscience-stricken at the thought of the theft, and overwhelmed with fear of the prison which he passes daily on the way to school, so he throws the books back into the classroom through the window. Twenty years later he is sentenced to this same prison, because his publications have given him a reputation as a political agitator. The second incident is also associated with books. After the death of the uncle who was his first guardian, he is entrusted to another uncle, Assouan Koffi, during his schooldays at Grand-Bassam. This uncle, more politically conscious, shows him pictures of a Negro in Haarlem being arrested for demonstrating on behalf of victimized brother Negroes, and another picture of Whites being beaten up by other Whites, presumably in the course of political riots or syndicalist activities. Climbié does not understand how such things can be, and his uncle gives him his first lesson in universal humanitarianism and anti-racism. We see in part two of the work how Climbié-Dadié puts this lesson into practice.

Yet, however militant the author may have become in his political writings and activities against the evils of colonialism and the victimization of his countrymen, the tone of *Climbié* is never violent. If anything the case is under-stated. Even when recounting his experiences in prison, which he does with economy, Dadié's tone is usually one of sober restraint. The bitterness may be subjacent, but it is never expressed. He is not incited to violent retaliation or thoughts of vengeance, but meditates on the meaning of the accusation cast at him of being 'anti-French' and reflects on general inequalities – the meagre opportunities for even well-qualified Black men and the different treatment he receives in gaol, compared with the naturalized Frenchmen.

Climbié ends on a note which reflects Dadié's fundamental optimism, his instinctive acceptance of the universality of human nature. Discharged from prison, he tells of his failure to sell the only thing of value he still possesses, in an attempt to support his family – his books. He expresses the hope that the day will come when bookshops and libraries will be well-used by his compatriots and educational qualifications will be honoured. He has learnt to understand even the racial discrimination that is current, ascribing this to self-defence on the part of the White man.

Climbié has undisputed value as a clear and sober document of an era. Firstly, it gives valuable, first-hand information on the educational system of A.O.F. as it tells of the hero's moves up the educational ladder from primary classes, through the Ecole Primaire Supérieure at Bingerville to the Ecole Normale Supérieure at Gorée, the William Ponty School. It also gives a picture of traditional rural African society, and finally of the life of an African pen-pusher, struggling to make ends meet on a sub-economic wage before the Second World War. We learn, too, how the relaxed relations between Black and White in Senegal deteriorate as strikes break out and racial hatred flares up.

However, Dadié's book is not simply of interest as a reference work to study a social or political background. While hardly deviating from autobiographical fact and owing little to the imagination, it has some claim to be regarded as a work of creative literature. Note the care with which the significant events have been selected over the thirty-four years of the author's existence and structured into a well-balanced and economical composition. The style is sober without monotony, the reserve with which deep emotional experiences are recounted giving way to lively descriptions of places and events. The characters who people the narrative are briefly but sharply defined. *Climbié* still ranks among the few really well-written autobiographical 'novels' from French Africa. It was completed in April 1953. Dadié never composed any other work in prose which made even minor concessions to the novel form. Between 1959 and 1968 he produced, interspersed with his poems, three travel books (see p. 320). However, in the post-Independence period, his inventive talents, his command of irony, his superb mastery of the poetic and humorous potential of the French language, have found their most original expression in the plays discussed in chapter 3, which are still, to date, among the most outstanding contribution to African drama in French.

Ferdinand Oyono

FERDINAND OYONO: *Une Vie de boy*. Paris, Julliard, 1956: re-ed. 1962. *Le Vieux Nègre et la médaille*. Paris, Julliard 1956.
   English translations: *Houseboy*, trans. John Reed. London, Heinemann, 1966; London, Ibadan, Nairobi, Heinemann Educational Books, 1966. Do. *Boy!* New York, Collier-Macmillan, 1970. *The Old Man and the Medal*, trans. J. Reed. London, etc., Heinemann Educational Books, 1967.

Ferdinand Oyono's novels reject the autobiographical element almost completely and offer the reflection of a period, without being a factual, objective documentary. Naturally, the author calls on his own experiences, as he does his own observations of the rural and small-town life of the Cameroon that he knew, but these are transposed and fused into fictional situations and characters to denounce the brutality and inhumanity of the colonial authorities, with a violent bitterness and cynicism unknown since René Maran's *Batouala*. Inspired by the same period and situation as his compatriot and contemporary, Mongo Beti, Oyono writes with more acerbity, his humour is more sarcastically lacerating than Beti's; his first and third novels include more violence, more melodramatic incident and demonstrate less fundamental compassion.

There is a certain obvious, if superficial, resemblance between Beti's *Poor Christ of Bomba* and Oyono's *Vie de boy*. In both cases the tale is told in the first person by a 'boy' employed by a missionary, and in both the Catholic missionaries are shown to be consciously or unconsciously in league with the colonial exploiters and so guilty of religious hypocrisy. But the differences between the two writers, their characters and the impact of their tales are profound. Because Oyono's hero-narrator, unlike Beti's observer of the drama, does not survive to recount his own history, Oyono contrives a more complex narrative technique. He imagines a double narrative, similar to that adopted by Prévost in his *Manon Lescaut*. Oyono supposes an anonymous narrator who is travelling in Spanish Guinea when the tom-toms announce that a 'Francès' (a Negro from neighbouring Cameroon) is dying. He crosses the forest to be present at the death-throes of his compatriot, who has had a lung pierced as the result of a brutal beating, and so comes into possession of two note-books in which the dead man, Toundi-Joseph, had written his story in the vernacular. The narrator translates this into French for publication, explaining that he has attempted to be as faithful as possible to the language and content of Toundi's journal. After this introduction the rest of the novel is devoted to the contents of the note-books, which form an equal part of the story with the rise and downfall of the houseboy. The narrative device is useful but hardly original. It has advantages but some improbabilities. At the beginning, it is wholly convincing: the youngster, educated by the missionary, Father Gilbert, wishes to put his new-found literacy to good effect and emulate the priest in keeping a diary. The language and style are appropriately naïve, and there are some touches which well illustrate the intelligence of young Toundi and his ambition for advancement, as when he quotes a word he does not understand, *maboule*, with the note that he will take the first opportunity of looking it up in a dictionary. But the illusion would have been more effective and the situation more probable if he were attempting his journal in French, and not in the vernacular. The pretext of the supposed translation from Ewondo poses other problems. It has the undoubted advantage of justifying a certain poverty of language and lack of idiomatic flexibility in French and gives the impression of being the authentic translation from a writer who has only a limited literacy. But the illusion is not consistent. One has suspicions that Oyono loses sight on occasions of the fact that the novel is supposed to be a translation from the indigenous tongue.

The appropriateness of the journal form is questionable in the second part of the novel and breaks down completely towards the end of the narrative, after Toundi's arrest and brutal treatment at the hands of the police inspector and prison officials. It supposes that he is able to retain possession of his note-books and be physically and mentally capable of recounting his experiences throughout his imprisonment, his torture, his hospitalization and finally his flight *in extremis* over the frontier. It is true that Oyono does attempt, by the occasional staccato style and greater rapidity of the narrative, an indication that Toundi is gradually succumbing to the ill-treatment he endures, but even here the illusion is not always maintained stylistically.

Because Toundi-Joseph is a quite different personality from Mongo Beti's Denis, we shall not find in *Une Vie de boy* the subtle effects of irony that Beti achieves by putting his narrative into the mouth of the observant but ingenuous, pious but credulous acolyte. Toundi's adherence to Christianity is more opportunist than profound. He may be ignorant of the ways of the White man (and woman), particularly in sexual matters, but he is far from naïve; the cynicism with which he records the obscenities of the local African community concerning Madame Decazy's physical charms and her easy virtue is clear indication that he is aware of their full implication. Moreover, he refers to the 'burning night' that this lady has spent with her lover, while her husband is away, and understands the little games being played by the commandant and the schoolmaster's wife. If he does not take advantage of the opportunity to spend a night with Sophie, this does not imply lack of sexual initiation, for he comments on the possibilities during Mass and Communion for taking rather blasphemous liberties with pretty girls, both Black and White. It seems that Sophie is simply not his type, rather than that he is unaware of the meaning of her invitation. Furthermore, when visited in prison by Obebé, the catechist, he cannot refrain from commenting that the pious gentleman 'is still suffering from the blenorrhagia he picked up before the war'. Toundi is reputed to be intelligent. It is true that he has profited from Father Gilbert's tuition to learn French and the ways of the White man's household, but he does not apply his intelligence to forestall the traps laid for him, because he is too sure of himself. His judgement of the members of the White community is sharp and satirically accurate, but it does not put him on his guard against the dangers of his position. When he still has an opportunity to escape and save his skin before the trumped-up charges are brought against him, he retains a quite unjustified faith in his employers, who are only waiting for some pretext to get rid of the witness to their shame, making him their innocent scapegoat.

If there is some inconsistency in the portrayal of the main character Toundi, there is all too much consistency in the picture of the African colonial community. Broadly speaking, Oyono ably satirizes the shallowness, the promiscuity, the racial prejudice, the brutality that would have been typical of this society. But the individual White personalities who are stereotyped, almost burlesque caricatures, are not always convincing in their actions or speech. However incensed the sanitary inspector might have been at the timid defence of the Africans attempted by the schoolmaster, it is doubtful if he would have permitted himself the very coarse term of abuse, *couillon*, in the commandant's drawing-room, and in the presence of ladies. Even if it was an authentic feature of colonial society to talk and act in front of African servants as if the latter were blind and deaf, if not actually invisible, it is doubtful if the prison governor would have entrusted verbal acceptance of Madame Decazy's rendezvous to Toundi, who had been sent with a written message, when it would have been simple and safer to write a note in reply. And a good deal of the comic effect of the central, if obscene, joke when Toundi finds the used condoms under his mistress's bed is spoilt by the extreme improbability of a furious Madame Decazy actually telling the uncomprehending 'Boy' what the objects are.

Because of these improbabilities, because, on the psychological level, Oyono's novel lacks subtlety, and because of the lack of finesse and consistency in the character of Toundi, our emotional reactions to his fate tend to be more stereotyped and less personal. Incontrovertible and undeserved as his sufferings are, we tend rather to view with horror a society and a political situation that can permit or condone such brutality than to be moved to profound pity for him as an individual victim. There is also the fact that many members of the community of Dangan are depicted as such grotesque caricatures that they fit incongrously into a genuinely tragic action. The preponderance of the burlesque in much of the characterization and description does not give a sense of inevitability to the final conclusion, which has the violence of melodrama rather than the fatality of tragedy.

In this first novel, Oyono shows his ability to create original action out of a typical colonial situation. He used his satirical gifts to suggest, with a certain amount of realism, a cross-section of small-town colonial society, with its pettiness, self-importance and low moral threshold. But his main purpose is not to satirize these White individuals or types, but to denounce all the sociological and political evils associated with brutal, vicious, ignorant officialdom. He applies a useful narrative technique to this end, but his command of the medium is not yet sure, with the result that, important as *Une Vie de boy* is as an original, imaginative contribution to a field which so far had leaned heavily on the autobiographical element, it is not a completely satisfactory novel. There are too many clichés in the characterization of the members of the White community and too much melodrama in the action that is inadequately motivated by either the weaknesses of the protagonists, who might thus be responsible for their own fate (as is the case with Father Drumont) or by the inevitability of circumstance. In the presentation of his hero, Oyono hesitates between the innocent and the cynic, the ingenuous and the opportunist, so that he undermines the inherent sympathy that the reader should feel. Finally, the mixture of burlesque and bloodshed is artistically unhappy. Many of these weaknesses are remedied in Oyono's next novel, which is more even in its composition and the level at which it operates.

Le Vieux Nègre et la médaille is more original in its central concept than *Une Vie de boy*: it is more compact in its structure, more consistent in its vision and succeeds better in its satirical intention because the burlesque comedy is not in conflict with tragedy. The action all takes place within a week, from the time the old man Meka is summoned to the District Commandant's office and informed that he is to be decorated with a medal by the Big White Chief from Paris, to the day after the ceremony when he returns to his village, the medal lost, having spent the night in prison for vagrancy. Without having recourse to any artifices of narrative composition, Oyono presents the whole situation with earthy realism and authenticity, devoid of folk-lore or artificial local colour, wholly through the eyes of the Black characters, who are at once the cast and the observers, the protagonists and the chorus. The action proceeds by a series of highly dramatic scenes, each leading to its own anti-climax, with a quota of convincing dialogue. This not only renders the mental processes and way of life of the inhabitants of the villages of Zourian and Douma, but is also evidence of Ferdinand Oyono's gifts for the theatrical, which he shares with his near-namesake, Oyônô-Mbia. A certain proportion of the narrative is presented in the form of free indirect speech, which allows us more access to the thoughts and changing reactions of Meka himself. The secondary characters of this novel include some of the Whites from *Une Vie de boy*, but the gallery of Black portraits is richer, more varied, and drawn with a detail that allows us to appreciate them more for their basic humanity, while at the same time we recognize some of the types who contribute to Oyônô-Mbia's comedies of Cameroonian village life; the ubiquitous catechist, the verbose and moralizing elders, the glutton hoping for more than his fair share of the viper.

The satire of *The Old Man and the Medal* is directed partly against the colonial authorities for their obtuseness and lack of human understanding, rather than for the brutality that Oyono attacks in *Une Vie de boy*, and partly against the Africans, who cling blindly to meaningless tradition. On the one hand he high-lights the exploitation by the colonists of an ignorant people; but the irony of the situation is accentuated by the fact that the latter are shown as willing and credulous victims. What is particularly original in Oyono's picture of colonial Africa is that he presents only the point of view of the older members of the indigenous society. In the whole tale of *The Old Man and the Medal* the only references to the young men of the communities are that they give up their seats in the shebeen to the 'men of mature years' (an expression which echoes like a *leitmotiv* through the narrative) and as the pretext for an outburst of indignation when Meka's nephew Mvondo, who, although bald and wrinkled, only acknowledges thirty years of age, has dared to eat the entrails of the sheep, which were reserved by tribal taboo for the elders. When Meka stands alone in the chalk circle at the medal-giving ceremony, in the double agony of full bladder and tight leather boots, newly bought for the occasion, he symbolizes a whole disorientated generation. They thought they had come to terms with the White Man's invasion of their country, because they accepted his religion and his authority, sent their sons to fight and die in his wars and gave up their best lands to the missions. They thought they were assimilated into the White Man's society because a token of gratitude, in the form of the medal, was offered. But in fact they still inhabit their no-man's-land between the worlds. There is no place in the future for their endless palavers, taboos and traditions. They are too inflexible to move with the times and they can hope for as little respect from the younger members among their congeners as they can from the Whites. The point is made incontrovertibly in the title of the novel: Meka may well be a 'man of mature years' for his contemporaries in his native village; for the rest he is just a *Vieux Nègre*, an old Negro, chosen to receive a meaningless honour, and eventually proving an embarrassment.

Oyono's central character as in *Une Vie de boy* is once more the victim of the system. However Meka, unlike Toundi, is not sacrificed physically; he does not give his life, having already given his two sons who died fighting for France. The real sacrifice that he makes in the course of the novel is that of his illusions over the colonial régime and the great White Chief. The end finds him weary and cynical, so weary that he cannot even find the words to defend himself after his unjust arrest; but it is clear that life in the village will go on, with a fair amount of optimism for the future, in spite of Meka's mortifying experience; the women will go back to wash in the streams, the men to their work in the fields: 'What is done is done and we can't change that. And we can't change the White people either . . .' said Meka, looking round, overcome with emotion. 'Perhaps one day . . .' (p. 208 [p. 169; pbk p. 167]).

The success of *Le Vieux Nègre et la médaille* is largely due to Oyono's capacity to use humour as an agent to distil the basic humanity out of all situations. The humour is not caustic or lacerating as in *Une Vie de boy*, but cathartic. The episode of Engamba and his goat is in the best tradition of rumbustious comedy. There is subtler ironic satire in the contrast between reality and the idealized dreams of personal aggrandizement that Meka and his brother-in-law Engamba enjoy, which include the possibility of the Big White Chief bringing Meka a White woman out from Paris, and even – greatest ambition of all – a few bottles of those spirits that were never allowed to be sold to natives. There is the organic realism of medieval farce in Meka's dilemma when the urgent need to relieve himself, the sweat pouring down his face, which he dared not wipe away, added to the agonizing pain from standing for an hour in his new boots, gradually usurps the main place in Meka's consciousness and diminishes the sense of dignity of the occasion: his new-found importance in the community recedes before his universal physical needs. Instead of despising all his compatriots, including the tribal chiefs whom he imagines bursting with envy, he would give the world – and his medal – to be squatting under the magnolia tree behind his hut, which did service for a privy.

When the social situation that called for the satire has become part of history and the point of the satire somewhat blunted thereby, *Le Vieux Nègre et la médaille* will hardly fail to retain its interest and its value as a lively, realistic and intensely comic novel.

Sembène Ousmane (more correctly Ousmane Sembène)[10]

SEMBÈNE OUSMANE: *Le Docker noir.* Paris, Nouvelles Editions Debresse, 1956. o.p.
Re-issued Présence Africaine, Livre de Poche, 1974. *O pays, mon beau peuple!*
Paris, Le livre contemporain, Amiot-Dumont, 1957. o.p. *Les Bouts de bois
de Dieu, Banty Mam Yall.* Paris, Le Livre Contemporain, 1960, o.p. Re-issued
Presses Pocket, 1972. *Voltaïque. Nouvelles.* Paris, Présence Africaine, 1962.
Re-issued 1971, Format de Poche, as *Voltaïque. La Noire de.... L'Harmat-
tan. I. Référendum.* Paris. Présence Africaine, 1964.
   English translations: *God's Bits of Wood,* trans. Francis Price. New York,
Doubleday, 1962; New York, Doubleday-Anchor, 1970; London, Ibadan,
Nairobi, Heinemann Educational Books, 1970. *Tribal Scars and other stories,*
trans. Len Ortzen. London etc., Heinemann Educational Books, 1974.

Sembène Ousmane is the most prolific of the African novelists writing in
French, with five full-length novels, one collection of short stories and two
important novellas to his name in sixteen years. He is also with Mongo
Beti one of the two main writers of the nineteen-fifties to continue producing creative fiction well after Independence. He had little formal education
and his novels reflect a steady progress from fumbling, unsure beginnings
to a complete mastery of his medium. His most recent publication, a novel
Xala (1973), came after an interval of eight years, during which he had
devoted himself to cinema production. Two novellas, *Le Mandat* and
Véhi-Ciosane (*White Genesis*) which had appeared in 1965, will be discussed
with the recent novel in the subsequent section devoted to the post-
Independence era.

   The subjects and scope of Ousmane Sembène's works of fiction follow
chronologically and geographically the author's own moves, experiences
and ideological orientation. *Le Docker noir* is set wholly in France, with
the exception of a brief introductory scene in and around Dakar, at the
homes of the hero's parents and relatives. It is inspired by Sembène's life
as a stevedore in Marseilles, and also reflects, incidentally, his experience
in the war. An accident which resulted in a fracture of the spine, immobiliz-
ing him for some months, gave him occasion for deep reflection on his own
principles and on the social problems of his people, as a consequence of
which he decided to return to Africa. His second novel, *O pays, mon beau
peuple!* is situated in a remote fishing village in Senegal, reminiscent of
his own birthplace in Casamance, to which a young Negro returns with
his White wife, and is a story astride two cultures. From then on, the
European scene recedes and Europeans are only secondary characters,
except for the White employers in the sardonic short story *La Noire*

[10] As with Camara Laye, his given name has been commonly confused with his patronymic.

*de...*in the collection, *Voltaïque.* All the novels subsequent to *O pays, mon beau peuple* are inspired by African social and political problems to which Sembène now turns his whole-hearted attention. In *Les Bouts de bois de Dieu* we see the application to a purely African situation of the socialism and militant trade-unionism that he had learnt as a dock-worker in Marseilles and which had found its first, primitive expression in *Le Docker noir. L'Harmattan*, a story of pure social realism, tells the story, as the sub-title indicates, of the Referendum of 1958 and the action of the militant socialists of pre-Independence. *Véhi-Ciosane*, set in a Senegalese village in 1950, stands alone as a timeless study of a human predicament, but *Le Mandat* and *Xala* return to social comment, this time of post-Independence African city life.

As might be expected, the plumber-bricklayer-soldier-stevedore, born in a little fishing village in Casamance, who supplements his lack of formal education with wide reading and composes his first novel in his early thirties, will not immediately produce a masterpiece. It is easy to find fault with *Le Docker noir* on literary grounds. Linguistically, Sembène is as yet unsure of the resources of the French language and he complicates his task by the multiplicity of stylistic levels at which the work operates. He is at his best when he can apply a kind of pastiche technique showing the influence of his reading which penetrates the straight descriptions of places, the newspaper reports of the murder and trial, and the extract from Diaw Falla's book, which is a fair example of rather flat, French, nineteenth-century narrative prose. In the many passages of dialogue and the long letter written by Diaw in prison to his uncle in Senegal, which forms the final part of the novel – a sort of epilogue – there are many linguistic inconsistencies. The worst examples of this type of inauthenticity come from Catherine, described as a simple, ignorant shop-girl, but who mixes her familiar, slangy expression with phrases like *Où est ta force d'antan?*[11] As for the hero, Diaw Falla, the autodidact dock-worker with literary aspirations, we can expect some fluctuations and hesitations in his command of language, from high-flown pedantry to crude dockside slang or Left Bank jargon. But the variations are not always appropriate to the company he keeps or the emotional level he wishes to convey. The difference between the fluent prose of his novel and the abrupt staccato and repetitive style of the letter is acceptable, inasmuch as the latter is written in a mood of deep mental distress, when he is not polishing his sentences. But then the clichés creep in and result in lapses into bathos and incongruity.

[11] The literal and stylistic equivalent would be 'Where is your strength of yesteryear?', echoing Villon's famous 'Ou sont les neiges d'antan', 'Where are the snows of yesteryear?'

Sembène is equally unsure of the psychological presentation of his main characters. Although Catherine's emotional level is shown to be shallow, there is inadequate preliminary preparation for her sudden and melo-dramatic downfall into both prostitution and alcoholism after Diaw's im-prisonment. With Diaw himself, the author has let himself be drawn into a series of contradictions and insuperable dichotomies. He is shown in the introductory chapter in Senegal as having acquired an apparently unjusti-fied reputation for living as a pimp in Marseilles, when in fact he has high ideals for the immigrant workers and tries to influence them to more reasonable and economic habits. He is intended as the symbol of the victimized Black proletariat and at the same time must be an individual whose fate is the reader's main concern. He is shown as capable of impulsive violence which can result in an accidental death, or at least manslaughter – in legal terms – if not murder, yet should give the impres-sion of being the victim of a miscarriage of justice. Although he has deep sympathy for the dock-hands and leads a wild-cat strike in protest against their working conditions (thereby losing his own chances of casual employ-ment), he seems incapable of real emotions for any individual person, as witness his reflections on his mistress Catherine.

In *Le Docker noir* Sembène has attempted a fairly complex narrative technique, given the relative simplicity of the plot. The first part of the novel introduces the main theme at the time of Diaw's trial for murder, seen first through the eyes of his despairing mother in Senegal, then of Catherine, his half-Melanesian, half-European mistress in Marseilles, seven months pregnant with his child and about to run away from her bullying African step-father; finally, but briefly, through the reactions of his friends and work-mates. The trial and the period of waiting for the verdict bring to an end the first part of the novel and are the occasion for Diaw to recollect the incidents that led up to his threatening Ginette Tontisane, who had had his novel published under her own name, and thus accidentally causing her death. This forms the substance of the second part and the majority of the total narrative and brings us to the moment of his sentence to hard labour for life. Part three, little more than a dozen pages, consists of Diaw's letter to his uncle, written after three years in prison, and is the vehicle for Sembène's explicit social comment.

The author cuts rapidly from one short episode or scene to another, anticipating his eventual involvement with film production and the more skilful application of this cinematographic technique to a maturer novel – *Les Bouts de bois de Dieu*. The structural weakness does not arise out of inability to manage the techniques he adopts, but the introduction of too much adventitious material and extraneous characters. The latter are clearly intended to suggest the teeming life of Marseilles and in particular the districts inhabited by the Black seamen and dock-hands; they only succeed in adding incoherence to what should have been a simple economical narrative with a social message. The most unsatisfactory aspect of the novel is the secondary episode, the illegal abortion performed on Andrée Lazare, her death and the subsequent imprisonment of her mother and the doctor responsible. Not only is this a bit of gratuitous melodrama, a cliché of pulp fiction, adding nothing to the presentation of Diaw Falla's predicament, but in a would-be realist narrative it leaves several important questions of logic and plausibility unanswered. How did a girl of Andrée's social background come to frequent the world of Black seamen and stevedores and become the mistress of Paul Sonko? Why did the doctor who had refused to terminate her pregnancy at a time when the intervention would have been relatively safe, yield eventually to Madame Lazare's pleas and perform the operation at the sixth month – performing too this hazardous surgery in his consulting room and letting the patient return home, unaccompanied...by tram?

If I note these weaknesses of structure, composition, psychology and language in some detail, it is for two reasons. Firstly, to indicate how far Sembène eventually comes in his later works from this fumbling beginning; and then to emphasize that, however unsure he might have been of his medium, he was convinced of his serious task as a committed writer and was impatient to express his message. He voices the purpose of his hard-earned literacy through Pipo, the Algerian spokesman for the dock-workers who says to Diaw: 'You hope to become a writer? You'll never be a good one as long as you don't defend a cause. You see, a writer should forge ahead, see things as they really are, have the courage of his own convictions. No-one else can defend us.' (p. 152).

While Diaw Falla writes a non-controversial novel about the horrors of slave-trading, espousing no topical cause, Sembène himself has a plethora of these which he is impatient to voice. His main purpose, in the body of the book, is to draw attention to the deplorable existence of the Black dockers in Marseilles, whose lot was aggravated by racial discrimination and lack of support from trade-unions. He illustrates the precariousness of their casual employment conditions, their consequent widespread unemployment, their exploitation and inadequate wages, their sickness and accident rate, the frequent deaths from tuberculosis, their eventual pauper's funeral. Because they can expect no help from outside or official sources – witness Diaw's vain intercession with the minister in Paris – and can only count on themselves, Sembène's task in relating his fellow-workers' and compatriots' lot, through the medium of fiction, is all the more urgent and imperative. And because his work will be read mainly by Frenchmen[12] he adds an epilogue in the form of Diaw's letter from prison. In this he widens the spectrum of social evils. It can be compared to Julien Sorel's statement at his trial and Meursault's emergence from indifference while in custody. Diaw, who had nothing to say when the verdict was pronounced and did not avail himself of the chance to appeal, now draws up his indictment of society, the law and the penal system. He challenges the latter which turns young delinquents into hardened recidivists. He asks 'What is the cause of crimes, abortions, poisonings, theft, prostitution, alcoholism and sodomy?' (unfortunately weakening his case by the final incongruous element) and gives the rather facile answer: unemployment. He draws attention to inadequate education, poverty, disease and vice that is rife in Africa. Finally, he makes some proposals for reform in an ambitious programme presented with redundancies, some naïveté, without order or logic, but containing many things which needed to be said. These literary weaknesses apart, *Le Docker noir* suggests a superficial comparison with Camus's *Etranger*, inasmuch as both Diaw Falla and Meursault are on trial not so much for a murder, but for refusing to take their place in society.

Some progress is discernible in Sembène's second novel, *O pays, mon beau peuple*, published a year later, though it still has many weaknesses. In *Le Docker noir*, he is primarily concerned with general social issues, to which the human situations are subservient. In the second work, still a novel of ideas, he sets his human problem in the forefront of the canvas, within the social framework. As in Socé's *Mirages de Paris*, he deals with racial prejudice inflamed by a mixed marriage, but presented here in reverse: the antagonisms are those encountered by Oumar Faye's White wife, Isabelle, when he returns with her to his native village in Casamance, after eight years spent in France. Sembène is still incapable of drawing his characters in depth. Isabelle's personality is not sufficiently well defined for us to share her sufferings or struggles for acceptance among her husband's family and people. We do not known enough about her background or ideas to allow adequate motivation for the curiously ambiguous episode when she allows her mother-in-law to practise witchcraft to cure her infertility. Oumar Faye is superficially presented as a proud, quick-tempered idealist whose dream is to improve the lot of the peasants by founding a model farm and co-operative. The secondary characters, with the exception of his old mother Rokhaya, are all puppets. The plot is

---

[12] Cf. his statement at the 1963 Dakar conference: 'Even written in French, by how many Africans is *Le Docker noir* read? Eighty-five per cent of the people here (in Senegal) are illiterate; the rest can read and write but they do not read African authors. That means that our public is in Europe.'

sketchy, all the action being subject to the exigencies of the author's ideology. A tragic ending is contrived to make Faye the victim of the vested interests of the colonists. After her husband has been ambushed and savagely beaten to death, Isabelle remains in the village to give birth to her child and show solidarity with Faye's *beau peuple*, now hers too.

O pays, mon beau peuple offers the thematic interest of being the first French-African novel to treat the problem of racial prejudice through the rejection of the White spouse by the Black people, instead of the stereotyped rejection of Black by the Whites. It is also a small contribution to the regional documentary, by the picture it gives of life among the fisherfolk and cultivators of the Casamance area. But it has no great literary qualities and certainly does not add significantly to the promise shown by Sembène in his first novel, where the deep and serious intention redeems some of the unsatisfactory aspects of the work.

After an interval of three years from the publication of *O Pays, mon beau peuple, Les Bouts de bois de Dieu* takes up the theme of the Black workers' struggle against White exploitation sketched with unsure hand in *Le Docker noir*. In this remarkably short time Sembène has reached his literary maturity. Now in full command of his medium, he produces a serious and important novel of near faultless structure and expression: covering a relatively large canvas with great economy of means, it is at once a historical document relating to an authentic episode – the 1947 strike of the Dakar–Niger railway workers – through the intermediary of fictional characters; a social statement – showing the sufferings of the workers and their families through their actions and, as a novel, a story of great human appeal. The title refers to a local superstition that by counting or enumerating people, their lives can be shortened, therefore pieces of wood are counted to represent people; this is essentially a story about the fate of people, men and more especially women and children although it has impact as a *roman à thèse*. In this respect, it bears comparison with other works of fiction inspired by similar actions – Zola's *Germinal*,[13] Malraux's *Les Conquérants*, Aragon's *Les Clochers de Bâle*, which retain their validity as literature when the subject central to the author's ideology has receded into the past.

Like Zola's Etienne Lantier among the coal miners of Northern France, Bakayoko develops an ascendancy over his fellow workers on the Dakar–Niger railway because of his literacy. But even better-read than Lantier

[13] Oulaye, the wife of Doudou, one of the militants, recalls at one point being taken to a cinema with her husband, by Bakayoko. The film took place in a coal-mine and the climax was the occurrence of a land-slide. Oulaye hadn't quite understood what was happening, particularly as the men on the screen looked like Blacks; Sembène could quite possibly have had the film of *Germinal* in mind.

(and also giving the impression of having better digested his reading), with his intelligence, his single-minded dedication to his mission and his principles, he reminds us more of Malraux's heroes, particularly Garine of *Les Conquérants*. He has his own small collection of books, including *La Condition humaine*, which must have impressed him deeply, and from which he quotes to his fellow-syndicalists the maxim: 'Pour raisonner, il ne s'agit pas d'avoir raison, mais pour vaincre, il faut avoir raison et non pas trahir'. Like Lantier, Bakayoko leads and encourages the strike movement, although he does not hold the centre of the stage throughout the action. In fact, he is not physically present until more than half-way through the narrative; but his influence is felt ubiquitously, his name is on everyone's tongue, and his inspiration, his leadership, his forceful personality contribute to the unity of the episodes as the action moves between the three main centres of Dakar, Thiès and Bamako. There is, however, one fundamental difference between Zola's novel and Sembène's. *Germinal*, in spite of the hope expressed in the symbolic title, ends on a note of pessimism. The miners' strike is beaten by hunger, sabotage and the superior power of the mine-owner; the men are forced to resume work with no hope for the betterment of their conditions. Sembène's on the other hand, ends authentically with the promise that some of the railwaymen's demands will be met. On moral grounds the book offers a message of optimism, too, in spite of the suffering and loss of life, for some of the characters have found redemption in espousing a cause and working together for the common good.

Like Aragon's novels, *Les Clochers de Bâle* and *Les Beaux Quartiers*, this novel of Sembène's is a picture of the clash of classes, not of races. The slogan of the railwaymen is 'Treat the bosses as enemies'. It is only incidental that the boss is White and the workers are Black. At the confrontation between the strikers' delegation and the representatives of the railway administration, this is made quite explicit by Lahbib, the assistant secretary of the Federation of Railway-workers at Thiès, addressing the head of the Thiès office: 'Sir, you do not represent here either a nation or a race, but a class. And we too represent a class whose interests are different from yours.' (p. 284 [p. 250]). Unlike Aragon, Sembène does not express an explicit Marxist doctrine; he and his mouth-pieces among the strike leaders represent a militant syndicalist view-point of the rights and interests of workers; nevertheless, the slight glimpses he gives us of the lives of the White railway officials at Thiès suggest a corrupt, vitiated bourgeoisie, whose decadence is aggravated by colonial existence – all of which would fit a Marxist definition.

A. C. Brench (in *The Novelists' Inheritance in French Africa*, ch. 6,

p. 113) suggests a parallel between *Les Bouts de bois de Dieu* and *La Condition humaine*. Sembène was undeniably influenced by Malraux's novel, as evidenced by the axiom quoted above, and which impels Tiémoko to study this work more deeply to find moral principles which will prove a surer guide than brute force; there are also undoubted parallels with *Les Conquérants*, not only because of the common theme – the organization of a strike, in Malraux's case for political, with Sembène for social ends – but because of the similar character of the two leaders. Like Malraux's hero, Garine, Bakayoko is deflected by nothing from his clear-sighted dedication to his cause. Twice he is accused, like Garine, who has sympathy for one man only, of having no human feelings. When he receives news that his adopted daughter has been injured and that his old mother has died as a result of police brutality, and when he hears of the death of Doudou, the secretary of the Railwayworkers' Federation at Thiès. Bakayoko could have retorted, obedient to Garine's credo: 'Have confidence only in a man's actions'.

From the point of view of the composition, *Les Bouts de bois de Dieu* has points of similarity with *L'Espoir*; in both we find a multiplicity of characters associated with a complex action initiated in different centres; short scenes in which one or other of the principle characters is high-lighted, with a cinema-like cutting from one scene to another to suggest simultaneous action, the whole proceeding inevitably and logically to a dénouement, in which the various elements are interrelated.

The role of the young apprentices of the Thiès railway workshops illustrates the skill with which Sembène uses apparently secondary characters as agents for the synthesis of the various stages of the action, contributing to the inevitability of the eventual dénouement. We meet this band of youngsters, aged between fourteen and seventeen, apparently irrelevantly occupied in the early stages of the narrative, when the strike action has been decided and the militia has been called in to charge the assembled workers and townsfolk in the market-place next to the station. For them the strike means only a welcome respite from work and the stimulus to play at soldiers themselves. We find them many weeks later, filling their idle days killing birds and reptiles with their catapults. Then, driven by boredom and daring, they penetrate the European quarter, aiming their stones and pellets at car-headlamps as well as at lizards, until the trigger-happy, nervy overseer Isnard shoots at the boys, killing two and wounding a third who subsequently dies of gangrene. When the procession of angry workers, headed by the women, lay the bodies on the doorstep of the Administrator's residence, the railway officials realize that the passive resistance of the workers has reached its limit and they can no longer refuse to receive the strikers' representatives with a view to reaching a settlement.

Linguistically, Sembène now has complete command of the European tongue which he uses as naturally and as flexibly as his original vernacular. The style of *Les Bouts de bois de Dieu* is sober, terse, astringent and always completely appropriate to the situation and the speaker, whether this be the Sérigne N'Dakarou – the spiritual leader of the Dakar Muslims – called in to harangue the women crowding into the railway administration offices; the workers' leader Tiémoko, unused to expressing his thoughts, struggling to find words, but anxious to convince the meeting that moral condemnation of the strike-breaker Diara will be a better deterrant than a brutal beating; or the precociously intelligent nine-year-old Ad'jibid'ji the adopted daughter of Bakayoko, conversing with her conservative old grandmother; or the various Whites, from the alcoholic Leblanc to the pretentious Béatrice Isnard. Sembène's vocabulary is simple but never impoverished. In the description of places, essential to justify the different reaction of his actors to their social situation, Sembène shows a power to evoke the atmosphere of the setting. Sometimes it is by the careful choice of the significant detail, elsewhere by an accumulation of effects to suggest the disordered poverty of lives spent in a sort of wasteland, the dumping-ground on the outskirts of Westernized existence that replaced the authentic African way of life. In relating the different episodes that punctuate the monotony of the months of hunger and inactivity, he alternates the tone of sombre poetry ('days passed and nights passed...the days were wretched and the nights were wretched') with that of tension or vivid drama in the shootings, the arrests, the outbreak of fire in the location. But the most moving incidents – the death of Maïmouna's baby, the killing of the apprentices, the shooting down of Penda as the marching women enter Dakar, are told with an economy, a sober restraint that minimizes any possible sense of melodrama and increases the readers' horrified compassion.

Ousmane Sembène shows an equally sensitive handling of the psychology of his large cast. Naturally more at home with his African characters, he nevertheless avoids for the most part the temptation to present his Whites as caricatures or stereotypes. Hard-core racists, to be true, they are nevertheless not brutes, but uncomprehending officials doing their job according to concepts on which they have built their lives. For them the idea of White superiority is as little open to question as the Divine Right of Kings would have been to Louis XIV's courtiers.

The Africans, as might be expected, are more sensitively distinguished. But there is no overall attempt to idealize them or sentimentalize their characters simply because they are engaged in an ideological struggle. Each reacts to the hardships, sufferings and challenges of the conflict according to the weakness or strength of his personality and of his possibly unproved potential. Some bend or break under the strain. Some are heroic for unheroic motives. Some are pitiful. Some demonstrate unexpected force of character. It is in the portrayal of the African women, in the variety of female characters, old and young, that Sembène shows his greatest skill and versatility. The author who had been so unsuccessful in drawing the heroines – Black or White – of his earlier novels, now reveals a greater understanding of the mentality and reactions of all types and ages of women than any African writer before or after him, to date. The lives of the women form, in fact, the central core of the drama. While the men hold meetings, talk and decide policy, the women for five, long, hungry months face the practical problems of existence, suffer the greatest hardships, feel most deeply the losses, and prove the true heroines of the struggle, even though at first they have little idea of the principles for which the men are in conflict. Seydou Badian, in his *Sous l'orage*, made his militant Sidi remark that the emancipation of women was a key issue in the programme for social advancement. Ousmane Sembène, in *Les Bouts de bois de Dieu*, shows this emancipation emerging naturally from a moment of crisis, when they rise to the occasion with all the resources they can muster.

The qualities of a mature writer that Ousmane Sembène demonstrates in *Les Bouts de bois de Dieu* are apparent in his next work of fiction, the collection of short stories, *Voltaïque*. We find the same authenticity and appropriateness of style in his dialogue of simple people; the same sober economy of effects by which he renders the reality of a setting; the tendency to understatement and restraint by which the dramas of everyday existence are related with moving poignancy; and with this a versatility in his narrative techniques according to the exigencies of each of the tales. There is a consistency of theme, too, that links the thirteen stories, though these range in time from slave-trading days to the present and topographically from Upper Volta to a slum garret in Marseilles, or a bourgeois villa in Antibes.

At the simplest level we have a contribution to the doctrine of Negritude in a return to traditional sources of fable and legend: *Communauté* is the old fable of the cat who went to Mecca, which we have met in Birago Diop's version, here revised with a political twist to prove that a 'community' headed by a traditional enemy is not to be trusted. *Le Voltaïque*, giving its title to the collection, re-tells the legend of Amoo's scarring of his beautiful daughter to save her from the slavers, which gave rise to the custom of that people wearing scars. In the stories situated in the present, the Negritude theme is expressed in attacks on false assimilation which causes the African people to lose their individuality and their sense of values. In *Prise de conscience* and *Devant l'histoire* Sembène shows his rare flashes of satirical humour; the first denounces the political opportunist, the Black neo-colonial who has learnt from the White colonials to oppress his fellows; the second is a study of the new Black bourgeoisie, a *drame de la rue* depicting individuals who symbolize a country that risks losing its equilibrium by a slavish and snobbish Westernization.

On the broadest level, the common element uniting the tales is a humanitarianism embracing the fate of humble folk. *Un Amour de la rue Sablonneuse* is a touching little story of a local romance, which seems to bring fortune and prosperity to the whole street, so that everyone is involved in the fate of the lovers. This note of simple happiness is rare. In most of the tales the theme is the suffering of men and women, particularly of women; tragedies that are not the result of chance or a cruel fate, but that inflicted by exploitation, oppression or simply insensitivity.

With his next full-length novel after *Les Bouts de bois de Dieu*, Sembène seems to have bent his talents too rigorously to the service of a political cause and the expression of social realism. His sense of humanity and his compassion, illustrated in *Les Bouts de bois* and *Voltaïque*, are far less in evidence here. His militant heroes and heroines, his fighters for Independence and scientific socialism are mouthpieces for propaganda, superhuman in their dedication and in their resistance to personal hardships or even torture, immune from normal human emotions and generally lacking in human dimensions, even beyond the single-minded Bakayoko.

In his notice to the reader, Ousmane explains that the scene of *L'Harmattan* is not intended to represent any particular French-speaking West-African state, but to be an amalgam of them all at the time of the 1958 Referendum. This may well be the weakness of the book, compared with *Les Bouts de bois*. The latter combines the authenticity of the historical documentary with the psychological plausibility of its main actors; it wins over the sympathies of the reader, not by polemics, or the exposition of political theories, but by the objectivity of its pitilessly accurate descriptions, its starkly simple narrative that reproduces the progress of the workers' struggle from their first unsure efforts, to their absolute conviction of the importance of their cause. *L'Harmattan*, on the other hand, is too undisguised in its didacticism, too doctrinaire. Its main characters, uncompromising exponents of partisan dedication, live and speak only within the framework of their political mission.

Sembène is happier when applying his observation of real people and his understanding of the light and shade of more complex existences, than in attempting to offer an ideal, exemplary model of the zealot. For this reason the minor characters of *L'Harmattan*, caught between their ancestral ways of life and thought and the pressures of the new society, are more successful than the single-minded protagonists. Among the former are the hunters of the forest, Bita Hien and Digbé, who introduce in the opening chapter the tensions of the pre-Referendum situation among the rural folk. They represent the ancestral past, in which a hunter can only live by hunting, the noble occupation of their forbears, which a colonial adminis-tration now calls poaching. The intermediate stage in the evolution of the typical West African society, with one foot in a conservative past, riddled with superstition and traditional beliefs, one foot in a progressive present, is represented by Mahn Kombéti. She has lived for fifty years without questioning her existence and without mental pressures. Now Tangara, the Black surgeon and newly appointed Hospital Director, wishes to exploit her knowledge of local simples, finds her an ad hoc post in his hospital and lodges her in his bungalow. She symbolizes most vividly the problems of improving the social conditions of rural Africa and the difficult-ies of uncompromisingly imposing new concepts of discipline and uncor-ruptibility which defy local custom and principles. She is quite prepared to make what she considers harmless concessions to satisfy the doctor's whims, and glad to be useful to him even in ways she does not understand, but she cannot accept that traditional family ties should be disregarded.

Tangara achieves his end in cleaning up the hospital, but he too falls into disgrace, made the scape-goat among his fellow intellectuals because he is basically a-political. The Harmattan of the title, the hot dry wind that was blowing across Black Africa in the fifties, was not only to clear away corrup-tion and superstition as obstacles to progress but political fellow-travellers and luke-warm supporters of 'NON'. The key thesis of this novel is that the only hope for the future lies in an unquestioning submission to the principles of African socialism, or the application of the Marxist-Leninist policy of the African Independence Party. We are dealing with creative fic-tion and not with a political tract, to which much of *L'Harmattan* com-pares. It is significant that the poet Lèye, who is probably the nearest of the militants to the author himself, has deliberately renounced literature in favour of painting and journalism; true he asserts he will not continue to enrich the literature of France with his creativity, but though this is not quite Sembène's own point of view, there is some parallel with his own political commitment. However, although the promised sequel to the first part of *L'Harmattan* has not yet appeared (1976), nor indeed the novel *Dombaye*[14]

[14] This was to be one hundred years in the life of a Senegalese family, from Faidherbe to the present day.

which Sembène had abandoned in favour of the work inspired by the Referendum in the early sixties, in the two novellas that follow *L'Harmattan*, he again shows his understanding of the private dramas of humble folk in a social setting depicted with objective realism and his latest novel, *Xala*, is a social satire, not a political document (see pp. 270–4).

Seydou Badian

SEYDOU BADIAN: *Sous l'orage*, part one. Avignon, Les Presses Universelles, 1957. o.p. Re-issued as *Sous l'orage (Kany)*. Paris, Présence Africaine, 1963.

Seydou Badian completed his only novel in 1954 when he was studying at the University of Montpellier. Without being polemical, its intention is strongly didactic and it is a contribution to the literature of Negritude: devoid of satirical elements, it is a novel of ideas rather than of character and incident.

The characters are all superficially drawn – chosen as types rather than as individuals. They represent the conflict between two generations. Kany, her brother Biramu, Samou, the man she wishes to marry and their various city friends are the enlightened younger elements of the new Africa, the product of Westernized education, rational and politically orientated. They reject the old traditions and despise the ignorance and superstitions of their fathers. They criticize the tests of endurance intended to harden the young men. They ridicule the custom of making sacrifices in times of epidemic in order to ward off evil, and do not accept that drought is a divine punishment for the misconduct of the young. They attack polygamy and more particularly the right of a father to dispose of his daughter in marriage without consulting her wishes. On the political level, they are beginning to question the colonial system, particularly the evils of forced labour, and the lack of local voice in local matters. The political demagogue, Sidi, sees woman's emancipation as the key issue in the programme of social advancement and so embraces Kany's cause enthusiastically, out of principle, not out of sentiment.

Foremost among the older generation are Benfu, Kany's father, an uncle Djigui and Sibiri, Kany's and Biramu's elder brother, all speaking with one voice; all nostalgic for the past governed by ancestral tradition and the experience and wisdom of age. They consider that marriage is an affair of the family, not of the individual and intend Kany to marry an elderly, wealthy, illiterate polygamist of the father's choice. Furthermore, the woman's role is purely to hold the family together and offer hospitality when required. Kany's mother is exemplary: while sympathizing with Kany's distress she sees no reason to revolt; women should continue to submit to their traditional lot, as she has done.

An intermediary between the two extreme views is required to resolve the conflict. Badian proposes as the voice of reason and his own mouth-piece, Tiéman, a man of maturity, a medical aide, the product of a Westernized education grafted on to the best in African ethics. Recognizing the evils of town life, where all is egotism and vanity, and the best of Africa's traditional ways are being sacrificed to a superficial cult of modernism and a taste for luxury, he decides to return to his native village before he loses his African personality. His philosophy is that one must choose between too close an adherence to the old customs, that enslave man and hinder his progress, and a total rejection of these in favour of Europeanization. Not a profound principle of life but one which Badian felt needed to be clearly expounded to his compatriots of the nineteen-fifties.

Tiéman, representing the wisdom of the middle path is also the *deus ex machina* who first sets the elders on the way to understanding the problems of the young and eventually to solving Kany's sentimental problems. Famagan is persuaded to withdraw his suit; Benfa does not lose face before his family; which all goes to show that sweet reason will prevail where hot-headed revolt will be useless.

The tone of the whole of Badian's novel is that of a moralizing tract addressed to the people of Sudan, with Independence round the corner, and the responsibility for organizing their own society in sight. The situation of the action, and every episode is thus chosen with a view to exposing or illustrating an idea or a principle. Badian places his characters first in a small town in the Sudan soon after the end of the Second World War. On Kany's refusal to accept the marriage plans, she is banished with her sympathetic brother Birama to their father's distant birthplace. The journey in the train allows for a discussion between a carefully selected group of passengers, who express their grievances and points of view in a contrived academic dialogue. The sojourn in the primitive village brings the 'city youngsters' into contact with African rural life where they are taught by their uncle Djigui to understand and appreciate the best of the old traditions. There is also vague and inconclusive reference to the continued existence of secret societies, a pretext for a lesson in the ancient tribal beliefs. The melodramatic introduction of the epidemic of cerebro-spinal meningitis, inadequately motivated, and unlinked to preceding or subsequent events, is used to show the reactions of the old and superstitious who think that disease is the result of a curse.

Seydou Badian has clearly an important message to convey to his compatriots and he has chosen the *roman à thèse* for the purpose. Although the novel will not have been read by large numbers of these, as it is written in a European tongue, he can justify himself by the fact that his lesson is addressed in the first instance to the young intellectuals, the product of Westernized schooling and White progress. As the ones who will take over responsibility when colonization comes to an end, they are advised to retain the best of the wisdom of Africa and keep a nice balance between the old and the new. The message comes over clearly; on this level the work is irreproachable. It is more open to criticism, if it is to be assessed as a contribution to original creative literature, in the genre that the author has adopted. The characters are not treated with profundity and so make little impact on the reader; the situations are contrived and the solution not psychologically motivated. But these reservations will fall away for those who place Badian's novel solely in the category of illustrative sociology.

When *Sous l'orage* was published in 1957 it was presumably intended to have a sequel, as the title read 'Part one'. The subtitle 'Kany' was added to the 1963 edition. So far no further parts have appeared and Badian has written no more works of fiction, his only other creative writing being his dramatic treatment of the death of Shaka, discussed in Chapter 2.

Mamadou Gologo

MAMADOU GOLOGO: *Le Rescapé de l'Ethylos.* Paris, Présence Africaine, 1963.

Mamadou Gologo warns the reader that his *Rescapé de l'Ethylos* (which he calls a *récit* to indicate that it has more of the documentary tale than of fiction) appears after ten years' delay. Its composition thus belongs to the early fifties, at a time when a traditional anti-colonial diatribe would have been more imperative than in 1963, when the politico-administrative structure of French Sudan had been changed for that of the Republic of Mali. In fact, there are indications that a factitious anti-colonial argument has been grafted on to an autobiographical chronicle. But *Le Rescapé de l'Ethylos* [The Survivor from the Ethylene Isles] turns out to be an anti-colonial tract with a difference – namely an element of the temperance homily: fortunate is the man who is rescued from ship-wreck on the Ethylene Isles and avoids the twin perils of Cythera, for which he would have a hard case to make the colonial régime responsible.

The book begins quite well as an authentic first person narrative, going back to the legendary founding of the author's native village in the Sudan by a wounded hunter – reminiscent of the similar episode in Jean Malonga's *Légende de M'Pfoumou Ma Mazongo*. He recounts his rural childhood, with some lively description of the malicious pranks played by the youngsters on the market merchants. Here a moralizing tone creeps in as Gologo, now Minister for Information for Mali, finds it necessary to excuse these petty larcenies. The description of his student years in Dakar are full of vivid and comic realism: first, during his studies at William Ponty, having imprudently opted, like Bernard Dadié, for a clerical training, with no particular aptitude, he is faced with a conflict with an intractable Remington. Then, discovering his real vocation, he transfers to the pre-clinical course for medicine, in which he makes good progress. There is wry humour in his account of his first experiences of Medical School, typical of the average young student thrown unprepared into the environment of hospital and lecture room, with the added disadvantage of the unfamiliarity of the Greco-Latin scientific jargon.

Unfortunately this light, but engagingly vivid manner of initiating us into the preoccupations and personalities of the student world (recalling Balzac's clerks and the younger male boarders of Madame Vauquer's establishment) is not maintained. Before long the Minister of Information remembers that he has promised us a temperance tract. So, with a frankness that could have done his personal reputation little good, he tells us how he allowed himself to fall victim to both women and wine, or more exactly fornication and spirits. The long moralizing interludes become increasingly tedious, as the style becomes proportionately ponderous and pretentious, with the introduction of precious periphrases, classical allusions, tired clichés, mixed with medical jargon that the layman can only find barbarous.

Here and there in the ensuing chronicle of the author's travels and the account of his eventual victory over his twin vices, we have a return to the vivid writing of the earlier chapters: the prosy moralizing is at times redeemed by a happy metaphor, an original image lights up a passage of description, or Gologo introduces an interesting historical interlude, as in the chapter 'En route vers la capitale de Kénédougou', where we learn the story of the heroic death of King Babemba, who drew a circle of gunpowder around his throne and set alight to it rather than capitulate to the French army in the seige of Sikasso of 1898. But because of the disconcerting unevenness of style and subject matter, *Le Rescapé de l'Ethylos* does not become the 'Voyage au boit de la nuit' that it might well have been. It certainly does not inspire cathartic horror or adequate pity.

Jean Ikelle-Matiba

JEAN IKELLE-MATIBA: *Cette Afrique-là*. Paris, Présence Africaine, 1963. Re-issued 1973.

Ikelle-Matiba's *Cette Afrique-là* [That Africa] also belongs to the preceding decade by its subject matter and its date of composition. The author tells us that he completed this biographical novel in 1955, eight years before its eventual publication. It tells of the suffering inflicted on the inhabitants of the Cameroon by the forced labour system under the French colonial régime, but the tone is sober and as objective as possible. The narrative purports to be the authentic story of the life of Franz Mômha, told by himself to the young people of his village. He was born at the end of the nineteenth century and lived a simple peasant existence in the midst of the Bassa folk until the coming of the Germans to the Cameroon. He was educated in schools founded by the Germans who applied Prussian methods of harsh discipline. Mômha is both horrified by their brutality and attracted by the efficiency and incorruptibility of the Prussian colonial system. A brilliant student, he is destined for higher studies in Germany, having become a civil servant in the colonial administration, when the First World War puts an end to his career and his personal happiness. He becomes both the witness and the victim of the chaos and confusion that ensue with the defeat of the Germans. Loyalty to his old teachers and masters makes him refuse to serve the French. He returns to the land, marries a simple girl who has had little formal education, but who had worked in a German household. Franz becomes a village personality, arousing thus bitter jealousy among the hereditary chiefs. When the French institute forced labour he is arrested for his defiance and treated with great brutality. The book ends with the beginning of the new era, Franz's sons explaining the meaning of the new parties, the programmes of the different candidates and the method of voting. The narrative has a sober objectivity and authenticity which makes one regret that the author has adopted the artifice of making Mômha tell his story over a series of evenings, which breaks the sequence and the structure of the composition.

The didactic intention, free from virulent indictment of past evils, of *Cette Afrique-là*, well illustrates both the period of its composition and its publication. The author's aim and that of the old, sage Mômha, is that the young generation should learn from the past: it is important that they should remember the past ignominies, not in order to continue to bear rancour, but to have a standpoint from which to build for the future.

1958–64: THE PERIOD OF TRANSITION: RELEASING THE
TENSIONS OF THE PAST AND DRAWING UP BLUE-PRINTS
FOR THE FUTURE

As the fifties drew to a close, bringing the end of French administration in the territories of A.O.F., the political transition from colonialism to independence was naturally reflected in the writing of the period. While roughly a score of novels in French by African writers had appeared between 1950 and 1957, the last two years of the decade saw a notable decrease in the publication of fiction. Of the more important authors, Mongo Beti published nothing for sixteen years, Dadié turned to travel chronicles until the late sixties when he found a new inspiration in satirical drama; Oyono was silent for four years, and when he produced *Chemin d'Europe* in 1960 the edge of his anti-colonial acerbity was blunted and he used his satirical gifts to produce a cynical and lewdly picaresque social comedy, demystifying the prestige of Westernized education and missionary proselytizing. When Sembène Ousmane took up his pen again in 1962, his commitment was, as before, more syndicalist than Negritude oriented, so that his post-Independence writings are predictably less indicative of a changing climate than those of the more specifically anti-colonial novelists.

If we consider the major works of fiction published in the five to six years that are astride the two decades, we find that broadly speaking they fall into one of three categories. Some make an attempt at an objective study of African society, both present and of the recent past, while recounting the experiences, usually autobiographical, of a young man faced with the problems of adapting to a changing world. These tend to continue the tradition of *Karim* and *L'Enfant noir*. Some writers, more conscious of their didactic mission, offer a rough blue-print for the future. A very few stoke the dying embers of anti-colonial polemics, but these we shall find are publishing in the early sixties manuscripts written some ten years previously.

Emile Cissé

EMILE CISSÉ: *Faraloko, roman d'un petit village africain. Liberté dans la paix.* Mamou, Guinea, published by the author, on sale from author, 1958.

The year of the Referendum saw the appearance of only one modest novel in French from West Africa, published by the author himself. Emile Cissé had patently a whole complex of urgent and laudable aims in writing his simple, regional story of life in a little African village. He consciously tries to evoke the mystique and mystery, the picturesqueness and epic past of his native Guinea. His book is also a story of family life and village intrigue, introducing the situation of the half-caste, the problems of sorcery, superstition, polygamy and the political implications of the old traditional ways. There are references to women's place in an African society, the importance of education and an attempt to define the 'civilization' to which this rural society can aspire without losing the best of the past. This is quite an ambitious programme for a novel of less than two hundred pages. In the event, the author does not manage to give very positive answers to his problems, through the medium of the fictional action. When his hero Nî, who personifies the best of both worlds, the Black and the White, goes mad after his mother has died a victim to sorcery and he loses his sweet-heart bitten by a rattle-snake, we are not left with much hope for the future. If, on the other hand, one discounts the didactic intention, and judges *Faraloko* simply as a village romance of love, jealousy and intrigue, it has a certain ingenuous charm. M. Diallo Saifoulaye, the then President of the Territorial Assembly of French Guinea, suggested in his preface that this novel 'free of the inferiority complex of the colonized and the superiority complex of the colonist', is reminiscent of Camara Laye and René Maran. It would be difficult for any author to combine the characteristics of such dissimilar writers. The best one can say is that Cissé's book has certain features recalling *L'Enfant noir*; but where Camara Laye's work is perhaps consciously poetic, Cissé's is more impoverished in style. In 1953 Laye was bitterly criticized by his compatriots for not producing a *témoignage* relevant to the problems of the day, although he did produce a masterpiece. Five years later, with his native Guinea in the birth-throes of her independence, which was to prove more radical than in any of the other ex-French colonies, Cissé's unpretentious rural romance, with its local colour and freedom from political implications, went unchallenged.

Aké Loba

Aké Loba: *Kocoumbo, l'étudiant noir.* Paris, Flammarion, 1960.

The watershed between colonialism and independence also witnessed a return to the autobiographical novel, telling the story of a young Black student, brought up in rural Africa, who is uprooted and transplanted to Paris. Two novels from the early sixties, of varying literary qualities, describe in moving fashion the dilemmas, the social, political or philosophical conflicts of a serious and sensitive young African, in the alien and sometimes hostile world of the West, based on the author's own experiences. Aké Loba and Sheikh Hamidou Kane, in their own way, take up the theme first introduced by Camara Laye in his *L'Enfant noir*. Like him they observe closely and describe with objectivity the consequences of the White man in the Africa of their childhood and early manhood. The problems that are associated with colonialism are analysed on a personal level, although certain general conclusions can be drawn as to the responsibility of the régime for the rootlessness of a whole generation of thinking Africans. In the case of Kane, we know that his manuscript was completed some ten years before it was eventually published. It could well be the case with Loba, that after the unpopularity of *L'Enfant noir* among the Black intellectuals, he waited for a more favourable moment before producing his chronicle, which in the earlier decade might also have been challenged for not contributing to the polemics of the time.

Aké Loba's *Kocoumbo* is not a remarkably original work, but it is by no means negligible. The structure of the composition is competent, following a simple chronological line, based on the most significant episodes in the hero's life, from his early youth in his native village, through his tribulations in France, to his eventual return to Africa, his law diploma in his pocket, to take up a post as a magistrate. The style is flat and rather monotonous. The characterization of some of the Black characters is mercilessly exact and Loba paints a vivid picture of the hardships and degradations to which Black students were exposed in Paris after the Second World War.

The opening chapter of *Kocoumbo* establishes the atmosphere of exotic, animist Africa hardly touched by the encroachment of Western civilization. Kocoumbo's father, the patriarch of the village, is an upholder of tradition. However, he has a great respect for France, which he thinks of as being similar to his village, with her patriarchs, in whom the gods have inspired much wisdom which has been preserved in big books. It is true that his son already knows all this wisdom from having studied all these books at school, and so has nothing more to learn . . . nevertheless, it would be useful to have a direct link between his village and the French sages, so Oudjo decides to send his son to France. Western clothes are bought in the nearest town, Kocoumbo says goodbye to his sweetheart Alouma and a black cat is sacrificed to the spirit of his ancestors. There follows the tragic-comic scene of his departure as he sets sets off alone for an unknown country draped in a heavy woollen suit, his feet tightly encased in two instruments of torture made of hard, dry leather, like the jaws of a crocodile.

On board ship Kocoumbo is prepared for the new life ahead by conversation with his fellow steerage passengers, some of whom are returning to France to resume their studies and give the newcomer the benefit of their experience and advice. This amounts to choosing one of the three lucrative professions which will also guarantee him prestige in White or Black society, namely medicine, government administration and law. Among these ship-mates four play a part in Kocoumbo's life in Paris. One, Joseph Mou a seminarist, has been promised to the priesthood by his father after the latter had been cured of a serious illness by a missionary: Joseph loses his faith, quits the seminary and joins the alcoholic flotsam of African expatriates in Paris. His story is told objectively as a simple statement of fact with no attempt at moralizing. Nadan, the son of a well-to-do neighbour from Kocoumbo's village, also corrupted by the *milieu*, sinks into a life of vice and ends up in prison. Douk, alias François Gogodi, a stowaway on the ship, more slightly sketched, is a typical adventurer and parasite, the jackal to Durandeau's lion. Durandeau, who proves Kocoumbo's evil genius, is the most vividly portrayed: an unscrupulous, mythomanic, francophile dandy who has discarded his barbaric name of Koukoto with its cacophonous k's. A highly intelligent opportunist, he lives on women, studies law and medicine, aims at power and eventually turns to politics.

In Marseilles, Kocoumbo's first impression is of the limpid French spoken by everyone, particularly of those admirable and effortless elisions, *mesdames-zé-messieurs*. The train journey to Paris is the first stage in his education. A kindly gentleman engages him in conversation, anxious to have his first-hand views on the 'African problem' which Kocoumbo equates to the endless arithmetic problems dinned into his ears at school. Nevertheless he is proud and impressed that for the first time a White person should talk to him man to man, particularly attaching so much importance to his native Africa. These early scenes show Loba to possess a talent for comic irony equal to that of his compatriot Dadié. However, the effect of the traumas of the subsequent years in France on his sensitive and nervous temperament proves stronger than his power to transmute his experiences into comedy. The tone of the rest of the novel is sombre without being bitter. Kocoumbo's first set-back is to discover that his *certificat d'études* which gained him such prestige in his native village is no qualification for higher study in France. By the good offices of the family of a colonial administrator he is admitted as a boarder at a provincial *lycée*, to find himself, at the age of twenty-one, classed with French schoolboys of thirteen to fourteen. After several years at school, suffering miseries of homesickness and loneliness, befriended only by the son of a peasant who admires his diligence and unfailing courtesy, he manages to reach the matriculation class. He leaves without sitting his examination when insulted by a new stupid and brutal *surveillant*. He returns to Paris, but again fails to obtain his *baccalauréat* through a complete breakdown in health due to overwork and privations. Loba here describes with merciless objectivity the life of the Black students in Paris in the fifties: their material and mental hardships, hunger, degradation, alienation; and the attempt of these *déracinés* to graft onto Paris something of the communal existence of Africa, but in fact enjoying the advantages of neither.

After four months in a student convalescent home, Kocoumbo finds employment as a factory worker. This is an equally alien world for the proud, reserved, a-political African, who had only one ambition – to continue his studies – and who refuses to make common cause with the White workers' grievances. Unable to keep a job, because of the hostility of the syndicalists, he is eventually taken in hand by Denise, a militant Communist, and Loba gives us a well-observed portrait of a belligerent, graceless, almost sexless 'comrade'. When his mistress is killed in an accident he is again adrift and sinks into the Pigalle underworld. He finds work in a night-club and poses for pornographic photographs which are sold in his native village, bringing disgrace on his family. He is finally redeemed by the retired colonial administrator who finds him white-collar work in an office, with sufficient leisure to complete his studies for his law diploma, when he returns to his home region to take up a post as a magistrate. This moving, dispassionate, authentic document ends with one unconvincing episode, necessary perhaps for poetic justice. The newly-appointed magistrate, who had always been a model of reserve, pacificism and good breeding, finally takes his revenge on Durandeau, who through his time-serving, is on his way to becoming politically powerful: he gives him a good thrashing – literally.

A. C. Brench, in his excellent study of *Kocoumbo*, which he compares to Dadié's *Un Nègre à Paris* and Kane's *L'Aventure ambiguë*, calls Loba's novel principally a *roman à thèse*, since 'the moral, social and political elements are by far the most important factors'. This is, of course, true, but the term *roman à thèse* does suggest a positive approach or at least some direct critical denunciation of evils, as well as exposition of problems. Loba's approach is essentially objective, negative and pessimistic. There is no overt attack on a system and no final suggestion of how the Black students of the future can avoid the experiences of Kocoumbo, Joseph Dou, Nadan and Durandeau, to whom he adds the Communist Abdou, insofar as their vicissitudes are the result of a system and not their own inherent character weaknesses. He could have said that it will be Africa's responsibility to build on her own stable traditions and introduce sufficient educational opportunities for her intelligent youth, without exposing them to an alien culture. He might have proffered a party-political solution. But Kocoumbo's association with the Parti Communiste Français is one of expediency: it temporarily fills an emotional and moral emptiness in his life and is quickly abandoned after Denise's death. Loba does not seem to indicate that the 'Africa Problem', which in his case is presented as the cultural problem of African youth facing the future, will be solved by Communism. Nor is assimilation the answer, if we are to take Durandeau as the suggested prototype. The progress of that smooth confidence trickster, ruthlessly pursuing his own successful career and his integration into Paris society, is not presented with the cynical irony of Oyono's Barnabas, happily discarding his moral principles on his way to Europe. Durandeau's example rather insists on the fact that assimilation is only possible for the completely unscrupulous and morally despicable. Although Loba makes sure he gets chastised at the end, we have a strong suspicion that Durandeau is on his way to join the ranks of political rope-dancers and gerrymanders of the new era and it is surprising not to find him among the characters from *Kocoumbo* whom Loba reintroduces into his next novel, *Les Fils de Kouretcha*, which deals with the post-Independence era.

The importance of *Kocoumbo* as a novel is that it is the first attempt at a non-idealized, objective presentation of a social situation, arising indirectly out of colonialism in Africa, but without any attack on the colonial administration or its officials. The majority of the action takes place in France, but with the exception of the brutal, stupid assistant school-master, none of the White characters gives evidence of overt racism, and the crises are not the result of racial prejudice but of tensions inherent in cultural and personality conflicts. The majority of the Europeans are shown to be sympathetic and helpful. If anything, Loba is more indulgent to his White characters than his Blacks. It is not because of racial prejudice, but Kocoumbo's own pride and his determination to hide any suggestion of his inner anguish, that they are unable to understand him and his dilemma more fully. *Kocoumbo* also has the added interest of being the first of the West African novels in French to attempt a mildly existentialist approach to the problems of human and social situations, with the suggestion that it is for Kocoumbo and his like to assume the responsibility for their own destiny.

Olympe Bhêly-Quénum

OLYMPE BHÊLY-QUÉNUM: *Un Piège sans fin.* Paris, Stock, 1960. *Le Chant du lac.* Paris, Présence Africaine, 1965. Repr. 1973.

In his notice to the reader, which precedes his first published novel, *Un Piège sans fin*, Olympe Bhêly-Quénum is at pains to point out that, although set in the colonial era, this work should not be interpreted as an attack on the oppression of Africans by the French colonial authorities. His ambition is to write a completely a-political novel, the vicissitudes of a man who could have been white or yellow or black. The endless snares to which his hero, Ahouna, is exposed are those inherent in the human condition. His story is intended to be the struggle to live a simple, uncomplicated existence in the face of the continual, irrational antagonism of fate – in essence then, an existentialist approach. *Un Piège sans fin* would thus be the first African novel in French, after Camara Laye's *Le Regard du Roi*, to have an universal human application.

Two years after the publication of this work, Bhêly-Quénum affirms his concept of the African novel and the role of the African novelist in an article 'On getting to know Black Africa through its literature', published in *La Vie Africaine* in March 1962. African writers of the second half of the twentieth century, he states, have the duty to purge their literature of false exoticism; to rectify the impression that the true face of Africa consists of mysterious tropical forests with giant trees and liana-creepers, populated with primitive tribesmen, half-way between the child and the savage, who live a bucolic existence interspersed with lion-hunts and ritual circumcision ceremonies. He holds no brief for the regional novels – among which he classifies Dadié's *Climbié* – which give a glimpse of a corner of Senegal, Benin or Ivory Coast, but no impression of the problems of 'eternal Africa'. The African novelist should, according to him, create characters who are not completely Senegalese, Beninian, Cameroonian, etc., but simply *African*, that is, in his definition, a synthesis of an archaic and unchangeable past, and a present given up to revolution and evolution. Yet, although he is concerned in this essay with defining the African vision and, to quote James Joyce, with seeking 'for the reality of an experience and to forge in the smithy of the soul the inborn conscience of one's race', in his own novel he aims to go even further in his progression from the particular to the universal: to offer a vision of the essence of man's isolation and his struggle against a hostile fate. Some indication of the measure of his success can be gained from the contradictory nature of the reviews which greeted the novel's appearance. Some critics were mostly impressed, in spite of the author's warning, by the picture of a primitive society, dominated by fetishism; others, mainly White, saw the greater universality of the essential theme. Jean Bouret writes in *Les Nouvelles Lettres*, 29.6.1960: 'What makes for the interest of this novel is particularly the simplicity with which the author initiates us into the customs – the very soul itself – of these African people, where both Islam and Christianity have still a long way to go before they can replace fetishism, which is solidly implanted.'

The African poet and critic Paulin Joachim sees *Un Piège sans fin* as the first authentically African work, the first manifestation of *l'âme nègre*, and 'all the sensitivity, all the emotional power of Negro-African peoples'. But it is difficult to understand what he means by his statement that 'there is in this book something that can largely contribute to changing the face of the world' (*Kokou*, January 1961). Halfway between the purely Negro-centric and the more universal interpretation is the judgement of the novelist Abdoulaye Sadji who thought that 'With this novel we really penetrate into the Black world, with its terrors, its passions, its tragedy, its strength...' An anonymous critic from *La Vie Africaine*, March 1961, is quite categoric in his wider interpretation:

Gone is the era of the 'good savage'. We open an African novel, written by an African, and it is the whole of humanity that is before our eyes...If universality is the criterion of human creativity, then *Un Piège sans fin* deserves to be known beyond all frontiers, for it has in addition a deeply spell-binding poetic quality.

There is, of course, a measure of accuracy in all these judgements. This is an ambitious and complex novel. The author's original intention was to illustrate by Ahouna's fate a philosophic and moral theme, and the perpetual backsliding to which mankind is prone, to be aware of which, he reminds us, it is not necessary to be a Christian. But the author may have been carried away by his subject, and it is possible that more may have been read into his work than he intended. Mercier and Battestini, in fact, list about twelve major themes that emerge, and also suggest echoes of both the Orpheus and the Orestes myths and of such modern works as Sartre's *Huis clos*, Dostoievsky's *Crime and Punishment* and Samuel Beckett's *End Game*. This might disconcert Bhêly-Quénum who, in the article quoted above, recommends that African writers seize their chance to do something different, leave the beaten tracks, avoid repetition of old formulae and not let themselves be inspired by French literature, even if they think they have found a master.

Yet none of these African novelists, writing in French, who have been subjected to a French literary training, can entirely free themselves from the unconscious influences of their Western and Classical reading. Far from being the exemplary exception that his theory suggests, Bhêly-Quénum's university degree in French and Classical literatures has left its indelible mark upon his creativity; sometimes, indeed, his erudition sits heavily upon him, as when the almost illiterate peasant Ahouno, discussing the possibility of escaping from prison, says he would like to escape because of his poor mother and his children but '...revenu de tout, cette tentative me paraît *a priori* vouée à l'échec';[15] or the old Dâko, meditating on the conflict with his family over avenging Kinhou's death, feels himself beaten in his task of 'clearing out the Augean stable'. The incorporation of mythic elements is not necessarily an objectionable feature of a modern novel: indeed the new school of mythocriticism has suggested an enriched interpretation of many contemporary works by uncovering hidden strata of myth in unsuspected places. An interesting approach to Bhêly-Quénum's novel, which might be taken up by students *en mal de thèse*, would be to assess the possible synthesis of African mythological influences with Judeo-Christian and Classical Greek myth.

The structure and style of *Un Piège sans fin* also betray unmistakable influences of French literature. There is a remarkable similarity between its narrative technique and composition and those of *Manon Lescaut*. It will be remembered that the 'Man of Quality' meets Des Grieux at a critical point in the latter's history and hears from him the story of his fortunes which fills the first part of Prévost's novel up to the lovers' deportation to the penal settlement; the second part being their trials in New Orleans and the eventual death of Manon. In Bhêly-Quénum's novel, the narrator, M. Houénou, an archeologist, travelling in the then Dahomey, meets the fugitive Ahouna, offers him hospitality, and hears from him the story of his life from his early childhood to the events which brought him to his present pass. Ahouna disappears in the night and the final details of his capture, imprisonment and death are told in the third person, with the narrator intervening occasionally in the first person. Unfortunately, the author's mastery of his narrative device is not complete: although we can accept the total recall by which Ahouna is able to tell in the minutest detail the story of some thirty years of his life, the introduction of the narrative within a narrative, when Ahouna reproduces the story of his brother-in-law Camara again in the first person, becomes clumsy and disturbing to the unity of tone and style of this first part. In the second part, there is a certain amount of confusion as to the source of the recital. Although some of the facts could have been told to the narrator by one of the prison officials, who is friendly to him and kindly disposed to the unfortunate Ahouna, and of others he is actually a witness, much that occurs could only be related by the omniscient author of conventional fiction.

Ahouna's story, as told by him to Houénou, is a regional bucolic, with anti-colonial overtones. His father Bakari was a prosperous and respected farmer from North Dahomey who had fought with the French in the 1914–18

---

[15] English stylistic equivalent would be (maintaining the unattached participle): 'disillusioned and cynical, this attempt seems to me *a priori* doomed to failure'.

war. The peaceful idyll of Bakari's family is disturbed by natural disasters
– a cholera outbreak that kills off his herds, a plague of locusts that
destroys his crops – but by diligence and united efforts they build up their
prosperity. The next intimation that this family is pursued by a hostile
fate comes when Bakari is impressed for forced labour by a brutal District
Commandant who ignores the tradition whereby a wealthy man could pay
a poor worker to do his service for him. The proud old man is humiliated
and violently beaten by the thuggish Commandant, and stabs himself,
before the eyes of his horrified son. Ahouna's brother-in-law, Camara,
assumes the role of patriarch to Bakari's family, initiating a new period
of rural bliss, during which Ahouna watches his flocks, plays his flute and
improvises songs. His music attracts Anatou from the other side of the
mountain, who is irresistibly drawn to him. Ahouna marries Anatou and
enjoys thirteen years of unblemished happiness with her. When the youngest of their four children is only nine months old, Anatou suddenly
becomes possessed with the demon of irrational jealously and the second
act of the drama begins, which continues without intermission until
Ahouna's destruction is accomplished. The atmosphere of mistrust rapidly
engendering hatred, Ahouna leaves home to escape from the temptation
to kill Anatou, and wanders for some weeks, weakened by hunger and
fatigue, into the unknown country of the South, where he cannot understand the dialect. One day, on a sudden impulse, as if to sublimate the
desire to avenge himself on his wife, he commits a completely gratuitous
murder, stabbing an innocent woman, the widow Kinhou. He is fleeing
from his victim's family when M. Houénou gives him refuge.

This first part has more unity both of action and of tone than the second
part, where the interest that should be intensified with the tragedy closing
in on Ahouna is dispersed over a number of incidents, with secondary
characters taking the centre of the stage. What now occurs, after Ahouna
finishes telling his story to Houénou, until the time of his death, is told
in a series of dramatic or tragic tableaux in which Ahouna is more often
an onlooker than the main actor. He is captured, fastened to a rough cross
and paraded through the streets of Ganmê by six prisoners, as an example
to the population, before being thrown in jail to await his trial. In this
grotesque parody of the Passion, however, our attention is diverted from
the suffering of the crucified Ahouna, to that of one of the prisoners,
one Affôgnon. This whole episode is told with such a wealth of trivial
and completely superfluous descriptive detail associated with secondary characters and situations as to detract from any symbolic or tragic
tonality.

There follow scenes of horror and violence in the prison and the quarries where Black and White, male and female prisoners, many of them condemned murderers, are sent to work. These prison scenes are also the occasion for some portrayals of stupid and brutal White officials. Then we move back to Zounmin, where Ahouna had killed Madame Kinhou some months earlier, and where the family of the victim is now bitterly divided over the question of their personal revenge, without waiting for the outcome of French justice. After they have engineered Ahouna's escape he is ambushed in the forest by the two sons and burnt alive. The narrator arrives with Camara and Ahouna's father-in-law, who had been alerted in the North of his imprisonment but only in time to perceive a red and smoking heap of ashes.

The lingering agony of Ahouna's death is thus the culmination of the drawn-out sufferings, both mental and physical, to which he had been prey since the irrational and illogical entered into his existence with Anatou's obsessive jealousy. He first become alienated from his home environment, then a wanderer in a strange country, a prisoner of society, subject to man's arbitrary justice, dominated by brutality and stupidity, and at the same time the prisoner of a hard and hostile Nature symbolized by the quarry. His own attitude is negative, passive to the point of nihilism. He is lucid enough to diagnose his own situation by explaining to Boullin, his fellow-prisoner, that he had lost his being, *son être* with the killing of Mme Kinhou. He had killed his own identity, his own will-power; he is now impelled onward by some external force, caught in the immense trap laid for man by fate or a vindictive divine power. Completely passive, he is nevertheless conscious of the emptiness of his existence and the vanity of any struggle to re-integrate or justify himself. In his own story the words *néant* and *nuit* (nothingness – or emptiness – and night) continually recur. He arouses the compassion of many people but they are all powerless to intervene on his behalf.

The incoherence, the unconvincing nature of some of the episodes, the lack of focus on the main character in the second part of the narrative might be attributed to a deliberate attempt to propound the theme of the absurd, which has no consistency. The author could claim that it is correct that Ahouna should now become the passive onlooker rather than the main actor in an illogical concatenation of adventures, such as the crucifixion parade and the quarry tragedies. It is noteworthy that in a novel which lays a certain emphasis on suicide, considered uncommon in African societies, Ahouna does not take his father's and Affôgnon's way out. Powerless to make a voluntary move for his own liberation he is condemned to life which must be a continual death until his final agony is accomplished.

Unfortunately the language and style of the second part of the novel are not always in harmony with this interpretation. The first part proceeds on the stylistic level of romantic lyricism, consistent with the bucolic idyll and with the sensitive *exalté* nature of the hero. The second part suffers from the lack of synthesis and unity of structure, from the confusion as to the source of the narrative, from a superfluity of trivial descriptive detail, from the cliché-ridden banality and often incongruity of the style. The digressions into ethnic lore, as with the descriptions of different funeral rites and the introduction of the moral fable told by Dâko to his family to warn them not to play with danger, also detract from the desired atmosphere of terror and tension, in a world dominated by invisible, inimical powers, determined on the destruction of their victim.

By presenting Ahouna as a submissive pawn, the victim of powers that inspire his uncontrollable impulse to kill, by never suggesting any condemnation of Houngbé's vicious action, by finally allowing him to be deported to take part in the war in Europe instead of being condemned to penal servitude, is Bhêly-Quénum re-affirming Houngbé's role as the instrument of superhuman forces against which all man's struggles are useless?

In his next novel, *Le Chant du lac*, a sequel to *Un Piège sans fin*, the supernatural powers are again present, the gods which haunt the lake with their presence and their song. Bhêly-Quénum now aims to exorcize their spell, desacralize their power, demythify the region of the lake. The second novel is more specifically a *roman à thèse* than its predecessor, with the didactic element overshadowing the philosophical: it is a plea for the abolition of superstition, if Africa is to look forward to a constructive future, rather than back to the destructive colonial past. It is a story of conflicts, oppositions – between the past and the future, between generations, beliefs, cultures and political aims.

Like *Un Piège sans fin*, *Le Chant du lac* is again a confusing and disconcerting book. It too has the making of the essential African novel, but it too is lacking in unity of structure and theme. Although it has more variety of style, particularly in the dialogue, which includes the realistic speech of the fishermen, the peasants' dialect and the colloquialisms of the students, there is much that is banal and cliché-ridden.

The first chapter is in reality a prologue to the main narrative. A group of Dahomean students return home from France for their holidays to the region beside the lake. The chapter is an amalgam of their conversations on the changing society in which they live, their differing attitudes from those of their elders, accounts of their life in France and, finally, the story recounted on the boat back to Dakar by Houngbé, a fellow passenger, who died from a rare form of typhoid. This is the Houngbé who was imprisoned at the end of *Un Piège sans fin* for the brutal vengeance inflicted on Ahouna and to whom the author now wishes to offer a quite unjustified apotheosis. His long monologue during his delirium leads up to his vow to return to the village by the lake from which his mother came and destroy the gods of the lake in order to free his compatriots from superstition.

This clumsily contrived introduction is also the occasion for Bhêly-Quénum to present his ideal for the young generation in whom the hope for the future of his country lies. Even if they disagree with their elders they feel it their duty to try to understand their point of view. Tolerant, understanding, charitable to the poor at home, these perfect youngsters also personify a healthy, pragmatic attitude to the practical realities of the present and the future, thereby justifying their European studies. They have no time for epic, legendary heroes of the past, stories of kings and princesses and mythological characters. Their hero is Houngbé, presumably because of his war exploits, though these are never made explicit and we only hear of his owing his life to two French soldiers. Their categorical and unsatisfactory explanation is that 'None of that [Houngbé's crime] interests us young people. We saw him die and for us Houngbé is a hero'. Later they state that their generation will not be formed by 'the words of the past', but by daily reality in which good intentions are rare, and which Houngbé's story is somehow intended to exemplify. The remainder of this part of the novel is devoted to the theme of the lake gods' destruction, the realization of Houngbé's dying wish.

At the opening of the second part we hear that Madame Noussi Ounéhou, the wife of an aspiring politican, has been most disturbed by this sacrilegious suggestion, for she is deeply imbued with traditional beliefs in the supernatural powers which haunt the lake. That night her sleep is disturbed and she is filled with premonitions of disaster, which the blood-red sunrise does nothing to dispel. She sets out across the lake to the market on the far shore, accompanied by her two children. It is the season of the harmattan. A thick fog descends and the canoe is carried away by the current. Many fishermen are drowned but Noussi and the children help the oarsman to the limit of their strength and finally escape from the fatal whirlpool, supposedly the haunt of the gods of the lake. These, according to local legend, were once two young lovers whose parents forbade their marriage. They went to bathe in the lake and disappeared, transformed into gods whose song always forecasts the death of others, for generation after generation have to pay the price for the parents' intransigence. On shore the students mock at this superstition and the fear that holds ignorant people in thrall. In the depths of the lake the call of one lover to the other predicts their own eventual destruction as the people of the nearby town prepare to revolt against the gods. This anguished dialogue between the spirits haunting the lake has a strong poetic quality, in contrast to the students' colloquialisms and the familiar speech of the fishermen. It is an anti-climax to discover that the elegiac gods whom a whole community adored and feared, are identified by one of the students as water-serpents, the thirty-foot long Cynopelamide, with a body like a boa and the head of a dog. The one which barked was the male and the one whose howl most nearly resembled a human voice was the female. These howls were the 'song of the lake'.

While this drama of the lake is continuing, on shore the local politicians, including Ounéhou, are holding an election campaign for the forthcoming cantonal elections. Some are in favour of the fetishists; some for the Christian parties against archaisms and taboos. Ounéhou is campaigning for a coalition party called R.G.D.W. (the author never bothers to explain what the initials stand for), whose main policy seems to be combatting reactionaries and obscurantism. Fortunately the last words of his speech are drowned in applause and the sacrilegious warning that the gods of the lake will sing no more is not heard.

Does this suggest a lack of finality, a reluctance on the author's part to take up a conclusive stand, although the general tone of the novel is that of a treatise against superstition? Those who had in fact destroyed the water-monster-gods are haunted by a sense of guilt which each tries to cover up in his own way, while expediency demands that the utmost discretion be maintained about the exploit, not for fear of the gods, but of the gods' supporters – men. Though the author reiterates that men are liberated by the death of the gods, their warning that the earth cannot do without them lingers in the words of Noussi, who feels that she has been exposed to an experience that is both mystic and dramatic. The story ends with the village in mourning for their dead divinities, which gives the impression that the final sympathies of the author are with the poetic, elegiac aspect of his tale, rather than with pragmatic, everyday rationalism.

Ferdinand Oyono

FERDINAND OYONO: *Chemin d'Europe*. Paris, Juillard, 1960.

In his third, and to date last novel[16] Oyono takes up the theme of *Une Vie de boy*, adds the burlesque, ironic humour and the naturalism of *Le Vieux Nègre et la médaille*, increases the dosage of lewdness and erotic

---

[16] As far back as 1960 a fourth novel, under the title *Le Pandémonium*, was announced as being 'in preparation', but so far (1976) there has been no sign of its appearance.

obscenities of the two preceding works, while refraining from any attack on colonial officials and reducing the virulence of his satire of the colonial situation generally. Where Toundi-Joseph's career might have ended in comedy, it is directed to bloodshed by the brutality, cynicism and self-interest of the White world into which he is plunged. But there is no question of Aki-Barnabas's destiny being governed by anything but his opportunism and his sense of humour, his lively taste for the comic to which he claims to reduce everything; in this he is the despair of his pious, slap-happy father and his long-suffering mother who wish to see quick returns for his mission education, his school certificate and particularly his competence in Greek and Latin.

Barnabas, like Toundi, expects to use the Catholic mission as a spring-board for his advancement; completely cynical, without the slightest moral scruple and devoid of any admirable sentiment, except some affection for his mother, he pushes his opportunism to the extreme, so that finally, after a series of set-backs, he finds himself realizing his ambition; on the road to Europe. By the time he reaches this goal, he is revealed as the typical anti-hero of a picaresque novel. He is first expelled from the seminary for a suspicious friendship. He is employed as a tutor to an eight-year-old French girl of premature sexuality and singularly depraved habits, whose father prefers the buxom charms of the local Black women to his pious, lachrymose spouse. Barnabas, a twentieth-century African Julien Sorel, imagines the latter in the role of Madame de Rênal, but it is only his mythomania that envisages Mme Gruchet falling into his bed. When she dismisses the importunate tutor, he sets about trying to get to Europe to improve his education. He lives on his mother's illicit brewing and acts as guide to Europeans staying at the local hotel who are avid for local folk-lore. Having been refused a bursary he finally finds his opportunity and his milieu by joining a moral rearmament group which is recruiting repentant sinners to exhibit throughout the world. We realize that Barnabas has already collected a more than average store of experiences which he can put to good use here, and there is no doubt that his imagination will not fail him in supplementing these where necessary.

A definite progression in the treatment of the colonial situation can be traced through Oyono's three novels, which reflect the evolving social and political climate of the nineteen-fifties. All are, in different degrees, satirical attacks on the colonial régime and aspects of colonial life. In *Une Vie de boy*, the author has not yet acquired full command of his literary expression nor of the resources of the novel. The subject, while original, is not deeply imaginative. Oyono invents melodramatic episodes and adopts an angry and bitter tone to inspire horror at the brutality of colonial officials and pity for his hero's fate. He indicates a gift for ironic humour which he does not exploit to the full. It seems clear that the composition of the novel belongs to an earlier period than that of *Le Vieux Nègre*, although both works are published in the same year, 1956. In the second novel he allows humour to take over and a healthier, more optimistic note to dominate. His White officials are obtuse and uncomprehendingly insensitive, but not so brutal. There is a suggestion of a positive moral, cynical as this may be: put no trust in the apparently friendly overtures of the colonial administrators; make no attempt to understand the Whites; simply *cultivez votre jardin* to quote *Candide*. There is a hint, by negative implication, that the future lies with the young generation, as not much material progress can be expected from Meka's ilk. This theme is taken up to form the core of *Chemin d'Europe* [Road to Europe]. We have now reached the watershed between colonialism and independence. The book still contains White characters, settlers and traders, but the only representative of the colonial administration is the quite benevolent M. Dansette, the official who tries to persuade Barnabas to enrol in the Centre d'Apprentissage when he cannot offer him a bursary. The White residents in the African colony, as well as the visiting Europeans, are attacked for their personal foibles, for their ambitions – usually frustrated – to make huge fortunes in Africa and live above their *petit bourgeois* origins, and mainly for their sexual morality. Oyono paints his African prostitutes with cynical and bawdy humour, but incidentally indicts the White man for his exploitation of the African woman. He launches a stray barb (which anticipates Yamba Ouologuem) at explorers and travellers in search of the picturesque Africa and folk-lore which they claim to know more about than the indigenous people. The chief target for his satire is, however, the missionaries: like Mongo Beti, he shows up their credulity in believing in the sincerity of their converts and their lack of comprehension of the mentality and motives of the Africans; he also accuses them of giving African youth a semblance of education which ill equips them for facing the problems of contemporary existence. Moreover, he makes some explicit and slanderous allusions to the missionaries' doubtful morals which indicate significantly the changed climate of opinion since Mongo Beti's *Pauvre Christ de Bomba* was banned four years previously.

If we accept that Oyono's aim in writing *Chemin d'Europe* was not merely to compose a lewdly picaresque, naturalist novel, nor to add much to the gallery of burlesque, caricatural portraits of White colonists who people contemporary African novels, we must examine more closely the role and significance of Aki-Barnabas himself. He is a bright young Cameroonian on the make. We are not expected to have any sympathy for his vicissitudes, which are never very serious, as he is sufficiently resourceful and unscrupulous to surmount all obstacles and set-backs. Oyono seems to be using him to demystify the situation of the young African intellectual and the faith put by his compatriots in a superficial Westernization. 'The time has past,' he seems to suggest, 'when a school certificate and an impressive pair of spectacles were an open sesame to success in life. All they are good for now is to offer an opening for degrading jobs and contact with the depravities of colonial existence. Now you must be prepared for a battle of wits.' In the final resort, with a cynical irony, worthy of Sacha Guitry's *Roman d'un tricheur* Barnabas is shown as owing the realization of his ambition to get to Europe to his lack of scruples and success in lying.

Irrespective of this latent didacticism, it is easy to understand the success that Oyono's novels enjoyed among African readers. The African critics who reproached Camara Laye with painting an idealized picture of Africa's mystic past, instead of facing the realities of her present and her future, hailed Oyono as an apostle of Negritude for the earthy realism of his novels.

Hamidou Kane

CHEIK HAMIDOU KANE: *L'Aventure ambiguë*. Preface by Vincent Monteil. Paris, Julliard, 1962. o.p. Re-issued Edits. 10/18, Paris, Union Générale des Editions, 1974.
English translation: *Ambiguous Adventure*, trans. by Katherine Woods. Introduction by Wilfred Cartey. New York, Collier, 1969. Repr. 1971.

Hamidou Kane admits that his *Aventure ambiguë* was completed ten years before it was published, and it is clear that by its basic theme it belongs to the fifties rather than to the sixties. Like *Karim*, *L'Enfant noir* and *Kocoumbo* it is a variation on the 'cross-roads' theme, that is a young Black man, representative of his generation, finding himself at the cross-roads, where two civilizations meet; he abandons or compromises his African origins and traditions, precipitated into, rather than choosing, Western civilization by his educational or professional ambitions, by economic necessity or political expediency. Like the above novels it is autobiographical: it is easy to identify the author with his hero Samba Diallo and to recognize his own personal dilemmas: those of the deeply spiritual man, torn from his basic moral and metaphysical anchorage and seeking for new guide-lines to existence in a Western European situation. But on the second level, Samba Diallo typifies the more general conflict between Afro-Islamic values and the demands and expediences of modern times which bedevilled the generation coming to maturity with Kane in the forties and fifties.

Lastly, Samba, belonging to the ruling family of the Diallobé, whose land is defeated and colonized, represents the hope for a return to sovereignty, if he can succeed in learning the secrets of the conquerer.

The date of publication of this novel is, however, significant. The political and material questions raised had already been largely solved, or faced early resolution with the end of the colonial era. The author's analysis of the spiritual, cultural, even theological conflicts resulting from colonization, which were even more urgent to him than the practical issues, would not have been popular with the militant anti-colonialists who were primarily concerned in the post-war years with denouncing the immediate practical evils of the régime. When the political struggle has been won, Kane then finds the moment propitious to remind his countrymen that the conflict for the affirmation of moral and spiritual values has still to be fought, and that here the opponent is a more insidious force. He goes further than the primary dictates of Negritude, the affirmation of Black consciousness, Black solidarity *qua* Black. At the Dakar conference on Negro-African literature in March 1963, he questioned the absolute community of interests and pre-occupations imposed solely by the black skin. He re-affirmed this point of view in an interview given to Irmelin Hossmann and published in *Jeune Afrique*, no. 134 (13–19 May 1963). While admitting that being Black is more dramatic than being White (though this would only be true in a White-majority society) and that the work of a Black writer is bound to be impregnated with this peculiarity of his condition, for Kane this is the limit of the common preoccupations. In his own case, as a Senegalese, a Musulman and trained in a French school, he must be fundamentally different from millions of Africans who had a different origin, religion and training. He shares the consciousness of Senghor that Black intellectuals must of necessity be cultural half-castes, but as a novelist transcends the purely cultural consequences of living at the meeting place of two worlds and he eludes attempts to enclose him in the Negritude net. When the French girl Lucienne challenges Samba Diallo with his 'Negritude' – 'I know now that you have Negritude at heart' – he parries with, 'I must admit that I don't like that word and I don't always understand what is at the bottom of it'. It is an over-simplification of all the issues to state that Samba Diallo's renunciation of Europe and return to Africa is a gesture of solidarity with Negritude, as Mercier and Battestini suggest; while the jacket note to the English translation (Collier, 1971) is a downright misinterpretation, when it describes *Ambiguous Adventure* as the 'novel of a black revolutionary's dilemma, telling how 'a modern African political revolutionary...attempts to win political freedom for his country by ridding it of foreign despotism'. Samba's dilemma is how to resolve his *crise de conscience* when he is torn from his service to God, rather than the political contingencies which preoccupy his aunt, 'La Grande Royale'; how to reconcile his training for sanctity with his responsibilities as a temporal leader of the Diallobé; how to continue his search for the absolute, faced with the conflicting teachings of Western philosophies and the Word of the Prophet. At the root of the novel is a fundamental, existentialist, universal dilemma and, as often in an existentialist situation, the final solution comes in the form of a tragic symbol of the absurd.

The anecdotal elements of *L'Aventure ambiguë*, right up to the tragic dénouement, are simple and largely traditional. Samba Diallo is given as a seven-year-old child, body and soul into the care of the ascetic Master of the Koranic school who recognizes all the potential spiritual purity of the boy. By the inhumanity of his treatment the Master deliberately aims at instilling a contempt for the flesh, an absolute exaltation, a sole passion for the mystery and the beauty of the Word of God, of which he feels his young disciple capable. But the child is snatched from this exclusive dedication to poverty and abnegation, solitude and prayer before his training is finished. His father's eldest sister, the 'Grande Royale', a woman shrewd in her understanding of the demands of reality, persuades the Chevalier of the Diallobé that the boy would be better trained for the changing times by being sent to the new French primary school for Africans: the 'school which only teaches how to bind wood to wood', in other words, how to be prepared for the practical material exigencies of the morrow. Her idea is also that Samba will learn from the conqueror the secrets of their victory in an unjust cause.

During the whole period of Samba's schooldays, with the introduction of the Lacroix family, whose children attend the African primary school, the Negro-centric unity of the book is maintained by the aura of unchildlike sadness that surrounds Samba like a wall of silence, cutting him off from his school-mates and making him less vulnerable than the average child. He is already preoccupied with the presence of death.

When he has completed his studies in the French schools of Senegal, already steeped in the philosophies of Descartes, Pascal and Nietzsche, he is sent to France to finish his university education. Hamidou Kane avoids the literary clichés of the Black student in the White society: there is no conventional love affair with a White woman, part of the stock-in-trade of the African novelists of the earlier decade. The French girl, Lucienne, who befriends Samba Diallo, a fellow philosophy student, feels she has the solution to the special problems of the colonized Black people and tries to convert him to Marxism. The daughter of a liberal-minded Protestant clergyman, she causes Samba to be welcomed into their relaxed and hospitable, cultured home. Nor is there any hint of racial prejudice in the milieux that he frequents in Paris. Lucienne is, however, the weakest character in the book from the point of view of psychological portrayal. She never really comes to life in the way that the slight portraits of Monsieur Lacroix and his son Jean indicate, in the first part of the book, something of their inner life and personality. Hamidou Kane is perfectly capable of a convincing psychological portrayal, where he sees his characters as persons, with deep human involvements. But this does not seem to be the case with Lucienne. Her role in the second part of Samba's ambiguous adventure is that of symbol of the attractions of Western logic, material preoccupations, political considerations, summed up in the Marxist doctrine, as opposed to the spiritual values of Diallo's Islamic Africa.

Samba refuses the temptation of the Communist solution, but he is conscious that in acquiring the knowledge and philosophies of Europe he has somehow betrayed God. He has abandoned the eternal and the absolute for the ephemeral and the contingent. His solitude is more intense than in his childhood because there is no longer the peace that he could enjoy in it before he had lost his faith. He returns to the country of his origins, but he does not resolve his spiritual and moral dilemma, nor that of his identity, the sense of having undergone an incomplete metamorphosis, and become a hybrid, as he explains to Lucienne's family when asked about his plans for the future. His return is not a triumph for the Negritude cause, but the step in the dark which brings him the only possible release from his existential anguish. The instrument for this liberation is the Madman, at whose hand he dies, absurdly, through an ambiguity, though in a sense he chooses this escape from his spiritual void.

The title of Sheikh Kane's sombre and poetic narrative reminds us that here are no simple issues nor clear-cut answers. Kocoumbo's problems of solitude, alienation and physical hardship could be solved by political independence, economic and educational autonomy of his native land. Samba's have a deeper, universally valid, metaphysical significance: to accommodate the material needs of a changing society, to assure its survival, without compromising with duty to God – or in fact, simply the choice between God and oneself. The ambiguous adventure of Samba Diallo is Everyman's allegorical quest for truth, reminding us of what André Breton said of Aimé Césaire in his preface to *Return to my Native Land*: 'And this Black man is not only a Black man but all mankind, expressing all man's anguish, all his hopes, all his ecstacy.'

Nevertheless we cannot discount the narrower issue of the confrontation between the European and the African cultures, Kane's answer to which is equally equivocal. He clearly cannot advocate either assimilation with the West, or complete rejection of the West. His hero, who cannot make the choice, dies, not tragically, but absurdly, almost accidentally, before the final responsibility for a decision is forced upon him. In the interview with Hossmann quoted earlier, when the author was asked about the pessimistic tone of his book, he replied that it was not intended to be devoid of hope. He intended the two extremes to be represented on the one hand by the Madman, the Fool who has been to Europe but, unable to understand or learn anything, returns with his mind deranged; and on the other by the Diallobés who represent the pure, undiluted, traditional Black society at its most conservative, deliberately shutting out the rest of the world. Kane goes on to suggest that with the ambiguous conclusion to his novel, the choice still remains open and that a synthesis is in fact possible. He himself believed in the possibility of a synthesis, although in his novel he only showed the Cartesian, pragmatic, materialist aspect of Europe. Since writing it he has discovered that the West, too, has her mystic and spiritual values.

The ambiguity of the subject, the ambivalence of the philosophical problems posed in Kane's novel, are nicely reflected in its structure. The composition, the characterization and, to some extent, the anecdote, have a duality which is expressed either in duplication or in opposition. The novel is divided into two uneven parts. The first, and longer, is situated entirely in Africa, from Samba's sixth year until he seems to be at the end of his secondary education. The only White characters introduced here are the thoughtful colonial administrator, Paul Lacroix, and his two small children who attend the same class as Samba in the African primary school. There is no explicit transition from this first part to the shorter second which corresponds with the end of Samba's studies in Paris for his Licentiate in Philosophy until his return to his native land and his death, a period which does not seem to cover more than a year. The transition and the trivial details of material preparations for the journey to France are superfluous, as this is a spiritual and not a geographical itinerary. But the second half has not the topographic unity of the first. There are scenes which cut back to the land of the Diallobé, a reminder that there has not been a final rupture in Diallo's existence.

A large portion of the narrative consists of a series of confrontations, occasioning a philosophical dialogue, which either oppose two points of view, or accentuate a major point of agreement. The shrewd, worldly-wise Grande Royale, representing the expediency of government, is thus opposed to her brother, the gentle, devout Chevalier; he in turn confronts with his mysticism the thoughtful and sensitive Lacroix, whose mind has been fed on Cartesian logic and scientific reasoning. The child Jean

Lacroix, on the other hand, at one moment at least when he finds himself isolated among the Black pupils, echoes the alienation and solitude of Samba Diallo. There is, of course, the obvious confrontation of Samba and Lucienne Martial, opposing spiritual values to Marxist dialectics. But in case this might be taken as an over-simplification of the Black/White, African/European relationships, we find the clergyman M. Martial duplicating or complementing the attitudes of Samba, in his frustrated wish to reject the material in favour of a return to a purity of faith. Finally, not long before his return home, there is the apparently inconsequential encounter with the old half-blind ex-magistrate from the Caribbean, who invites Samba to his home to meet the rest of his family. Pierre-Louis represents the Negro cultural hybrid (is it fortuitous that Kane portrays him with one eye dimmed by a cataract?) but as such he would not have had enough to contribute to the continual unresolved debate that is pursued throughout the novel. His real significance is as the symbol of the old revolutionary fighter for liberty that his semi-senile ramblings reveal him to have been. This rather grotesque re-incarnation of the spirit of Saint-Just causes Samba to meditate on the nature of revolution and the place of revolutionary action in his own time and to realize that he can no more envisage a violent resolution of contemporary problems than he could espouse Marxism. Arousing out of this chance encounter comes Samba's meeting with Pierre-Louis's grand-daughter Adèle, the young Mulatto, born on the banks of the Seine, who also reminds Samba that he too is an exile and a cultural half-caste. By affirming the plenitude of his African heritage, he helps her to find her own identity by accepting her own Black heritage.

In this economical, carefully constructed, dense narrative, there are no superfluous characters, no gratuitous incidents, no unnecessary details to reinforce a superficial realism. The characters are human and convincing, although there is not a single one who is base or despicable; this is not because Hamidou Kane rejects the presence of evil in mankind, but because his hero Samba Diallo, by his own nobility and deep spirituality seems impervious to the presence of meanness or brutality. The language of the narrative is soberly poetic, matching the nobility of the subject. The dialogue is unfailingly authentic, ranging from the deliberate effects of translation from Fula of the beggar-disciples' chants, to the familiar Parisian colloquialisms of the Pierre-Louis family. *L'Aventure ambiguë* is a profound and accomplished novel, with the epic qualities of heroic literature and the universality of allegory.

Charles Nokan

CHARLES NOKAN: *Le Soleil noir point*. Paris, Présence Africaine, 1962.

This modest piece was composed when Charles Nokan was a twenty-three-year-old student at the University of Poitiers in 1959, at the time when a conflict was raging between the Eburnean left-wing students and the rulers of Ivory Coast. The independence of his native land was already a reality when his book was published, but Nokan feared that the 'Black Sun' whose dawning he celebrated would not illumine the structure of African socialism for which he had sketched the working drawing.

Le Soleil noir point [The black sun is dawning] was born of an ideological and a personal inspiration: a two-fold romantic drama, with some references to factual experiences, is told with great reserve and delicacy. Into this is woven an equally economical account of the struggle for progress of a poverty-stricken, backward, rural community. Hardly a novel by its dimensions or even a novella in its form, it is a series of sixty-four short, apparently disconnected episodes, called *tableaux* – some consisting of only two or three lines, the longest of as many pages – which take place in France and in Ivory Coast. It passes from a third person narrative in poetic prose to an exchange of letters and to interior monologue in the first person; it includes passages of dramatic dialogue and others of recognizable verse. The links are formed by the two central figures of Tanou and Aube.

The first twenty-seven short tableaux tell of Tanou's love for Amah, his departure to study in France, his loneliness and nostalgia and include the lovers' brief but passionate correspondence. Amah waits patiently and faithfully, rejecting another suitor, while Tanou is unable to resist the advances of his landlady's daughter, Sarah. As his studies in France are prolonged and his parents can no longer send him money, poverty forces Tanou to share his room with three other poor Black students. When he is discharged from hospital after having had a testicle accidentally crushed and finds that Sarah has been unfaithful to him, his solitude is greater than ever. The knowledge of his personal sterility turns his thoughts to working for the future of a whole people; his own suffering will take on its rightful importance when confronted with that of his race. He returns home to his village of Gnassé where Amah has married his rival and he is saddened by the lives of hardship of his countryfolk. He has a dream of the struggle uniting men of all colours in love and fraternity against injustice and slavery.

The central figure of the next ten tableaux is the Princess Aube, an impassioned idealistic adolescent who lives in a world of unrealized dreams.

She is finally liberated from her negative obsessions and sees her way through pity and sorrow to a constructive future.

The final act of the drama unites the destiny of Tanou and Aube. Aware of their mission to transmit their culture and learning to their own people, they start classes for young and old, encourage carving, poetry, music and drama and create a co-operative to improve the coffee crop. The book ends on a note of hope and a promise that though some have died and others are still in prison, their example will not be forgotten and the Black Sun will soon dawn on the horizon and illuminate their deliverance.

Though set in the colonial era, *Le Soleil noir point* differs from earlier political novels in that it makes no direct attack on colonial exploitation. It is the local chiefs, who now have a semblance of power and a great many vested interests, who dissolve Tanou's Co-operative Association of Gnasséens, suppress his lectures and teachings and ban his public appearances.

But the real originality of this little, unclassifiable work is in its form and the charm exerted by its style. The passages of inner monologue and correspondence lend a poignant sincerity to personal episodes that could have been stereotyped. The brevity and rapidity of the sketches also prevent any monotony or banality in these scenes: the universal themes of love and infidelity, suffering and death are glimpsed, suggested as in an impressionist painting, rather than boldly outlined. The personal dramas are acted out in the chiaroscuro of a dream-world in which it is difficult to distinguish imagination from reality. The didactic purpose of the book is always evident: to illustrate how dignity, prosperity and independence can be attained through a people's corporate efforts – physical toil and education going hand in hand. But the composition is saved from becoming a tedious piece of moralizing propaganda by the elegiac lyricism of the style and the discreetly interwoven personal dramas of Tanou and the symbolically named Aube [Dawn].

1964–74: In the light of Independence

FAMILIAR WRITERS – NEW INSPIRATIONS

It took about half a decade before the fact of Independence was fully reflected in the French-African novel. By the mid-sixties it was finally appreciated that Negritude as a political war-cry had served its purpose and that literature need no longer express the demand for the liberation of a race from the cultural or political domination of other races. Literature still serves to express political ideals or ideologies in some regions, but in the French-speaking areas of Black Africa it no longer features the confrontation of oppressed colonized Blacks with White colonizing exploiters except in a historical context. Polemical writing, if effective, tends to have a built-in self-destructive mechanism in that it stimulates amelioration of the social or political structure and eliminates the evils that gave it birth. In the Independent Africa of the nineteen sixties, then, the well of inspiration which fed so many of the novels of the fifties, seemed to have dried up. Of the major satirical writers of the pre-Independence decades, Ferdinand Oyono found no new themes to replace the evils of the colonial society and has published nothing since 1960. Camara Laye made a belated attempt to redeem his earlier fall from grace with his politically oriented compatriots by making an unhappy sally into the fields of committed fiction, after which he, too, retreated into silence. Bernard Dadié continued to use his satirical gifts in historical dramas and travel chronicles which wickedly pin-point the foibles of contemporary society and human nature, which are only incidentally White and Occidental.

Ousmane Sembène was the first of the earlier generation of committed novelists to show that his rich and varied talents can continue to find new inspiration in the evolving world of decolonized Africa. Mature and confident in his use of the medium of fiction, he continues to observe his contemporary society with intuitive perceptiveness and compassion, describing the lives and dilemmas of simple people in satirical but uncommitted novels. Aké Loba, who had left his Kocoumbo on the way back to his native Ivory Coast, now, like the hero of his first novel, devotes his serious attentions to the problems of building up a new nation, in two works which broke a ten-year silence. It was even longer – sixteen years – before Mongo Beti joined the ranks of newer writers, who, finally liberated from their inferiority complexes, indict their own society, attack their own leaders and governments, exposing weaknesses, corruption, tyranny or injustice, in a new type of political novel.

In the previous sections of this chapter on the novel, I have presented the works by each author in the chronological order of first publication: this has allowed a perspective of the development of styles, inspirations and themes. In this final section I shall depart from this approach and deal first with the authors mentioned above, who returned to fiction after a greater or lesser interval after Independence, before going on to study the works of a new generation of young novelists, who have not known the orthodoxy of Negritude, and dare to write primarily about human emotions and universal values. Some of them deal incidentally with traditional social and tribal patterns, or the problems arising from the changing pattern of African life. Others inaugurate the new political novel, to which Mongo Beti eventually contributes.

Sembène Ousmane

SEMBÈNE OUSMANE: *Véhi-Ciosane ou Blanche-genèse*, followed by *Le Mandat*. Paris,
    Présence Africaine, 1965. Re-issued in Format de poche as *Le Mandat*,
    preceded by *Véhi-Ciosane*, 1970. *Xala*. Paris, Présence Africaine, 1973.
    English translation: *The Money Order*, with *White Genesis*, trans. by Clive Wake.
    London, Heinemann Educational Books, 1972.

Véhi-Ciosane is a story of village life in Senegal in the 1950s, after the
War in Indo-China. The Chief of the Santhiu Niaye brings disgrace
and tragedy to his family in begetting a child by the daughter of his
eldest wife. But this is no psychological analysis of passion or lust,
but a private drama of moral decadence which is felt to be symbolical
of the gradual decline of the whole community. The young people are
leaving the locality one by one for Dakar, attracted by the better
employment opportunities and the pleasures of city life: the catastrophe
in the life of one family resumes the spiritual and material denudation of
the whole society.

Sembène now manifests complete mastery of an economical, dense and
compelling narrative. The seduced mother of the child conceived in incest
hardly appears; the father who is responsible for the disgrace is also a
secondary character. The whole tragedy is presented through the anguished
incomprehension of the wife, Ngoné War Thiandum. At the beginning of
the story, she has become aware of the shame brought on her noble origins
by her daughter and her husband. She then turns painfully to questioning
the traditional supremacy and superiority of the master of the African
household, and the position of women. As in his most successful novel,
Les Bouts de bois de Dieu, Ousmane Sembène again shows himself the
champion of the cause of the African woman, which he submits with
insight and sober restraint, not in the form of a pamphlet, but through
the tortured thoughts of Ngoné War Thiandum herself. Unable to bear
the weight of social censure for herself and the mother of the unborn child,
as well as the disrepute into which her husband has fallen, she poisons
herself just before her daughter's child is born, so that she will never have
to set eyes on it. Before she dies she first declares that the child must be
called Véhi Ciosane (White Genesis) in the hope that the shame of its
conception will be redeemed by its existence. The village elders cannot
decide what punishment must be meted out by the community to the
incestuous father, the tradition that would have demanded his death having
weakened. A dramatic climax satisfying poetic justice is achieved by one
of the sons, who has gone mad from fighting in the Indo-Chinese War,
stabbing his father to death. The young mother is driven out with her child

born of sin. The author's preface tells us that she still lives alone in Dakar in 1965. He addresses the child as follows:

For you Véhi Ciosane Ngoné War Thiandum (White Genesis) may you prepare the genesis of our new world. For it is from the blemishes of our old world already condemned that this new world will be born, a new world that we have so long awaited, dreamed of so long. (p. 17 [p. 6])

After this clarification of his intention in the preface, Sembène does not labour his moral which is presented with delicate restraint, making the tale all the more moving, contrary to his works of fiction dictated by partisan commitment.

The story which accompanies *Véhi-Ciosane*, *Le Mandat*, is set in post-Independence Senegal. Sembène here exploits his gift for political satire which was briefly viewed in *Voltaïque*, particularly in the story *Prise de conscience* and also in the portrait of the opportunist Black Prime Minister of *L'Harmattan*. However *The Money Order* is not only a telling satirical comment, but also a profound psychological study of a man caught between two worlds, a study we shall find again in Ahmadou Kourouma's novel, *Les Soleils des Indépendances*, with which Sembène's *novella* has much in common. Ibrahima Dieng, unemployed, in debt, but still retaining his dignity, receives a money order from his nephew in Paris, with instructions to pay certain remittances for him. His tribulations begin when he tries to cash the order, as he is caught up in a spider's web of bureaucracy. He is also the victim of the machinations of the local shop-keepers, his neighbours, relatives and 'friends' who all swarm around at the news of his windfall. In the end, more in debt than ever, he is swindled of the money order by a wide boy of a relative, who impresses the ignorant and credulous Ibrahima by his standard of living, which has all the appurtenances of Westernized bourgeois existence. *Le Mandat* is an ironic, pathetic, sometimes comic, trenchant study of the life of poor and humble folk, still ignorant, unlettered, torn from the shelter of a rural community governed by tradition, and unable to cope with the sophistications and bureaucratic complications of city life.

For many years after the publication of these two short novels, Ousmane devoted all this time and talents to film productions. Then, in 1973, he produced another novel rather similar to *Le Mandat*, an ironic, closely observed comment on contemporary Senegalese urban society, concentrating his camera on the profiteers of the New Order. *Xala*[17] is part comedy of manners, part comedy of character, part merciless, savage burlesque with an unequivocal moral intention. The hero, El Hadji Abdou Kader

---

[17] *Xala*, pronounced, so the author tells us, 'Hâla'.

Bèye, belongs to the same family as Bernard Dadié's Monsieur Thôgô-Gnini and Ayi Kwei Armah's Koomson, of *The Beautyful Ones are not yet Born*. He is the nouveau-riche political turn-coat, time-server and profiteer, taking advantage of the changing social order to become an exploiter of the poor – the new colonizer of his own compatriots. Opulent, middle-aged and uxorious, he is punished for his rapacity in a way no wealth or power can compensate: he is suddenly stricken with the *xala*, that is absolute impotency, before he can consummate his union with his third wife – an appetizing young nineteen-year-old virgin. He becomes the laughing-stock of the town. Convinced that the *xala* can only be the result of a curse put on him by an enemy, he suspiciously reviews all the possible sources, in particular his two senior wives who are most likely to be jealous. He implores them to lift the spell, for they too cease to benefit from their share of his conjugal attentions. Exemplifying his synthesis of two cultures – middle-class European and feudal African – he consults in turn the sorcerers who still practise their profession on the outskirts of the city, and the psychiatrists at the local hospital who find him an interesting case but can offer no cure. As El Hadji loses face, so he loses friends and what is more important – credit. In his final desperation he allows his chauffeur to take him to Serigne Mada, a holy man who lives far in the bush and is reputed able to effect miraculous cures. As they travel over rough country roads, forced eventually to abandon the Mercedes for a farm-cart, Abdou Kader Bèye is travelling symbolically back to his origins, and to the time when he was a humble primary school teacher, and is more and more dependant on his chauffeur. But still he does not realize the moral lesson of his humiliations.

Abandoned by everyone except his chauffeur and his loyal and resigned senior wife, Adja Awa Astou, he finally discovers that the curse of the *xala* has been put on him by a beggar who sits all day outside his business premises and whose monotonous chanting had long irritated him. This same beggar now offers to cure him. Two days later the 'cure' takes place, in the form of the beggar's vengeance. In the scene reminiscent of Buñuel's *Viridiana* (and we must remember that Sembène's major preoccupation over the past ten years has been with film production) the beggar invades the villa of Adja Awa Astou, where El Hadji has taken refuge, leading a procession of all the inhabitants of a modern *Cour des Miracles*. This ragged, filthy, scarred, deformed, rheumy-eyed, degenerate horde of cripples, lepers and other outcasts of society, ransack and defile the house. The beggar is obtaining his payment in advance for the cure that he is about to perform, and his vengeance for having been expropriated, imprisoned on a false charge and, on his discharge, brutally beaten by Abdou's friends more than twenty years before. The cure itself, the means by which El Hadji Abdou Kader Bèye can hope to regain his complete manhood, consists of standing naked before all these wretched of the earth and allow them each in turn to spit solemnly on him three times, without making any move to wipe away the sickening materialization of their opprobrium.

Xala is a satirical indictment of the society that allows the El Hadji Abdou Kader Bèyes to batten on their victims and also a serious morality tale. In spite of its originality of theme and the powerful impact of the dénouement, it is also a somewhat unsatisfactory work. This is partly because of a confusion over genre and partly because of the lack of sympathy evoked by the majority of the secondary characters. As far as genre is concerned, Sembène gives the impression in the early part of the novel that he is going to treat his theme, which has Rabelaisian potential, in a satirico-comic vein. This is the promise of the lascivious comments of Abdou's fellow-members of the Chamber of Commerce, the descriptions of the wedding celebrations, the account of the machinations of the young bride's family to get the best out of the match, and the jealousies of the two senior wives. However, acerbity and a more sombre moral tone gradually dominate the burlesque potential, without compensating by winning over our sympathies for any of El Hadji's victims or any of the members of his entourage, with the possible exception of Adja Awa Astou. But in the final analysis the worthy Adja is too colourless and lymphatic a personality to command our deep sympathies. Her eldest daughter, Rama, represents the new generation of intellectuals, a student at Dakar University, so fiercely nationalist that she refuses to speak French, denounces polygamy and the subservience of women generally in the traditional African Muslim society, but is as out of touch with the realities of suffering as her father and his opportunist friends. In the final scene, she is as helpless and uncomprehending in the face of the horde of beggars and their vengeance as her parents. The element of compassion that is present in the best of Sembène's works is completely absent here. He leaves us with the impression that he had become disillusioned and cynical, finding little hope for redemption in a society as much populated with self-centred, grasping individuals as the world of El Hadji. There is no positive message in this morality tale; there is little hope that he will have been washed clean by the spittle and will be ready to turn over a new leaf or that anyone will have learnt any fundamental lesson from the retribution meted out to Abdou Kader. *Xala* is the most pessimistic of Ousmane Sembène's novels since he has not replaced his earlier partisan commitment with any positive spiritual message. And here, where we might have expected the therapy of laughter we are treated to an emetic. But we cannot deny his originality of treatment

of a theme which is becoming part of the stock-in-trade of satirical com-
mentators on the New African society. With this novel, Sembène confirms
his unique place among the French African writers. He offers the sole
example of the novelist who served his literary apprenticeship in the ranks
of the most heavily committed school of Negro-African authors, to emerge
as one of the most accomplished of contemporary novelists. His early work
was more laudable for its promise than for its performance. For long he
showed himself an uneven writer. In *Les Bouts de bois de Dieu* he transcended the ideological and partisan theme by his deeply understanding
study of the repercussions on individuals and families of their political
involvements. He does not maintain this level of human understanding in
L'Harmattan (*Référendum*), whose characters are paste-board and whose
interest will probably be purely academic when the events that inspired
it have receded into the past. However, I would venture to prophesy that
the three short novels, *Véhi-Ciosane*, *Le Mandat* and *Xala*, some of the
short stories of *Voltaïque*, and the one novel *Les Bouts de bois de Dieu*, will
guarantee him a permanent place among the important African novelists
of the mid-century.

Camara Laye

CAMARA LAYE: *Dramouss*. Paris, Plon, 1966.
   English translation: *A Dream of Africa*, trans. J. Kirkup. London, Collins, 1968.

I have already drawn attention (p. 193) to the hostility with which African
intellectuals, in France particularly, greeted *L'Enfant noir*, reproaching the
author with insisting on universalities rather than specifically African values
and for high-lighting the mysterious and the supernatural which lacked
relevance to contemporary problems. Thirteen years after his first autobiographical novel, Camara produced its sequel, *Dramouss* – the answer
to his African critics and the sop to his conscience for having shown small
enthusiasm for the policies of his one-time friend Sékou-Touré. He dedicated his new book to the young people of Africa, claiming to have written
it 'in order that African ways of thinking, reintegrated and restored... may
be a new force – not aggressive but fruitful'. But, in fact, what we find
most clearly emerging is the divided personality of the writer. The work,
ambivalent in inspiration and intention, is a mixture of autobiography,
lacking the freshness, originality and poetry of *L'Enfant noir*, and political
tract, in the form of a would-be mystico-supernatural parable, which fails
to inspire the sense of awe in the face of powerful forces pervading both
the two earlier works. Its mediocrity also inspires doubts as to how these
can all be from the same pen.

The author, thinly disguised as Fatoman, returns to Conakry after six years in France. In an attempt, not entirely successful, to vary the narrative techniques, the events of the preceding years are presented in flashback, as Fatoman recalls his life since he left Kouroussa: his struggles as a poor student in Paris, typical of so many of his compatriots. The details of Fatoman's work as a porter at Les Halles and on the assembly line at the Simca motor works, his affair with the French girl, Françoise, all give the impression of being the unworked extracts from a diary, the raw material of literature on the level of social realism. The scenes, the characters, are superficially evoked with no creation in depth. Laye seems to have lost the art of recalling scenes from the past with vivid colour and observation, which form the web of memory in *L'Enfant noir*.

The author – 'hero' is revealed as a very serious, long-suffering, self-righteous young man, whose excessive virtue is rather a bore. He is polite, subservient even, to his superiors, while not hesitating to reprimand both strangers and friends for their wrong values. He is prepared to be a martyr to bring salvation to his fellows, but, in a parable revealed in a dream, he learns that he can, in turn, be saved if he does not compromise his principles. It is the little snake of his childhood who brings him this message. Immediately upon his arrival in Conakry, Fatoman finds his childhood sweetheart, Mimie (the Marie of *L'Enfant noir*), and they are unceremoniously bundled into bed by his uncle who explains that they are already married by Muslim custom. Mimie proves a rather tenuous character. Although she seems the *évoluée* young African career girl, she does not prove, on further acquaintance, to have any real personality or psychological depth.

The father of Fatoman, just like Laye's father in *L'Enfant noir*, is the key to the mystic-supernatural element in *Dramouss*, which is first introduced by the re-appearance of the little black snake, which shares its master's hut and seems to have a real means of communicating with him; and then, at the very end of the novel, by the incident of the sparrow-hawk which has flown off with a young fowl and which the old smith summons back to the court-yard and forces to deposit its prey. But the main supernatural element is introduced in the episode which gives the book its title: Dramouss is a genie who usually adopts the guise of a beautiful woman, but sometimes that of a huge white silhouette, seemingly clad in a shroud, who will reveal the future to the man who sleeps with a white ball under his pillow. This ball is given to Fatoman by his father, who neglects, however, to tell him that Dramouss is a jealous spirit and that he must not spend the night with his wife when he wishes to summon her. The revenge that she takes is to set alight to the hut, from which Fatoman and Mimie barely escape with their lives. Meanwhile Dramouss does reveal to him in a nightmare vision what the world of the future will be: a starving, impoverished people, living in a huge prison, where violence is the only law, surrounded by a wall that reaches to the skies, dominated by a vicious jailer-judge-torturer-executioner. Finally a pure, strong Black Lion would set the people free and bring peace and prosperity to the land.

This key episode is a circumlocutory, unconvincing attempt to recapture the Kafka-esque nightmare and visionary allegory of *Le Regard du Roi*, where Man is trapped in a labyrinth from which he can only escape – gain redemption – by the force of his aspirations and purity of his ideals. The parable of Dramouss and the Black Lion is not only the core of the book but also the link between the magic and the political elements, for most of the novel operates on the level of a political tract. We are left in no doubt of the author's intention in the very first chapter, when Fatoman is driving in the bus from Conakry Airport to the city and his neighbour inveighs against the colonial system. Fatoman/Laye makes his first plea for suspended judgement till the moment comes when his compatriots can prove themselves superior to the colonists. Later, when asked what reply he would have given if asked to speak at the meeting of the Rassemblement Démocratique Africaine, he is just as equivocal. This is in 1953. When Fatoman returns again from France to Guinea, presumably after Independence (*Dramouss* was published in 1966), he finds that the first part of the prophetic nightmare vision is being realized, as are the activities of political agitators which he had formerly denounced. His friends have been the victims of violence, either executed or in exile. 'The government shoots our children on the slightest pretext', his father tells him. 'There is no meat in the land, not a grain of rice'. According to the old man's philosophy, the present misery is the punishment for neglecting the adoration of the Almighty, but after some years of this chastisement He will send his Redeemer (the Black Lion). On this pious note the book ends.

The father is also the mouthpiece for another message – regret for the disappearance of traditional crafts, which were for the old generations of artists more than aesthetic creativity; they were a rite, an expression of spirituality, and act of worship in the art's constant relationship with fire, which purifies and fuses.

The final level at which *Dramouss* operates, still in the area of nostalgia for the creative expressions of traditional ethnic culture, is as a framework for the resuscitation of old legends, in this case the tale, told by the *griot* Moussa, of the jealousy of a wealthy, respected Imam, cuckolded by a hideous, vile and filthy shepherd in his own employ. This rather scabrous little fable, in spite of its moral, seems incongruous and gratuitous in view of the elevated ideological intentions of the book as a whole. But its introduction is characteristic of the literary weaknesses of the work. The author has clearly been confused by too many theses which he feels the need to defend and of which he has made *Dramouss* the vehicle. None of these theses emerge with real conviction, and the literary merit of the composition suffers at all levels. As a semi-autobiographical novel based on real experience, as was the case of *L'Enfant noir*, there is little or no depth of observation, no rich description of setting, no penetration beneath the superficialities of the anecdote, nor of the psychology. The dialogue is stilted, unconvincing, not adapted to differences of social and geographic milieu or personalities; the hero, Fatoman, himself falls into the error for which he reproaches his countrymen – and with which opinion his father concurs – that of perpetrating too much speechifying. In this work of fiction purporting to be dominated by mysticism and spiritual powers, the oneiric, symbolic element which pervades *Le Regard du Roi* fuses badly with the pragmatic, practical problems and political realities of the situation the author wishes to confront. The symbolism remains superficial, artificial even, not an integral part of the events, not emerging as the main axis for the narrative, as the title would lead us to expect. Only here and there does one sense Laye's power to feel his subject poetically and to express it compellingly, as he did in his earlier works. It is clear that his main purpose was to offer a philosophico–political tract, spelling out unambiguously his own attitude to the doctrines of Negritude, but the didactic message is lost in a mass of verbiage and the lack of coherence seriously detracts from the impact of the work.

Aké Loba

AKÉ LOBA: *Les Fils de Kouretcha*. Paris, Brussels, etc., Edits. de la Francité. (Coll: Romans contemporains) 1970. *Les Dépossédés*. Paris, Brussels, etc., Edits. de la Francité, 1973.

Aké Loba, is one of the few pre-Independence novelists to make a return to fiction writing with new post-Independence inspirations. While First Secretary at the Eburnean Embassy in Rome, he completed his second novel, situated entirely in Africa. With no sociological thesis or political axe to grind, he tries to depict the problems facing a primitive community in adjusting to a new mode of life and the way different individuals react to new standards according to their different temperaments, personal backgrounds and relationships with one another and the authorities. It is another in the series of new novels of transition, to which Ousmane Sembène's *Le Mandat* and Kourouma's *Les Soleils des Indépendances* are notable contributions. Loba also permits himself at one stage a brief personal note when he makes the Black Préfet, Tougon, presumably his mouth-piece, speak of the progress of Negro-African literature and the difficulties facing the African writer. (Surprisingly he seems a little uncertain as to the normally accepted orthography of his fellow-authors' names and works.) To the Frenchman Demblin's confession of ignorance about the true nature of Africa, her society, her laws, her religions, her cities, he asks:

'Haven't you read our authors: Mongo Betti, Sunben Ousman, Bernard Dadié?'
'Yes, but they don't attach much value to the forest and its poetry. Dadié, in his famous book Krimbié, scarcely mentions it at all, at least not enough for me.'
(p. 123)

Aké Loba's *Les Fils de Kouretcha* [The sons of Kouretcha] was completed in 1966, but did not appear until 1970, when it went virtually unnoticed. The author's note indicates that it is intended as a sequel to *Kocoumbo* and we certainly recognize the rascally Douk, now a successful merchant, managing a store in the rural area of Ivory Coast, where the action takes place. This attempt to establish continuity with the earlier novel is however quite arbitrary, as neither the main characters nor the incidents of the two works are in any way related. The central figure of the book is Pierre Dam'no, a sexagenarian to whom Independence has brought no joy. He is one of the elders of the tribe which takes its name from the River Kouretcha, in the neighbourhood of which they have established their villages and which they worship as a god. Dam'no had been the first literate man of his tribe and had enjoyed a position of prestige and authority amongst his own people by virtue of the post of senior copying clerk that he held with the colonial administration.

The new Black Administration, headed by the Préfet Tougon, accords him neither privilege nor honour. What is more, they are preparing to affront the River Divinity, Kouretcha, by building a barrage, to supply electricity and so improve the economy and standard of living of the area. The whole of the novel consists of the confrontation between individuals and groups associated with the power project, and the presentation of rivalries associated with personal complexes, jealousies and ambitions within the life of the community. The construction work on the barrage is eventually interrupted by torrential rains, causing floods, washing away material, bringing deaths from drowning and crocodiles. All this substantiates the belief that it is the angry god himself avenging the profanation of the sacred waters and surrounding territory. Unrest grows among the villagers, with rumours of a plague of scorpions descending on the area and more violent deaths being perpetrated, culminating in that of Moussa Dombyia at the hands of Dam'no himself.

Les Fils de Kouretcha is an honest and original attempt to recount the combined private and public dramas of a small rural community of modern Africa, in the new period of transition from colonialism to self-determination. The rivalries over personal issues are not always convincing or, at best, are versions of somewhat stereotyped social situations; the resolution of the plot at the end is arbitrary. But the character of Dam'no, presented without sentimentalization or bias, makes a notable contribution to the gallery of portraits of the Old Men in the New Society, which we are beginning to find in increasing numbers in post-Independence Negro-African fiction.

The idea of combining an individual and a national history informs Aké Loba's second post-Independence novel, *Les Dépossédés* [The dispossessed], which he indicates was written over the period 1967–71, immediately after the completion of *The Sons of Kouretcha*. I have the feeling that he may well have had second thoughts about publishing as late as 1973 a novel whose title betrays a clearly anti-colonial theme; he seems to have been impelled to graft a kind of prologue on to a fairly traditional story of an average Eburnean's evolution during the first sixty years of this century, to introduce the parallelism between his hero's existence and that of the city of Abidjan: 'The curious thing is that he (Païs) confuses the story of his own existence with that of the city of Abidjan, whose birth he had witnessed, to the extent that for him Abidjan represented his own personality. "Everything here begins with myself," he states' (p. 16). Loba then goes on to suggest that 'the whole story of Africa has been cancelled out by the town of Abidjan' and that it is sufficient to know the life of Païs, the museum-keeper, to know all that there is to know about the capital. And so he goes on to recount the reminiscences of the sexagenarian: his departure from his native village to obtain sufficient schooling for exemption from forced labour; his first happy marriage to a fifteen-year-old village girl, with whom he settles in Abidjan, still an undeveloped little port, dominated by the neighbouring Grand Bassam and the then capital, Bingerville. Of average intelligence and mediocre schooling, Païs obtains employment in a hardware shop, accepts the rough treatment of his employer as natural, thinks his modest wage a fortune, becomes involved in a tribal feud with a fellow-employee, serves a term in prison, takes to himself two new wives, thereby introducing discord into his once peaceful and happy home, and is finally abandoned by his first wife after the death by drowning of one of his youngest children in a storm-water drain being dug outside his home.

There is no apparent echo in the Colony of the events racking the world during the two wars that punctuate the half century covered by the narrative. Nor is there any attempt to bridge the period from Païs's divorce (he must have been between forty and fifty) to the present, in the early sixties. The story ends abruptly with the semi-burlesque funeral ceremony for the dead child, at which the missionary Father Tourbillon is called to officiate by his avowedly Christian mother, while the animist bearers proceed to the traditional 'smelling out' of the person responsible for the death, until a well-placed boot of the priest sends them scuttling at indecorous speed to the cemetery. This final scene is intended, presumably, to sum up the ambiguity of the society inhabiting the native township of Abidjan in the decade preceding Independence.

To counter the anachronistic nature of his subject, Aké Loba makes an honest attempt at dispassionate *reportage*, kept deliberately low-key in the account of the brutal treatment meted out to prisoners and villagers recruited for forced labour. Païs's attitude of resigned acceptance of his fate pervades the whole narrative. On the positive side, Loba frequently mentions actual advantages that colonization brought to his native land – not only in the proud growth of the city of Abidjan. The generation gap finds a new expression in the musings of sixty-year-old Païs, regretting that contemporary youth does not have the benefits he himself enjoyed with his colonial upbringing:

The White man taught me the meaning of work; he also taught me justice and plain-speaking. If he demanded my maximum exertions, he gave in return security and confidence in the established order of things. What we thought then was lack of understanding, was really an apprenticeship in mutual help and courage: 'You give me your labour, I'll give you methods of organization; you give me your toil, I'll provide you with care in your hour of need'. Whereas all these Independence profiteers, have they any idea where their little game is leading us? (p. 13)

Loba makes an equally honest attempt at understanding the problems of the colonial authorities, typified by the Police Chief, Guillot. He is shown as a zealous, but credulous idealist, the victim of suspicion from his fellow colonists and autochtones alike, and eventually abandoning his efforts to introduce justice and understand the 'native mentality' and resorting to indiscriminate brutality in his disillusionment. In a moment of rare insight, Loba makes Guillot exclaim to his wife: 'My poor Rose, the real dispossessed ones are ourselves' (p. 145).

If we can deduce any lesson from this novel, it is pessimistic, if not nihilistic. Firstly, comes the explicit submission that there was no hope of understanding between alien cultures, that is patent in every episode where Whites and Blacks are confronted; but in the introductory pages, situated in the post-Independence years, Loba insinuates that his average Eburnean sees little improvement in his lot. The most satisfactory level on which *Les Dépossédés* operates, is when the author forgets to make any political inference, omits references to social growth of the city and abandons himself to the tale of an average polygamous family, which he does, unexcitingly, but with sound psychological understanding, particularly of his female characters.

Mongo Beti

MONGO BETI: *Remember Ruben*, Paris, 10/18 Union Générale d'Editions (Coll: La Voix des Autres) 1974. *Perpétue et l'habitude du malheur*. Paris, Buchet/Chastel, 1974.

Published within a few months of each other, *Remember Ruben* covers the period from before the Second World War to the proclamation of Independence and *Perpétue* takes up the story about 1965. *Remember Ruben* has certain features in common with *Cercle des Tropiques* discussed later on (p. 312); indeed when the latter appeared, and I was trying unsuccessfully to pierce the anonymity of the author, I suspected – wrongly – that Alioume Fantouré was but another pseudonym adopted for political expediency by Alexandre Biyidi, for this seemed just the sort of book that Mongo Beti might have conceived in his known mood of post-Independence cynicism. Both novels take place in an un-named French colony, where the vicissitudes of a simple peasant are the pretext for an indictment of the political intrigues, election-rigging and manoeuvring for power surrounding the granting of independence. In both cases the central figure is a friendless orphan – here called Mor-Zamba – who becomes a prey to the machinations of the city wide boys and almost unwittingly involved in a revolutionary movement, led by a defender of democratic rights, who seeks to prevent the forthcoming independence from becoming a continuance in another form of the evils and oppressions of colonialism.

However, *Remember Ruben* is a vastly inferior novel to *Cercle des Tropiques*, unsatisfactory by most standards and certainly disappointing from the author of *The Poor Christ of Bomba* and *Mission to Kala*. It gives the impression that Mongo Beti's deep involvement with the political issues, and his own personal bitterness did not allow him sufficient distance from his subject to compose a work of art. The polemical contingencies have overshadowed imaginative creativity as, in part two, we are continually reminded of his pamphlet, *Main basse sur le Cameroun*, published two years previously, in which he vituperates against President Ahidjo, presumably the model for Baba Toura, the puppet Chief of State of the novel (see my page 207 above). Although the author precedes his story with the traditional disclaimer that 'any resemblance to past events, real characters or known countries is only apparent, and even, to some extent, regrettable', this is discounted by his dedication 'To Diop Blondin, that proud Black youth, my brother, assassinated in the infamous gaols of an African ruler. Africa, unnatural mother who has given birth to too many mercenary tyrants!'

Part one consists of a series of loosely connected episodes from the childhood and early manhood of Mor-Zamba, a mysterious orphan who wanders one day into the village of Ekoumdoum and becomes the victim of a vicious but unexplained xenophobia on the part of the local inhabitants, with the exception of one childless old widower who adopts him and gives him his name, and a fiercely independent, bellicose youngster, Abéna, who becomes his inseparable friend. On the death of his guardian, Mor-Zamba is betrayed by the villagers to the forced-labour recruiting gang. Abéna goes in search of his adoptive brother and finds him in a labour camp on the outskirts of the city of Oyola. Meanwhile war has broken out in Europe and Abéna disappears, and we learn much later that he has volunteered for service in the French army. Mor-Zamba escapes from forced labour when he is involved in the shooting down of his unarmed comrades by a posse of trigger-happy police; 'a rebel in spite of himself' he reaches the capital, Fort Nègre, hoping to find news of Abéna.

In the longer second part, to which the preceding forms an introduction, we follow the next twenty years of Mor-Zamba's existence in the native township of Kola-Kola on the outskirts of the capital. Illiterate, politically and socially naïve, of few positive principles except his loyalty to the memory of his friend Abéna, of unusual physical strength, he becomes one of the henchmen of a crooked Black businessman and, by accident rather than conviction, a follower of the revolutionary leader, Ruben, whom he helps to rescue from the police. Although there is frequent mention of Ruben, he only appears in the action during this one incident of his torture and rescue. His partisans eventually learn of his assassination at the hands of the new government, and the slogan 'remember Ruben' becomes their rallying cry. Abéna, who had volunteered for service in Indo-China at the end of the war in Europe, now turns out to be the man on whom Ruben's mantle has descended and, under the name of 'Hurricane-Viet' continues the struggle. He appears briefly at the end of the novel to reveal to Mor-Zamba the rather improbable facts of his mysterious childhood, which he has somehow gleaned in the interim: he is the son of the former deposed Chief of Ekoumdoum, whose mother had been exiled with her children and who had died wandering insane about the countryside.

Mor-Zamba is exhorted to return to his legitimate home, reclaim his rightful heritage and 'Remember Ruben'.

The narrator being ostensibly one of the older inhabitants of Ekoumdoum, Beti has recourse to many artifices in order to try – not very successfully – to bridge the gaps between the different episodes and situations. A large number of secondary characters and incidents are introduced, which militate against any unity of theme and action or concentration of interest. The language is often pedantic or weighted with a heavy facetiousness that is far from the Voltairian irony of the best of Mongo Beti's earlier novels.

In spite of Mor-Zamba's central position in the action of the two parts of the novel, neither his continual martyrdom at the hands of the villagers of Ekoumdoum, his sufferings in the labour-camp of Oyolo or torture in the prison of Fort Nègre fully succeed in eliciting our sympathies for him as an individual. He remains a shadow-hero, the symbol for a whole oppressed people, his misfortunes the pretext for a political tract. The first part of this is in the form of a somewhat belated affidavit (in 1974) from which the 'civilized world would learn with horror and stupefaction of the daily practices current in the Colony, the cruelty of the 'Saringalas [Black mercenaries], racial discrimination in every field, all the excesses with which life in the Colony was cursed' (p. 223). The second part cynically expresses the little hope that can be nourished with the coming of Independence for any improvement in conditions. The actual words of the tract clandestinely printed and circulated by Abéna, after the assassination of Ruben, exhorting the members of the Popular Progressive Party to continue the struggle, best sum up the message of the novel and give a fair idea of its linguistic style:

With Baba Toura, De Gaulle's Black *gauleiter*, independence will just be the continuation of colonization... under a different disguise, perhaps. This independence will in no way correspond to the aims of the P.P.P. Far from turning out to be the indispensable instrument for the full development of the people, it will prove to be the yoke by means of which the agents of colonialism and imperialism who hide behind Baba Toura will continue to oppress the people of this country – people who will continue to go hungry and barefoot in a country overflowing with natural resources. If this nazi experiment succeeds – and only our party is resisting it – then those who stand to gain most by it will extend its application further and further. (p. 270)

This is the theme taken up in *Perpétue*, when 'His Beloved Excellency' Sheikh Baba Toura has been in power for many years in a corrupt and fascistic state from which the last traces of Ruben's party have been ruthlessly eradicated. Essola, a former Rubenist, is finally released after six years in a concentration camp and allowed to return to his home region on promising to organize mass manifestations in favour of Baba Toura, to strengthen the support for the Dictator's single party régime. Essola's main preoccupation, however, is to try to find out under what conditions his young sister Perpétue died during his imprisonment.

The novel proceeds on two levels, with unequal success. On the one hand it recounts the deplorable fate of Perpétue, married by her rapacious mother, while still a schoolgirl, to a weak, slow-witted, bullying, low-grade government clerk in Oyolo (presumably Douala). On the other, it is a diatribe against the government of this thinly-veiled state, in which the worst evils of colonialism are perpetuated and exacerbated by a compound of venality and mediocrity, as the authorities deliberately keep the people physically and intellectually under-developed. While adding to the usual polemics against tyrannical dictatorships, Mongo Beti also raises his voice to decry two unsuspected plagues that ravage Africa: alcoholism and the French language. While people's moral and physical fibre is being sapped by a home-brewed rot-gut, now openly distilled and consumed in suicidal quantities, the continued insistence on a close knowledge of the niceties of the former colonists' tongue is equally a factor in retarding normal intellectual development:

Just as in the hey-day of colonization, the absolute supremacy of the French language was a poisoned humus on which only feeble plants could grow: the never-ending apprenticeship required to obtain a knowledge of its refinements kept people in a state of infantilism; the inevitable or calculated exclusion of the immense majority of the population from this paradise, produced obscurantism, social and political stagnation, as well as mass frustration. The infinitesimal rarity of this intellectual élite, this superior class, who surmount all obstacles and manage to acquire a diploma, caused them to be treated like sickly shrubs, enclosed in the hot-house of separate residential areas, where they eventually lost touch with their own national character. (p. 132)

This invective is inspired by the episode of the civil-service examination, through which Perpétue's husband hopes to obtain his promotion. Without a suspicion of irony or the humour that leavens *Mission to Kala*, Beti expounds at length on the unsuspected snares of past participles and infinitives in examination dictation passages. He puts a long, pedantic lesson in French grammar into the mouth of the fifteen-year-old Perpétue, fresh from her convent school, which does not endear the bride of three months to her less erudite and slower-witted husband. Nor does the reader find these pages, lifted direct from a grammar manual, particularly palatable in a novel.

The above quotation (of which I have tried to retain in English the stylistic peculiarities) illustrates the ponderous, laboured manner – more suited to the pamphlet than the novel – in which Mongo Beti denounces the politics of this fictional decolonized state. On the other hand, his attack on one of the traditional social evils persisting in some parts of Independent Africa, is woven into the fabric of the novel itself: namely the practice of selling girls in marriage and thereby condemning them to virtual slavery, which is the substance of Perpétue's history. Whereas Mor-Zamba, in the first of these two new novels, is more of a symbol than an individual, Perpétue is a clearly defined personality – in spite of her unusual name, which is obviously intended to convey her symbolic role. So that, when Mongo Beti neglects to 'remember Ruben' and simply recounts the wretched marriage and death of this intelligent, high-principled, fiercely independent girl, crushed and depraved by her circumstances, the narrative is convincing and moving.

Though superior as a work of imaginative fiction to the first part of the diptych, *Perpétue* still does not add any significantly original element to the post-Independence African novel, either in theme, style, structure or narrative techniques. Nor does it substantially add to Mongo Beti's reputation as a novelist, gained by his three pre-Independence works. These two new publications only confirm the impression that the political novel offers the most snares even to the experienced writer.

NEW VOICES IN FICTION

René Philombe (pseud. of Philippe-Louis Ombède)

René Philombe: *Lettres de ma cambuse*. Yaoundé, CLE (Coll: Abbia) 1964. *Sola, ma chérie*. Yaoundé, (Coll: Abbia) 1966. *Un Sorcier blanc à Zangali*. Yaoundé, CLE (Coll: Abbia) 1969. *Histoires queue de chat (quelques scènes de la vie camerounaise)*. Yaoundé, CLE, 1971.

René Philombe's *Lettres de ma cambuse* [Letters from my shack] inevitably invite a superficial comparison with Daudet's *Lettres de mon moulin*. Afflicted with a chronic disease at the age of twenty-five, Philombé withdrew to a tumble-down hut on the outskirts of Yaoundé to be near the consulting rooms of the doctor–friend who was treating him. With whimsical humour he does his best to see in his peri-urban slum the advantages of the genuine countryside which he adores! In the isolation of his *cambuse* he sharpens his powers of observation on the limited views from his veranda, and learns to weave out of his very immobility the stuff of charming tales. The miniature daily dramas of the market-place, the visit of a friend, the irrepressible impertinences of his co-tenants, the mice, are all pretexts for descriptive vignettes, philosophic meditations or fables recounted with verve and humour and an engaging style that here and there echoes, not unhappily, Molière and La Fontaine.

Sola, ma chérie [Sola, my darling] is an insufficiently motivated, badly constructed novelettish love-story with some well-intentioned reflections on rural superstitions and on the social evils of prostitution, alcoholism, bride price and forced marriage. The situations are exaggerated and the characters either caricatural or thin. Sola, an intelligent, city-educated girl, is married off by her callous father to a wealthy, elderly planter, Nkinda. She is repulsed by her gross, violently jealous husband who savagely ill-treats her, and by the filth and hardships of peasant existence to which the miserly Nkonda condemns her. Yet the author suggests that the only alternative to the misery of this forced marriage would have been prostitution, which seems hardly credible in 1958, when an intelligent girl with a secondary-school education must have been able to find some sort of honest employment in Yaoundé.

This first attempt by Philombe at a novel has little to commend it except his good intentions, and the melodramatic treatment of an unconvincing plot does little to help establish his theses. In his next and longer novel, he is much more successful in marrying his romanticism with a moralizing theme; but the basic interest lies in the bigger moral conflict rather than in the story of personal redemption through hardship and communal labour.

Un Sorcier blanc à Zangali [A White sorcerer in Zangali] is set in the early colonial era of Cameroon. Though the author begins with a brief evocation of the suffering of the indigenous population first under the Germans and then the French, his purpose is not to add a belated voice to the pre-Independence vociferations against the colonizers and conquerors. However the establishment of the historical period – a time when missionaries were murdered by hostile tribes – is as important to the development of the action as the geographical setting in Zangali, in the heart of Beti fetishist country.

The Reverend Father Marius, an austere and dedicated priest in the tradition of Mongo Beti's 'Poor Christ' volunteers to go on a dangerous civilizing mission to the savage, heathen district of Zangali, where the previous missionary has recently been murdered by tribesmen particularly hostile to the White Fathers. He decides to travel in mufti, accompanied by his young Black acolyte Etienne. When they arrive at Zangali Father Marius is faced with the decision either to keep up the pretence of being an administrator to protect their lives, or to declare himself a priest in order to realize his mission, so risking death. In fact, the Elders of Zangali are preparing to murder him like his predecessor, but the Chief advises them that they risk merciless reprisals now that the Germans have withdrawn and the French are well established. Instead, the little party is given a 'concession' by being placed in a sinister, inhospitable region, a little distance from the village, full of human bones and reputed to be haunted, where it is expected that they will not survive for long. But they manage to build up a little settlement, joined by some villagers whom the missionary cures of the *maladie des fantômes* with which the area is cursed, and which he diagnoses as blackwater fever. But the peaceful communal existence and the evangelizing mission come to an abrupt end when the priest, horrified by the sacrilegious mockery of the Communion, rashly breaks up a rite in which the tribesmen are placating the spirits which send the 'ghosts' sickness'. He is savagely beaten and condemned to death for his blasphemy of the fetishist ritual, but is saved by the intervention of his converts. The French Commandant hears of his ordeal and comes with the order for the execution of the Chief in reprisal. Marius pleads in vain for mercy, for he has forgiven his torturers, but he sees all his efforts collapse. Like the Reverend Father Drumont and his successor Le Guen, he is faced with the realization that he has not been working for Christ's mission, but in the service of colonialism.

The comparison between *Un Sorcier blanc à Zangali* and *Le Pauvre Christ de Bomba* is interesting. Of exactly the same age but writing at different periods and from the standpoint of their widely differing temperaments, the two compatriots approach the subject of the Catholic missionary in colonial Cameroon with quite distinct literary intentions. Beti, educated at a mission school, later reacted violently against the Christian faith and mercilessly attacks all activities of Catholic missionaries, while not doubting the sincerity of his Father Drumont. Philombe not only shows clear admiration for the courage and dedication of his Father Marius, but he does not denounce evangelizing activities in his country. Against Beti's robust and practical cynicism, which makes him such a formidable satirist, Philombe opposes a romantic idealism, a philosophic nature more given to indulgence towards others' laudable intentions. Where Beti is concerned with indicting a principle, Philombe concentrates on personal qualities and high-lights a moral conflict. The period of composition, too, is important: *The Poor Christ* was written when the most imperative issue was the rejection of colonialism with all its cultural and religious implications. Published thirteen years later, in the light of Independence, *Un Sorcier blanc* aims more at recapturing the realities of an historical situation. More objective in its approach, but more romanticized in its treatment – in particular, of the Utopian existence in the heart of the inhospitable forest

– Philombe's novel lacks the originality and the powerful impact of Beti's satirical work. But, following the amateurish *Sola, ma chérie*, it demonstrates a capacity for a well-constructed work of fiction with convincing characterization of the good Father Marius, his young neophyte Etienne and the engaging little Princess Andela.

In his next publication Philombe returns to the form in which he had first shown his promising literary talents – the short story. *Histoires queue de chat* are not 'cock-and-bull-stories', but more pragmatic and didactic scenes of Cameroonian life than the earlier *Lettres de ma cambuse*. But these edifying pills are coated with sufficient irony and human understanding for the dose to be completely palatable and for the stories to have a literary as well as a therapeutic quality. A two-fold programme runs through the tales: how to deal with the inroads of both superstition and corruption in the Cameroonian society of today.

Francis Bebey

FRANCIS BEBEY: *Le Fils d'Agatha Moudio*. Yaoundé, Edit. CLE, 1967. *Embarras & Cie*. Yaoundé, Edit. CLE, 1968. *La Poupée ashanti*. Yaoundé, Edit. CLE, 1973.
English translation: *Agatha Moudio's Son*, trans. J. Hutchinson. London, Ibadan, Nairobi. Heinemann Educational Books, 1971.

Francis Bebey was already known as a poet and a musician when he produced in quick succession his first novel, which was awarded the Grand Prix Littéraire de l'Afrique Noire, and a collection of short stories interspersed with poems. His *Fils d'Agatha Moudio* is one of the few really accomplished African novels in French of the post-colonial era to be completely liberated from the stranglehold of political protest. It has the sense of humanity of Ousmane Sembène's *Véhi-Ciosane* or *Le Mandat* with the addition of a most attractive dry humour. The story is simplicity itself, deeply rooted in a traditional tribal society, hardly touched by Europeanization. It takes place during the colonial era, but the emphasis is on the tragi-comedy of human relations.

A young fisherman, known as 'La Loi' [The law] since the day when he proudly announced to some White hunters the French version of his African name Mbenda, enjoys a formidable reputation for his daring, his good looks and his great physical strength, being the champion wrestler of the region. He would indeed be a law unto himself, were it not for the indomitable authority of his widowed mother, supported by all the traditions of the tribe. His independence and audacity in confronting the party of White hunters and demanding payment of a fee to the villagers for the right to shoot monkeys on their land, earns him a term of imprisonment, the increased esteem of his contemporaries and in particular the attentions of Agatha Moudio, a girl of easy virtue. Mbenda, for his part, is completely bewitched by Agatha's charms although he knows she is frivolous and would be worthless as a wife. Before his death his father had made a solemn promise that his only child should wed the first daughter of his closest friend, although the chosen bride had not yet been conceived. Mbenda's mother and the village elders now hastily arrange the marriage with the scarcely nubile Fanny, hoping to cut short Mbenda's scandalous association with Agatha. When Mbenda refuses to consummate his union, on the pretext that Fanny is still a child, she takes her revenge by presenting him with a daughter, whom he is forced to recognize as his or else publicize his dubious marital state. Eventually he insists on taking Agatha as his second wife, in spite of the opposition of his mother, supported, by the whole village, and the dissension that this brings into his far from tranquil home. She duly gives birth to a son, who turns out to be unmistakably White, thus completing Mbenda's mortification and realizing his mother's prophecy that no good can come of the match.

Francis Bebey lets his hero tell his own tale, which he does with an unfailing surety of touch. Every scene, every character, every reaction, is presented through Mbenda's eyes and understanding, which makes for a double focus and perspective. We are aware that he is no illiterate; he has attended school but feels more inclination for the freedom and open-air life of a fisherman than the pen-pushing job for which his school certificate might qualify him. He is, however, lucid enough to analyse and recount his own vicissitudes with a mixture of self-knowledge and ingenuousness that puts a subtle double edge on the irony. The story is told with just the right lightness of tone for the burlesque potential of the situation to be apparent without ever dominating. Where African writers of lesser talent have made of arranged marriage a subject for melodrama or treated it with ponderous pathos, Bebey tackles it with gentle humour and elegant understatement. There is no revolt, no tragic despair, no overthrowing of social traditions. All his characters work within the framework of convention, philosophically making the best they can of their situation; not least in initiative is the little Fanny, who, young and inexperienced as she may be, is clearly capable of looking after her own interests. And Mbenda, too, realizing his total responsibility for his own fate, ruefully puts a good face on his final discomfiture.

In the eight short stories of *Embarras & Cie* (the title comes from one of the poems inserted between the tales), the author speaks in his own name, sometimes recounting a brief personal experience, sometimes an incident purporting to have occurred in his native Cameroonian village, or have been told to him by a fellow-traveller. For the most part they are as light and transparent as gossamer and as smoothly textured as velvet – woven out of gentle raillery, mock self-deprecation, pseudo-naïveté and disarming understatement. But under cover of this reassuring bonhomie, Bebey shoots off little barbed shafts and sometimes the gossamer is the web woven by a spider hidden in its heart to catch its prey. His exposition of a sorcerer's difficulties in making ends meet in this enlightened age is innocent enough, or his mockery of marriage customs and the one-upmanship of rural African society in *Le Mariage d'Edda*, where the whole hierarchy of status symbols is revealed, ranging from a brick house to the ultimate in coveted possessions – a tropical pith helmet. But the dart sinks deeper in *Jimmy et l'égalité*, aimed at the ambiguous position of the Westernized Negro – the 'Black Frenchman' – and at the whole master-servant relationship of Black Africa, inherited from the colonial era.

With only two works of fiction to his name, Bebey showed that he was an accomplished prose writer as well as a poet. With his sure sense of the ironic effects to be drawn from the simplest, colloquial language, with his humorous tolerance of human foibles, spiced at times with subtle malice, Francis Bebey's writing in his first novel and short stories has the same impact as that of his countryman Bernard Dadié, Like him, too, he manages to imply criticism without dogmatism or any overt attacks. If he trails a wisp of Negritude after him, it is a Negritude freed from any complexes, any protest, any hatred or even cynicism. It is compounded of a concern for honesty – which means for him writing as an African – and a preoccupation with getting through to his reader.

Unfortunately, when Francis Bebey attempts another full-length novel, more ambitious than his *Son of Agatha Moudio*, his sure touch abandons him completely. In *La Poupée ashanti* he makes an unfortunate incursion into the field of political fiction and *roman à thèse*, producing a lamentable novelettish romance, spiced with melodrama and unrelieved by the irony and human understanding that have formed the basic qualities of his previous prose works. 'My Ashanti Doll' is the nick-name that Spio, a young Ghanaian civil-servant gives to the extremely beautiful but illiterate and not overly intelligent young market-woman with whom he falls in love; after a certain number of peripeteia he marries her, on the last page, presumably to live happily ever after, in spite of certain ominous indications that he will find many areas of incomprehension and differing moral standards in his charming, ignorant little Edna.

Bebey places his story in Ghana in the months immediately following the withdrawal of the British colonial authorities from the then Gold Coast.

The centre of the action is the Accra market-place and the central characters old Mam, an influential market-woman and her orphaned grand-daughter, Edna. The political situation is precisely indicated, with special reference to the power wielded in the recent elections by the said market-women, whose support had been instrumental in the return to power of the Prime Minister, referred to as 'The Doctor' (Nkrumah's name is not mentioned). The crux of the plot is the withdrawal of the vendor's licence from Amiofi, whose daughter was engaged to marry a member of the Doctor's opposition, who has been imprisoned. There is some irony introduced over the so-called democratic régime and the one-party state. The market-women, led by Mam, stage a march on the Parliament buildings in protest against the injustice done to one of their colleagues. The police open fire on the defenceless women, several of whom are wounded, including Edna, who becomes the heroine of the moment. Strangely enough, this incident, which rings far more true than some of the other violent episodes, is recounted by the author with a certain casual insouciance, without any apparent desire to evoke our horror at the brutality or relief that complete tragedy is averted. With unusually ponderous didacticism Bebey then devotes space to eulogies of the virtues of the African market-women, however ignorant or illiterate, who are not to be underestimated by the side of their educated urban sisters. He has already indicated the political weight they carry and the envy they inspire because of their wealth. (This is an interesting contrast with Abdoulaye Sadji's Maïmouna, of twenty years earlier, whose punishment is to be condemned to follow her mother's wretched existence as a market-woman – she who had dreamt of the joys of city life – and now, dishonoured and disfigured, cannot hope to find a husband.)

The moral and social themes are relieved by the jealousies of Edna and her two more sophisticated friends Gin and Angela, which give rise to several melodramatic interludes. The diffuse but thin narrative is padded out with digressions, irrelevancies and long passages of trivial dialogue, purporting to give verisimilitude to the everyday situations, but couched in such uniformly stilted, pedantic language that it bears no relationship to the individual characters and their social and educational level. What we most miss in this latest venture into fiction of Francis Bebey is the charm of his ironic humour, which is here replaced by a monotonous, ponderous facetiousness.

Guy Menga

Guy Menga: *La Palabre stérile*. Yaoundé, Edit. CLE (Coll. Abbia) 1968. Repr. 1970.

We have already noted the paucity of creative writing in French from Equatorial Africa, compared with the rich output from the Western regions. Among the few authors from the Congo of the past decade, Guy Menga has been seen as a dramatist with two successful satirical plays to his name: *La Marmite de Koko-Mbala* and *l'Oracle*. His first venture into fiction was the short novel, *La Palabre stérile*. [The sterile palaver]. This seems, in its opening chapter, to be about to exploit the same vein as the plays: attacking superstition and commenting on social custom in a traditional tribal community of Central Africa, soon after the Second World War. The hero, Vouata, in his early twenties, revolts against the stranglehold that the fetishists and the elders have, with their insistence on absolute obedience to the laws of the ancestors and recognition of the powers of the spirits, against all the dictates of reason and the normal human emotion. Vouata's father has just died following ordalic rites and he is banished under a curse, because he has been moved to tears by his loss, in defiance of the edict against weeping over such a death. The chapters devoted to Vouata's initiation into life in Brazzaville and his struggle to make a living as a rickshaw-pusher, take up the theme of African colonial society in transition, found in early West African novels. The book owes its title to Vouata's childless marriage, but it also becomes – with a bit of mental prestidigitation – a political novel, as Vouata finds consolation for the shame of sterility by devoting himself to an underground movement working for liberation from colonial rule, founded by André Matswa. An adept of Matswanism and marijuana, he feels he is born anew. But his new lease of life is short, as, soon after his 'conversion', he is arrested and shipped up river to Chad where he spends nearly sixteen years in a prison camp. Released at the declaration of the Independence of Congo-Brazzaville, he is repatriated, accompanied by the five-year-old son he now learns he had fathered. He is welcomed on his arrival at Brazza airport by two other unknown offspring. So ends Vouata's sterility! Presumably his personal liberation from his complexes and his incarceration, with the promise of further fertility, now coincides with his country's era of promise.

In spite of the award of the *Grand Prix Littéraire de l'Afrique Noire*, *La Palabre stérile* is a disappointing novel. It might have been considered fairly outstanding in the early years of Negro-African fiction, in the period marked by Ousmane Socé, Abdoulaye Sadji and Menga's compatriot, Jean

Malonga (who encouraged him to write). But in the mid-sixties, it does not make a strikingly original contribution to the African novel in French. The characterization is thin; the language, particularly in the dialogue, is stilted; the action lacks unity and the structure balance and proportion. There is no trace of the talent for comedy with which Guy Menga treated social problems in *L'Oracle*. The pungent satire with which he treated a society in transition from superstition to reason in *La Marmite* has been blunted by a rather ponderously sententious approach to political commitment, and an urge to add what might be called a post-script to anti-colonial literature.

François-Borgia Marie Evembe

FRANÇOIS-BORGIA MARIE EVEMBE: *Sur la terre en passant*. Paris, Présence Africaine, 1966. o.p.

Between 1966 and 1968 four ambitious, completely original and outstanding works of fiction emerged from French-speaking Black Africa. They were all the first novels of hitherto unknown writers and none conformed to the rather tired stereotypes of their predecessors. In style and structure, theme, setting and characterization, these works have an inherent 'Africanness' which replaces the self-assertive Negritude of French-African literature of the colonial era. The first of these successful works by a newcomer, *Sur la terre en passant*, is not merely a promising first novel, but a powerful and important work by any standards, economically composed, rich in social implications and philosophical significance. Like Ousmane Sembène's shorter work, *Le Mandat*, it operates on one level as the study of a man's struggles for survival when pitted against the alien and hostile society of the new African city. Malick Fall and Ahmadou Kourouma take up this theme, adding to it their own particular interpretation and enrichment in *La Plaie* and *Les Soleils des Indépendances* respectively. However, *Sur la terre en passant* is more than a satirical tragi-comedy of the problems of existence under an African bureaucracy that has replaced a colonial authority. Sembène's and Kourouma's heroes are men of advanced years, unadaptable, ill-equipped to come to terms with a new order. Evembe's Iyoni is a young man of artistic potential, entering the most fertile period of his life, who cannot find employment, partly because he lacks the right influence. But he is also in the terminal stage of cancer. The title of the novel, and the commonplace tone of the allusion ('Ce genre de personnes d'ailleurs ne vivent jamais longtemps. On a l'impression qu'ils sont sur la terre en passant' [This sort of person never lives long. You get the feeling that they're only in transit on earth]) belie the richer, philosophic treatment of a simple theme: a man fighting indomitably, not so much for his life, but to retain his human dignity.

In the periods of respite from the crises of his illness, when the charity of the friends who house and help him has worn thin, Iyoni tries desperately to find employment, any employment on any terms to regain his self-respect and independence. Work, when found, may bear no relationship to qualifications or experience; it may involve waiting three months, penniless, for the first salary, starving for five days out of seven, going cap in hand from door to door. But when Iyoni inveighs against the system, he is not indulging in African auto-criticism, except inasmuch as the urbanization of African society has drawn it into line with the pattern of Western city life and imposed new economic and sociological problems. Similarly, when Iyoni appeals to an old friend who has become a Minister in the new government, and Evembe adds to the gallery of satirical portraits of the New Men of Independent Africa that we find in recent novels in English and French, the characteristic features of the arriviste politician dispensing charity, the situation is not peculiar to Africa. Evembe's presentation of Iyoni's predicament is all the more moving because it has universal application.

Pungent and pertinent as these passages of social criticism are, they do not in themselves bring any fundamentally new themes into the ambit of the African novel. Only the blindly partisan ideologue could have claimed that Independence would see the birth of a perfect man in a perfect society, so it was to be expected that satirical novelists would continue to find their targets in the human suffering associated with oppression, cruelty, injustice, violence or mere indifference, when these are no longer identifiable with White Imperialism. But Evembe's novel is more than a topical satire, it is a parable and a philosophical meditation.

The hospital with its labyrinth of endless corridors empty of human contact, deserted courtyards, doctors' consulting-rooms besieged by crowds of anxious sufferers is an epitome of a world. Iyoni's helpless wanderings, his confrontations with indifferent medical aides to whom he seems invisible, his humble self-effacement before the priorities of other patients, his timid concern for a woman's predicament which brings momentary forgetfulness of his own, his collapse in the latrines and his dragging himself back to consciousness amid blood, vomit and faeces, can all be seen as symbols of the peripeteia of existence. Iyoni is not merely pitted against a coldly impersonal system; he is engaged in an ineluctable, inexorable, absurd encounter with life and death.

Evembe describes in clinical detail the somatic erosions of Iyoni's disease. But his descriptions of the morbid disintegration of a man are not mere virtuoso exercises in the sordid, the squalid, the degraded condition of the infirm body. He emphasizes the fight that Iyoni's lucidity and will-power can put up against his ruthless enemy for the dignity and autonomy of his person and the nobility of his death; inevitably, he loses the battle and dies in the street, collapsed like a drunkard in his own vomit. The general sombre pessimism of the theme is in part redeemed by the grim humour with which Evembe treats the existential theme of his novel. Iyoni's struggle with his failing physical strength is described in terms of an industrial dispute between management and workers:

In Iyoni's factory a serious dispute had broken out: the brain laconically announced that the machines were in such a deplorable state that the management would have to discharge the workers. Conscience retorted that as long as there had been no interview with the medical personnel in charge of hospitalization, any discharge would be contrary to regulations governing working conditions and to the discredit of the firm's reputation for reliability, since all the contracts with clients had not been honoured. If the Brain was not in agreement it couldn't be helped, but it must be understood that this was really not the moment to start a dispute between the management and the workers' union. (*Sur la terre*, p. 30)

Evembe's novel is not a faultless masterpiece. He does not avoid the pitfalls of hackneyed expression, nor of labouring the theme that life is a struggle. The very last sentence of the book, instead of leaving his allegory to its unambiguous message, diminishes its impact with a puerile, sentimental note that underrates the intelligence of the reader, heavily underscoring the significance of the title. But *Sur la terre en passant* is still among the most moving as well as the most original of West African novels in French, particularly of the post-colonial era. It expresses a universal human predicament with a mixture of realism and wry humour. It shows the way for a Negro-African school of novelists who will continue to define certain universal notions, metamorphosing neo-realism into an art which analyses man in preference to society. The weakness of Evembe's work is that he did not have sufficient confidence to offer Iyoni's story as a commentary on our common destiny, or sufficient skill to develop with force the symbol, which he presumably wished to imply, of a cancer which threatens the existence of our civilization or the bases on which contemporary society is built. He suggests a syndrome compounded by materialism, corruption, contempt for certain ill-defined ideals. 'For Iyoni', says the narrator, commenting on his death, 'the world was built on ideals and not on petty interests'. (p. 110)

Malick Fall

MALICK FALL: *La Plaie*. Paris, Albin Michel, 1967.
　English translation: *The Wound*, trans. Clive Wake. London, etc., Heinemann
　Educational Books, 1973.

Malick Fall's *La Plaie* treats a similar subject to Evembe's *Sur la terre en passant*, but brings to it a greater subtlety of treatment, more poetry, a rich and complex symbolism and far-ranging philosophical implications, while avoiding any hint of sentimentality. It is among the most original and possibly the most successful of the attempted existentialist novels to have come out of Black Africa. The theme is again that of a man at war with an infirm body, by reason of which his human dignity is diminished. Magamou Seck, like Iyoni, fights to maintain his independence and his integration with society, in the face of the erosions of disease. Iyoni's cancer is invisible but incurable; his enemy is invincible, but he can show himself a worthy adversary, fighting to the last, rather than surrendering with ignominy. Magamou's ulcer is not fatal in itself, but he risks its associated gangrene spreading through his whole body; he can save his life at the price of a limb, but he has a seemingly irrational prejudice in favour of maintaining his body intact, of 'being a man like other men' ('être un homme comme les autres'). Iyoni becomes an object of charity, Magamou of revulsion and public vindictiveness.

　Within an apparently simple framework this novel is expertly structured and rich in characterization, poetry and irony – a human document of wide philosophical implication, psychological complexity and occasional humour. Magamou Seck, *l'homme-à-la-plaie*, [the-man-with-the-running-sore] as an adolescent in his native village, is already a rebel because he is a lucid idealist. Either by intuition or by perception, he has become aware of the bluffs, the shabbiness, the moral vacuity of his fellows and the existential slime in which this society of spineless, gelatinous creatures is engulfing him with their *mauvaise foi*. His only solution, his only salvation is escape, and his only possible avenue of escape is to the city. With his head full of dreams he sets out in search of true freedom and his lost illusions, of the possibility of finding an idyllic universe where good deeds are rewarded and errors punished, where 'things had human virtues and animals their code of honour'.

　Hitch-hiking to the city, he is the victim of a stupid accident when the lorry on which he is travelling overturns and he sustains a deep wound in his leg, which becomes infected. The ulceration spreads, taking on alarming proportions and reducing his whole body to the limitations of his swollen, stinking leg and the apparently incurable, purulent sore. Having escaped the mental imprisonment of his village environment, with which he was so out of step, he becomes the prisoner of his own body and finally of society. Having rejected the despised life of mendicity imposed by the routine of the Koranic school, he is now reduced to becoming a permanent beggar in order to satisfy his barest needs, and just keep his putrefying body alive. Having left his village with its limitations in the hope of fulfilling himself, he is reduced to the lowest depths of existence and the knowledge that he is only a *mort en sursis*, a condemned man enjoying a temporary stay of execution.

The ironic absurdities of Magamou's lot are legion and are paralleled by the contradictions in his character. He is a sombre figure, full of vituperative spleen, but with his own brand of sardonic humour. A solitary and disillusioned misanthrope, he has, in fact, a need for society and a deep hatred of solitude which he must populate with his memories and his reveries, at the end of each day recounting to himself that day's experiences to convince himself of his own existence as well as to recreate his world to suit his own needs. A militant and a rebel, his guiding principles are a passionate devotion to freedom, an absolute obedience to the imperatives of human dignity which, with his ebullient optimism, demand a continuation of the fight to heal his ulcer, even when he is reduced to the utmost degradation. Aware that he is a prisoner of things, he is nevertheless extremely sensitive to the poetry of things, whose touch brings him integration into the real world that society refuses him. Repudiated by men, he finds companionship with animals; stray cats, mongrels and even a vulture, the only creatures to whom he can still offer something, the share of his misery, a little human warmth, a sense of equality.

The novel opens with Magamou's arrest for vagrancy and his incarceration among the mental patients of the local hospital, after the authorities have finally decided to act on the market-women's continual complaints about his unsavoury presence and his petty larcenies. He suffers bitterly from the loss of his freedom, worries about the fate of his stray cats and mongrels and is affronted by the physical hardships and indignities to which he is subjected. He indulges in a continual monologue, reviewing his present condition, recalling his past and outlining his homespun philosophy. His habit of thinking aloud, interspersed with vituperations against his jailers, reinforces the conviction that he is mad. His two main enemies are revealed as the alcoholic White doctor and the illiterate Black hospital interpreter: the one determined to persuade Magamou to accept amputation, the other to admit his insanity. The passages of verbal sparring between Dr Bernardy and Cheikh Sar, with Magamou the involuntary buffer between them, are often scenes of high burlesque comedy – a crazy dialogue of complete mutual incomprehension. It is difficult to decide which of the three is the most sane, but Magamou is certainly not the least lucid. We are not surprised when Bernardy becomes completely deranged. Magamou, on the other hand, has the necessary grip on reality to engineer his own escape and to release all the other mental patients at the same time.

The second half of the novel is the story of the use Magamou makes of his new-found freedom. His situation is more critical than before his incarceration: his make-shift shelter has been destroyed and he is homeless; he must keep clear of the market-place for fear of re-arrest, and he is without means of subsistence or earning a living; the ulceration of his leg is spreading alarmingly. He feels more a prisoner than when shut up in his cell, enclosed in a huge prison, with invisible walls. Officially, too, he has ceased to exist, as the rumour that he died after his escape has spread and been accepted in the city. He contemplates suicide but, with only his favourite mongrel pup for company and support, he continues to cling to a life-line of hope. 'Everyone drags around his own ulcer, but one must keep on one's feet.' He determines to stand up to society, hold out the hand of friendship. He fells the need of love, to clothe himself in human warmth.

So, having decided that the only posture worthy of a man is upright, advancing on his two feet, the first priority is to heal his infected leg. Once the desire is there the cure is easy but, like Columbus's egg, it is necessary to know how. He first visits a saintly *marabout*, interested in saving souls not bodies, who can only offer him prayers. The *marabout* does, however, advise him to consult an elderly healer, Khar-l'Ancien, who has a sound reputation for achieving cures by his knowledge of traditional simples. Khar prescribes bathing the purulent wound daily in the sea until it is completely disinfected. To aid healing he gives him a herbal powder and specific leaves for a dressing. In six weeks Magamou is completely cured.

Now he realizes for the first time the reality of his destiny which he has rejected – to be *l'homme-à-la-plaie*. Healed, he has no existence and no identity. When he returns to the market-place, hungry for human warmth, he is taken for a ghost and disseminates panic. Re-assuming his dialogue with himself, he comes to the conclusion that he has repudiated his real self and his singular destiny. His isolation is all the more complete as even his strays abandon him, since the only friend they knew was the man with the stinking sore, not the healthy Magamou. He has made certain progress in the pursuit of his own existential significance, since he set out to escape from the mediocrity and *mauvaise foi* of the village society. He has learnt that only the man of no imagination fears to deviate from the familiar pattern, hiding his nullity in conformity. He has learnt that he needed his ulcer; Magamou the idealist, with the vision of a poet, knows now that he must assume his blemishes and his taints as the price of his individuality. Now, even if he could re-integrate himself into society, he would be diminished in his personality. His injury had given him an identity, made him an object of interest. His ulcer, his vermin, his stench, had been his *titres de noblesse*, his patent of nobility, the proof of his existence as an individual; whereas now he has become an anonymous cipher.

The *marabout*, Sérigne Massall, had warned Magamou that man could not aspire to perfection. ('No man is perfect. Without the kernel the mango would be ideal, as would the guava without its pips. Imagine the sea rid of its salt, humanity without its dross; we'd all be saints!') Magamou again debates with himself the various possible solutions to his plight. Nowhere does he see the road to happiness and the meaning to life which he sought. He decides to drown himself but fate intervenes. It is election time. On his way to a suitable bridge he is caught up in a brawling crowd in a narrow lane, trampled underfoot and left for dead. His mortal remains are taken to the hospital where the interpreter recognizes the former patient, whose death had once before been reported soon after his escape from detention. In the morgue the corpse sits up and sneezes. When completely recovered and discharged from hospital, only the worse for the loss of one eye, Magamou makes his peace with his enemies, Dr Bernardy and Cheikh Sar. Bernardy remains haunted by the memory of his strange patient's handshake, and with the assistance of his alcoholic excesses declines into complete insanity himself.

Magadou wanders all night through the familiar streets and districts of the city, each aspect of which recalls a part of his own existence, with one firm decision in mind – this time not to bungle his own death. Yet each time the occasion is denied him. At dawn, the sight of a procession of prisoners emerging from the jail to empty their slops gives him his final assessment of the meaning of life: 'What! Emptying chamber-pots! A man, emptying chamber-pots! Incredible!...To sink so low!...And yet these prisoners with so little to live for, perhaps under sentence of death, still cling to life.' (p. 249 [p. 148–9])

Gradually everything assumes its correct proportions for Magamou: the prisoners are just workers doing a job; his missing eye is merely a ball of jelly; money is simply an attribute of the rich. The market is a garden of Eden, the city a mistress, a mother, his own situation a paradise: 'Magamou would eat hungrily of the *couscous* of life; he would drink deep draughts at the magnificent springs of delight; he would steep himself indefinitely in living.' (p. 250 [p. 149])

Exultant in his final decision, he makes his way to the market-place, bursts upon his old acquaintances shouting, 'Long live life!', seizes a knife from a butcher's stall and deliberately hacks at his right ankle till the flesh is reduced to mince-meat. Once more recognizable as *l'homme-à-la-plaie*, he collapses, murmuring confused words that might have been 'Cheikh' or 'cher', 'Bernardy' or 'paradis'.[18]

La Plaie is one of the most original and best composed of all the West African fiction in French. It is in the tradition of the 'quest' novel: the search for self-knowledge and self-acceptance, for an ideal of happiness through social integration and the disillusionment that comes with experience. *La Plaie* can also be read as a conflict between the individual and society, for whom the non-conformist eccentric is a running sore.[19] Although not a political novel, whether Malick Fall intended it or not we are tempted to see parallels between Magamou's detention in the mental cells of the hospital and the incarceration in mental asylums of intellectual recalcitrants in the Soviet Union. The symbolism is too obvious to need labouring. However, *La Plaie* has universal moral and philosophical implications that give it a dimension and an importance beyond any temporary or topical allusions.

Ahmadou Kourouma

AHMADOU KOUROUMA: *Les Soleils des Indépendances.* Montréal, Presses de l'Université de Montréal, 1968. Repr. Paris, Edit du Seuil, 1970.

La Plaie did not receive the attention it deserved in French-speaking circles, but I have no doubt that its reputation will continue to grow and to spread now through the English-speaking world with the publication of an English translation. Likewise, Ahmadou Kourouma's *Les Soleils des Indépendances* [The suns of the independences] has not yet been evaluated at its true worth, although the review *Etudes Françaises* of Montreal recognized its quality and awarded it their annual literary prize. It is a novel that is profoundly African in style and subject, inspiration and expression. It could be considered the first real African novel, in which the fact that it is written in French seems almost incidental. It might almost be deemed to manifest those values that Jean-Marie Abanda Ndengue calls *Négrisme*,[20] which he defines as the result of a fruitful marriage between the culture of the Negro-African world (Negritude) and those values introduced by the influence of Western colonization – whether military, economic, political or cultural. In the case of Ahmadou Kourouma, we

---

[18] There is a double pun here as Fall is playing on the fact that the title of Sheikh (Cheikh or Cheik) is pronounced *cher* (dear) in Senegal.

[19] I would join issue with Dr Clive Wake over the title of his otherwise excellent English translation of this novel: his use of 'the wound' does not render the associations surely inherent in the French title and evades the symbolic overtones.

[20] See *De la Négritude au Négrisme: Essais polyphoniques*, Yaoundé, Edit. CLE, 1970.

find a Malinké who has adopted the most popular literary form of the modern Western world – the novel, and mastered the literary language of the former colonists; but he writes a French which seems the spontaneous, indigenous tongue of Africa, such as only Birago Diop had used before for his *Contes d'Amadou Koumba*, and L. S. Senghor for his poems, and composes a novel which owes little to traditional Western European models. His language is neither the laboured high-school exercise of African novelists of mediocre talent or inadequate literacy, nor the polished, flexible medium of the best of his compatriots. Like Senghor and Diop he has – probably unconsciously – emancipated himself from the attitude of awed respect for the French vocabulary and syntax bearing the seal of the Académie Française. He has evolved a rich, spontaneous expressiveness that seems the natural idiom of his Musulman, Malinké hero, Fama Doumbouya, expostulating, vociferating, vituperating or merely meditating in his own vernacular.

A detailed study of the resources of Kourouma's style would be a rewarding subject for academic research, but there is not space for it here. Briefly, it will be found to owe its kaleidoscopic and exotic effect only in small degree to the introduction of local terms, which are far fewer than in Birago Diop's prose. More frequent are exclamations and expletives that seem to be translated directly from local usage to convey contumely and irascible indignation. Kourouma's vocabulary is also enriched with picturesque neologisms which have not yet found their *droit de cité* in Larousse or Robert, and the local stylistic flavour ensured by a plentiful seasoning with proverbs, aphorisms and images, clearly transposed from indigenous lore. These are sometimes mildly obscene, occasionally salacious, usually racy and epigrammatic.

While lending a new African dimension to the French language, Ahmadou Kourouma also manipulates with flexible virtuosity the free indirect speech. By this means we follow through soliloquy, reminiscence, inner monologue, interspersed with atrabilious vituperations against his lot and his enemies, the story of Fama and his wife Salimata – his nostalgia for the honours and dignities to which he was heir in pre-Independence Horodougou. Because so much of the narrative is presented from within the experience and sentiments of these two main characters, it is consistent that the stylistic tone should be familiar rather than elevated, and serio-comic rather than tragic. The comic dimension depends for the most part on the reader's entering intimately into the lives of the protagonists, while at the same time retaining his objectivity. Thus the comedy, even when verging on the bawdy is never gratuitously salacious or scatalogical, but arises spontaneously from the dichotomy of man's personality, half sensual, half spiritual. This can best be illustrated by the description of Fama's continual lapses in the mosque into sacrilegiously erotic thoughts, when his prayers for lifting Salimata's sterility are interspersed with savoury appreciation of his wife's still appetizing physical charms. As far as the tragic tone is concerned, this is diluted with irony and made palatable by the dominating principle of Islam that death is a normal attribute of existence and the precept of Allah, forbidding mourning for the deceased.

Superficially, the theme of *Les Soleils des Indépendances* seems to be, as in *La Palabre stérile*, that of a childless marriage, which is not only a personal tragedy but also a source of social inferiority in an African society. But Fama's barren union is only one aspect of his tragedy; moreover, it is treated with much more profundity, originality, psychological insight and elaboration of dramatic and episodic detail than in Guy Menga's novel. The true subject, of which Fama's sterility is only the individual symbol, is the collapse, with no hope of regeneration, of the only society into which he was fully integrated. This is an extension of the 'Things-Fall-Apart' theme, originally illustrating the catastrophic impact of colonization on African rural society, now applied ironically to the disillusionment and eventual tragedy that Independence brings to those for whom the colonial era was a time of prosperity and privilege.

Les Soleils des Indépendances is a novel symmetrically structured in the shape of a parabola. The first of the three parts presents Fama at the nadir of his social humiliations and personal despair at the impossibility of his twenty-year-old monogamous marriage to Salimata ever bearing fruit. In part two, his fortunes rise to a summit, with the possibility of his re-integration as the honoured chief of his native village and the promise of a nubile young bride who seems capable of being 'as fertile as a mouse'. Part three tells of Fama's decline and death after vicissitudes worse than he had ever anticipated in the miseries of his earlier existence. The tragic equilibrium of the novel is likewise assured by the presentation of Fama as the victim of circumstance and of his own character. Irascible and arrogant, susceptible and superstitious, intractable and uncompromising, born to riches, honour, autocracy and ostentation, ambitious but politically naïve, he is incapable of accommodating himself to poverty, compounding with sycophancy, or quite simply of understanding the realities of his present existence. For Fama Doumbouya, last legitimate descendant of the princes of Horodougou, a region of the fictitious 'Ebony Coast', the colonial era had been a time of prosperity, in that it favoured the free-trading enterprise in which he was engaged. Independence has brought Fama nothing but an identity card, a membership ticket of the single party in power, poverty and the humiliation of a life of quasi-beggary. Too old to return to the land, the last prince of Horodougou is unfortunately completely illiterate, so could hope for none of the perquisites of power in the new régime. The man whose totem was the royal panther is reduced to earning his living as a 'hyena', a 'vulture', that is a professional assistant at Musulman funeral rites, which even with Independence are long and complicated.

To Fama's troubles is added the curse of his sterile marriage to Salimata, by reason of which the line of Doumbouya will become extinct. Part one of *Les Soleils des Indépendances* is as much Salimata's story as Fama's. She in turn, relives her memories, trying to explain her life to herself. All through the day, as she sells her porridge in the market-place, she muses on the curse of her sterility, recalling the hopes aroused by a pseudo-cyesis – a hysterical pregnancy that lasted two years, to be followed by the shame of the gradual subsidence of her swollen belly. There is a counterpart to Fama's visit to the mosque and his evening prayer, in Salimata's visit to the marabout sorcerer, Hadj Abdoulaye. While Fama entreats Allah to end his wife's sterility, Salimata pins her hopes on the powerful marabout's exorcism and his abilities to read the auguries.

In part two, Fama returns to his native village of Togabala, now part of a separate independent territory, the Republic of Nikinei, to attend the funeral rites of his cousin who had inherited the chiefdom, until he too had been dispossessed at Independence. With the possibility of a permanent improvement in his fortunes, Fama is tempted to stay in Togobala for good. But he decides to return to the capital, accompanied by his new young wife, Mariam, his legacy from the deceased cousin, to tell Salimata of his plans. This journey is the beginning of his final undoing.

Part three opens on a note of farce, with Fama's troubles increased by the introduction of the co-wife Mariam into the exiguous domicile. It is easy to imagine the problems caused by Salimata's jealousy, enhanced by propinquity in the single bedroom with the creaking mattress that the triangular ménage shares. Before there is any possibility of Mariam's realizing her promised fertility, Fama is forced to renounce all claim to conjugal bliss. Like Guy Menga's Vouata, he had earlier tried to compensate for his sterility by involvement in politics, when there was a question of working towards the expulsion of the colonists. Now he joins a movement to unseat the governing and only legal party. Repressive measures are quickly enforced. Ministers, Members of Parliament, Councillors, are arrested, imprisoned, exiled or simply disappear. Fama does not heed warnings, continuing to concern himself with politics, even after some of his friends have disappeared. The episode that begins with farce ends in tragedy. He is arrested and sent to an internment camp for his part in the attempted *coup*. He is released when the President declares a general amnesty at a time when he is seeking a general reconciliation of the people for political ends. Broken and disillusioned, abandoned by both his wives during his imprisonment, unable to accept or adapt to the new régime, Fama tries to return to his native Togobala. The frontier is now closed for diplomatic reasons. Notwithstanding, Fama sets out across the bridge separating the two territories, shouting 'See Doumbouya, the prince of Horodougou!...Admire me, sons of Independence!' (p. 199) The arrogant words are Fama's last. Unable to find his way through the wire barring the other end of the bridge, to enter the Republic of Nikinai, he drops down into the river, sure that the sacred crocodiles will not attack a legitimate heir to the chiefdom. He is dragged unconscious from the river on the Nikinai side and taken by ambulance to the capital, the road to which passes through Togobala. His wish to end his days in his native village is fulfilled. The novels ends exactly as it began, with the news of the death of a Malinké, and the announcement of days of mourning and prolonged funeral rites.

Les Soleils des Indépendances is not a novel that can be neatly tagged and docketed like many earlier French-African works of fiction. It is not simply a political, sociological, psychological or anthropological study. Fama Doumbouya is manifestly the victim of a changing world to which his inculcated principles, lack of formal education and inflexible temperament prevent him from adapting. But his story is not simply that of a society in transition, the novel of metamorphosis. Similarly, while the author throws light on social custom, details of the female excision, consultation of sorcerers, these passages are not included for their exotic interest and to enrich the local colour, but are closely integrated into the psychological study of Salimata's predicament. Like many creative Black writers of the last decade, no longer committed to the anti-colonial cause, nor to any partisan issues, Ahmadou Kourouma can permit himself ironic comment on contemporary African politics and politicians, without passing final judgement on the situation. He merely suggests, with objective and lucid intelligence, that all is not a Utopia in the territories illuminated by the suns of Independence. The conclusion to be drawn is consistent with the Muslim African inspiration and texture of the novel: no political change can bring Paradise on earth to mortal existence plagued by: 'Colonization, District Commandants, Epidemics, droughts, Independence, the single party and revolution...all kinds of curses invented by the devil.' (p. 137)

Yambo Ouologuem

YAMBO OUOLOGUEM: *Le Devoir de violence*. Paris, Edit. du Seuil, 1968.
English translation: *The Wages of Violence*, trans. R. Manheim. London, Secker
& Warburg, 1968. Also as *Bound to Violence*. New York, Harcourt, Brace,
Javanovich, 1971; London etc., Heinemann Educational Books, 1971.

No literary work out of Africa since *Batouala* has attracted so much
attention or aroused so much controversy as Yambo Ouologuem's first
novel. The last word has yet to be said in this matter and the final
judgement still to be made. When *Le Devoir de violence* appeared in 1968,
to be awarded the Prix Renaudot (after the Prix Goncourt, the major
French literary prize for a novel, judged on talent and originality), it caused
a sensation in France such as no other Black writer's work – even including
Batouala – has ever known. The acclaim from France was followed by
enthusiasm from the Anglo-Saxon world, particularly from America, on
the publication of the English translation, under the title *Bound to Violence*.
Glowing American reviews followed glowing French reviews. *Le Monde*
greeted the work as 'perhaps the first African novel worthy of the name'.
In a notice in *African Literature Today*, Ouologuem's novel was compared
to George Orwell's *Burmese Days*, by Hena Maes Jelineck. In brief, the
consensus of judgement was that this was a 'truly African novel' and a
masterpiece to boot. Robert Kanters, a critic who usually manifests a
reasonably balanced judgement, called *Le Devoir* 'un livre très beau et très
fort', and also picked up an interesting comparison in his review in *Le
Figaro littéraire*:

Violent, sensual, dramatic, heavy with the smell of the earth and the flesh of Africa
. . . In spite of some flaws, some concessions to doubtful tastes at present in vogue,
it is a more authentic novel and one which serves its cause better than that of M.
Schwarz-Bart which belongs to the same category. (18.9.68, p. 17)

One dissenting voice from the chorus of praise came from that usually
percipient Nigerian critic, Abiola Irele, who denounced Ouologuem's novel
as 'a meandering succession of sordid happenings, excesses and extravagances, presented as an historical narrative of a fictitious but "typical"
African empire' and condemned the work for indicating that 'the past has
only bequeathed to the present generation of Africans a legacy of crime
and violence'.[21] (The last clause quoted indicates, however, that Irele's
reservations may also be inspired by a certain element of African
chauvinism.)

The storm, which brought red faces to the firm of Le Seuil and

[21] Article entitled 'A new mood in the African novel', in *West Africa*, 20.9.69, p. 115.

eventually to Heinemann, who were bringing out the English version in England, broke in 1971, when Eric Sellin, Professor of French at Temple University, Pennsylvania, first challenged Ouologuem with plagiarism, proving by clear illustrations that the resemblances between the African novel and Schwarz-Bart's *Le Dernier des justes* (the Goncourt prize-winning novel of 1960) was not simply one of categories, but were also textual. The periodical which published Sellin's submission (and incidentally his retraction of his former eulogies over the novel in his notice in the *French Review*) possibly has a circulation limited to the few specialists in the field. But the echoes spread wider and the controversy became more bitter when *The Times Literary Supplement* of 5 May 1972 printed an article submitting the striking resemblance between two pages of Ouologuem's work and an extract from an early novel by Graham Greene – *It's a Battlefield*, published in 1934. The similarity was noticed by a research student in Australia, a devotee of Graham Greene, when he read the English translation of *Le Devoir*. M. Schwarz-Bart expressed himself completely unconcerned by the use that the Black writer had made of his work, in fact maintaining that he was 'deeply touched, overwhelmed even' and 'happy that his apples should be . . . taken and planted in different soil'. Mr Greene was somewhat less enchanted about the indirect flattery of this unacknowledged debt. M. Ouologuem was asked by his French publishers to re-write the offending parts of his text, while the first edition was hastily withdrawn from sale. Publication was also halted of the American paperback version of *Bound to Violence*. It is not my intention to resume here the literary polemics that raged for a time over Ouologuem's book, but to try to assess as objectively as possible what it does contribute to Negro-African fiction in French, when we discount the borrowed passages (and there is no certainty that there may not be others from sources that have not yet been identified).

Much play has naturally now been made of Ouologuem's vituperative essay 'Lettre aux pisse-copie, nègres d'écrivains célèbres,[22] in his *Lettre à la France nègre*, which appeared shortly after the novel. In this *Letter*, the author proposes a blue-print for successful composition to other aspirant Black novelists, which consists of cutting promising sections out of the works of established writers and fitting them together to form a sort of literary jig-saw. He submits some models of the technique. Eric Sellin, in his previously mentioned article, first suggested that 'the essay . . . with

---

[22] This title could be translated as 'Letter to literary hacks, ghost-writers for famous writers', but betraying both the insinuations and the play on words of the original: in journalistic jargon 'pisser de la copie' is 'to churn it out' and *un nègre* (a ghost-writer) is also a stooge, a drudge, as well, of course, as literally 'a nigger'.

its formula for literary brain-picking, now emerges not as the satire it appears to be but as an all-too-real *modus operandi*'.[23]

While not claiming to have the last word in the matter, I would like to add this little postscript on the question of plagiarism, for which I am indebted to Una Pope-Hennessy's book, *Charles Dickens* (Reprint Society, London, by arrangement with Chatto & Windus, 1947). She is speaking of the death of the Duke of Wellington in 1851:

A panegyric on the dead duke was delivered in the House of Commons by the leader of the Conservative Party, Disraeli. His speech reminded some reporters of something they already knew and the *Morning Chronicle* made a scoop by hunting up Thiers' oration on Marshal Mortier and printing it in parallel columns with Disraeli's speech: they were identical. Pleased with their astuteness, they went on to an extract from *Venetia*, the character of Lord Cadurcis, and printed it side by side with the character of Lord Byron drawn by Mr Macaulay in the *Edinburgh Review*, in which all contributors were anonymous. The explanation offered by Disraeli was that he copied anything that struck him and did not know afterwards whether he had written the extracts or not. Macaulay ignored the incident. (p. 322)

We can accept that *Le Devoir de violence* is an African *Le Dernier des justes*: the chronicle of the fictional Empire of Nakem, situated somewhere in the Sudan, from the thirteenth century to just after the Second World War. But with this difference – there are no Just Men, with the exception of the Bishop Henry, who is an observer, on the sidelines of the games between the vicious and intriguing parties of the present century. At the very end, he enters the game directly – the famous game of chess with its symbolical innuendoes – which ends of course in check-mate. The link from century to century is the despotic, tyrannical rule of the African Potentates – the Saïfs – who created and perpetuated a brilliant, barbaric society, based on slavery, intrigue and the most ruthless violence. From century to century they elaborated ever more subtle means of consolidating their power, enslaving the masses and eradicating their rivals – which in more recent times included the colonial authorites. The last, and most ruthless of the Potentates, Saïf ben Isaac El Heït, Master of Nakem-Ziuko, brings the story of rapine, civil wars, slavery and bestial violence to its horrifying climax by inventing the most sophisticated refinements of torture, subjugation and assassination. His subjects are reduced to 'Zombies' by means of drugs and his enemies are liquidated by vipers, trained

---

[23] Readers interested in the 'Affaire Ouologuem' will find more details of the controversy in the following publications: an article in *The Times* 5.5.72, by Tim Devlin; *Research in African Literatures*, vol. 2, no. 2 and vol. 4, no. 1 carries Prof. Sellin's article and subsequent correspondence; see also, *West Africa*, 21.7.72 (pp. 939–41) and *Transition*, no. 41, 1972 (pp. 64–8); interviews with Ouologuem before the storm, appeared in *New York Times Book Review*, 7.3.71, p. 7, and *Cultural Events in Africa*, no. 61, 1969, p. I–II.

through the application of Pavlovian conditioned reflexes, to bite the designated victims.

It is possible that Ouologuem intended to perpetrate a literary spoof, or to create a literary forgery, for which he subsequently revealed the techniques if not the complete recipe – in which case he can be said to have created a minor masterpiece in the tradition of the canvasses of Van Meegeren. It also seems likely from internal as well as external evidence – among other incidents, his studied insolence to his publisher and host at the lunch given to celebrate the Renaudot award – that the young author was moved by an aspiration that has nothing to do with literature: to thumb his nose at European liberal enthusiasm for the African Renaissance. This may have been responsible for some of the passages of sheer bad taste which seem to rub readers' noses in viscera and vomit, or, to quote Saïf's own metaphor, making them 'gargle with poison from the bloody cup of violence'. This view is substantiated by the almost simultaneous appearance of *Lettre à la France nègre*, which he must have been working on at the same time as *Le Devoir*, and in which, inspired by a similar state of jaundiced prejudice against Europeans, he probes the seamy side of the noble sentiments sometimes expressed in France about Africa, by 'bogus liberals and paternalists' (K.W., reviewing *Lettre à la France nègre*, in *West Africa*, no. 2729, 20.8.68). It seems improbable that Ouologuem would have done a *volte-face*; the *Letter* can surely be considered the manifesto of which *Le Devoir* is the illustration, in this as in other aspects.

The author claims that he spent two years collecting the documentation for the historical background for his work, which is based on recorded documents as well as accounts handed down by the oral tradition, from the time of the African Warrior Emperors, through the period of the Arab conquests to that of European colonization. But it is not his intention to write an historical novel. His avowed aim is to demonstrate that the character of the Black man of West Africa and the texture of his society has been formed by the bloody violence of his history – that he is the product of this social heritage. Now this is a sociological thesis, and Yambo Ouologuem is a student of sociology. (At the time of the publication of *Le Devoir*, he was preparing a doctorate at the Sorbonne.) It is true that large numbers of Negro-African novelists have composed didactic novels with the purpose of illustrating arguments dear to their heart. But the novel, as opposed to the thesis, is an art form and must to some extent transcend purely functional, polemical or educational purposes. The means that Ouologuem adopts for the submission and support of his argument is to recount a series of episodes from the history of his Empire of Nakem, loosely bound together by the tyrannical power of the current Saïf, each more ruthless than the last, assuring the continuity of a slavery that neither began with the arrival of the White slavers nor ceased with the laws promulgated in Europe for its abolition. Into this sanguinary warp is woven a pattern of savage, ruttish eroticism. The monstrous kyrielle of sadism and erotica proceeds from the most stereotyped ingredients of melodrama to refinements arising from the author's own imagination.

For example, in the last period of the chronicle the centre of the stage is taken by Raymond Spartacus Kassoumi, the son of a slave who becomes Saïf's protégé and straw man, serving after the war as a front behind which the Potentate can continue his intrigues and his crimes while retaining diplomatic relations with France. But before that he has lived through more frightful vicissitudes than it is usually given to imagine. When he was still a schoolboy, his mother had been raped by two of Saïf's creatures, and in her shame seeks a horrifying death by hanging herself among the excrement of the pit-privies. Raymond is then sent to continue his studies in France. He celebrates his success in the *baccalauréat* by indulging in a sextuplet orgy in the region of Pigalle, only to find that his partner, a plump Negress, is his own sister, who has found her way to Paris, and inevitably the whore-house, after being seduced and abandoned by a French merchant. She informs Raymond that his fiancée is dead, one of Saïf's victims, that his father has been sold into slavery in the South, that two of his brothers have been drugged into complete madness. The new-found sister is soon lost again, when a sadistic client introduces a razor-blade into the cake of soap she uses at her bidet, so that she slits herself open and bleeds to death. Having no further heart for his studies, Raymond loses his bursary and drags out his days and nights in bistros in the Latin Quarter until he becomes the male doxy of a well-to-do Frenchman . . . But well before this point the violence has ceased to lacerate our sensitivities; the sordid has ceased to shock or repel; the very accumulation of monstrous episodes blunts our powers to react with pity or terror. There is no catharsis, but it is possible that Ouologuem never intended any. What remains is a certain admiration for the sheer inventiveness of the story and the virtuosity displayed in its telling, particularly in the extraordinary variety of tone and styles manifested in the different parts of the narrative, from the loftiest epic eloquence to the most colloquial or familiar jargon of Left Bank student or Place Blanche slut. But remembering the debt owed by Ouologuem to Graham Greene and Schwarz-Bart, I cannot help wondering if this very rich texture of language and style might not be due to the unacknowledged collaboration of other, as yet unidentified, writers. In 1972 Yambo Ouologuem was reported to be working on a sequel to *Le Devoir de violence*. To date (1976) it has not appeared, but in 1969 he published another work with the suggestive title of *Les Mille et Une Bibles du sexe* [The thousand and one bibles of sex] (Paris, Edit. du Dauphin) under the pseudonym of Utto Rudolph – not a novel,[24] but a series of semi-fictional pieces, purporting to be factual, which further confirms Ouologuem as a master of *pastiche* and literary bluff.

Rémy Médou Mvomo

RÉMY MÉDOU MVOMO: *Afrika Ba'a.* Yaoundé, Edit. CLE (Coll: Abbia), 1969.

Mvomo's novel is a far more modest *roman à thèse* with a strong moralizing intention. His undisguised message is clearly directed at his own compatriots, and in particular those who have a certain basic education which makes them despise the life of the primitive bush. His thesis is that, since the dawn of Independence, the rural areas in particular need the co-operation of the intelligent youth, to win over the conservative elders with their 'colonized' mentality, to a positive programme of self-regeneration.

The fictitious but presumably typical little village of Cameroon that gives its name to the novel, has fallen on evil days since the colonial authorities have withdrawn. The inhabitants had imagined that Independence would herald an immediate Utopia. Instead, young and old are slowly starving to death. Huts are collapsing in disrepair; brawling is the only diversion; prostitution and parasitism are the only way of life of the young; drunkenness and awaiting death that of the old. Kambara, a young man with a certain education, realizes that the remedy must lie in their own hands, but unaided he cannot persuade his people to become the architects of their own regeneration. Despondent, he leaves the village, in traditional fashion, to seek employment in the neighbouring town, where he is engulfed in the thousands of unemployed, struggling for existence in the sub-civilization of urban slums. He decides to return to Afrika Ba'a and encourage his people to work for their own rehabilitation, with the educated élite setting the example.

Rapidly, in the last twenty-five pages, Mvomo sketches the miraculous rebirth of Afrika Ba'a. Kambara overcomes the lethargy of sufficient of the young and old to win their co-operation in revolutionizing their way of life. Eventually a modern progressive 'Kibbutz'-type village is flourishing on the basis of self-help and communal activity, which becomes an example to the rest of the country. Mvomo does not commit himself as to the ideology which presided over the scheme. His Kambara himself does not know whether this is Communism, African Socialism or if in fact any

[24] Although Jahn & Dressler list it as such in their usually authoritative bibliography.

known 'ism'. He concludes that the only fundamental principle was 'a great faith, an acute desire to live...'.

Mvomo's novel may be simplistic, but within its unpretentious compass it is well presented, giving a realistic, if unshaded picture of some of the social problems of rural and urban life of post-Independence Cameroon. As a moral tract it is certainly better reading than some, and can even be compared in a modest way with Jean Giono's *Regain*.

Cheik Aliou Ndao

CHEIK ALIOU NDAO: *Buur Tilleen, Roi de la Médina*. Paris, Présence Africaine, 1972.

In this first novel, Cheik Ndao paints the portrait of the respected elder of an earlier society, who cannot adapt to changing customs and standards – as does Aké Loba in *Les Fils de Kouretcha*. His hero, though, Gorgui Mbodj, known derisively among the inhabitants of Dakar's slums, as 'Buur Tilleen', the King of the Medina, has little in common with Pierre Dam'no, except his intractable conservatism. The latter, unscrupulous, vain, ambitious for self-advancement, deliberately tries to impede material progress where this runs counter to his own interests and he is the instrument of confusion and tragedy which affects the whole community. Gorgui Mbodj, a man of honour and principle, preferring personal humiliation rather than not uphold the proud traditions of his race and caste, makes himself and his family the victims of his stiff-necked intolerance. Dam'no's vicissitudes are closely related to the socio-political developments of the coming of Independence. Ndao makes only one indirect reference to the end of the colonial era, his story illustrating more specifically a sempiternal generation gap than a contemporary social evolution. Gorgui, the proud descendant of princes, had some years previously been banished from his region for affronting a District Commandant who had humiliated him before his own subjects. Since then he has lived in poverty in the Medina, his only link with his proud past is his stallion Sindax, from whom he has refused to be separated; his only consolation for his wretched condition is to ride through the streets of the Medina in the afternoon, reliving the glory of the court of Walo. He has refused to sanction his daughter's marriage with a man of inferior caste and prefers to turn her out on the streets, in time-honoured melodramatic fashion when she becomes pregnant.

There are clearly many predictable ingredients in the plot of *Buur Tilleen*, which culminates in Raki's death in childbirth together with that of her infant. On the other hand, the portrayal of the complex character of 'Buur Tilleen' is authentic and moving. The conflict between his sense of honour and his real affection for his wife and child is presented with economy and understanding. In the end, when he reverts to animist practices to try to conjure the threat of death to Raki, we realize how irrevocably the pattern of his life has been rent, even before the final tragedy, and how real will be his remorse. Cheik Aliou Ndao has succeeded in portraying the tragedy – albeit on a small canvas – that ensues when noble aspirations go hand in hand with human weakness. He has attempted to make us enter more deeply into the emotions and dilemmas of Gorgui and his wife Maram by adopting the technique of the inner monologue for the opening passages which present the immediate crisis in their lives and the background of their past history. It is a pity that he is not consistent in using this narrative technique throughout, as it might have infused a little more life into the other protagonists, in particular Raki and Bougouma, the two lovers and representatives of the younger generation.

Alioum Fantouré

ALIOUM FANTOURÉ (pseud.): *Le Cercle des Tropiques*. Paris, Présence Africaine, 1972.

French African writers of the post-Independence era have ventured with the utmost caution into the field of the political novel, or the novel with a dominantly political theme. Not that there were large numbers of really successful political novels in the preceding era, although personal ideologies and commitment to the anti-colonial struggle inspired many of the better-known post-war works of fiction. The urgent necessity to high-light the evils and suffering of the colonial régime offered novelists a positive literary programme and imposed a certain moral pressure on representatives of the Black intelligentsia, then entering the field of creative writing, to voice the grievances of their less articulate countrymen. It is also significant that they did not seem to run any serious risks of reprisals from the colonial authorities, however outspoken the censures expressed in their satirical fiction. Not one of the committed writers we have studied here came under any ban, suffered any term of imprisonment, because of his writings of this nature, with the exception of Gadeau's *Les Recrutés de M. Maurice*, a very minor dramatic work, whose performance was banned in Ivory Coast in 1942 because of its attack on the forced labour system. Mongo Beti's *Pauvre Christ de Bomba* was banned in 1956, in Cameroon, on the grounds of the supposed slur on the Catholic Church, rather than because of the political implications. Bernard Dadié's imprisonment in Ivory Coast at the time of the strikes after the Second World War was not on account of his creative writings, but for his active participation in political demonstrations. This tolerance by the colonial authorities, as well as the Metropolitan government, of criticism in the form of imaginative literature, has not been enjoyed in all the ex-colonies. The coming of independence has seen a changing literary climate which has not encouraged attacks on political régimes, except in the most veiled and discreet terms. This is partly due, of course, to the instability of many of the new governments; witness the numerous *coups d'état* they have known. The other reason for the diminishing popularity of the political theme in fiction is the relaxing of the solidarity, based on the common cause of anti-colonialism, which united Black writers from all the French African territories, as well as those from the West Indies. Writers opposing or criticizing their own country's political situation were likely to find themselves as lone voices, as well as risking banning, exile or imprisonment.

One of the really outstanding post-Independence African novels in French does deal with a political theme, but the author, understandably, hides behind a pseudonym, and his publishers refuse to divulge his real identity. Their jacket-note tells us that 'Alioum Fantouré' was born in 1938 (being thus thirty-four when his first work of fiction appeared) in Forécariah. This is an important town in Guinea halfway between Conakry and the Sierra Leone border, and presumably the centre of the region that Fantouré calls Les Marigots du sud [the Southern Marshes] in his novel *Le Cercle des Tropiques*. The capital of Porte Océane can presumably be identified as Conakry. However, by setting his satire of the tyrannical rule of a messianic leader in a fictional state, Fantouré not only gives himself some protection against possible reprisals from Sékou Touré, but also indicates that this sort of régime is not uncommon in Africa today – indeed it suggests echoes of 'Papa Doc' Duvalier's Haïti and his *tonton macoutes*, described in Graham Greene's novel *The Comedians* (not that I am implying that Alioum Fantouré has followed the example of Yambo Ouologuem in literally taking a leaf or two out of Graham Greene's book). He has succeeded in creating an atmosphere of political intrigue and ruthless tyranny that I find far more convincing and subtle than Ouologuem's story of violence, in spite of the horrific nature of many of the events in 'Tropical Circle'.

Fantouré narrates his sly adaptation of the 'simple-peasant-come-to-town' theme simply and effectively in the first person, which ensures cohesion and the sense of authentic history. His hero Bohi Di, whose name means in his own language 'son of the soil', is an orphan, driven by hardship, persecution and poverty to try his fortune in the capital, Porte Océane; this is the stereotyped basic plot of much neo-African fiction. He is sufficiently literate to be able to tell his own tale, which he does in an unsophisticated, familiar style, giving the impression of a spoken narrative, with the casual punctuation, repetitions and limited vocabulary of an autodidact. Bohi Di, by a combination of circumstances which by no means stretches credibility, becomes an actor in and, at the same time, an eye-witness to the power struggles of two rival political parties immediately preceding the declaration of independence of his country. The party representing the Workers' Club, led by the philanthropic Dr Malekê, Mellé Houré and their followers is defeated owing to the unscrupulous ruses employed by the Social Party of Hope, whose Messianic Leader, Baré Koulé, becomes the ruthless, dictatorial first President of the Republic of the Southern Marshes. The second part of Bohi Di's chronicle tells of the people's suffering under the tyrannical rule of a man drunk with power; of the systematic repression of all opposition in a single party state; of the conspiracy by the followers of Dr Malekê and Mellé Houré, joined by some of the military leaders; of the eventual *coup d'état* and the death of the 'Messie-Koï' the Messianic Leader, Baré Koulé. Justice is done; hope dawns again for the people of the Marigots du sud. And yet . . . on the next page, a brief, brutal, cynical epilogue reminds us that there is no hope, that tyrannical rule is a hydra-headed monster: 'A few months later, Dr Malekê, Mellé Houré, who had just returned from exile, Colonel Hof, Lieutenant Fairweather and Salimata were mysteriously assassinated.' (facing p. 252) The procedure adopted by Fantouré reminds me of a similar postscript to the temporary triumph of justice in the face of venal, ruthless authority in Costa-Gavaras's film, *Z*, based on Vassilikis's novel of that name, about the rule of the Colonels after their overthrow of the monarchy in Greece in the nineteen-sixties.

Le Cercle des Tropiques operates on a double level of interest as Bohi Di's personal destiny becomes inextricably linked to the political conflicts. He first becomes the unwitting and then unwilling stooge of Baré Koulé's men; later, he comes under the protection of Mellé Houré and is enrolled as a member of the Workers' Club. Having realized his ambition to become a qualified motor mechanic, he is an indispensable member of the latter's entourage, not only serving as a driver, but also a living illustration of the possible rise from destitution of the peasant. But he is not a mere tool or bystander; he has his own personal existence. Implicit in the inexorable progress of the political tug-of-war is the life of the little 'son of the soil' that he personifies. The story is thus balanced nicely between Bohi Di's brief moments of happiness with wife and children, temporary improvements in his lot, alternating with reversals of fortune, and the dramatic incidents which mark the rise and fall of the Master of the Social Party of Hope.

One of the virtues of Alioum Fantouré's novel is that he does not make himself the advocate of any political ideology. He does not offer any facile solution to the situation, but makes us feel acutely the fate of a typical inhabitant of the 'Third World', caught in the wheels of the political machinery as his country moves forward to 'progress'. His unfolding of the fictional events in *Le Cercle des Tropiques* is fascinating, dramatic and profoundly disquieting.

Pierre Makambo Bamboté

PIERRE MAKAMBO BAMBOTÉ: *Princesse Mandapu*. Paris, Présence Africaine, 1972.

Ahmadou Kourouma, Ousmane Sembène, Aké Loba, Cheik Ndao – each in his own way has portrayed with more or less compassion the vexations, rebuffs or tragedies that Independence has introduced into the lives of representatives of the older generation. Fama Doumbouya, Ibrahima Dieng, Pierre Dam'no, Gorgui Mbodj, are all either innocent victims or justly impeached for their inadaptability to the New Society. To the hero of Bamboté's novel, Alphonse Batila – nicknamed 'Monsieur Boy' by some long-forgotten colonist – Independence is far from bringing any decline in fortune. Monsieur Boy is a grotesque, ruthless monster of a patriarch. A veteran of the First World War, enjoying the privileges of some undefined official post in the little town of Uandja, some 400 miles to the north of Bangui, he considers himself the *bon papa public* of the local inhabitants. He rules autocratically over his servants, his three wives and many children – whom he continues to procreate in spite of his advanced age – and hands out largesse as the whim takes him or brutal chastisement to man or woman who offends him. The way in which he abuses his authority strains credibility. But Bamboté's novel does not operate solely on the level of realism, although all the events are taken straight from the life of the inhabitants of the little community.

The action proceeds by inference rather than by exposition. This includes a series of significant events over a period of several years, into which the little Mandapu of the title seems to stray almost incidentally. In the final, irrational *dénouement*, the child is scalded to death when a cauldren of boiling water overturns. We have been told that the name 'Mandapu' means 'the price of this affair'. There is a veiled suggestion that the child's life has been in forfeit since her birth, the midwife who officiated seeming to be in some unexplained way in league with Boy's principal enemy, a wily merchant, Mokta. There are several oblique references to 'business' between Boy and Mokta, possibly to do with illicit diamond dealing. But

Bamboté clearly does not intend clarification of these secondary details to add to the force of his narrative.

Much is thus left unexplained in this loosely connected, baroque narrative, which mingles violence with poetry in what is the best, if not the only example of literature of the absurd among the works of the French-African writers. The style, presentation and form of the novel reveal the author's complete independence from previous influences, just as the subject matter cannot be said to present any of the traditional themes. Sometimes we seem to be following the events through a glass darkly; sometimes they impinge on our consciousness and lacerate our sensitivities with their violence and subjacent passion. Often we share in the emotions of the protagonists only by virtue of an inner monologue which betrays their secret unspoken thoughts. This adds an aura of authenticity to the pageant of events which is more poetic and more convincing than any laboured explanations. Bamboté's style is equally original; he takes liberties with the French language, sacrifices its traditional clarity. He proceeds by jerky half-sentences, exclamations, hermetic allusions, like thoughts half-formulated, as though moved by the desire to economize his expression. The reader's attention is solicited; there is much confusion; he is invited to participate by filling in the gaps, the silences in the expression.

Bamboté, who had published some collections of poetry before this novel, often wanders over the borderline into the form of the prose poem, just as he deliberately presents some of the aspects of his narrative with the blurred outline of a dream, or as though seen through a heat haze in the tropical landscape in which the action unfolds. What is clear is that he breaks new ground in his *Princesse Mandapu*. He has shown himself completely emancipated from the contingencies of the Negro-African novel of sociological demonstration or political commitment. He is as unconcerned with the view he gives of an African society – favourable or unfavourable? – as he is with neatly parcelling up his plot, or relating specifically to a temporal reality. After *Le Devoir de violence* and *Les Soleils des Indépendances* which were each in turn hailed as the ultimate, authentic, original African novel – the latter with more justification than the former – I would suggest that *Princesse Mandapu* introduces the African 'New Novel'.

CONCLUSION

A conclusion to a study of the Negro-African novel in French up to 1972 will serve to tie together the various strands which can be traced through this survey of all the literary genres that have been adopted by African writers in the half-century since the beginning of the Black Renaissance. It was in fiction early in the nineteen-twenties that they first tentatively tried their hands at original composition in French based on local inspiration. I take my *terminus a quo* as 1920, when the Senegalese schoolteacher, Ahmadou Mapaté Diagne, composed his moral tale *Les Trois Volontés de Malick*. This inspired the fourteen-year-old Birago Diop, and was closely followed by René Maran's sombre and satirical *Batouala* and, some five years later, by Bakary Diallo's naïve but lyrical Rousseauesque *Force Bonté* with his eulogies of Franco-Senegalese fraternity. The story of the evolution of the French-African novel is linked to the political and cultural awakening of French-speaking Africa. First, a relative outsider, a man who declares himself 'a Frenchman with a black skin', tries to show the true face of Africa in his novels and denounces the abuses rife in colonized territories, without, however, making common cause with the whole of Black Africa. Throughout the rest of the inter-war period there was little original fiction-writing; the first prose efforts of the supporters of the Negritude movement being to preserve the historical and cultural traditions of their past. These bore fruit in collections of folk-tales and fables recreated in French, the best of which demonstrated the authors' original creative style. At this time Paul Hazoumé pioneered the African historical novel with his *Doguicimi*, a field in which he has had few disciples. However, the Black dramatists took up the challenge and, thirty years after the first dramatic essays of the William Ponty pupils, historical subjects formed the inspiration of at least half of the Negro-African drama in French.

The aggressiveness of the militant Negritude apostles that inspired the poetry of Césaire, Damas and other Caribbean poets, most concerned with questions of race and colour, did not immediately find its way into original French fiction from Africa. The novels of Ousmane Socé were limited to a statement of the problems associated with the confrontation of Black and White, but started a long line of fictional works dealing with the *déraciné*, either in a society in transition in Africa proper, or transplanted to the alien soil of Europe. After the Second World War, the novel became the most popular vehicle for the exposition of the problems and experiences peculiar to the Black man in a White-dominated society. Some writers attempted, rarely with great success, psychological novels in the European tradition. More numerous and better observed are those which concentrated on a sociological study. Singularly few – and notable among them is Camara Laye – escaped from the field of political polemics or sociological comment to reveal the serenity and mystery of Africa; the *mot d'ordre* being not to look to the ancestral past but to work rigorously for a better future.

Because the Black writer belonged to the élite of his generation and his people, he was adjured to a collective commitment. This involved explaining to the masses the social and political obstacles in the way of their progress, suggesting the means of their liberation and the solutions to their problems. In many respects pre-Independence African literature corresponds to the Romantic literature of Europe, without the introspection, the effusions of the heart, the *mal du siècle*. What is left is the insistence on a national inspiration, an actuality of subject, a rejection of tyranny and foreign domination. In drama, this is expressed in the historical episode, lauding the exploits of the national hero; in fiction it takes the form of the political or social realist novel. Considering the numbers, there were very few successful political novels from French-speaking Africa. Those who reiterated the battle-cry mentioned above forgot that the 'masses' to whom the novelist was supposed to be addressing his message, were incapable of reading, much less of reading French. In fact, the élitist Black writer was addressing a small public of élitist White readers, and they were usually won over to sympathy for his cause in the first instance. And, if he was not preaching to the converted, he had not taken sufficient steps to assure the impact of his message. This commitment to didacticism is at the root of much of the weakness of pre-Independence creative literature from Africa, particularly in fiction. 'Didactic' of course means a concern with instruction, but literature, if it is to be effective, especially in the field of polemics, must *move* as well as inform. We have seen how one of the plays on a historical subject – an attempt to rehabilitate the Warrior–Emperor Lat Dior – fails in dramatic impact because large sections of it are like pages out of a French equivalent of *Hansard*, instead of being a moving justification for the hero. I remember the distinction made by De Quincey between the 'Literature of Knowledge' and the 'Literature of Power': where the first is content to inform – and the best vehicle is the pamphlet, essay, or report appealing directly to the intellect – the second appeals to the emotions, charging the subject with human understanding. The amount of power wielded by the creative writer, novelist or playwright, is in direct proportion to the shared emotions inculcated into the reader or spectator. As novels and plays are concerned with people – their existence and their problems – involvement with their fates is also dependent on their credibility, and the author's power to appeal to the emotions. In this respect he will be guided, subconsciously, by the collective psychology of an age. The effectiveness of the didacticism of Rousseau's *Nouvelle Héloïse* or Dickens's *Oliver Twist* was largely due to the facility with which contemporary readers could be moved to tears by Julie's virtue and death or the miserable fate of a parish orphan in Victorian England. The more pragmatic and rationalist character of the mid-twentieth century requires fewer lachrymatory ingredients and more convincing characterization of the protagonists in its literature if readers' sensibilities are to be quickened by the exposition of wrongs and injustices. Alternatively, the other and usually successful formula for didactic literature is ridicule, burlesque humour, irony. The African novelists and dramatists who have learnt to wield this weapon with skill (Mongo Beti, Ferdinand Oyono, Bernard Dadié) have usually transmitted their message more effectively than those who ignore the powers of laughter to win sympathizers to their cause.

One major theme of Western literature that has been little exploited by French-African novelists of the pre-Independence era, is that of the universal human condition, as opposed to the problems presented to the individual by race, colour and politics. Certain critics have attempted to establish subjective thematic categories by which African novels in French can be classified. Among these are: a happy childhood in a rural environment; mother and child relationship; romantic love and jealousy; various metaphysical preoccupations and moral problems. In fact these are rarely the dominant feature of novels of this period, although they can all be found in different works in different proportions. *Le Regard du Roi* is exceptional in its allegorical treatment of the search for the absolute; *L'Enfant noir* for the part played by mystery and universal love; *Mission terminée* can be read as a burlesque *Sentimental Education* while *Piège sans fin* is the exposition of existential absurdity, as its title indicates. *Aventure ambiguë* treats a subject similar to *Le Regard du Roi* with critical realism rather than allegory.

The coming of Independence to French African colonies marks the watershed in the evolution of the novel from these territories. The rupture was less marked in poetry, while drama only began to flourish in the sixties and for long continued to look back to the pre-colonial and anti-colonial themes. This was mainly because the indigenous drama, although in French, was addressed directly to the local populations, whereas fiction and poetry had been addressed primarily to the West. When novelists were simultaneously liberated from colonial rule and the shackles of commitment, the most talented began to exploit a new, original range of subjects, and to a lesser degree, forms. The last ten years have seen some remarkable works, indisputably African in setting and inspiration: treating the theme of social maladjustment to a new transitional era, we have Ahmadou Kourouma's *Les Soleils des Indépendances*; the problems of existential malaise and aspirations to human dignity are explored in Malick Fall's *La Plaie* and Evembe's *Sur la terre en passant*. Under the new autonomous, but often autocratic or oppressive régimes of the African republics, writers tend to be more cautious in handling political themes than when inspired by Black solidarity to denounce the colonial oppressor. The noteworthy exception to the mediocrity of the African political novel is Alioum Fantouré's *Le Cercle des Tropiques*. There are still, among the novelists, no real pioneers in structure, form, narrative techniques, who can compare with the best of the poets – Senghor and Tchicaya U Tam'si – for the original imprint they have put on the language and form of their verse. The most outstanding of the novels are still in the tradition of nineteenth-century realism or naturalism, inspired by Balzac, Flaubert, Zola. The only notable master from the twentieth century is not Proust but André Malraux. Some tentative experimentation with form and language can be found in *La Plaie*, while Bamboté's *Princesse Mandapu* offers the hope that African French literature may still produce its *avant garde*. The balance sheet of half a century's production in the field of fiction is on the credit side.

APPENDIX TO CHAPTER 4

BERNARD DADIÉ'S TRAVEL NOTES

Un Nègre à Paris. Paris, Présence Africaine, 1959.
Patron de New York. Paris, Présence Africaine, 1964.
La Ville où nul ne meurt (Rome). Paris, Présence Africaine, 1968.

Dadié stands out from the other writers of his generation in coming late to Europe. His formal education ceased when he left the William Ponty Normal School in 1935 and entered the service of the Education Department in Dakar. Twenty years passed before he made his first journey to France, to spend barely three weeks in the capital, which nevertheless gave him the material for the closely observed, rich and ironic chronicle of his experiences, *Un Nègre à Paris*.[25] From then on, his travels in Europe and America, full of continual meditation on the human condition and on societies that have been subject to differing historical and sociological influences, form the basis of works that are devoid of any political, ideological, partisan bias, but which assert overtly or in veiled terms, the contribution of Africa to the cultural heritage of the world. Without falling back on any of the clichés about the enriching nature of travel, Dadié is aware of the clear, fresh vision he brings to the Old World and the New. One must not be misled by the apparent ingenuousness of his expression: he is no innocent abroad. His wonderment at sights and customs in his travels is nothing but a mock naïveté, the better to ensure the ironic, satirical impact of his observations. Nevertheless, there is a genuine freshness in

[25] The usually authoritative bibliography of Jahn and Dressler, 1971 edition, lists *Un Nègre à Paris* as a novel, not even qualified as 'autobiographical' as with *Climbié*. For Dadié's own disclaimer, I refer the reader again to the 'Dialogue with a work and a poet' that forms part four of Quillateau's study. He then goes on to discuss his literary progress from poetry to the expression of the more philosophical side of his nature. See especially pp. 152–3.

his perception and receptivity to what have become commonplaces in the life and tourist attractions of Paris, New York and Rome.

Each of the books is constructed on the same lines, following fairly rigidly the course and chronology of the author's travels, except that in *Un Nègre à Paris* he adopts the artifice of a supposed long epistle from 'Tanhoé Bertin' to his African correspondent, telling of his impressions of Paris. In each case we follow the author through the preliminaries of his journey, which are recounted with light-hearted humour. Then Dadié takes as a key symbol one of the travel formalities to be overcome or the first feature that strikes him on arrival, which may be a commonplace of everyday life. In *Un Nègre à Paris*, it is the Metro which is the key to his explorations of Paris, the means of penetrating into the geographical and emotional heart of the city, with its spider-web ramifications, the Ariadne's thread to guide him in his meditations, whose starting-point is the motto *Fluctuat nec mergitur*. In *Patron de New York*,[26] the American eagle, the stars of the national flag and, of course, the Statue of Liberty, form the main points of his reference system. In *La Ville où nul ne meurt* [The town where no-one dies], his travels start with an emphasis on the importance of the amount of currency he is allowed to take from France, and on his arrival in Rome, faced with the ubiquitous presence in the Holy City of the *Banco di Santo Spirito*, he is drawn to muse on the evolution of Society since Christ had declared that man could not serve both God and Mammon.

It has become a commonplace to compare *Un Nègre à Paris* to Montesquieu's *Lettres persanes*, with which it has, of course, many shared features. The principal one is the satirical device of making a foreigner express his comments on French manners, customs, social and political institutions to his correspondents at home. The impact of Montesquieu's satire arises from his distancing himself from his compatriots by imagining how the Persian travellers would react to his contemporary society, thereby expressing his own pungent criticisms of social institutions or his preoccupations with graver matters of politics or religion. Dadié never lets us forget that he is himself the Negro, the man of different complexion and different cultural heritage, seeing for the first time the external manifestations of Western history in which his reading had steeped him, as well as a myriad idiosyncrasies of daily existence, for which no reading had prepared him, and to which familiarity has blinded Western eyes. This is at the root of an important difference in the mood and content of the two books: Montesquieu is light-heartedly ironic about the insularity, ignorance and chauvinist complacency of his eighteenth-century compatriots, in the celebrated 'Comment peut-on être persan?' [How can one be Persian?] Dadié invites us, seriously, although without rancour, with the wry humour that Wole Soyinka also catches in his poem 'Telephone Conversation', to consider: 'Comment peut-on être nègre?'

Dadié's keenly observant eye and equally receptive ear are attentive to every aspect of daily life during his first short stay in the capital, as he travels in the Metro,

---

[26] There is a pun here, which is lost in translation. 'Patron' means pattern or model, but also boss. I feel that Dadié deliberately left the meaning ambiguous, viz. 'the physical outlines, sky-lines, impressions of the city that imposed itself at the time as the "model" capital of the Western world, imposing itself in a "patronizing" way on lesser cities and capitals'.

sits in cafés, walks the streets and visits monuments. His comments range from French history to unmarried mothers, with subliminal references to his own African norms, suggesting the possibility of re-evaluating Western concepts of social behaviour and institutions. In many respects his ability to exploit his experiences and observations of a foreign culture as material for philosophic reflection, reminds us as much of Voltaire's *Lettres anglaises* as of the *Lettres persanes*. But where Volatire's comparisons to the disadvantage of his own country's institutions are coloured with corrosive irony, Dadié's suggestions that France can learn from Africa never lose their bonhomie.[27]

The next subject for a travel chronicle was, chronologically, Dadié's short visit to Rome in 1959, but the book that was its fruit, *La Ville où nul ne meurt*, did not appear until 1968: he presumably needed as many years to mature the observations and experiences of a ten-day visit to the focal point of Western cultural and spiritual traditions. The humour, the facility of expression, are still present, but one is less struck by the freshness of Dadié's account of his Roman experiences, compared to the stylishness of his first Parisian chronicle: although Dadié constantly makes comparisons between the inhabitants, the manners and customs of Rome and Paris, their differences are possibly not so fundamental for his observations to have the same fresh, critical impact as his first book. Dadié's erudition, surprisingly, also seems to run short when he confuses Augustus Caesar with his ancestor Julius, ascribing to the former the crossing of the Rubicon, the conquest of Gaul, the associated sayings *Alea jacta est* and *Veni, vidi, vici* and also the death by the assassins' daggers.

When he visits the New World in 1963, everything solicits his keen observation and penetrating judgement and is food for a richly satirical analysis of the way of life of the new chosen people in the hey-day of the J. F. Kennedy era. The acerbity of his judgements is moreover increased by the fact that he is making his first pilgrimage to the home of his distant cousins – the descendants of African slaves. With pitiless accuracy he pin-points the absurdities, the incongruities, the contradictions, of the American paradise, whose gates are guarded by the giant goddess originating in France. The humour of *Un Nègre à Paris* and Dadié's ambivalent guilelessness are still in evidence, but we also glimpse some of the more ferocious satire of his dramatic works of recent years. Where *Un Nègre* suggested kinship with Voltaire's *Lettres philosophiques* as well as the obvious comparison with the *Lettres persanes*, *Patron de New York* seems unconsciously or consciously to have recourse to the effective satirical procedures of the *Encyclopédie*. The typical device is to proceed from an anodyne observation on a non-controversial issue to more tendentious matters and the associated innuendo, just as the *encyclopédistes* offered the unsuspecting reader the bait of an objective scientific definition of, say, the plant *Agnus Scythicus*, to make him swallow attacks on prejudice, superstition and injustice. An example of Dadié's progression is to take as his starting-point some observations on the institution of marriage in the United States, 'making a good match', courting customs, then the ceremony with the bride in white – the symbol

---

[27] The best critical analysis of *Un Nègre à Paris*, including some pertinent comments on Dadié's prose style, can be found in A. C. Brench's *The Novelists' Inheritance in French Africa*, ch. v, devoted to the theme of 'Africans in Paris' pp. 86–91. However, I do not agree with Brench's reference to this work as a novel.

of her sacrificial state. There follow more serious comment on the inhuman conditions under which women are often employed in North America.

The description and role of the American woman occupies a large place in Dadié's impressions, together with comments on paper napkins, artificial flowers, one-way streets, unseasoned salads, American cuisine generally, a football match between Michigan and West Point, difficulties of pronunciation of 'th' and American speech in general, wineless restaurants; and inevitably there is an effortless progression towards some more serious implication: militarism, American imperialism, the power of the dollar, the real meaning of liberty, the status of the American Indian and the ubiquitous Negro problem.

Dadié once again, as in *Un Nègre à Paris*, demonstrates his virtuosity in handling the French language, particularly in squeezing an idiomatic expression to extract the original juices of its allusiveness, or slyly adding a new dimension to a worn-out cliché. Such examples are untranslatable, as their ironic impact cannot be dissociated from the normal usage of the phrase in French. This sensitivity to the infinite resources of the French language, and the virtuosity with which he juggles with idiom, cliché, discreetly punning on occasion, always bringing fresh vision to eyes clouded by generalizations, makes Dadié stand out among the French African prose writers. He is only rivalled by the poet Senghor, the professor *agrégé* of classical and modern language and literature. He is a master of the discursive essay which proceeds from personal experience and observation to moral and philosophical reflections – never very profound, but expressed with humorous verve and bland irony. In this genre he also stands alone among the Negro-African writers, the only one to follow the path first marked out by Montaigne, clearly blazed by the eighteenth-century *philosophes* and leading through to Alain. To these predecessors Dadié is a worthy successor, by his command of expression as well as by his humanism.

Bibliographical notes

The most important critical works on the various subjects dealt with above are listed under the individual chapters concerned.

GENERAL BIBLIOGRAPHIES

There are several bibliographies of creative and critical writing from Africa, usually including that in English as well as in French, and sometimes other European and African languages. The most useful are:

Thérèse Baratte, comp. and ed. *Bibliographie d'auteurs africains et malgaches de langue française.* 2nd ed., Paris, OCORA, 1968. Covers historical and political writing as well as creative literature, but is not yet brought up to date.

Janheinz Jahn and Claus Peter Dressler, comp. *Bibliography of Creative African Writing.* Nendeln, Kraus Thompson Organization Ltd, 1971. Covers every region and language of Africa. The most complete and authoritive bibliographical reference with regional arrangement. Includes all translations and notes on apocryphal works. Invaluable up to its publication date. I have noted in the course of discussion the compilers' tendency to list as novels works more properly essays or chronicles.

Donald E. Herdeck, ed. *African Authors, A Companion to Black African Writing.* Vol. I, 1300–1973. Washington, Black Orpheus Press. Has some slightly more up to date material than Jahn & Dressler, but not so complete a coverage of the whole of Africa. Has short biographical notes on authors and résumés of works.

Hans Zell and Hélène Silver, eds., *A Reader's Guide to African Literature.* London, Ibadan, Nairobi, Heinemann Educational Books, revised ed., 1972. An annotated bibliography of writing in French and English, including political literature, children's books, literary articles and periodicals, publishers and book dealers. About half the publication is taken up by potted biographies of some fifty writers.

GENERAL REFERENCE WORKS ON AFRICAN LITERATURE
AND ITS BACKGROUND

Kofi Awoonor: *The Breast of the Earth.* New York, Anchor Press Doubleday, 1975. Fulfils its claim to be 'a survey of the history, culture and literature of Africa South of the Sahara'; gives brief account of pre-colonial period, and traces arrival of Europeans, the Islamic penetration and moves to independence. Deals concisely with links between philosophical systems of Africa and traditional art forms. Presents various genres of oral literature as well as writing in African and received languages by representative authors.

Jacques Chevrier: *Littérature nègre, Afrique, Antilles, Madagascar.* Paris, Armand Colin, (Coll: U prisme) 1974. A very useful study for the student. Covers evolution of Negro-African literature in French from beginnings in the Caribbean, through the Negritude movement to the present. An interesting section is devoted to the problems of the committed writer, to oral literature and to the possibility of a literature in the vernacular languages.

Janheinz Jahn: *Muntu. An Outline of Neo-African Culture,* (trans. from German by M. Grene. London, Faber & Faber, 1961. New York, Grove Press, 1961. 7th print, 1969.

Neo-African Literature. New York, Grove Press, 1969.

J. Jahn & J. Ramsaran: *Approaches to African Literature.* Ibadan, University Press, 1959. Though not up to date, as it stops before the post-Independence period, Jahn's analysis of the non-English writings of West Africa is useful.

Robert Pageard: *Littérature négro-africaine.* Paris, Le Livre Africain, 2nd ed. 1966. A brief introduction to the subject with notices on the most important writers, including those whom the author calls the 'theorists of the Negro-African personality'. Makes some attempt to place fiction in categories, e.g. 'social and reforming', 'philosophical', 'psychological', 'satirical', not very successfully to my mind, as these so frequently overlap in many authors' works and often in any one novel.

Claude Wauthier: *L'Afrique des Africains. Inventaire de la négritude.* Paris, Editions du Seuil, 1964. 2nd ed. 1973.

The Literature and Thought of Modern Africa. A Survey, trans. of above by Shirley Kay. London, Pall Mall Press, 1966. Places the birth of a literature in its political and sociological climate. Gives an outline of the history of Africa south of the Sahara, mentioning the work of some 150 authors writing in French or English up to 1963. The 1973 edition brings the political situation up to date and devotes a chapter to the main literary publications of the last decade.

Revue de littérature comparée, nos. 191–2, July-Sept. & Oct.-Dec. 1974, nos 3–4. Paris, M. Didier. Special volume devoted to African literature. Compares the relative quantative decline of French writing with the rise in English productions. Reassesses the ideology of Negritude. An excellent study by Mohamadou Kane on the debt owed by African novelists to the traditional forms, themes and techniques of oral literature (pp. 536–68).

Introduction: Background to a literature

Historical review

As always, when history concerns a victor and a vanquished, it is difficult to find an objective, neutral point of view. For this reason I would first recommend works by English writers:

John Anderson: *History of West Africa in the Nineteenth and Twentieth Centuries.* London, Heinemann, 1971. Intended as a school text-book to cover West

African Education Certificate 'O' Level History Syllabus, this is a useful introduction for the general reader, with maps and photographs.

Basil Davidson: *Old Africa re-discovered. The Story of Africa's Forgotten Past.* London, Gollancz, 2nd ed. 1960. Chapter III is useful on the realms of Ancient Sudan.

The African Past. Chronicles from Antiquity to Modern Times. London, Longmans, 1964. Not a history but an anthology of illustrative passages, 'records of chiefs and kings, tales of travellers and merchant adventurers, poets and pirates, soldiers and men of learning'. The chapter on the nineteenth century has extracts on El Hadj Omar and Shaka that are of interest.

Virginia Thompson & Richard Adloff: *French West Africa.* London, Allen & Unwin, 1958. The first part gives a brief historical survey (from the European colonist's standpoint), with some geographical precisions and light on ethnological and religious aspects of African society, government and administrative policy up to the immediate post-Second World War period. Part III is devoted to social and cultural fields including education. There are some useful maps.

Most useful works in French:

C. Coquery-Vidrovitch and H. Moniot: *L'Afrique noire de 1800 à nos jours.* Paris, Presses Universitaires Françaises, 1974. A most complete, scholarly, factual, up-to-date reference book, covering historical, political, sociological development of the whole of Africa, with very exhaustive bibliographies.

Robert and Marianne Cornevin: *Histoire de l'Afrique, des origines à la seconde guerre mondiale.* Paris, Payot, 3rd ed., revised, 1970. The third and revised edition of M. Cornevin's *History* which first appeared in 1966, contains a rapid survey of the main facts of the history of the whole continent. It is not easy to find one's way in, since it attempts to pack so much into a small volume.

R. Cornevin: *Histoire de l'Afrique. II: Du tournant du XVIe au tournant du XXe siècle.* Paris, Payot, 1966.

L'Afrique noire de 1919 à nos jours. Paris, P.U.F. 1973.

M. Cornevin: *Histoire de l'Afrique contemporaine de la deuxième guerre mondiale à nos jours.* Paris, Payot, 1972.

Maurice Delafosse: *Haut-Sénégal-Niger,* 3 vols, Paris, Maisonneuve et Larose, 1912, new, ed, 1972 with pref. by R. Cornevin. An important historical, geographical and ethnographical study by one of the pioneers in the field.

Boubou Hama et Jean Boulnois: *L'Empire de Gao, Histoire, coutumes et magie des Sonrai.* Paris, Adrien-Maisonneuve, 1954. A specialized study.

Djibril Tamsir Niane and J. Suret-Canale: *Histoire de l'Afrique occidentale.* Paris, Présence Africaine, 1961. Originally hurriedly produced as a school text-book, immediately after the proclamation of Independence by Guinea, to replace the old *Manuels d'Histoire de l'A.O.F.,* it has been revised, with maps and many illustrations. Although basically a school book, it is a useful manual for the reader who wants a quick introduction to the history of West Africa.

Yves Person: *Samori – Une Révolution Dyula.* Dakar, Edit. IFAN vol. 1, 1968; vol. 2, 1973; vol. 3, 1973. A very detailed study of the Samorian Empire and campaigns, for the serious student of African history.

Jean Suret-Canale: *Afrique noire, occidentale et centrale.* Paris, Edit. Sociales. vol. I, *Géographie, civilisations, histoire,* 3rd ed. 1968; vol. II, *L'Ere coloniale* (*1900–1945*), 1962. In spite of the author's evident bias in favour of certain political ideologies, and his quite justifiable intention to correct the colonial view of African history, this work is scholarly and full of useful facts, especially about the Great Empires and the lives of the Warrior Sultans. It is the most detailed and documented study that exists. The geographical section and the maps clarify some of the confusion as to geographical nomenclatures at different periods of history.

L'Almamy Samory Touré, article in *Recherches Africaines.* Etudes guinéennes (Nouvelle Série), nos. 1–4, quarterly Jan.-Dec. 1959. A slightly more detailed version of the life and career of Samory than appears in Suret-Canale's *Afrique noire.*

Negritude

This is the aspect of Negro-African writing that has inspired the greatest number of critical studies and articles. I mention here a selection in English and French. The reader who wishes to pursue this subject further should consult Jahn and Dressler's *Bibliography of Creative African Writing,* items S138–S205 (pp. 25–33).

Stanislas Adotevi: *Négritude et négrologues.* Paris, 10/18 Union Générale d'Editions, 1972. A book which, according to the publisher's note, 'brings us up to date with the political aspect of the last fifty years' struggle for the intellectual emancipation of the Negroes, and offers an erudite explanation of the concept of Negritude...'

Honorat Aguessy: *La Phase de la négritude,* in *Présence Africaine,* no. 80, 1971, pp. 33–48.

Roger Bastide: *Variations sur la négritude,* in *Présence Africaine,* no. 36, 1961, pp. 7–17.

Variations on Negritude (English version of above) in *Présence Africaine,* English edition, vol. VIII, 1961, pp. 83–91.

Dorothy S. Blair: *Negritude:* I (Black Renaissance) in *Contrast,* vol. I, no. 2, Cape Town, 1961, pp. 38–48.

Negritude: II (Black Orpheus Arising), in *Contrast,* vol. I, no. 3, 1961, pp. 38–49.

Whither Negritude? in *The Classic,* vol. 2, no. 2, Johannesburg 1966, pp. 5–10.

Léon Damas: *The Birth of Negritude,* in *AMSAC Newsletter,* vol. 7 no. 5, New York, Feb. 1965, pp. 1–3.

Laminé Diakhaté: *Le Processus d'acculturation en Afrique noire et ses rapports avec la négritude,* in *Présence Africaine,* no. LVI, 1965, pp. 68–81.

Albert Franklin: *La Négritude: réalité ou mystification?* Reflections on *Orphée noir,* in *Présence Africaine,* no. 14: 'Les étudiants noirs parlent', pp. 287–303.

Albert Gérard: *Origines historiques et destin littéraire de la négritude,* in *Diogène,* no. 48, Paris, 1964, pp. 14–37.

Abiola Irele: *A Defence of Negritude. A Propos of Black Orpheus by Jean-Paul Sartre,* in *Transition,* vol. 3, no. 13, Kampala, March/April 1964, pp. 9–11.

Negritude or Black Cultural Nationalism, in *The Journal of Modern African Studies*, vol. 3, no. 4, London, Dec. 1965, pp. 499–526.

Lilyan Kesteloot: *Introduction à la littérature négro-africaine de langue française.* Doctoral thesis in romance philology Bruxelles: Université Libre, 1960.) Re-issued as *Les Ecrivains noirs de langue française: naissance d'une littérature*, Université Libre de Bruxelles, 3rd ed. 1965. A pioneering work when it first appeared, still a basic reference book. Traces the influences bearing on the growth of the Negritude movement in the colonial period and analyses thematically the work of the major Negro-African writers up to 1960.

Lilyan Kesteloot: *Black Writers in French, A Literary History of Negritude*, trans. by E. C. Kennedy. Philadelphia, Temple University Press, 1974.

Thomas Melone: *De la négritude dans la littérature africaine.* Paris, Présence Africaine, 1962. Solely an exposition of the doctrine of Negritude in literature before Independence.

John Reed: *The Relevance of Negritude*, in *The Central African Examiner*, vol. 5, no. 1, Salisbury, June 1961.

Gregory Urban Rigsby: *Negritude: A Critical Analysis.* Dissertation presented at Howard University, Washington, D.C., 1968.

Jean-Paul Sartre: *Orphée noir*, in Senghor: *Anthologie de la nouvelle poésie nègre et malgache de langue française*, Paris, Presses Universitaires de France, 1948. 2nd ed. 1969. Also in J.-P. Sartre: *Situations*, vol. III.

Erica Simon: *La Négritude et les problèmes culturels de l'Afrique contemporaine (A propos de l'oeuvre de Cheikh Anta Diop)*, in *Présence Africaine*, no. 47, 1963, pp. 145–72.

Negritude and cultural problems of contemporary Africa, English version of above, in *Présence Africaine*, English Edition, vol. XIX, 1963, pp. 122–46.

Louis-Vincent Thomas: *Panorama de la négritude*, in *Actes du colloque sur la littérature africaine d'expression française*, Dakar, 26–9 mars, 1963. Dakar, l'Université, 1965.

1: The transition from yesterday to today

General

There is no very detailed study of the influence of folk-lore on neo-African literature. Reference to the well-known works of Lévi-Strauss will, of course, be useful for the reader particularly interested in mythocriticism as applied to Negro-African literature. We would otherwise recommend:

D. Biebuyck and Kahombo Mateene: *Anthologie de la littérature orale nyanga.* Bruxelles, Académie royale des sciences d'outre-mer, 1970. Texts in French and Nyanga from Central African Congo regions.

R. Colin: *Les Contes noirs de l'Ouest africain. Témoins majeurs d'un humanisme.* Préface de Léopold S. Senghor, Présence Africaine, 1957.

R. Finnegan: *Oral Literature in Africa*, O.U.P., 1970. Some useful comments will be found here on the *griot* on pages 96–7.

Albert Gérard: 'Preservation of tradition in African creative writing', in *Research in African Literature*, vol. 1, no. 1, Spring 1970, pp. 35–9.

The *Série africaine* of the 'UNESCO Collection of Representative Works' published by Gallimard, Paris, contains the following titles on African traditional literature. *Textes sacrés d'Afrique noire*, chosen and presented by Germaine Dieterlen, Préface by Amadou Hampaté Ba. Paris, Gallimard, 1965. W. H. Whiteley, *La Prose africaine*. This would be a translation of Whiteley's *Selection of African Prose*, Oxford, The Clarendon Press, 1964. I can find no confirmation of the date when Gallimard brought out the French version. D. Biebuyck and J. Jacobs: *Littérature épique d'Afrique noire*. (Publication date not available at time of going to press.) P. Mercier: *Chants et poèmes d'Afrique noire*. (Do. for publication date.)

Some studies of the folk-lore of different regions

Contes Wolof du Baol (Sénégal) Collected by Jean Copens and Philippe Couty; translated by Ben Khateb Dia, Dakar, O.R.S.T.O.M. Centre de Dakar-Hann, 1968. Some verbatim transcriptions of traditional Wolof tales, many of a very scabrous nature, presented with a foreword and an analysis of the tales according to theme and style.

Anthologie de la vie africaine du Congo-Gabon: Documents collected and annotated by Herbert Pepper, ethno-musicologist at the O.R.S.T.O.M. A set of three records issued by Ducretet-Thomson, numbers 320 C126–C128, with a preface by L. S. Senghor, entitled 'Le langage intégral des Négro-Africains'.

Contes du Nord Cameroun, Yaoundé, Edit. CLE, 1970. Local tales, recounted and illustrated by the pupils of the Lycée Garona, under the guidance of their teacher, Henriette Maysall.

History and legend

Robert Pageard: *Soundiata Keita et la tradition orale*, in *Présence Africaine*, no. XXXVI, 1st quarter 1961, pp. 51–70.

Edit. Fernand Nathan, Paris, in their collection 'Classiques du monde' have a series 'Littérature africaine', which includes four short volumes devoted to the Da Monzon epic.

Da Monzon de Ségou, épopée bambara, texts collected and edited by Lilyan Kesteloot, with the collaboration of Amadou Hampaté Ba. Paris, Fernand Nathan, 1972. Vol. 1: *Introduction historique, Da Monzon et Bassi de Samaniana*; vol. 2: *Biton Koulibaly, Ngolo Diarra, Le Dibi de Niamina, Da Monzon et Diétékoro Kārta*; vol. 3: *Bakari Dian et Bilissi, Da Monzon trahit Bakari Dian, Bakari Dian et les Peuls de Kounari, Da Monzon et Djon Goloni*; vol. 4: *Silimaka du Macina, Da Monzon et Koré Douga, Da Monzon et Karta Tiéma*.

Studies of some writers

R. Mercier and M. and S. Battestini: *Birago Diop, Textes commentés*. Paris, F. Nathan (Series: Littérature africaine, 'Classiques du monde') no. 6, 1964.

Bernard Dadié, Textes commentés. Do, no. 7, 1964. These 'textes commentés' are intended for secondary school classes and are preceded by biographical notes and an analysis of the main aspects of the work. The study devoted to Dadié does not deal specifically with his folk-tales, but gives an introduction to the author and his work generally.

C. Quillateau: *Bernard Binlin Dadié, l'homme et l'oeuvre.* Paris, Présence Africaine, 1967.

Mohamadou Kane: *Les Contes d'Amadou Coumba, du conte traditionnel au conte moderne d'expression française.* Dakar, Publications de la Faculté des Lettres et Sciences Humaines (Series: Langues et Littératures) no. 16, 1968.

Originally presented as a doctoral thesis, Mohamadou Kane's work is invaluable, both as a study of the traditional elements of the African fable and folk-tale, as well as an analysis of the *Contes* of Birago Diop. He includes a most exhaustive bibliography of the African folk-literature and folk-lore, and of all studies of Birago Diop. It is therefore unnecessary to reproduce this here.

English translations

Birago Diop: *Tales of Amadou Koumba*, trans. with intro. by Dorothy S. Blair. London, O.U.P., 1966. (A selection of the stories from the three volumes by B. Diop.)

D. T. Niane: *Sundiata. An Epic of Old Mali*, trans. G. D. Pickett. London, Longmans (Forum Series) 1965.

2: Dramatic literature

Studies on the theatre

Robert Cornevin: *Le Théâtre en Afrique noire et à Madagascar.* Paris, Le Livre Africain, 1971.

Monsieur Cornevin, one of the most distinguished historians of Africa, and permanent Secretary of the Académie des Sciences d'Outre-Mer, draws on his vast and unique collection of documents and some 40 years personal experiences, to tell the story of the growth of dramatic art and literature among the French-speaking Negro-African populations. His approach is chronological and regional. He quotes generously from unpublished sources to illustrate contemporary reactions to theatrical performances. Although he does not attempt any real synthesis or critical evaluation of a literary form, M. Cornevin's book is valuable to students of the theatre and dramatic arts, particularly as a social phenomenon.

Bakary Traoré: *Le Théâtre négro-africain et ses fonctions sociales.* Paris, Présence Africaine, 1958.

This first critical study devoted to the contemporary French African theatre is, as its title indicates, the work of a sociologist. M. Traoré traces the development of dramatic entertainment and its place in the community, and analyses some of the major productions of the pre-Independence era. He devotes an important chapter to an explanation of the aesthetics of the traditional African theatrical spectacles and how these differed from those of Europe.

His book has not been revised since 1958, the date of its first publication, and thus includes no mention of the important dramatic literature of the post-Independence era.

The periodical *Eburnea*, no. 66, December 1972, contains a useful article by R. Bonneau entitled 'Quarante ans de théâtre ivoirien' (pp. 17–32), outlining the important contribution of Eburnean writers to French African dramatic art and literature. Together with the usual explanation of the development of the contemporary theatre from traditional sources, M. Bonneau gives a useful bibliography and, for easy reference, alphabetical notes on Eburnean drama and dramatists. He also includes a recent interview with Mme Béart on her memories of the Bingerville and William Ponty drama.

Colloque sur l'art nègre, Premier festival mondial des arts nègres, Dakar, 1–24 avril 1966. Complete proceedings, published in French and English (1967 and 1968 respectively), Paris, Présence Africaine. In a section entitled 'Fonction et signification de l'art nègre dans la vie du peuple et pour le peuple' (30 mars–6th avril), Bakary Traoré contributes a paper on 'La signification et fonction du théâtre négro-africain traditionnel', without, however, adding much to what he has already said in his book.

Actes du colloque sur le théâtre négro-africain (organised at the University of Abidjan 15–29 April 1970). Paris, Présence Africaine, 1972. Of interest are papers on the genesis of the Negro-African theatre; the sources of its inspiration; its impact on the public and the universality of the Negro-African drama.

Texts printed in periodicals

Otherwise unpublished texts of early dramatic productions by the William Ponty Normal School can be found in the following:

Education Africaine, no. 86, April-June 1934, pp. 73–89, 'Un Mariage au Dahomey' (anon.)

Education Africaine, nos. 90–1, April-Sept. 1935, pp. 181–9, 'L'Election d'un roi au Dahomey' (anon.)

Présence Africaine, no. 1, Nov.-Dec. 1947, pp. 62–77, 'La Mort du Damel', Amadou Cissé Dia.

Présence Africaine, 1948, pp. 627–741, 'Sokamé' (anon.)

Traits d'Union, no. 11, pp. 68–96, has the play 'Fasi' by Anoumou Pedro Santos, for which this revue offered a prize. The play was never performed.

English translations

Publishers have so far been cautious about bringing out translations of dramatic literature, claiming that there is not sufficient readership, as compared to the large public interested in the African novel, or even poetry. Oyônô-Mbia, who, like Samuel Beckett, is completely bilingual, has himself been responsible for the English versions of two of his plays, in fact *Until Further Notice* was actually produced in English by the B.B.C. before being translated into French by the author. (See ch. 3, p. 132.)

S. Badian: *La Mort de Chaka*, trans. by C. Wake, as *The Death of Chaka*. Nairobi, etc., O.U.P., 1968.

L. S. Senghor: *Chaka*, trans. by J. Reed & C. Wake, in their *Selected Poems*. London, O.U.P., 1964.

Gu. Oyônô-Mbia: *Trois prétendants... un mari*, as *Three Suitors, One Husband*, with *Jusqu'à nouvel avis*, as *Until Further Notice*. London, Methuen, 1968. Repr. 1975.

3: Negro-African poetry: from Negritude to disengagement

For the bibliography of Negritude see pages 327–8

L. S. Senghor

A large corpus of critical work has been published on Senghor in volumes and in periodicals. I mention here only a few works on his poetry that throw light on his contribution to literature: in case I am accused of an important omission, I must point out that J. L. Hyman's book, subtitled 'An intellectual biography', concentrates on the political and sociological aspects of Senghor's ideology and their expression in his writings, whether poetic, political or philosophical.

Ulli Beier: 'The theme of the ancestors in Senghor's poetry', in *Black Orpheus*, no. 5, May 1959, pp. 15–17.

Alain Bosquet: 'Les "engagements" de Léopold Sédar Senghor', In *Nouvelle Revue Française*, XII, November 1964, pp. 879–84.

Armand Guibert: *Léopold Sédar Senghor, l'homme et l'oeuvre*. Paris, Présence Africaine, 1962.

Abiola Irele: 'Léopold Sédar Senghor as a poet', in *Odu – a Journal of West African Studies*, no. 1, 1969.

H. de Leusse: *Senghor: Des 'Poèmes' aux 'Lettres d'hivernage': Analyse critique*. Paris, Hatier (Coll: Profil d'une oeuvre) 1975.

S. Okechukwu Mezu: *Léopold Sédar Senghor et la défense et illustration de la civilisation noire*. Paris, Didier, 1968. After a first part devoted to an analysis of the socio-historical background to Senghor's life and work, Dr Mezu offers the most complete and objective critical analysis of all Senghor's poetry, its themes and its aesthetics. He has an interesting chapter on comparisons with Senghor's predecessors and contemporaries, including Gobineau, Claudel and Saint-John Perse. There are twenty pages of bibliography for further reference.

The Poetry of L. S. Senghor. London, Heinemann, 1973.

Gerald Moore: 'Léopold Sédar Senghor, Assimilation or Negritude', in *Seven African Writers*, London, O.U.P., 1962.

Marcien Towa: *Léopold Sédar Senghor: Négritude ou servitude?* Yaoundé, Edit. CLE (Coll. 'Point de vue') 1971.

Sylvia Washington Bâ: *The Concept of Negritude in the Poetry of Léopold Sédar Senghor.* Princeton University Press, 1973. Originally thesis for the degree of Ph.D. presented at Fordham University, New York, 1967.

A special number of the periodical *Francité*, published at St Louis University, Missouri, namely no. 2, Spring, 1973, was devoted to L. S. Senghor. It contains the following articles.

Dorothy S. Blair: 'La présence française dans la poésie de L. S. Senghor, pp. 1–36. (Unfortunately this article has been so mutilated by clumsy editing and uncorrected printer's errors that in parts it only marginally reflects the writer's intentions.)

M. J. Hoog: 'Chaka de Senghor', pp. 37–57.

Janice Spleth: 'Le feu de brousse', pp. 57–73.

Robert O'Connor: 'Senghor et l'animisme', pp. 74–84.

Birago Diop

See bibliography on pages 329–30 referring to chapter 2. Nothing has been published specifically on his verse.

David Diop

Ulli Beier: Review of *Coups de pilon*, in *Black Orpheus*, no. 5, May 1959, pp. 57–8.

Gerald Moore: 'Poet of the African Revolution', in *Seven African Writers*, London, O.U.P., 1962.

Bernard Dadié

See bibliography on page 330. Quillateau's book contains some rather elementary commentaries on some of Dadié's poems.

Also: Ulli Beier: Review of *La Ronde des jours*, in *Black Orpheus*, no. 5, May 1959.

Joseph Bognini

Jacques Howlett: Review of *Ce dur appel de l'espoir*, in *Présence Africaine* no. 36, 1st quarter 1961, pp. 165–7.

Ellen Conroy Kennedy: 'Four African Poets', in *African Forum* vol. 2, no. 1, Summer 1966, pp. 103–7.

Gérald Félix Tchicaya U Tam'si

Anna Greki: Review of *Epitomé*, in *Jeune Afrique* no. 99, 10–16 Sept. 1962.

Janheinz Jahn: Review of *Epitomé* in *La Presse*, 7.10.1962. (This is a translation of text by Jahn which had appeared in *Blätter und Bilder*.)

G. D. Killam (ed.) *African Writers on African Writing*, London, Heinemann, 1973.

Gerald Moore: 'Surrealism and Negritude in the poetry of Tchikaya (sic) U Tam'si', in *Black Orpheus* no. 13, Nov. 1963, pp. 100–9.

'Surrealism on the River Congo', in *African Literature and the Universities*, Ibadan University Press, 1965, pp. 41–51.

Introduction to *Selected poems of Tchicaya U Tam'si*. Translated into English, London, Ibadan, Nairobi, Heinemann Educational Books (African Writers' Series) 1970.

African Literature and the Universities, Record of the seminars held at University of Dakar and Fourah Bay College, the University College of Sierra Leone, in March and April 1963. Ibadan University Press, 1965. Chapter 6: 'The writers speak', pp. 62–3, contains Tchicaya U Tam'si's contribution to the discussion, his own testimony on his poetry.

Muriel Rukeyser: Review of *Feu de Brousse*, in *African Forum*, vol. 1, no. 1, Summer 1965, pp. 145–8.

Per Wästberg (ed.): *The Writer in Modern Africa*, Uppsala, Scandinavian Institute of African Studies & New York, Africana Publishing Corp. 1969. This contains Tchicaya's own contributions to the discussions at the African–Scandinavian Writers' Conference held in Stockholm in February 1967.

Cultural Events in Africa, no. 60, 1969, pp. III, II, IV. This contains the record of an interview with the poet by Edris Makward, during the African Studies Association Conference, held in Montreal in October 1969. This item has been reprinted in more accessible form in: G. D. Killam (ed.) *African Writers on African Writing*, London, Heinemann, 1973.

General

Janheinz Jahn: 'Rhythm and Style in African Poetry', in *African Literature and the Universities*, Ibadan University Press, 1965, pp. 51–6.

Clive Wake: Introduction to his *Anthology of African and Malagasy Poetry in French*. London, Ibadan, Accra, Nairobi, O.U.P., 1965.

English translations

English verse translations of most of the poets dealt with in chapter 3 have been included in anthologies, of which we recommend the following.

Darkness and Light, ed. P. Rutherfoord. London, Faith Press, 1958. A pioneering work, including some of the first English versions of poems by D. Diop and Senghor.

A Book of African Verse, ed. J. Reed and C. Wake. London, Heinemann, 1964. Repr. 1969.

West African Verse, ed. D. I. Nwoga. London, Longmans, 1967.

French African Verse, ed. J. Reed and C. Wake. London, Heinemann, 1972.

The Negritude Poets, An Anthology of Translations from the French, ed. with introductions by Ellen Conroy Kennedy, New York, The Viking Press, 1975.

To date, the most complete anthology for the reader with no French. Though few of the translations do justice to the rhythms, harmonies and poetic qualities generally of the poems, they give a good impression of the range of subject and style of the major French-African poets. Apart from sections devoted to the Caribbean and Indian Ocean writers, that dealing with Africa proper contains works by Senghor, B. Diop, F.-D. Sissoko, A.-R. Bolamba, Dadié, D. Diop, M. Sinda and Tchicaya U Tam'si. Also contains useful bibliographies.

3000 Years of Black Poetry, ed. by A. Lomax & R. Abdoul. New York, Dodd, Mead & Co., 1970. The French-African poets represented are Senghor, Joachim, Dadié and Tchicaya U Tam'si, reproduced from other anthologies.

Isolated poems in translation occur in the review *Black Orpheus*, of which it is impossible to list all the numbers concerned. My articles, listed on p. 327, contain translations of some poems also. So far only collections of English translations of verse by Senghor, David Diop and Tchicaya U Tam'si have been published.

L. S. Senghor: *Selected Poems*, trans. J. Reed and C. Wake. London, O.U.P., 1964.
    Prose and Poetry, ed. and trans. J. Reed and C. Wake. London, O.U.P. (Three Crowns), 1965.
    Nocturnes, trans. J. Reed and C. Wake. London, Heinemann, 1972.
Tchicaya U Tam'si: *Selected Poems*, trans. G. Moore. London, Heinemann, 1970.
David Diop: *Hammerblows and Other Writings*, ed. and trans. by Simon Mpondo and Frank Jones. Bloomington and London, Indiana University Press, 1973.

4: The African novelist and the Negro-African novel in French

Works already mentioned will not be noted again here, unless they have a predominant reference to the novel.

General

Actes du colloque sur la littérature africaine d'expression française, Dakar, 26–9 March 1963. Dakar: L'Université, 1965.
African Literature and the Universities, ed. with introduction by Gerald Moore. Ibadan, University Press, 1965. (The same as above in English.)
Sunday Ogbonna Anozie: *Sociologie du roman africain. Réalisme, structure et déterminisme dans le roman moderne ouest-africain*. Paris, Aubier-Montaigne (Coll: Tiers Monde et Développement.) 1970.

Anozie offers a systematic study of novels in English and French from West Africa from 1947 to 1967, as illustrating the role of the novelist in the changing political and social situation today. Those parts of his work which are most relevant to the novel in French are chapters III, IV, VII and VIII of part II, where he applies his sociological observations to *Le Regard du Roi, L'Aventure ambiguë, Un Piège sans fin* (ch. III & VII); *Dramouss, Afrique, nous t'ignorons*, (ch. IV), *Sous l'orage, Une Vie de boy, Le Pauvre Christ, O Pays, mon beau peuple!* and *Maïmouna*, in ch. VIII, mainly.

A. C. Brench: *The Novelists' Inheritance in French Africa*. London, etc. O.U.P. (Three Crowns) 1967.

Sound critical essays on the following novelists and their works to date, presented under themes, which refer to the novels, or birthplace or character of the writer, which makes the grouping a little arbitrary: Birago Diop (whom I would hardly consider a novelist); A. Sadji, Camara Laye, F. Oyono, Mongo Beti, Jean Malonga, Bernard Dadié (here again I do not agree that *Un Nègre à Paris* is really a novel; Brench does not mention *Climbié*), Aké Loba, Ch. Hamidou Kane and Sembène Ousmane (only for *Les Bouts de bois de Dieu*).

Wilfred Cartey: Whispers from a Continent. The Literature of contemporary Black Africa. New York, Random House, 1969.

Deals with fiction in English and in French. The French works studied are as follows. *L'Enfant noir*, in chapter 1 on autobiographical themes, and chapter 2 on 'Disillusionment and break-up of the colonial world'. And chapter 5 entitled 'Exile and Return'. *Le Regard du Roi*: In ch. 4, under the heading 'The Movement Back'. *L'Aventure ambiguë*: In ch. 1, and ch. 4, under the heading 'The search'. *Mission accomplie*: In ch. 1 – so for Cartey, the main issue of this work is the autobiographical element. *Le Vieux Nègre et la médaille, Cœur d'Aryenne, O Pays, mon beau peuple!, Batouala, Vie de boy, Le Pauvre Christ de Bomba* and *Ville cruelle* are all analysed in ch. 2 under the general heading of 'Disillusion and break up', applied to 'the colonial world', 'Destruction of self', 'Disintegration of society', 'Degradation of society'. *Les Bouts de bois de Dieu*: In ch. 4 illustrates 'The Lost Generation' and 'Urban Reality'.

Edouard Eliet: *Panorama de la littérature négro-africaine* (*1921–1962*). Paris, Présence Africaine, 1965.

Deals with literature in French from the Caribbean and Madagascar as well as Black Africa. The second part, devoted to the novel, with long illustrative passages, discusses *Batouala, Climbié, Le Vieux Nègre, Le Pauvre Christ, Le Regard du roi*. This part is little more than an anthology of extracts with brief introductory notes.

Judith I. Gleason: *This Africa. Novels by West Africans in English and French*. Evanston, Northwestern University Press, 1965.

A chatty, superficial survey, mainly dealing with the plot of works by seven English-speaking writers and eighteen from French West and Equatorial Africa, all of whom the author manages to accommodate in chapters entitled 'The Styles of the Conquerors', 'The Heroic Legacy of Africa', 'Village Life', 'City Life' and 'The Inner Life'. (She devotes much space and enthusiasm to G. Bolombo's *Kavwanga* which is probably not by an African.)

Mohamadou Kane: 'Naissance du roman africain francophone'. In *African Arts/Arts d'Afrique*, vol. 2, no. 2, Winter 1969. pp. 54–8. A brief review of the origins of the French African novel.
　'Sur les "Formes traditionnelles" du roman africain', in *Revue de Littérature Comparée*, nos. 191–2, July-Sept. & Oct.-Dec. 1974, pp. 536–8.
Gerald Moore: *Seven African Writers*. London, O.U.P. 1962. New edit. 1966.

Only two of the seven writers in question are novelists, writing in French: Camara Laye and Mongo Beti, of whose works Moore gives a useful analysis.

James Olney: *Tell me Africa. An Approach to African Literature*. Princeton, N.J. Princeton University Press, 1973. This 'approach' is limited to an interpretation of autobiographical novels, which the author claims can help the non-African reader to understand communal African life. Thus a more sociological than strictly literary criterion. More English than French African works dealt with.

Jarmila Ortová: *Etude sur le roman au Cameroun*. Prague, Publishing House of the Czechoslovak Academy of Sciences, 1971. An attempt to assess the specific contribution of the Cameroonian novelists to French African literature. Miss Ortová deals conscientiously with each of the authors she treats, but fails to show what are the essentially Cameroonian characteristics of their works, which she claims to be part of her aim. The rather approximate nature of the French expression does not always make her arguments easy to understand.

Eustace Palmer: *An Introduction to the African Novel*. London, Heinemann, 1972.

Out of the twelve authors whom Palmer chooses to study, only two are African novelists writing in French, namely Camara Laye and Mongo Beti. Palmer offers the most percipient and judicious analysis to date of the weaknesses and greatness of Camara Laye's novels. He is also the only critic to see what I feel is the main issue and intention of *Mission to Kala*.

Adrien A. Roscoe: Mother is Gold. A Study in West African Literature. London, C.U.P. 1971.

Although this deals mainly with African English writing, the first chapter is useful for the comparison made between the situation in the French and English-speaking territories and their respective return to the traditions of the past.

Books and articles on specific authors, not including chapters or essays in works under ' General' above

MONGO BETI

Thomas Melone: 'Mongo Beti et la terre camerounaise'. In *Annales de la Faculté des Lettres et Sciences Humaines*, vol. 1, no. 1, Yaoundé, 1969, pp. 87–118.
Mongo Beti: l'Homme et le Destin. Paris, Présence Africaine, 1971. The only complete study of the pre-Independence novels.

OLYMPE BHÊLY-QUÉNUM

A.C. in *Présence Africaine*, nos. 34–5, Oct. 1960–Jan. 1961, pp. 230–2.
R. Mercier and M. and S. Battestini: *Olympe Bhêly-Quénum, écrivain dahoméen* (Textes choisis et commentés). Paris, Nathan, 1964.

CH. HAMIDOU KANE

Dominique Desanti: 'Le conflit des cultures et *L'Aventure ambiguë*', in *African Arts/Arts d'Afrique*, vol. 1, no. 4, Summer 1968, pp. 60–1.
R. Mercier and M. and S. Battestini: *Cheikh Hamidou Kane* (Textes commentés). Paris, Nathan, 1964.

CAMARA LAYE

Janheinz Jahn: *Camara Laye – an interpretation.* In *Black Orpheus*, no. 6, Nov. 1959, pp. 35–38.

A.B., 'Trois écrivains noirs', in *Présence Africaine*, no. 16, 1954, pp. 419–20.

J. A. Ramsaran: 'Camara Laye's symbolism. An interpretation of *The Radiance of the King*'. In *Black Orpheus*, no. 3, May 1958, pp. 55–7.

R. Mercier and M. and S. Battestini: *Camara Laye, écrivain guinéen* (Textes choisis et commentés). Paris, Nathan, 1964.

FERDINAND OYONO

Gerald Moore: 'Ferdinand Oyono et la tragi-comédie coloniale'. In *Présence Africaine*, no. XLVI, 2nd quarter, 1963, pp. 221–33.

R. Mercier & M. & S. Battestini: *Ferdinand Oyono, écrivain camerounais* (Textes choisis et commentés). Paris, Nathan, 1964.

Novels published in English translation

Bebey, Francis: *Le Fils d'Agatha Moudio*, trans. by Joyce Hutchinson as *Agatha Moudio's Son*. Heinemann, 1971.

Beti, Mongo* : *Mission terminée*, trans. by P. Green as *Mission Accomplished*. New York, Macmillan, 1958. In England, as *Mission to Kala*, Heinemann, 1964. Repr. 1966.

Le Roi miraculé, trans. as *King Lazaras* (tr. anon.). London, Muller, 1961; Heinemann, 1970.

Le pauvre Christ de Bomba, trans. by Gerald Moore as *The Poor Christ of Bomba*. Heinemann, 1971.

Dadié, Bernard: *Climbié*, trans. by Karen Chapman as *Climbié*. New York, Africana Publishing House, 1971; also Heinemann, 1971.

Fall, Malick: *La Plaie*, trans. by Clive Wake as *The Wound*. London, Heinemann, 1973.

Kane, Hamidou: *L'Aventure ambiguë*, trans. by Katherine Woods as *Ambiguous Adventure*. New York, Walker & Co., 1963; Collier Books-Macmillan, 1969; Heinemann, 1972.

Laye, Camara: *L'Enfant noir*, trans. by J. Kirkup as *The Dark Child*. London, Collins, 1955. Also as *The African Child*, Fontana books, 1959; and New York, Collier Books–Macmillan, 1969.

Le Regard du Roi, trans. by J. Kirkup as *The Radiance of the King*. London, Collins, 1956; Fontana Books, 1965; New York, Collier Books–Macmillan, 1965.

Dramouss, trans. by J. Kirkup, as *A Dream of Africa*. London, Collins, 1968.

Ouologuem, Yambo: *Le Devoir de violence*, trans. by R. Manheim as *The Wages of Violence*. London, Secker & Warburg, 1968. Also as *Bound to Violence*, New York, Harcourt, Brace, Jovanovich, 1971; London, Heinemann, 1971.

Oyono, Ferdinand: *Une Vie de boy*, trans. by J. Reed as *Houseboy*. London, Heinemann, 1966. Also as *Boy!*, New York, Collier Books–Macmillan, 1970.

Le Vieux Nègre et la médaille, trans. by J. Reed as *The Old Man and the Medal*. London etc., Heinemann, 1967.

Sembène, Ousmane: *Les Bouts de bois de Dieu*, trans. by Francis Price as *God's bits of Wood*. New York, Doubleday, 1962; New York, Doubleday–Anchor, 1970; London, Heinemann, 1970.

Le Mandat, suivi de *Véhi-Ciosane*, trans. by Clive Wake as *The Postal Order*, with *White Genesis*. London, Heinemann, 1972.

Voltaïque, trans. by L. Ortzen as *Tribal Scars & Other Stories*. London etc., Heinemann, 1974.

Xala, trans. Clive Wake, London etc., 1976.

---

* Since this book went to press the anon. trans. to Mongo Beti's *Perpetue* has appeared in Heinemann's African Writers' Series, 1976.

Index

In the interest of space, the English titles of works, whether published translations exist or not, will not be listed separately here. Reference should be made to the author and the French title. For individual stories or poems see the title of the collected work.